I0528497

www.ingramcontent.com/pod-product-compliance
Lightning Source LLC
Chambersburg PA
CBHW051313120626
46547CB00015B/2210

* 9 7 8 1 9 5 7 1 0 9 3 6 7 *

ירמיהו

THE
ISRAEL
BIBLE

JEREMIAH

EDITED BY

Rabbi Tuly Weisz

ISRAEL
365

The Israel Bible: Jeremiah

First Edition, 2021

The Israel Bible was produced by Israel365 in cooperation with Teach for Israel and is used with permission from Teach for Israel. All rights reserved. The English translation was adapted by Israel365 from the JPS Tanakh. Copyright © 1985 by the Jewish Publication Society. All rights reserved.

Cover images used under license from Shutterstock.com

ISBN 978-1-957109-36-7

A CIP catalogue record for this title is available from the British Library

The Israel Bible: Jeremiah is a holy book that contains the name of God and should be treated with respect.

Table of Contents

iv   Introduction to *The Israel Bible*

ix   Foreword

xii   Introduction to *Sefer Yirmiyahu* (Jeremiah)

xiv   Map of the Two Kingdoms of Israel

1   *Sefer Yirmiyahu* (Jeremiah)

131   List of Transliterated Words in *The Israel Bible*

145   Photo Credits

146   Map of Modern-Day Israel and its Neighbors

Introduction

The Hebrew Bible is commonly known as the *Tanakh* which stands for *Torah* (the Five Books of Moses), *Neviim* (the Prophets) and *Ketuvim* (the Writings). The *Tanakh* consists of 24 books that are considered by Jews to be the word of God. While these books have been referred to as the "Old Testament," many Jews reject this label since it implies the replacement of the Hebrew Bible with something newer and prefer the more authentic Jewish name.

The *Tanakh* is not only the most important book known to man, it is God's word that is perfect and absolute. It is therefore a daunting undertaking to publish an edition of the *Tanakh*, and the responsibilities are awesome. There is no room for error or carelessness in dealing with the eternal word of God. Further, upon embarking on such a serious initiative, we ask ourselves if our efforts are gratuitous. Considering the many editions of the Bible in print, is there truly a need for yet another one?

While there are numerous Bibles in circulation today, its most central aspect – the Land of Israel – has often been overlooked. References to Israel appear on nearly every page, and the city of Jerusalem is specifically referred to hundreds of times throughout the Bible. The essential link between Israel and *Torah* is emphasized repeatedly in verses such as, "For instruction (*Torah*) shall come forth from *Tzion*, the word of *Hashem* from *Yerushalayim*" (Micah 4:2).

The miraculous return of the People of Israel to the Land of Israel in our own generation provides the perfect moment for a new volume to fill this void in biblical literature. *The Israel Bible* includes many special features elucidating God's focus on Israel throughout *Tanakh* and there are many additional, multimedia features available on our website **www.theisraelbible.com**.

Ordering and Presentation – In presenting *The Israel Bible*, our goal is to spread awareness of the biblical significance of the Land of Israel as well as the Jewish people's eternal connection to the land, based on the text of the *Tanakh*, the Hebrew Bible. We aim to honor "the God, the People and the Land of Israel" from an Orthodox Jewish perspective. To that end, *The Israel Bible* follows the traditional Jewish ordering of the books and the customary Hebrew division of chapters. Therefore, for example, we count 24 books of *Tanakh* with *Sefer Divrei Hayamim* (Chronicles) appearing last. It is our hope that our rich content will speak to all Jews and non-Jews who appreciate Israel as the God given land of the Jewish people.

English Translation – Throughout history, Jews have studied the Bible in Hebrew, as any form of translation would miss much of the nuance of the original holy tongue in which *Torah* has been transmitted since the days of Moses. However, as many Jews settled in America in the 19th Century, the need for an English translation became necessary. To be sure, there were already English translations prepared over the centuries by Christians, but in the words of the original editors of the Jewish Publication Society (JPS), "The Jew cannot afford to have his Bible translation prepared for him by others. He cannot have it as a gift, even as he cannot borrow his soul from others."

JPS set out in the late 1800s to publish an authoritative English translation "in the spirit of Jewish tradition." It was compiled over decades by some of the leading Jewish scholars of the time. They formed committees and subcommittees to compare existing English versions, considering medieval and modern Jewish commentators. The monumental JPS translation, originally published in 1917, has been updated in recent years, and *The Israel Bible* is proud to utilize the 1984 New Jewish Publication Society (NJPS) version with its modern, clear language, as well as its wide-ranging acceptance as an accurate and high-quality translation. We applied the NJPS translation verbatim, except for a select list of nouns which we replaced with their traditional Hebrew names. This is true even when we found the NJPS translation to be different than the popular translation of a word or phrase and when the NJPS switched the order of the text for the sake of clarity (see, for example, Ezekiel 24:22–24).

Hebrew Transliteration – To give our readers an authentic *Tanakh* experience, every verse that has commentary is transliterated from Hebrew into English. The Hebrew alphabet chart includes our standards for transliteration and pronunciation of Hebrew verses, enabling readers of *The Israel Bible* to decipher key biblical passages in the holy language. Readers can hear the entire Bible read in Hebrew on our website **www.theisraelbible.com**.

There are various standards when it comes to transliterating Hebrew words into English. While we have relied primarily on the classical Hebrew transliteration, we have occasionally deviated for the sake of simplicity, clarity and to reflect common usage.

In addition to whole verses, we have also transliterated many proper nouns in the English translation so that our readers can learn the names of key biblical figures and locations in their Hebrew form. As a rule, we chose to transliterate names of people that were central in the establishment and functioning of the nation of Israel, as well as significant places in the Holy Land. Therefore, regarding Adam's sons, for example, only *Shet* (Seth) is transliterated since it was from him that *Noach* (Noah), and ultimately *Avraham* (Abraham), descended. For this reason, there might be verses or sections of *The Israel Bible* that contains multiple names and only some of them are transliterated.

For the same reason, we have transliterated the names of the books of *Tanakh* when referring to them in our introductions and commentary. When referencing a specific chapter or verse, however, we use the English names of the books in our citations for clarity. We also transliterated ideas and concepts that are central to Judaism such as *Shabbat* (Sabbath), the names of the Jewish holidays and the *Beit Hamikdash* (Temple), as well as biblical measurements. Finally, the name of God is transliterated. Out of respect, Orthodox Jews generally refer to the Lord as *Hashem*, which literally means 'the Name.' Referring to God as *Hashem* reminds us that we feel close to Him but also recognize our distance at the same time. To stress this moniker, we transliterated both the Tetragrammaton as well as the name *Elohim* as *Hashem*.

Study Notes – Our unique commentary was compiled by Orthodox Jewish scholars who live in Israel. It is an anthology in the sense that most of the commentary is not original, but draws from traditional teachings of early Jewish Sages and modern rabbinic commentators. We also include quotations from individuals who have played a significant part in the past century of modern Israeli history including Israeli prime ministers, poets and military leaders.

Our commentary can be broken into four categories, three of which are identified by an icon at the beginning of the study note:

 Israel lessons are indicated with an icon bearing the map of Israel and focus on the Land of Israel and the modern State of Israel.

 Jewish lessons are indicated with a *Torah* scroll and teach a concept in Judaism or a classic idea from rabbinic thought.

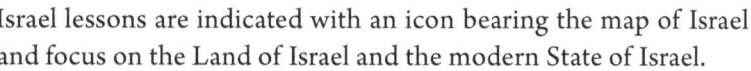 Hebrew lessons are represented by an icon bearing the letter *aleph* and focus on the meaning of a Hebrew word or phrase.

All other comments are considered general comments and are not assigned an icon.

Supplemental Material – In addition to our unique translation and original commentary, *The Israel Bible* offers supplementary material to enrich the learning experience of our readers. Before every book of *Tanakh*, we provide an introduction, as well as information, generally in the form of a map, a chart or a list, which is central to the specific book.

Maps – As the purpose of *The Israel Bible* is to highlight the biblical significance of the Land of Israel, significant time was spent researching and preparing maps to bring the physical contours of the holy land to life with great accuracy. However, since there is a lack of information regarding the precise locations of certain ancient cities, some of the places on our maps are approximate or subject to debate. In these cases, we followed the opinion that we are most comfortable with, but acknowledge that there is room for disagreement. We continue to produce new maps, which are available on our website **www.theisraelbible.com/maps**.

Torah **Readings** – The *Torah* is not just a work that is studied privately, it is also read out loud in synagogue. Every *Shabbat* and holiday a portion of the *Torah* is read, as well as a related section from *Neviim*, the prophets, called the *haftarah*. We included the blessings recited before and after the reading of the *Torah*, a list of the weekly *Torah* portions and their corresponding *haftarot*, and a chart of the *Torah* readings for special days with their corresponding *haftarot*. Readers can always find the current week's *Torah* portion by visiting **www.theisraelbible.com/weekly-torah-portion**. In this volume, we indicate where a new *Torah* portion begins by highlighting the Hebrew verse number with a gray box so readers can follow along with the communal *Torah* readings. Furthermore, we have included prayers for the State of Israel and the soldiers of the Israel Defense Forces (IDF) that are generally recited following the *Torah* reading in synagogue. It is our constant prayer that God watch over the State of Israel and the members of the IDF, who defend Israel every hour of every day.

In 1948, the State of Israel was created providing a modern answer to Isaiah's ancient question, "Is a nation born all at once?" (Isaiah 66:8). *The Israel Bible* was first published in the 70th year of God's miraculous restoration of the People of Israel to the Land of Israel. Jewish wisdom teaches that 70 is a significant number: *Moshe* (Moses) translated the *Torah* into 70 languages for all 70 nations of the world. From our very origins, the Jewish people were meant to be a light unto the 70 nations, spreading God's truth to the masses.

In the seven decades since the modern rebirth of the State of Israel, God's plan has been unfolding with unprecedented speed, dramatic highs and heartbreaking lows. Never has Israel been at the forefront of the world's attention as it is in our generation. Efforts to vilify the Jewish State seem to spread every day across the globe. At the same time, so does the growing movement of millions of non-Jewish biblical Zionists who stand with the nation of Israel as an expression of their commitment to God's word. As we seek to understand the clash of these two conflicting worldviews, the need for *The Israel Bible* has never been so important.

Standing on the great shoulders of those who came before us and emanating from the land that has always served as the birthplace for the Bible, we conclude with a heartfelt prayer: May the Almighty bless our efforts in offering this *Tanakh* to influence the hearts, minds and actions of its readers. In this way, it is our hope to spread God's name so that the publication of *The Israel Bible* brings us one step closer to the final redemption of Israel and the entire world.

Rabbi Tuly Weisz
Editor, *The Israel Bible*

Foreword

The mandate to study God's word daily is interestingly not found in the Five Books of Moses (Pentateuch), but rather in the first book of our prophetic writings: "Let not this Book of the Teaching cease from your lips, but recite it day and night, so that you may observe faithfully all that is written in it. Only then will you prosper in your undertakings and only then will you be successful" (Joshua 1:8). Charged with bringing the Israelites into the land covenantally promised to Abraham, Isaac and Jacob, God ensures Joshua of His protection if the nation observes His ways as dictated in the Divine constitution known as the *Torah*.

In Jewish tradition, Joshua (1:8) is directly linked with Deuteronomy (11:14), "You shall gather in your new grain and wine, and oil."[1] Our Sages deduced from this scriptural combination the importance of merging *Torah* study with a profession. Completely dedicating oneself to the study of *Torah* without having the financial means to sustain this lifestyle can lead one to eventually straying from observance of God's will. Poverty and crime can have an intimate relationship.

We must also be careful that our work does not affect our daily study of Scripture. The addiction of becoming a workaholic and not making *Torah* study a priority can also lead one into temptations that can violate our personal relationship with Him as well as our fellow human beings. The goal is to achieve a healthy balance between our study of God's word and our daily work.

The Deuteronomic verse quoted above is part of the second section of the Shema[2] that discusses the concept of reward and punishment. Sanctifying God by fulfilling His commandments results in the Land of Israel practically benefitting from rains that occur in the right season and reaping the abundance from the fields. However, if the nation follows pagan gods and practices, the consequences are devastating – famine and death. The Land of Israel is intrinsically linked with the keeping of the *Torah*. Covenant Land comes with covenant responsibility.

---

1. Talmud Bavli Berachot 35b
2. Consisting of three sections within the Five Books of Moses (Deut. 6:4–8; 11:13–22 and Numbers 15:37–42), the *Shema* is proclamation of accepting God's Kingdom in our lives, loyalty to His commandments and remembering His redemptive act of liberating us from Egypt. Jews recite the *Shema* twice a day as stated in Deut. 6:7.

Born into slavery, Joshua is now leading His people into the Promised Land. More than 500 years separates him from his ancestral forefather Abraham. The historical narratives that took place between Abraham leaving everything behind to follow God in Genesis 12 and the death of Moses in the last chapter of Deuteronomy are filled with intrigue, suspense, joy, sorrow and hope. What began as a family is now a nation actualizing its mission to be a kingdom of priests to the world. However, for the Israelites to succeed in the Land of Israel, they must see the *Torah* as the only compass to direct their lives.

The biblical episodes after our first entry into the land are well known. Our ancestors' triumphs and sins are all on public record. We learned the harsh reality of Leviticus (18:28) "So let not the land spew you out for defiling it as it spewed out the nation that came before you." Twice, we lost the privilege to be stewards of the Land of Israel and to fulfill our nation state mandate to be a light to the world. However, when the annals of history were ready to archive the Jewish people after the Holocaust, God kept His covenantal promise and gathered us from the four corners of the globe to come home. The year 1948 was a game changer. Biblical prophecies were and are being realized. We are now living in the birth pangs of the messianic era.

In our morning prayers, we recite a series of blessings over the *Torah* that include petitioning God to have a sweet tooth for His word, to study it without any ulterior motive and to have Him to teach it to us. They are some congregations that invoke the following liturgical prayer after the completion of these blessings: *May the Torah be my faith and El Shaddai my help. Blessed be the name of His glorious kingdom forever and all time.*

According to Jewish tradition, the neglect of not blessing the *Torah* before engaging in its study was one of the reasons for the destruction of the Temple.[3] This is deduced from the redundancy of words in Jeremiah (9:12) that talks about Israel not following God: "...Because they forsook the teaching I had set before them. They did not obey Me and they did not follow it [did not make a blessing before studying it]." Our inability to properly cherish God's greatest gift to the world, the *Torah*, led to our eventual exile from our land.

On Israel's Independence Day, Jews around the world recite Psalms 113–118 to express our gratitude to God for His Divine hand in helping establish the State of Israel. We have learned from our past and realize the privilege to see firsthand the land, people and *Torah* operating all together in our generation.

---

3. Babylonian Talmud Nedarim 81a

When Rabbi Tuly Weisz approached me about his intent to publish *The Israel Bible* that would highlight commentary about the special relationship between the land and people, I saw this project as another way to publicly demonstrate our appreciation to God for having the State of Israel. In addition, it is another educational tool to ensure biblical literacy. If we are to truly enjoy the Land of Israel, it is incumbent upon us to continually study the *Torah*. Isaiah once prophesied that the Jewish people would return to Zion with songs, "crowned with everlasting joy" (35:10). *The Israel Bible* provides us the lyrical content to express our joy in living in the land that God calls holy.

Rabbi Shlomo Riskin
Chief Rabbi of Efrat
Founder of the Center for Jewish-Christian
Understanding & Cooperation (cjcuc)

Introduction to Sefer Yirmiyahu
The Book of Jeremiah

Introduction and commentary by Rabbi Yaakov Beasley

Yirmiyahu (Jeremiah) lives during the tragic final years of Israel's southern kingdom, *Yehuda*, just before its destruction in 586 BCE at the hands of Babylonia. He prophesies for forty years, beginning during the reign of King *Yoshiyahu*, a strong point in the history of the kingdom of *Yehuda*, and ending after the small remnant of Jews left in *Yerushalayim* following the Temple's destruction flees to Egypt.

Yirmiyahu's prophecy is intensely personal; we know much more about his personal life than we know of the life of any other prophet. Born to a priestly family in *Anatot* (1:1), he becomes a prophet at a very young age. He is commanded by God not to marry or raise children, to symbolize His plan to destroy the next generation (16:1–4). His prophecies contain many predictions of doom and a desperate cry to Israel to accept the upcoming upheaval and submit to Babylonian rule – a demand that earns him the title of traitor among his own people.

In truth, *Yirmiyahu* loves his people too much to stand by while they commit national suicide. As such, he never ceases to speak to them, and even when his prophecies are proven true, his only response to the destruction and exile is devastation. This response finds its eloquent and heartbreaking voice in *Megillat Eicha*, which, according to tradition, was also authored by *Yirmiyahu*. *Sefer Yirmiyahu* also includes several sections which describe the emotional price of being the lone voice of a painful truth.

Sefer Yirmiyahu is not structured chronologically. The first 35 chapters are a collection of prophecies directed to the kingdom of *Yehuda* about the upcoming destruction. They describe the sins which are the cause of the impending devastation, and include the ultimately futile request for the people not to rebel against Babylonian dominion. *Yirmiyahu* also intersperses promises that *Hashem* will return His scattered people to live in Israel in peace. Of specific interest is a prophecy to the Jews who are exiled, that their exile will last for seventy years. After this, however, the prophet states that the Babylonian empire will fall, and their descendants will have the opportunity to return to *Eretz Yisrael* (29:5–14). Chapters 36–38 include *Yirmiyahu's* personal sufferings and 39–44 describe the downfall of *Yerushalayim*. In the final chapters of the book, *Yirmiyahu* prophesies against the nations that participated in, or cheered at, Israel's downfall, for the Lord does not forgive the insult against His people.

While *Yirmiyahu* is known as the prophet of doom, his prophecies also contain much promise. By the time he becomes a prophet, the destruction of *Yehuda* and the *Beit Hamikdash* is almost inevitable. *Yirmiyahu* tries one last time to awaken the Israelite nation to return to *Hashem*, but they refuse to listen and are exiled from their land. However, even in exile, far from their land, the Jewish people are not to abandon hope. As *Hashem* promises through *Yirmiyahu*, "I will delight in treating them graciously, and I will plant them in this land faithfully, with all My heart and soul" (32:41).

Map of the Two Kingdoms of Israel

After King *Shlomo*'s death, the united Kingdom of Israel splits into two: the northern kingdom of *Yisrael* under the leadership of *Yerovam*, and the southern kingdom of *Yehuda* under the leadership of *Rechovam* son of *Shlomo*. The kingdom of *Yehuda* was made up primarily of the tribes of *Yehuda* and *Binyamin*, and the kingdom of *Yisrael* was made up of the other ten tribes. By *Yirmiyahu*'s time, *Yisrael* had already been exiled by the Assyrians and "lost," and *Yehuda* was on the verge of being exiled as well. As a prophet, *Yirmiyahu*'s job was to speak to the people of *Yehuda* and try to urge them to repent in order to prevent the final exile and destruction of the kingdom. The following is a map delineating the boundaries of the two kingdoms of Israel, *Yehuda* and *Yisrael*, at the time that the kingdom split.

1 ¹ The words of *Yirmiyahu* son of *Chilkiyahu*, one of the *Kohanim* at *Anatot* in the territory of *Binyamin*.

א דִּבְרֵי יִרְמְיָהוּ בֶּן־חִלְקִיָּהוּ מִן־הַכֹּהֲנִים אֲשֶׁר בַּעֲנָתוֹת בְּאֶרֶץ בִּנְיָמִן:

² The word of *Hashem* came to him in the days of King *Yoshiyahu* son of *Amon* of *Yehuda*, in the thirteenth year of his reign,

ב אֲשֶׁר הָיָה דְבַר־יְהֹוָה אֵלָיו בִּימֵי יֹאשִׁיָּהוּ בֶן־אָמוֹן מֶלֶךְ יְהוּדָה בִּשְׁלֹשׁ־עֶשְׂרֵה שָׁנָה לְמָלְכוֹ:

³ and throughout the days of King *Yehoyakim* son of *Yoshiyahu* of *Yehuda*, and until the end of the eleventh year of King *Tzidkiyahu* son of *Yoshiyahu* of *Yehuda*, when *Yerushalayim* went into exile in the fifth month.

ג וַיְהִי בִּימֵי יְהוֹיָקִים בֶּן־יֹאשִׁיָּהוּ מֶלֶךְ יְהוּדָה עַד־תֹּם עַשְׁתֵּי עֶשְׂרֵה שָׁנָה לְצִדְקִיָּהוּ בֶן־יֹאשִׁיָּהוּ מֶלֶךְ יְהוּדָה עַד־גְּלוֹת יְרוּשָׁלַ͏ִם בַּחֹדֶשׁ הַחֲמִישִׁי:

⁴ The word of *Hashem* came to me:

ד וַיְהִי דְבַר־יְהֹוָה אֵלַי לֵאמֹר:

⁵ Before I created you in the womb, I selected you; Before you were born, I consecrated you; I appointed you a *Navi* concerning the nations.

ה בְּטֶרֶם אֶצָּורְךָ [אֶצָּרְךָ] בַבֶּטֶן יְדַעְתִּיךָ וּבְטֶרֶם תֵּצֵא מֵרֶחֶם הִקְדַּשְׁתִּיךָ נָבִיא לַגּוֹיִם נְתַתִּיךָ:

⁶ I replied: Ah, *Hashem*! I don't know how to speak, For I am still a boy.

ו וָאֹמַר אֲהָהּ אֲדֹנָי יְהֹוִה הִנֵּה לֹא־יָדַעְתִּי דַּבֵּר כִּי־נַעַר אָנֹכִי:

⁷ And *Hashem* said to me: Do not say, "I am still a boy," But go wherever I send you And speak whatever I command you.

ז וַיֹּאמֶר יְהֹוָה אֵלַי אַל־תֹּאמַר נַעַר אָנֹכִי כִּי עַל־כָּל־אֲשֶׁר אֶשְׁלָחֲךָ תֵּלֵךְ וְאֵת כָּל־אֲשֶׁר אֲצַוְּךָ תְּדַבֵּר:

⁸ Have no fear of them, For I am with you to deliver you – declares *Hashem*.

ח אַל־תִּירָא מִפְּנֵיהֶם כִּי־אִתְּךָ אֲנִי לְהַצִּלֶךָ נְאֻם־יְהֹוָה:

⁹ *Hashem* put out His hand and touched my mouth, and *Hashem* said to me: Herewith I put My words into your mouth.

ט וַיִּשְׁלַח יְהֹוָה אֶת־יָדוֹ וַיַּגַּע עַל־פִּי וַיֹּאמֶר יְהֹוָה אֵלַי הִנֵּה נָתַתִּי דְבָרַי בְּפִיךָ:

¹⁰ See, I appoint you this day Over nations and kingdoms: To uproot and to pull down, To destroy and to overthrow, To build and to plant.

י רְאֵה הִפְקַדְתִּיךָ הַיּוֹם הַזֶּה עַל־הַגּוֹיִם וְעַל־הַמַּמְלָכוֹת לִנְתוֹשׁ וְלִנְתוֹץ וּלְהַאֲבִיד וְלַהֲרוֹס לִבְנוֹת וְלִנְטוֹעַ:

¹¹ The word of *Hashem* came to me: What do you see, *Yirmiyahu*? I replied: I see a branch of an almond tree.

יא וַיְהִי דְבַר־יְהֹוָה אֵלַי לֵאמֹר מָה־אַתָּה רֹאֶה יִרְמְיָהוּ וָאֹמַר מַקֵּל שָׁקֵד אֲנִי רֹאֶה:

vai-HEE d'-var a-do-NAI ay-LAI lay-MOR mah a-TAH ro-EH
yir-m'-YA-hu va-o-MAR ma-KAYL sha-KAYD a-NEE ro-EH

Blossoming almond tree in *Yerushalayim*

א 1:11 I see a branch of an almond-tree In his first vision, *Yirmiyahu* is shown an almond branch, *makel shaked* (מקל שקד in Hebrew. *Hashem* explains that the branch symbolizes His watching over His word to perform it. The Hebrew word he chooses for 'watch', *shoked* (שקד), also means 'to hasten.' *Yirmiyahu* deliberately chose this word since it is similar to the word for 'almond,' *shaked* (שָׁקֵד). Commenta-

tors give two explanations for this wordplay. First, just as the almond tree blossoms quickly, so too *Hashem* will hasten to punish Israel. Furthermore, the almond tree is the first to blossom in *Eretz Yisrael*. When all else is dead, the almond trees awaken the countryside from its winter slumber. So too, although the people are spiritually dead, God's word, like the almond blossoms, will awaken the nation.

שקד

Jeremiah

12 *Hashem* said to me: You have seen right, For I am watchful to bring My word to pass.

יב וַיֹּאמֶר יְהֹוָה אֵלַי הֵיטַבְתָּ לִרְאוֹת כִּי־שֹׁקֵד אֲנִי עַל־דְּבָרִי לַעֲשֹׂתוֹ:

13 And the word of *Hashem* came to me a second time: What do you see? I replied: I see a steaming pot, Tipped away from the north.

יג וַיְהִי דְבַר־יְהֹוָה אֵלַי שֵׁנִית לֵאמֹר מָה אַתָּה רֹאֶה וָאֹמַר סִיר נָפוּחַ אֲנִי רֹאֶה וּפָנָיו מִפְּנֵי צָפוֹנָה:

14 And *Hashem* said to me: From the north shall disaster break loose Upon all the inhabitants of the land!

יד וַיֹּאמֶר יְהֹוָה אֵלָי מִצָּפוֹן תִּפָּתַח הָרָעָה עַל כָּל־יֹשְׁבֵי הָאָרֶץ:

15 For I am summoning all the peoples Of the kingdoms of the north – declares *Hashem*. They shall come, and shall each set up a throne Before the gates of *Yerushalayim*, Against its walls roundabout, And against all the towns of *Yehuda*.

טו כִּי הִנְנִי קֹרֵא לְכָל־מִשְׁפְּחוֹת מַמְלְכוֹת צָפוֹנָה נְאֻם־יְהֹוָה וּבָאוּ וְנָתְנוּ אִישׁ כִּסְאוֹ פֶּתַח שַׁעֲרֵי יְרוּשָׁלַם וְעַל כָּל־חוֹמֹתֶיהָ סָבִיב וְעַל כָּל־עָרֵי יְהוּדָה:

16 And I will argue My case against them For all their wickedness: They have forsaken Me And sacrificed to other gods And worshiped the works of their hands.

טז וְדִבַּרְתִּי מִשְׁפָּטַי אוֹתָם עַל כָּל־רָעָתָם אֲשֶׁר עֲזָבוּנִי וַיְקַטְּרוּ לֵאלֹהִים אֲחֵרִים וַיִּשְׁתַּחֲווּ לְמַעֲשֵׂי יְדֵיהֶם:

17 So you, gird up your loins, Arise and speak to them All that I command you. Do not break down before them, Lest I break you before them.

יז וְאַתָּה תֶּאְזֹר מָתְנֶיךָ וְקַמְתָּ וְדִבַּרְתָּ אֲלֵיהֶם אֵת כָּל־אֲשֶׁר אָנֹכִי אֲצַוֶּךָ אַל־תֵּחַת מִפְּנֵיהֶם פֶּן־אֲחִתְּךָ לִפְנֵיהֶם:

18 I make you this day A fortified city, And an iron pillar, And bronze walls Against the whole land – Against *Yehuda*'s kings and officers, And against its *Kohanim* and citizens.

יח וַאֲנִי הִנֵּה נְתַתִּיךָ הַיּוֹם לְעִיר מִבְצָר וּלְעַמּוּד בַּרְזֶל וּלְחֹמוֹת נְחֹשֶׁת עַל־כָּל־הָאָרֶץ לְמַלְכֵי יְהוּדָה לְשָׂרֶיהָ לְכֹהֲנֶיהָ וּלְעַם הָאָרֶץ:

19 They will attack you, But they shall not overcome you; For I am with you – declares *Hashem* – to save you.

יט וְנִלְחֲמוּ אֵלֶיךָ וְלֹא־יוּכְלוּ לָךְ כִּי־אִתְּךָ אֲנִי נְאֻם־יְהֹוָה לְהַצִּילֶךָ:

2 1 The word of *Hashem* came to me, saying,

ב א וַיְהִי דְבַר־יְהֹוָה אֵלַי לֵאמֹר:

2 Go proclaim to *Yerushalayim*: Thus said *Hashem*: I accounted to your favor The devotion of your youth, Your love as a bride – How you followed Me in the wilderness, In a land not sown.

ב הָלֹךְ וְקָרָאתָ בְאָזְנֵי יְרוּשָׁלַם לֵאמֹר כֹּה אָמַר יְהֹוָה זָכַרְתִּי לָךְ חֶסֶד נְעוּרַיִךְ אַהֲבַת כְּלוּלֹתָיִךְ לֶכְתֵּךְ אַחֲרַי בַּמִּדְבָּר בְּאֶרֶץ לֹא זְרוּעָה:

3 *Yisrael* was holy to *Hashem*, The first fruits of His harvest. All who ate of it were held guilty; Disaster befell them – declares *Hashem*.

ג קֹדֶשׁ יִשְׂרָאֵל לַיהֹוָה רֵאשִׁית תְּבוּאָתֹה כָּל־אֹכְלָיו יֶאְשָׁמוּ רָעָה תָּבֹא אֲלֵיהֶם נְאֻם־יְהֹוָה:

4 Hear the word of *Hashem*, O House of *Yaakov*, Every clan of the House of *Yisrael*!

ד שִׁמְעוּ דְבַר־יְהֹוָה בֵּית יַעֲקֹב וְכָל־מִשְׁפְּחוֹת בֵּית יִשְׂרָאֵל:

5 Thus said *Hashem*: What wrong did your fathers find in Me That they abandoned Me And went after delusion and were deluded?

ה כֹּה אָמַר יְהֹוָה מַה־מָּצְאוּ אֲבוֹתֵיכֶם בִּי עָוֶל כִּי רָחֲקוּ מֵעָלָי וַיֵּלְכוּ אַחֲרֵי הַהֶבֶל וַיֶּהְבָּלוּ:

6 They never asked themselves, "Where is *Hashem*, Who brought us up from the land of Egypt, Who led us through the wilderness, A land of deserts and pits, A land of drought and darkness, A land no man had traversed, Where no human being had dwelt?"

ו וְלֹא אָמְרוּ אַיֵּה יְהֹוָה הַמַּעֲלֶה אֹתָנוּ מֵאֶרֶץ מִצְרָיִם הַמּוֹלִיךְ אֹתָנוּ בַּמִּדְבָּר בְּאֶרֶץ עֲרָבָה וְשׁוּחָה בְּאֶרֶץ צִיָּה וְצַלְמָוֶת בְּאֶרֶץ לֹא־עָבַר בָּהּ אִישׁ וְלֹא־יָשַׁב אָדָם שָׁם:

7 I brought you to this country of farm land To enjoy its fruit and its bounty; But you came and defiled My land, You made My possession abhorrent.

ז וָאָבִיא אֶתְכֶם אֶל־אֶרֶץ הַכַּרְמֶל לֶאֱכֹל פִּרְיָהּ וְטוּבָהּ וַתָּבֹאוּ וַתְּטַמְּאוּ אֶת־אַרְצִי וְנַחֲלָתִי שַׂמְתֶּם לְתוֹעֵבָה:

8 The *Kohanim* never asked themselves, "Where is *Hashem*?" The guardians of the Teaching ignored Me; The rulers rebelled against Me, And the *Neviim* prophesied by Baal And followed what can do no good.

ח הַכֹּהֲנִים לֹא אָמְרוּ אַיֵּה יְהֹוָה וְתֹפְשֵׂי הַתּוֹרָה לֹא יְדָעוּנִי וְהָרֹעִים פָּשְׁעוּ בִי וְהַנְּבִיאִים נִבְּאוּ בַבַּעַל וְאַחֲרֵי לֹא־יוֹעִלוּ הָלָכוּ:

9 Oh, I will go on accusing you – declares *Hashem* – And I will accuse your children's children!

ט לָכֵן עֹד אָרִיב אִתְּכֶם נְאֻם־יְהֹוָה וְאֶת־בְּנֵי בְנֵיכֶם אָרִיב:

10 Just cross over to the isles of the Kittim and look, Send to Kedar and observe carefully; See if aught like this has ever happened:

י כִּי עִבְרוּ אִיֵּי כִתִּיִּים וּרְאוּ וְקֵדָר שִׁלְחוּ וְהִתְבּוֹנְנוּ מְאֹד וּרְאוּ הֵן הָיְתָה כָּזֹאת:

11 Has any nation changed its gods Even though they are no-gods? But My people has exchanged its glory For what can do no good.

יא הַהֵימִיר גּוֹי אֱלֹהִים וְהֵמָּה לֹא אֱלֹהִים וְעַמִּי הֵמִיר כְּבוֹדוֹ בְּלוֹא יוֹעִיל:

12 Be appalled, O heavens, at this; Be horrified, utterly dazed! – says *Hashem*.

יב שֹׁמּוּ שָׁמַיִם עַל־זֹאת וְשַׂעֲרוּ חָרְבוּ מְאֹד נְאֻם־יְהֹוָה:

13 For My people have done a twofold wrong: They have forsaken Me, the Fount of living waters, And hewed them out cisterns, broken cisterns, Which cannot even hold water.

יג כִּי־שְׁתַּיִם רָעוֹת עָשָׂה עַמִּי אֹתִי עָזְבוּ מְקוֹר מַיִם חַיִּים לַחְצֹב לָהֶם בֹּארוֹת בֹּארֹת נִשְׁבָּרִים אֲשֶׁר לֹא־יָכִלוּ הַמָּיִם:

kee sh'-TA-yim ra-OT a-SAH a-MEE o-TEE a-z'-VU m'-KOR MA-yim kha-YEEM lakh-TZOV la-HEM bo-ROT bo-ROT nish-ba-REEM a-SHER lo ya-KHI-lu ha-MA-yim

14 Is *Yisrael* a bondman? Is he a home-born slave? Then why is he given over to plunder?

יד הַעֶבֶד יִשְׂרָאֵל אִם־יְלִיד בַּיִת הוּא מַדּוּעַ הָיָה לָבַז:

Plastered water cistern found at Qumran

2:13 They have forsaken Me, the Fount of living waters Water is a precious resource. While in some locations there were natural springs that provided water for the ancient Israelites, the people also carved out many cisterns in which to store rain water, to ensure they would have enough to drink. Although ancient workers developed a special kind of plaster that was used to line the inside of the cisterns to prevent the water from seeping out, cracks would often develop, causing the water to be lost. *Yirmiyahu* compares *Hashem* to a fountain of natural spring water, while the false gods are likened to cracked and broken cisterns. Though the fountains provide life-giving waters, the people foolishly choose to drink from cisterns which cannot contain their water, relying on meaningless idols rather than God, the true source of life.

¹⁵ Lions have roared over him, Have raised their cries. They have made his land a waste, His cities desolate, without inhabitants.

טו עָלָיו יִשְׁאֲגוּ כְפִרִים נָתְנוּ קוֹלָם וַיָּשִׁיתוּ אַרְצוֹ לְשַׁמָּה עָרָיו נצתה [נִצְּתוּ] מִבְּלִי יֹשֵׁב:

¹⁶ Those, too, in Noph and Tahpanhes Will lay bare your head.

טז גַּם־בְּנֵי־נֹף ותחפנס [וְתַחְפַּנְחֵס] יִרְעוּךְ קָדְקֹד:

¹⁷ See, that is the price you have paid For forsaking *Hashem* your God While He led you in the way.

יז הֲלוֹא־זֹאת תַּעֲשֶׂה־לָּךְ עָזְבֵךְ אֶת־יְהוָה אֱלֹהַיִךְ בְּעֵת מוֹלִכֵךְ בַּדָּרֶךְ:

¹⁸ What, then, is the good of your going to Egypt To drink the waters of the Nile? And what is the good of your going to Assyria To drink the waters of the Euphrates?

יח וְעַתָּה מַה־לָּךְ לְדֶרֶךְ מִצְרַיִם לִשְׁתּוֹת מֵי שִׁחוֹר וּמַה־לָּךְ לְדֶרֶךְ אַשּׁוּר לִשְׁתּוֹת מֵי נָהָר:

¹⁹ Let your misfortune reprove you, Let your afflictions rebuke you; Mark well how bad and bitter it is That you forsake *Hashem* your God, That awe for Me is not in you – declares the lord God of Hosts.

יט תְּיַסְּרֵךְ רָעָתֵךְ וּמְשֻׁבוֹתַיִךְ תּוֹכִחֻךְ וּדְעִי וּרְאִי כִּי־רַע וָמָר עָזְבֵךְ אֶת־יְהוָה אֱלֹהָיִךְ וְלֹא פַחְדָּתִי אֵלַיִךְ נְאֻם־אֲדֹנָי יְהוִה צְבָאוֹת:

²⁰ For long ago you broke your yoke, Tore off your yoke-bands, And said, "I will not work!" On every high hill and under every verdant tree, You recline as a whore.

כ כִּי מֵעוֹלָם שָׁבַרְתִּי עֻלֵּךְ נִתַּקְתִּי מוֹסְרֹתַיִךְ וַתֹּאמְרִי לֹא אעבד [אֶעֱבוֹר] כִּי עַל־כָּל־גִּבְעָה גְּבֹהָה וְתַחַת כָּל־עֵץ רַעֲנָן אַתְּ צֹעָה זֹנָה:

²¹ I planted you with noble vines, All with choicest seed; Alas, I find you changed Into a base, an alien vine!

כא וְאָנֹכִי נְטַעְתִּיךְ שֹׂרֵק כֻּלֹּה זֶרַע אֱמֶת וְאֵיךְ נֶהְפַּכְתְּ לִי סוּרֵי הַגֶּפֶן נָכְרִיָּה:

²² Though you wash with natron And use much lye, Your guilt is ingrained before Me – declares *Hashem*.

כב כִּי אִם־תְּכַבְּסִי בַּנֶּתֶר וְתַרְבִּי־לָךְ בֹּרִית נִכְתָּם עֲוֹנֵךְ לְפָנַי נְאֻם אֲדֹנָי יְהוִה:

²³ How can you say, "I am not defiled, I have not gone after the Baalim"? Look at your deeds in the Valley, Consider what you have done! Like a lustful she-camel, Restlessly running about,

כג אֵיךְ תֹּאמְרִי לֹא נִטְמֵאתִי אַחֲרֵי הַבְּעָלִים לֹא הָלַכְתִּי רְאִי דַרְכֵּךְ בַּגַּיְא דְּעִי מֶה עָשִׂית בִּכְרָה קַלָּה מְשָׂרֶכֶת דְּרָכֶיהָ:

²⁴ Or like a wild ass used to the desert, Snuffing the wind in her eagerness, Whose passion none can restrain, None that seek her need grow weary – In her season, they'll find her!

כד פֶּרֶה לִמֻּד מִדְבָּר בְּאַוַּת נפשו [נַפְשָׁהּ] שָׁאֲפָה רוּחַ תַּאֲנָתָהּ מִי יְשִׁיבֶנָּה כָּל־מְבַקְשֶׁיהָ לֹא יִיעָפוּ בְּחָדְשָׁהּ יִמְצָאוּנְהָ:

²⁵ Save your foot from going bare, And your throat from thirst. But you say, "It is no use. No, I love the strangers, And after them I must go."

כה מִנְעִי רַגְלֵךְ מִיָּחֵף וגורנך [וּגְרוֹנֵךְ] מִצִּמְאָה וַתֹּאמְרִי נוֹאָשׁ לוֹא כִּי־אָהַבְתִּי זָרִים וְאַחֲרֵיהֶם אֵלֵךְ:

²⁶ Like a thief chagrined when he is caught, So is the House of *Yisrael* chagrined – They, their kings, their officers, And their *Kohanim* and *Neviim*.

כו כְּבֹשֶׁת גַּנָּב כִּי יִמָּצֵא כֵּן הֹבִישׁוּ בֵּית יִשְׂרָאֵל הֵמָּה מַלְכֵיהֶם שָׂרֵיהֶם וְכֹהֲנֵיהֶם וּנְבִיאֵיהֶם:

²⁷ They said to wood, "You are my father," To stone, "You gave birth to me," While to Me they turned their backs And not their faces. But in their hour of calamity they cry, "Arise and save us!"

כז אֹמְרִים לָעֵץ אָבִי אַתָּה וְלָאֶבֶן אַתְּ ילדתני [יְלִדְתָּנוּ] כִּי־פָנוּ אֵלַי עֹרֶף וְלֹא פָנִים וּבְעֵת רָעָתָם יֹאמְרוּ קוּמָה וְהוֹשִׁיעֵנוּ:

Jeremiah

28 And where are those gods You made for yourself? Let them arise and save you, if they can, In your hour of calamity. For your gods have become, O *Yehuda*, As many as your towns!

29 Why do you call Me to account? You have all rebelled against Me – declares *Hashem*.

30 To no purpose did I smite your children; They would not accept correction. Your sword has devoured your *Neviim* Like a ravening lion.

31 O generation, behold the word of *Hashem*! Have I been like a desert to *Yisrael*, Or like a land of deep gloom? Then why do My people say, "We have broken loose, We will not come to You any more?"

32 Can a maiden forget her jewels, A bride her adornments? Yet My people have forgotten Me – Days without number.

33 How skillfully you plan your way To seek out love! Why, you have even taught The worst of women your ways.

34 Moreover, on your garments is found The lifeblood of the innocent poor – You did not catch them breaking in. Yet, despite all these things,

35 You say, "I have been acquitted; Surely, His anger has turned away from me." Lo, I will bring you to judgment For saying, "I have not sinned."

36 How you cheapen yourself, By changing your course! You shall be put to shame through Egypt, Just as you were put to shame through Assyria.

37 From this way, too, you will come out With your hands on your head; For *Hashem* has rejected those you trust, You will not prosper with them.1

3 1 [The word of *Hashem* came to me] as follows: If a man divorces his wife, and she leaves him and marries another man, can he ever go back to her? Would not such a land be defiled? Now you have whored with many lovers: can you return to Me? – says *Hashem*.

2 Look up to the bare heights, and see: Where have they not lain with you? You waited for them on the roadside Like a bandit in the wilderness. And you defiled the land With your whoring and your debauchery.

כח וְאַיֵּה אֱלֹהֶיךָ אֲשֶׁר עָשִׂיתָ לָּךְ יָקוּמוּ אִם־יוֹשִׁיעוּךָ בְּעֵת רָעָתֶךָ כִּי מִסְפַּר עָרֶיךָ הָיוּ אֱלֹהֶיךָ יְהוּדָה:

כט לָמָּה תָרִיבוּ אֵלָי כֻּלְּכֶם פְּשַׁעְתֶּם בִּי נְאֻם־יְהֹוָה:

ל לַשָּׁוְא הִכֵּיתִי אֶת־בְּנֵיכֶם מוּסָר לֹא לָקָחוּ אָכְלָה חַרְבְּכֶם נְבִיאֵיכֶם כְּאַרְיֵה מַשְׁחִית:

לא הַדּוֹר אַתֶּם רְאוּ דְבַר־יְהֹוָה הֲמִדְבָּר הָיִיתִי לְיִשְׂרָאֵל אִם אֶרֶץ מַאְפֵּלְיָה מַדּוּעַ אָמְרוּ עַמִּי רַדְנוּ לוֹא־נָבוֹא עוֹד אֵלֶיךָ:

לב הֲתִשְׁכַּח בְּתוּלָה עֶדְיָהּ כַּלָּה קִשֻּׁרֶיהָ וְעַמִּי שְׁכֵחוּנִי יָמִים אֵין מִסְפָּר:

לג מַה־תֵּיטִבִי דַּרְכֵּךְ לְבַקֵּשׁ אַהֲבָה לָכֵן גַּם אֶת־הָרָעוֹת למדתי [לִמַּדְתְּ] אֶת־דְּרָכָיִךְ:

לד גַּם בִּכְנָפַיִךְ נִמְצְאוּ דַּם נַפְשׁוֹת אֶבְיוֹנִים נְקִיִּים לֹא־בַמַּחְתֶּרֶת מְצָאתִים כִּי עַל־כָּל־אֵלֶּה:

לה וַתֹּאמְרִי כִּי נִקֵּיתִי אַךְ שָׁב אַפּוֹ מִמֶּנִּי הִנְנִי נִשְׁפָּט אוֹתָךְ עַל־אָמְרֵךְ לֹא חָטָאתִי:

לו מַה־תֵּזְלִי מְאֹד לְשַׁנּוֹת אֶת־דַּרְכֵּךְ גַּם מִמִּצְרַיִם תֵּבוֹשִׁי כַּאֲשֶׁר־בֹּשְׁתְּ מֵאַשּׁוּר:

לז גַּם מֵאֵת זֶה תֵּצְאִי וְיָדַיִךְ עַל־רֹאשֵׁךְ כִּי־מָאַס יְהֹוָה בְּמִבְטַחַיִךְ וְלֹא תַצְלִיחִי לָהֶם:

ג א לֵאמֹר הֵן יְשַׁלַּח אִישׁ אֶת־אִשְׁתּוֹ וְהָלְכָה מֵאִתּוֹ וְהָיְתָה לְאִישׁ־אַחֵר הֲיָשׁוּב אֵלֶיהָ עוֹד הֲלוֹא חָנוֹף תֶּחֱנַף הָאָרֶץ הַהִיא וְאַתְּ זָנִית רֵעִים רַבִּים וְשׁוֹב אֵלַי נְאֻם־יְהֹוָה:

ב שְׂאִי־עֵינַיִךְ עַל־שְׁפָיִם וּרְאִי אֵיפֹה לֹא שֻׁגַּלְתְּ [שֻׁכַּבְתְּ] עַל־דְּרָכִים יָשַׁבְתְּ לָהֶם כַּעֲרָבִי בַּמִּדְבָּר וַתַּחֲנִיפִי אֶרֶץ בִּזְנוּתַיִךְ וּבְרָעָתֵךְ:

3 And when showers were withheld And the late rains did not come, You had the brazenness of a street woman, You refused to be ashamed.

4 Just now you called to Me, "Father! You are the Companion of my youth.

5 Does one hate for all time? Does one rage forever?" That is how you spoke; You did wrong, and had your way.

6 *Hashem* said to me in the days of King *Yoshiyahu*: Have you seen what Rebel *Yisrael* did, going to every high mountain and under every leafy tree, and whoring there?

7 I thought: After she has done all these things, she will come back to Me. But she did not come back; and her sister, Faithless *Yehuda*, saw it.

8 I noted: Because Rebel *Yisrael* had committed adultery, I cast her off and handed her a bill of divorce; yet her sister, Faithless *Yehuda*, was not afraid – she too went and whored.

9 Indeed, the land was defiled by her casual immorality, as she committed adultery with stone and with wood.

10 And after all that, her sister, Faithless *Yehuda*, did not return to Me wholeheartedly, but insincerely – declares *Hashem*.

11 And *Hashem* said to me: Rebel *Yisrael* has shown herself more in the right than Faithless *Yehuda*.

12 Go, make this proclamation toward the north, and say: Turn back, O Rebel *Yisrael* – declares *Hashem*. I will not look on you in anger, for I am compassionate – declares *Hashem*; I do not bear a grudge for all time.

13 Only recognize your sin; for you have transgressed against *Hashem* your God, and scattered your favors among strangers under every leafy tree, and you have not heeded Me – declares *Hashem*.

14 Turn back, rebellious children – declares *Hashem*. Since I have espoused you, I will take you, one from a town and two from a clan, and bring you to *Tzion*.

15 And I will give you shepherds after My own heart, who will pasture you with knowledge and skill.

ג וַיִּמָּנְעוּ רְבִבִים וּמַלְקוֹשׁ לוֹא הָיָה וּמֵצַח אִשָּׁה זוֹנָה הָיָה לָךְ מֵאַנְתְּ הִכָּלֵם:

ד הֲלוֹא מֵעַתָּה קָרָאתי [קָרָאת] לִי אָבִי אַלּוּף נְעֻרַי אָתָּה:

ה הֲיִנְטֹר לְעוֹלָם אִם־יִשְׁמֹר לָנֶצַח הִנֵּה דברתי [דִבַּרְתְּ] וַתַּעֲשִׂי הָרָעוֹת וַתּוּכָל:

ו וַיֹּאמֶר יְהוָה אֵלַי בִּימֵי יֹאשִׁיָּהוּ הַמֶּלֶךְ הֲרָאִיתָ אֲשֶׁר עָשְׂתָה מְשֻׁבָה יִשְׂרָאֵל הֹלְכָה הִיא עַל־כָּל־הַר גָּבֹהַ וְאֶל־תַּחַת כָּל־עֵץ רַעֲנָן וַתִּזְנִי־שָׁם:

ז וָאֹמַר אַחֲרֵי עֲשׂוֹתָהּ אֶת־כָּל־אֵלֶּה אֵלַי תָּשׁוּב וְלֹא־שָׁבָה ותראה [וַתֵּרֶא] בָּגוֹדָה אֲחוֹתָהּ יְהוּדָה:

ח וָאֵרֶא כִּי עַל־כָּל־אֹדוֹת אֲשֶׁר נִאֲפָה מְשֻׁבָה יִשְׂרָאֵל שִׁלַּחְתִּיהָ וָאֶתֵּן אֶת־סֵפֶר כְּרִיתֻתֶיהָ אֵלֶיהָ וְלֹא יָרְאָה בֹּגֵדָה יְהוּדָה אֲחוֹתָהּ וַתֵּלֶךְ וַתִּזֶן גַּם־הִיא:

ט וְהָיָה מִקֹּל זְנוּתָהּ וַתֶּחֱנַף אֶת־הָאָרֶץ וַתִּנְאַף אֶת־הָאֶבֶן וְאֶת־הָעֵץ:

י וְגַם־בְּכָל־זֹאת לֹא־שָׁבָה אֵלַי בָּגוֹדָה אֲחוֹתָהּ יְהוּדָה בְּכָל־לִבָּהּ כִּי אִם־בְּשֶׁקֶר נְאֻם־יְהוָה:

יא וַיֹּאמֶר יְהוָה אֵלַי צִדְּקָה נַפְשָׁהּ מְשֻׁבָה יִשְׂרָאֵל מִבֹּגֵדָה יְהוּדָה:

יב הָלֹךְ וְקָרָאתָ אֶת־הַדְּבָרִים הָאֵלֶּה צָפוֹנָה וְאָמַרְתָּ שׁוּבָה מְשֻׁבָה יִשְׂרָאֵל נְאֻם־יְהוָה לוֹא־אַפִּיל פָּנַי בָּכֶם כִּי־חָסִיד אֲנִי נְאֻם־יְהוָה לֹא אֶטּוֹר לְעוֹלָם:

יג אַךְ דְּעִי עֲוֹנֵךְ כִּי בַּיהוָה אֱלֹהַיִךְ פָּשָׁעַתְּ וַתְּפַזְּרִי אֶת־דְּרָכַיִךְ לַזָּרִים תַּחַת כָּל־עֵץ רַעֲנָן וּבְקוֹלִי לֹא־שְׁמַעְתֶּם נְאֻם־יְהוָה:

יד שׁוּבוּ בָנִים שׁוֹבָבִים נְאֻם־יְהוָה כִּי אָנֹכִי בָּעַלְתִּי בָכֶם וְלָקַחְתִּי אֶתְכֶם אֶחָד מֵעִיר וּשְׁנַיִם מִמִּשְׁפָּחָה וְהֵבֵאתִי אֶתְכֶם צִיּוֹן:

טו וְנָתַתִּי לָכֶם רֹעִים כְּלִבִּי וְרָעוּ אֶתְכֶם דֵּעָה וְהַשְׂכֵּיל:

¹⁶ And when you increase and are fertile in the land, in those days – declares *Hashem* – men shall no longer speak of the *Aron Brit Hashem*, nor shall it come to mind. They shall not mention it, or miss it, or make another.

טז וְהָיָה כִּי תִרְבּוּ וּפְרִיתֶם בָּאָרֶץ בַּיָּמִים הָהֵמָּה נְאֻם־יְהֹוָה לֹא־יֹאמְרוּ עוֹד אֲרוֹן בְּרִית־יְהֹוָה וְלֹא יַעֲלֶה עַל־לֵב וְלֹא יִזְכְּרוּ־בוֹ וְלֹא יִפְקֹדוּ וְלֹא יֵעָשֶׂה עוֹד:

¹⁷ At that time, they shall call *Yerushalayim* "Throne of *Hashem*," and all nations shall assemble there, in the name of *Hashem*, at *Yerushalayim*. They shall no longer follow the willfulness of their evil hearts.

יז בָּעֵת הַהִיא יִקְרְאוּ לִירוּשָׁלַם כִּסֵּא יְהֹוָה וְנִקְווּ אֵלֶיהָ כׇל־הַגּוֹיִם לְשֵׁם יְהֹוָה לִירוּשָׁלָםִ וְלֹא־יֵלְכוּ עוֹד אַחֲרֵי שְׁרִרוּת לִבָּם הָרָע:

¹⁸ In those days, the House of *Yehuda* shall go with the House of *Yisrael*; they shall come together from the land of the north to the land I gave your fathers as a possession.

יח בַּיָּמִים הָהֵמָּה יֵלְכוּ בֵית־יְהוּדָה עַל־בֵּית יִשְׂרָאֵל וְיָבֹאוּ יַחְדָּו מֵאֶרֶץ צָפוֹן עַל־הָאָרֶץ אֲשֶׁר הִנְחַלְתִּי אֶת־אֲבוֹתֵיכֶם:

¹⁹ I had resolved to adopt you as My child, and I gave you a desirable land – the fairest heritage of all the nations; and I thought you would surely call Me "Father," and never cease to be loyal to Me.

יט וְאָנֹכִי אָמַרְתִּי אֵיךְ אֲשִׁיתֵךְ בַּבָּנִים וְאֶתֶּן־לָךְ אֶרֶץ חֶמְדָּה נַחֲלַת צְבִי צִבְאוֹת גּוֹיִם וָאֹמַר אָבִי תִּקְרְאוּ [תִּקְרְאִי] לִי וּמֵאַחֲרַי לֹא תָשׁוּבוּ [תָשׁוּבִי]:

v'-a-no-KHEE a-MAR-tee AYKH a-shee-TAYKH ba-ba-NEEM v'-e-ten
LAKH E-retz khem-DAH na-kha-LAT tz'-VEE tziv-OT go-YIM
va-o-MAR a-VEE tik-r'-ee LEE u-may-a-kha-RAI LO ta-SHU-vee

²⁰ Instead, you have broken faith with Me, as a woman breaks faith with a paramour, O House of *Yisrael* – declares *Hashem*.

כ אָכֵן בָּגְדָה אִשָּׁה מֵרֵעָהּ כֵּן בְּגַדְתֶּם בִּי בֵּית יִשְׂרָאֵל נְאֻם־יְהֹוָה:

²¹ Hark! On the bare heights is heard The suppliant weeping of the people of *Yisrael*, For they have gone a crooked way, Ignoring *Hashem* their God.

כא קוֹל עַל־שְׁפָיִים נִשְׁמָע בְּכִי תַחֲנוּנֵי בְּנֵי יִשְׂרָאֵל כִּי הֶעֱווּ אֶת־דַּרְכָּם שָׁכְחוּ אֶת־יְהֹוָה אֱלֹהֵיהֶם:

²² Turn back, O rebellious children, I will heal your afflictions! "Here we are, we come to You, For You, *Hashem*, are our God!

כב שׁוּבוּ בָּנִים שׁוֹבָבִים אֶרְפָּה מְשׁוּבֹתֵיכֶם הִנְנוּ אָתָנוּ לָךְ כִּי אַתָּה יְהֹוָה אֱלֹהֵינוּ:

²³ Surely, futility comes from the hills, Confusion from the mountains. Only through *Hashem* our God Is there deliverance for *Yisrael*.

כג אָכֵן לַשֶּׁקֶר מִגְּבָעוֹת הָמוֹן הָרִים אָכֵן בַּיהֹוָה אֱלֹהֵינוּ תְּשׁוּעַת יִשְׂרָאֵל:

²⁴ But the Shameful Thing has consumed The possessions of our fathers ever since our youth – Their flocks and herds, Their sons and daughters.

כד וְהַבֹּשֶׁת אָכְלָה אֶת־יְגִיעַ אֲבוֹתֵינוּ מִנְּעוּרֵינוּ אֶת־צֹאנָם וְאֶת־בְּקָרָם אֶת־בְּנֵיהֶם וְאֶת־בְּנוֹתֵיהֶם:

ארץ חמדה

3:19 A desirable land – the fairest heritage of all the nations *Yirmiyahu* describes the Land of Israel as *eretz chemda* (ארץ חמדה), 'a desirable land.' The commentator *Radak* explains that *Yirmiyahu* uses this description since *Eretz Yisrael* is desired by all the nations. *Hashem*'s holy presence is so palpable there, that everyone senses its holiness and wants it. One needs to look no further than the morning newspapers or the nightly news to appreciate the accuracy of the *Radak*'s words. Despite its small size, Israel is a "desired land" sought after by "all the nations."

Israel365 tour group visits *Chevron*

²⁵ Let us lie down in our shame, Let our disgrace cover us; For we have sinned against *Hashem* our God, We and our fathers from our youth to this day, And we have not heeded *Hashem* our God."

נִשְׁכְּבָה בְּבָשְׁתֵּנוּ וּתְכַסֵּנוּ כְּלִמָּתֵנוּ כִּי כה לַיהֹוָה אֱלֹהֵינוּ חָטָאנוּ אֲנַחְנוּ וַאֲבוֹתֵינוּ מִנְּעוּרֵינוּ וְעַד־הַיּוֹם הַזֶּה וְלֹא שָׁמַעְנוּ בְּקוֹל יְהֹוָה אֱלֹהֵינוּ:

4 ¹ If you return, O *Yisrael* – declares *Hashem* – If you return to Me, If you remove your abominations from My presence And do not waver,

אִם־תָּשׁוּב יִשְׂרָאֵל נְאֻם־יְהֹוָה אֵלַי א ד תָּשׁוּב וְאִם־תָּסִיר שִׁקּוּצֶיךָ מִפָּנַי וְלֹא תָנוּד:

² And swear, "As *Hashem* lives," In sincerity, justice, and righteousness – Nations shall bless themselves by you And praise themselves by you.

וְנִשְׁבַּעְתָּ חַי־יְהֹוָה בֶּאֱמֶת בְּמִשְׁפָּט ב וּבִצְדָקָה וְהִתְבָּרְכוּ בוֹ גּוֹיִם וּבוֹ יִתְהַלָּלוּ:

³ For thus said *Hashem* to the men of *Yehuda* and to *Yerushalayim*: Break up the untilled ground, And do not sow among thorns.

כִּי־כֹה אָמַר יְהֹוָה לְאִישׁ יְהוּדָה ג וְלִירוּשָׁלַם נִירוּ לָכֶם נִיר וְאַל־תִּזְרְעוּ אֶל־קוֹצִים:

⁴ Open your hearts to *Hashem*, Remove the thickening about your hearts – O men of *Yehuda* and inhabitants of *Yerushalayim* – Lest My wrath break forth like fire, And burn, with none to quench it, Because of your wicked acts.

הִמֹּלוּ לַיהֹוָה וְהָסִרוּ עָרְלוֹת לְבַבְכֶם ד אִישׁ יְהוּדָה וְיֹשְׁבֵי יְרוּשָׁלָם פֶּן־תֵּצֵא כָאֵשׁ חֲמָתִי וּבָעֲרָה וְאֵין מְכַבֶּה מִפְּנֵי רֹעַ מַעַלְלֵיכֶם:

⁵ Proclaim in *Yehuda*, Announce in *Yerushalayim*, And say: "Blow the *shofar* in the land!" Shout aloud and say: "Assemble, and let us go Into the fortified cities!"

הַגִּידוּ בִיהוּדָה וּבִירוּשָׁלַם הַשְׁמִיעוּ ה וְאִמְרוּ וְתִקְעוּ [תִּקְעוּ] שׁוֹפָר בָּאָרֶץ קִרְאוּ מַלְאוּ וְאִמְרוּ הֵאָסְפוּ וְנָבוֹאָה אֶל־עָרֵי הַמִּבְצָר:

⁶ Set up a signpost: To *Tzion*. Take refuge, do not delay! For I bring evil from the north, And great disaster.

שְׂאוּ־נֵס צִיּוֹנָה הָעִיזוּ אַל־תַּעֲמֹדוּ כִּי ו רָעָה אָנֹכִי מֵבִיא מִצָּפוֹן וְשֶׁבֶר גָּדוֹל:

s'-u NAYS tzi-YO-nah ha-EE-zu al ta-a-MO-du KEE ra-AH
a-no-KHEE may-VEE mi-tza-FON v'-SHE-ver ga-DOL

⁷ The lion has come up from his thicket: The destroyer of nations has set out, Has departed from his place, To make your land a desolation; Your cities shall be ruined, Without inhabitants.

עָלָה אַרְיֵה מִסֻּבְּכוֹ וּמַשְׁחִית גּוֹיִם נָסַע ז יָצָא מִמְּקֹמוֹ לָשׂוּם אַרְצֵךְ לְשַׁמָּה עָרַיִךְ תִּצֶּינָה מֵאֵין יוֹשֵׁב:

⁸ For this, put on sackcloth, Mourn and wail; For the blazing anger of *Hashem* Has not turned away from us.

עַל־זֹאת חִגְרוּ שַׂקִּים סִפְדוּ וְהֵילִילוּ כִּי ח לֹא־שָׁב חֲרוֹן אַף־יְהֹוָה מִמֶּנּוּ:

Jeremiah

Nes Tziona

🔶 **4:6 Set up a signpost: To *Tzion*** After the sentry alerts the nation to the invaders from the north, the people flock to *Yerushalayim* for protection. To guide and direct them, signposts will be established on the roadways. The Hebrew term *nes tziona* (נס ציונה), 'a signpost: To *Tzion*,' became the name of one of the first towns established in Israel by returning Jews at the end of the nineteenth century. In 1891, a man by the name of Michael Halperin gathered a group of people in Central Israel and unfurled a blue and white flag emblazoned with the words *nes tziona* written in gold. This location became the modern-day city of *Nes Tziona*, and Halperin's banner became the model for the future Israeli flag.

9 And in that day – declares *Hashem* – The mind of the king And the mind of the nobles shall fail, The *Kohanim* shall be appalled, And the *Neviim* shall stand aghast.

ט וְהָיָה בַיּוֹם־הַהוּא נְאֻם־יְהֹוָה יֹאבַד לֵב־הַמֶּלֶךְ וְלֵב הַשָּׂרִים וְנָשַׁמּוּ הַכֹּהֲנִים וְהַנְּבִיאִים יִתְמָהוּ:

10 And I said: Ah, *Hashem*! Surely You have deceived this people and *Yerushalayim* saying: It shall be well with you – Yet the sword threatens the very life!

י וָאֹמַר אֲהָהּ אֲדֹנָי יֱהֹוִה אָכֵן הַשֵּׁא הִשֵּׁאתָ לָעָם הַזֶּה וְלִירוּשָׁלַ͏ִם לֵאמֹר שָׁלוֹם יִהְיֶה לָכֶם וְנָגְעָה חֶרֶב עַד־הַנָּפֶשׁ:

11 At that time, it shall be said concerning this people and *Yerushalayim*: The conduct of My poor people is like searing wind From the bare heights of the desert – It will not serve to winnow or to fan.

יא בָּעֵת הַהִיא יֵאָמֵר לָעָם־הַזֶּה וְלִירוּשָׁלַ͏ִם רוּחַ צַח שְׁפָיִים בַּמִּדְבָּר דֶּרֶךְ בַּת־עַמִּי לוֹא לִזְרוֹת וְלוֹא לְהָבַר:

12 A full blast from them comes against Me: Now I in turn will bring charges against them.

יב רוּחַ מָלֵא מֵאֵלֶּה יָבוֹא לִי עַתָּה גַּם־אֲנִי אֲדַבֵּר מִשְׁפָּטִים אוֹתָם:

13 Lo, he ascends like clouds, His chariots are like a whirlwind, His horses are swifter than eagles. Woe to us, we are ruined!

יג הִנֵּה כַּעֲנָנִים יַעֲלֶה וְכַסּוּפָה מַרְכְּבוֹתָיו קַלּוּ מִנְּשָׁרִים סוּסָיו אוֹי לָנוּ כִּי שֻׁדָּדְנוּ:

14 Wash your heart clean of wickedness, O *Yerushalayim*, that you may be rescued. How long will you harbor within you Your evil designs?

יד כַּבְּסִי מֵרָעָה לִבֵּךְ יְרוּשָׁלַ͏ִם לְמַעַן תִּוָּשֵׁעִי עַד־מָתַי תָּלִין בְּקִרְבֵּךְ מַחְשְׁבוֹת אוֹנֵךְ:

15 Hark, one proclaims from *Dan* And announces calamity from Mount *Efraim*!

טו כִּי קוֹל מַגִּיד מִדָּן וּמַשְׁמִיעַ אָוֶן מֵהַר אֶפְרָיִם:

16 Tell the nations: Here they are! Announce concerning *Yerushalayim*: Watchers are coming from a distant land, They raise their voices against the towns of *Yehuda*.

טז הַזְכִּירוּ לַגּוֹיִם הִנֵּה הַשְׁמִיעוּ עַל־יְרוּשָׁלַ͏ִם נֹצְרִים בָּאִים מֵאֶרֶץ הַמֶּרְחָק וַיִּתְּנוּ עַל־עָרֵי יְהוּדָה קוֹלָם:

17 Like guards of fields, they surround her on every side. For she has rebelled against Me – declares *Hashem*.

יז כְּשֹׁמְרֵי שָׂדַי הָיוּ עָלֶיהָ מִסָּבִיב כִּי־אֹתִי מָרָתָה נְאֻם־יְהֹוָה:

18 Your conduct and your acts Have brought this upon you; This is your bitter punishment; It pierces your very heart.

יח דַּרְכֵּךְ וּמַעֲלָלַיִךְ עָשׂוֹ אֵלֶּה לָךְ זֹאת רָעָתֵךְ כִּי מָר כִּי נָגַע עַד־לִבֵּךְ:

19 Oh, my suffering, my suffering! How I writhe! Oh, the walls of my heart! My heart moans within me, I cannot be silent; For I hear the blare of *shofarot*, Alarms of war.

יט מֵעַי מֵעַי אֹחִילָה [אוֹחִילָה] קִירוֹת לִבִּי הֹמֶה־לִי לִבִּי לֹא אַחֲרִישׁ כִּי קוֹל שׁוֹפָר שמעתי [שָׁמַעַתְּ] נַפְשִׁי תְּרוּעַת מִלְחָמָה:

20 Disaster overtakes disaster, For all the land has been ravaged. Suddenly my tents have been ravaged, In a moment, my tent cloths.

כ שֶׁבֶר עַל־שֶׁבֶר נִקְרָא כִּי שֻׁדְּדָה כָּל־הָאָרֶץ פִּתְאֹם שֻׁדְּדוּ אֹהָלַי רֶגַע יְרִיעֹתָי:

21 How long must I see standards And hear the blare of *shofarot*?

כא עַד־מָתַי אֶרְאֶה־נֵּס אֶשְׁמְעָה קוֹל שׁוֹפָר:

22 For My people are stupid, They give Me no heed; They are foolish children, They are not intelligent. They are clever at doing wrong, But unable to do right.

כב כִּי אֱוִיל עַמִּי אוֹתִי לֹא יָדָעוּ בָּנִים סְכָלִים הֵמָּה וְלֹא נְבוֹנִים הֵמָּה חֲכָמִים הֵמָּה לְהָרַע וּלְהֵיטִיב לֹא יָדָעוּ:

23 I look at the earth, It is unformed and void; At the skies, And their light is gone.

כג רָאִיתִי אֶת־הָאָרֶץ וְהִנֵּה־תֹהוּ וָבֹהוּ וְאֶל־הַשָּׁמַיִם וְאֵין אוֹרָם:

24 I look at the mountains, They are quaking; And all the hills are rocking.

כד רָאִיתִי הֶהָרִים וְהִנֵּה רֹעֲשִׁים וְכָל־הַגְּבָעוֹת הִתְקַלְקָלוּ:

25 I look: no man is left, And all the birds of the sky have fled.

כה רָאִיתִי וְהִנֵּה אֵין הָאָדָם וְכָל־עוֹף הַשָּׁמַיִם נָדָדוּ:

26 I look: the farm land is desert, And all its towns are in ruin – Because of *Hashem*, Because of His blazing anger.

כו רָאִיתִי וְהִנֵּה הַכַּרְמֶל הַמִּדְבָּר וְכָל־עָרָיו נִתְּצוּ מִפְּנֵי יְהוָה מִפְּנֵי חֲרוֹן אַפּוֹ:

27 For thus said *Hashem*: The whole land shall be desolate, But I will not make an end of it.)

כז כִּי־כֹה אָמַר יְהוָה שְׁמָמָה תִהְיֶה כָּל־הָאָרֶץ וְכָלָה לֹא אֶעֱשֶׂה:

28 For this the earth mourns, And skies are dark above – Because I have spoken, I have planned, And I will not relent or turn back from it.

כח עַל־זֹאת תֶּאֱבַל הָאָרֶץ וְקָדְרוּ הַשָּׁמַיִם מִמָּעַל עַל כִּי־דִבַּרְתִּי זַמֹּתִי וְלֹא נִחַמְתִּי וְלֹא־אָשׁוּב מִמֶּנָּה:

29 At the shout of horseman and bowman The whole city flees. They enter the thickets, They clamber up the rocks. The whole city is deserted, Not a man remains there.

כט מִקּוֹל פָּרָשׁ וְרֹמֵה קֶשֶׁת בֹּרַחַת כָּל־הָעִיר בָּאוּ בֶּעָבִים וּבַכֵּפִים עָלוּ כָּל־הָעִיר עֲזוּבָה וְאֵין־יוֹשֵׁב בָּהֵן אִישׁ:

30 And you, who are doomed to ruin, What do you accomplish by wearing crimson, By decking yourself in jewels of gold, By enlarging your eyes with kohl? You beautify yourself in vain: Lovers despise you, They seek your life!

ל וְאַתְּ [וְאַתְּ] שָׁדוּד מַה־תַּעֲשִׂי כִּי־תִלְבְּשִׁי שָׁנִי כִּי־תַעְדִּי עֲדִי־זָהָב כִּי־תִקְרְעִי בַפּוּךְ עֵינַיִךְ לַשָּׁוְא תִּתְיַפִּי מָאֲסוּ־בָךְ עֹגְבִים נַפְשֵׁךְ יְבַקֵּשׁוּ:

31 I hear a voice as of one in travail, Anguish as of a woman bearing her first child, The voice of Fair *Tzion* Panting, stretching out her hands: "Alas for me! I faint Before the killers!"

לא כִּי קוֹל כְּחוֹלָה שָׁמַעְתִּי צָרָה כְּמַבְכִּירָה קוֹל בַּת־צִיּוֹן תִּתְיַפֵּחַ תְּפָרֵשׂ כַּפֶּיהָ אוֹי־נָא לִי כִּי־עָיְפָה נַפְשִׁי לְהֹרְגִים:

5 1 Roam the streets of *Yerushalayim*, Search its squares, Look about and take note: You will not find a man, There is none who acts justly, Who seeks integrity – That I should pardon her.

ה א שׁוֹטְטוּ בְּחוּצוֹת יְרוּשָׁלַיִם וּרְאוּ־נָא וּדְעוּ וּבַקְּשׁוּ בִרְחוֹבוֹתֶיהָ אִם־תִּמְצְאוּ אִישׁ אִם־יֵשׁ עֹשֶׂה מִשְׁפָּט מְבַקֵּשׁ אֱמוּנָה וְאֶסְלַח לָהּ:

2 Even when they say, "As *Hashem* lives," They are sure to be swearing falsely.

ב וְאִם חַי־יְהוָה יֹאמֵרוּ לָכֵן לַשֶּׁקֶר יִשָּׁבֵעוּ:

3 *Hashem*, Your eyes look for integrity. You have struck them, but they sensed no pain; You have consumed them, but they would accept no discipline. They made their faces harder than rock, They refused to turn back.

ג יְהוָה עֵינֶיךָ הֲלוֹא לֶאֱמוּנָה הִכִּיתָה אֹתָם וְלֹא־חָלוּ כִּלִּיתָם מֵאֲנוּ קַחַת מוּסָר חִזְּקוּ פְנֵיהֶם מִסֶּלַע מֵאֲנוּ לָשׁוּב:

4 Then I thought: These are just poor folk; They act foolishly; For they do not know the way of *Hashem*, The rules of their God.

ד וַאֲנִי אָמַרְתִּי אַךְ־דַּלִּים הֵם נוֹאֲלוּ כִּי לֹא יָדְעוּ דֶּרֶךְ יְהֹוָה מִשְׁפַּט אֱלֹהֵיהֶם:

5 So I will go to the wealthy And speak with them: Surely they know the way of *Hashem*, The rules of their God. But they as well had broken the yoke, Had snapped the bonds.

ה אֵלֲכָה־לִּי אֶל־הַגְּדֹלִים וַאֲדַבְּרָה אוֹתָם כִּי הֵמָּה יָדְעוּ דֶּרֶךְ יְהֹוָה מִשְׁפַּט אֱלֹהֵיהֶם אַךְ הֵמָּה יַחְדָּו שָׁבְרוּ עֹל נִתְּקוּ מוֹסֵרוֹת:

6 Therefore, The lion of the forest strikes them down, The wolf of the desert ravages them. A leopard lies in wait by their towns; Whoever leaves them will be torn in pieces. For their transgressions are many, Their rebellious acts unnumbered.

ו עַל־כֵּן הִכָּם אַרְיֵה מִיַּעַר זְאֵב עֲרָבוֹת יְשָׁדְדֵם נָמֵר שֹׁקֵד עַל־עָרֵיהֶם כָּל־הַיּוֹצֵא מֵהֵנָּה יִטָּרֵף כִּי רַבּוּ פִּשְׁעֵיהֶם עָצְמוּ משבותיהם [מְשׁוּבוֹתֵיהֶם]:

*al KAYN hi-KAM ar-YAY mi-YA-ar z'-AYV a-ra-VOT y'-sho-d'-DAYM
na-MAYR sho-KAYD al a-ray-HEM kol ha-yo-TZAY may-HAY-nah
yi-ta-RAYF KEE ra-BU pish-ay-HEM a-tz'-MU m'-shu-vo-tay-HEM*

7 Why should I forgive you? Your children have forsaken Me And sworn by no-gods. When I fed them their fill, They committed adultery And went trooping to the harlot's house.

ז אֵי לָזֹאת אסלוח־[אֶסְלַח־] לָךְ בָּנַיִךְ עֲזָבוּנִי וַיִּשָּׁבְעוּ בְּלֹא אֱלֹהִים וָאַשְׂבִּעַ אוֹתָם וַיִּנְאָפוּ וּבֵית זוֹנָה יִתְגֹּדָדוּ:

8 They were well-fed, lusty stallions, Each neighing at another's wife.

ח סוּסִים מְיֻזָּנִים מַשְׁכִּים הָיוּ אִישׁ אֶל־אֵשֶׁת רֵעֵהוּ יִצְהָלוּ:

9 Shall I not punish such deeds? – says *Hashem* – Shall I not bring retribution On a nation such as this?

ט הַעַל־אֵלֶּה לוֹא־אֶפְקֹד נְאֻם־יְהֹוָה וְאִם בְּגוֹי אֲשֶׁר־כָּזֶה לֹא תִתְנַקֵּם נַפְשִׁי:

10 Go up among her vines and destroy; Lop off her trailing branches, For they are not of *Hashem*. (But do not make an end.)

י עֲלוּ בְשָׁרוֹתֶיהָ וְשַׁחֵתוּ וְכָלָה אַל־תַּעֲשׂוּ הָסִירוּ נְטִישׁוֹתֶיהָ כִּי לוֹא לַיהֹוָה הֵמָּה:

11 For the House of *Yisrael* and the House of *Yehuda* Have betrayed Me – declares *Hashem*.

יא כִּי בָגוֹד בָּגְדוּ בִּי בֵּית יִשְׂרָאֵל וּבֵית יְהוּדָה נְאֻם־יְהֹוָה:

12 They have been false to *Hashem* And said: "It is not so! No trouble shall come upon us, We shall not see sword or famine.

יב כִּחֲשׁוּ בַּיהֹוָה וַיֹּאמְרוּ לֹא־הוּא וְלֹא־תָבוֹא עָלֵינוּ רָעָה וְחֶרֶב וְרָעָב לוֹא נִרְאֶה:

13 The *Neviim* shall prove mere wind For the Word is not in them; Thus-and-thus shall be done to them!"

יג וְהַנְּבִיאִים יִהְיוּ לְרוּחַ וְהַדִּבֵּר אֵין בָּהֶם כֹּה יֵעָשֶׂה לָהֶם:

A lion at the Ramat Gan safari

5:6 The lion of the forest strikes them down In ancient times, the Land of Israel was filled with a variety of animal species, including lions, wolves and leopards, some of which are still found in Israel today. When the Jewish people were obedient to *Hashem*, these animals would not pose a threat, as it says in *Sefer Vayikra* (26:6), "I will grant peace in the land…I will give the land respite from vicious beasts." Should the people sin, however, the animals would become their enemy (Leviticus 26:22). Reflecting these verses, *Yirmiyahu* describes the dangers that await the besieged Israelites by comparing them to wild animals preparing to attack.

¹⁴ Assuredly, thus said *Hashem*, The God of Hosts: Because they said that, I am putting My words into your mouth as fire, And this people shall be firewood, Which it will consume.

לָכֵן כֹּה־אָמַר יְהֹוָה אֱלֹהֵי צְבָאוֹת יַעַן דַּבֶּרְכֶם אֶת־הַדָּבָר הַזֶּה הִנְנִי נֹתֵן דְּבָרַי בְּפִיךָ לְאֵשׁ וְהָעָם הַזֶּה עֵצִים וַאֲכָלָתַם:

¹⁵ Lo, I am bringing against you, O House of *Yisrael*, A nation from afar – declares *Hashem*; It is an enduring nation, It is an ancient nation; A nation whose language you do not know – You will not understand what they say.

הִנְנִי מֵבִיא עֲלֵיכֶם גּוֹי מִמֶּרְחָק בֵּית יִשְׂרָאֵל נְאֻם־יְהֹוָה גּוֹי אֵיתָן הוּא גּוֹי מֵעוֹלָם הוּא גּוֹי לֹא־תֵדַע לְשֹׁנוֹ וְלֹא תִשְׁמַע מַה־יְדַבֵּר:

¹⁶ Their quivers are like a yawning grave – They are all mighty men.

אַשְׁפָּתוֹ כְּקֶבֶר פָּתוּחַ כֻּלָּם גִּבּוֹרִים:

¹⁷ They will devour your harvest and food, They will devour your sons and daughters, They will devour your flocks and herds, They will devour your vines and fig trees. They will batter down with the sword The fortified towns on which you rely.

וְאָכַל קְצִירְךָ וְלַחְמֶךָ יֹאכְלוּ בָּנֶיךָ וּבְנוֹתֶיךָ יֹאכַל צֹאנְךָ וּבְקָרֶךָ יֹאכַל גַּפְנְךָ וּתְאֵנָתֶךָ יְרֹשֵׁשׁ עָרֵי מִבְצָרֶיךָ אֲשֶׁר אַתָּה בּוֹטֵחַ בָּהֵנָּה בֶּחָרֶב:

¹⁸ But even in those days – declares *Hashem* – I will not make an end of you.

וְגַם בַּיָּמִים הָהֵמָּה נְאֻם־יְהֹוָה לֹא־אֶעֱשֶׂה אִתְּכֶם כָּלָה:

¹⁹ And when they ask, "Because of what did *Hashem* our God do all these things?" you shall answer them, "Because you forsook Me and served alien gods on your own land, you will have to serve foreigners in a land not your own."

וְהָיָה כִּי תֹאמְרוּ תַּחַת מֶה עָשָׂה יְהֹוָה אֱלֹהֵינוּ לָנוּ אֶת־כָּל־אֵלֶּה וְאָמַרְתָּ אֲלֵיהֶם כַּאֲשֶׁר עֲזַבְתֶּם אוֹתִי וַתַּעַבְדוּ אֱלֹהֵי נֵכָר בְּאַרְצְכֶם כֵּן תַּעַבְדוּ זָרִים בְּאֶרֶץ לֹא לָכֶם:

²⁰ Proclaim this to the House of *Yaakov* And announce it in *Yehuda*:

הַגִּידוּ זֹאת בְּבֵית יַעֲקֹב וְהַשְׁמִיעוּהָ בִיהוּדָה לֵאמֹר:

²¹ Hear this, O foolish people, Devoid of intelligence, That have eyes but can't see, That have ears but can't hear!

שִׁמְעוּ־נָא זֹאת עַם סָכָל וְאֵין לֵב עֵינַיִם לָהֶם וְלֹא יִרְאוּ אָזְנַיִם לָהֶם וְלֹא יִשְׁמָעוּ:

²² Should you not revere Me – says *Hashem* – Should you not tremble before Me, Who set the sand as a boundary to the sea, As a limit for all time, not to be transgressed? Though its waves toss, they cannot prevail; Though they roar, they cannot pass it.

הַאוֹתִי לֹא־תִירָאוּ נְאֻם־יְהֹוָה אִם מִפָּנַי לֹא תָחִילוּ אֲשֶׁר־שַׂמְתִּי חוֹל גְּבוּל לַיָּם חָק־עוֹלָם וְלֹא יַעַבְרֶנְהוּ וַיִּתְגָּעֲשׁוּ וְלֹא יוּכָלוּ וְהָמוּ גַלָּיו וְלֹא יַעַבְרֻנְהוּ:

²³ Yet this people has a wayward and defiant heart; They have turned aside and gone their way.

וְלָעָם הַזֶּה הָיָה לֵב סוֹרֵר וּמוֹרֶה סָרוּ וַיֵּלֵכוּ:

²⁴ They have not said to themselves, "Let us revere *Hashem* our God, Who gives the rain, The early and late rain in season, Who keeps for our benefit The weeks appointed for harvest."

וְלֹא־אָמְרוּ בִלְבָבָם נִירָא נָא אֶת־יְהֹוָה אֱלֹהֵינוּ הַנֹּתֵן גֶּשֶׁם וִירָה [יוֹרֶה] וּמַלְקוֹשׁ בְּעִתּוֹ שְׁבֻעוֹת חֻקּוֹת קָצִיר יִשְׁמָר־לָנוּ:

²⁵ It is your iniquities that have diverted these things, Your sins that have withheld the bounty from you.

עֲוֺנוֹתֵיכֶם הִטּוּ־אֵלֶּה וְחַטֹּאותֵיכֶם מָנְעוּ הַטּוֹב מִכֶּם:

Jeremiah

26 For among My people are found wicked men, Who lurk, like fowlers lying in wait; They set up a trap to catch men.

כו כִּי־נִמְצְאוּ בְעַמִּי רְשָׁעִים יָשׁוּר כְּשַׁךְ יְקוּשִׁים הִצִּיבוּ מַשְׁחִית אֲנָשִׁים יִלְכֹּדוּ:

27 As a cage is full of birds, So their houses are full of guile; That is why they have grown so wealthy.

כז כִּכְלוּב מָלֵא עוֹף כֵּן בָּתֵּיהֶם מְלֵאִים מִרְמָה עַל־כֵּן גָּדְלוּ וַיַּעֲשִׁירוּ:

28 They have become fat and sleek; They pass beyond the bounds of wickedness, And they prosper. They will not judge the case of the orphan, Nor give a hearing to the plea of the needy.

כח שָׁמְנוּ עָשְׁתוּ גַּם עָבְרוּ דִבְרֵי־רָע דִּין לֹא־דָנוּ דִּין יָתוֹם וְיַצְלִיחוּ וּמִשְׁפַּט אֶבְיוֹנִים לֹא שָׁפָטוּ:

29 Shall I not punish such deeds – says *Hashem* – Shall I not bring retribution On a nation such as this?

כט הַעַל־אֵלֶּה לֹא־אֶפְקֹד נְאֻם־יְהֹוָה אִם בְּגוֹי אֲשֶׁר־כָּזֶה לֹא תִתְנַקֵּם נַפְשִׁי:

30 An appalling, horrible thing Has happened in the land:

ל שַׁמָּה וְשַׁעֲרוּרָה נִהְיְתָה בָּאָרֶץ:

31 The *Neviim* prophesy falsely, And the *Kohanim* rule accordingly; And My people like it so. But what will you do at the end of it?

לא הַנְּבִיאִים נִבְּאוּ בַשֶּׁקֶר וְהַכֹּהֲנִים יִרְדּוּ עַל־יְדֵיהֶם וְעַמִּי אָהֲבוּ כֵן וּמַה־תַּעֲשׂוּ לְאַחֲרִיתָהּ:

6 1 Flee for refuge, O people of *Binyamin*, Out of the midst of *Yerushalayim*! Blow the *shofar* in *Tekoa*, Set up a signal at Beth-haccerem! For evil is appearing from the north, And great disaster.

א הָעִזוּ בְּנֵי בִנְיָמִן מִקֶּרֶב יְרוּשָׁלַ͏ִם וּבִתְקוֹעַ תִּקְעוּ שׁוֹפָר וְעַל־בֵּית הַכֶּרֶם שְׂאוּ מַשְׂאֵת כִּי רָעָה נִשְׁקְפָה מִצָּפוֹן וְשֶׁבֶר גָּדוֹל:

2 Fair *Tzion*, the lovely and delicate, I will destroy.

ב הַנָּוָה וְהַמְּעֻנָּגָה דָּמִיתִי בַּת־צִיּוֹן:

ha-na-VAH v'-ha-m'-u-na-GAH da-MEE-tee bat tzi-YON

3 Against her come shepherds with their flocks, They pitch tents all around her; Each grazes the sheep under his care.

ג אֵלֶיהָ יָבֹאוּ רֹעִים וְעֶדְרֵיהֶם תָּקְעוּ עָלֶיהָ אֹהָלִים סָבִיב רָעוּ אִישׁ אֶת־יָדוֹ:

4 Prepare for battle against her: "Up! we will attack at noon." "Alas for us! for day is declining, The shadows of evening grow long."

ד קַדְּשׁוּ עָלֶיהָ מִלְחָמָה קוּמוּ וְנַעֲלֶה בַצָּהֳרָיִם אוֹי לָנוּ כִּי־פָנָה הַיּוֹם כִּי יִנָּטוּ צִלְלֵי־עָרֶב:

5 "Up! let us attack by night, And wreck her fortresses."

ה קוּמוּ וְנַעֲלֶה בַלָּיְלָה וְנַשְׁחִיתָה אַרְמְנוֹתֶיהָ:

6 For thus said the Lord of Hosts: Hew down her trees, And raise a siegemound against *Yerushalayim*. She is the city destined for punishment; Only fraud is found in her midst.

ו כִּי כֹה אָמַר יְהֹוָה צְבָאוֹת כִּרְתוּ עֵצָה וְשִׁפְכוּ עַל־יְרוּשָׁלַ͏ִם סֹלְלָה הִיא הָעִיר הָפְקַד כֻּלָּהּ עֹשֶׁק בְּקִרְבָּהּ:

6:2 The lovely and delicate In describing the coming invasion, *Yirmiyahu* describes *Tzion* as "lovely and delicate." Some commentators suggest that this is a mocking reference to the women of *Yerushalayim*, whose extravagant tastes and styles contrast with the simple and honest manners

Israel's green hills and rolling pastures

of the country dwellers. *Rashi*, however, understands the phrase "lovely and delicate" as a description of the Land of Israel itself. Her gentle green hills and rolling pastures provided perfect grounds for shepherds to graze their flocks, as described in the next verse.

7 As a well flows with water, So she flows with wickedness. Lawlessness and rapine are heard in her; Before Me constantly are sickness and wounds.

כְּהָקִיר בור [בַּיִר] מֵימֶיהָ כֵּן הֵקֵרָה רָעָתָהּ חָמָס וָשֹׁד יִשָּׁמַע בָהּ עַל־פָּנַי תָּמִיד חֳלִי וּמַכָּה:

8 Accept rebuke, O *Yerushalayim*, Lest I come to loathe you, Lest I make you a desolation, An uninhabited land.

הִוָּסְרִי יְרוּשָׁלִַם פֶּן־תֵּקַע נַפְשִׁי מִמֵּךְ פֶּן־אֲשִׂימֵךְ שְׁמָמָה אֶרֶץ לוֹא נוֹשָׁבָה:

9 Thus said the LORD of Hosts: Let them glean over and over, as a vine, The remnant of *Yisrael*. Pass your hand again, Like a vintager, Over its branches.

כֹּה אָמַר יְהֹוָה צְבָאוֹת עוֹלֵל יְעוֹלְלוּ כַגֶּפֶן שְׁאֵרִית יִשְׂרָאֵל הָשֵׁב יָדְךָ כְּבוֹצֵר עַל־סַלְסִלּוֹת:

10 To whom shall I speak, Give warning that they may hear? Their ears are blocked And they cannot listen. See, the word of *Hashem* has become for them An object of scorn; they will have none of it.

עַל־מִי אֲדַבְּרָה וְאָעִידָה וְיִשְׁמָעוּ הִנֵּה עֲרֵלָה אָזְנָם וְלֹא יוּכְלוּ לְהַקְשִׁיב הִנֵּה דְבַר־יְהֹוָה הָיָה לָהֶם לְחֶרְפָּה לֹא יַחְפְּצוּ־בוֹ:

11 But I am filled with the wrath of *Hashem*, I cannot hold it in. Pour it on the infant in the street, And on the company of youths gathered together! Yes, men and women alike shall be captured, Elders and those of advanced years.

וְאֵת חֲמַת יְהֹוָה מָלֵאתִי נִלְאֵיתִי הָכִיל שְׁפֹךְ עַל־עוֹלָל בַּחוּץ וְעַל סוֹד בַּחוּרִים יַחְדָּו כִּי־גַם־אִישׁ עִם־אִשָּׁה יִלָּכֵדוּ זָקֵן עִם־מְלֵא יָמִים:

12 Their houses shall pass to others, Fields and wives as well, For I will stretch out My arm Against the inhabitants of the country – declares *Hashem*.

וְנָסַבּוּ בָתֵּיהֶם לַאֲחֵרִים שָׂדוֹת וְנָשִׁים יַחְדָּו כִּי־אַטֶּה אֶת־יָדִי עַל־יֹשְׁבֵי הָאָרֶץ נְאֻם־יְהֹוָה:

13 For from the smallest to the greatest, They are all greedy for gain; *Kohen* and *Navi* alike, They all act falsely.

כִּי מִקְּטַנָּם וְעַד־גְּדוֹלָם כֻּלּוֹ בּוֹצֵעַ בָּצַע וּמִנָּבִיא וְעַד־כֹּהֵן כֻּלּוֹ עֹשֶׂה שָּׁקֶר:

14 They offer healing offhand For the wounds of My people, Saying, "All is well, all is well," When nothing is well.

וַיְרַפְּאוּ אֶת־שֶׁבֶר עַמִּי עַל־נְקַלָּה לֵאמֹר שָׁלוֹם שָׁלוֹם וְאֵין שָׁלוֹם:

15 They have acted shamefully; They have done abhorrent things – Yet they do not feel shame, And they cannot be made to blush. Assuredly, they shall fall among the falling, They shall stumble at the time when I punish them – said *Hashem*.

הֹבִישׁוּ כִּי תוֹעֵבָה עָשׂוּ גַּם־בּוֹשׁ לֹא־יֵבוֹשׁוּ גַּם־הַכְלִים לֹא יָדָעוּ לָכֵן יִפְּלוּ בַנֹּפְלִים בְּעֵת־פְּקַדְתִּים יִכָּשְׁלוּ אָמַר יְהֹוָה:

16 Thus said *Hashem*: Stand by the roads and consider, Inquire about ancient paths: Which is the road to happiness? Travel it, and find tranquillity for yourselves. But they said, "We will not."

כֹּה אָמַר יְהֹוָה עִמְדוּ עַל־דְּרָכִים וּרְאוּ וְשַׁאֲלוּ לִנְתִבוֹת עוֹלָם אֵי־זֶה דֶרֶךְ הַטּוֹב וּלְכוּ־בָהּ וּמִצְאוּ מַרְגּוֹעַ לְנַפְשְׁכֶם וַיֹּאמְרוּ לֹא נֵלֵךְ:

17 And I raised up watchmen for you: "Hearken to the sound of the *shofar*!" But they said, "We will not."

וַהֲקִמֹתִי עֲלֵיכֶם צֹפִים הַקְשִׁיבוּ לְקוֹל שׁוֹפָר וַיֹּאמְרוּ לֹא נַקְשִׁיב:

18 Hear well, O nations, And know, O community, what is in store for them.

לָכֵן שִׁמְעוּ הַגּוֹיִם וּדְעִי עֵדָה אֶת־אֲשֶׁר־בָּם:

¹⁹ Hear, O earth! I am going to bring disaster upon this people, The outcome of their own schemes; For they would not hearken to My words, And they rejected My Instruction.

יט שִׁמְעִי הָאָרֶץ הִנֵּה אָנֹכִי מֵבִיא רָעָה אֶל־הָעָם הַזֶּה פְּרִי מַחְשְׁבוֹתָם כִּי עַל־דְּבָרַי לֹא הִקְשִׁיבוּ וְתוֹרָתִי וַיִּמְאֲסוּ־בָהּ:

²⁰ What need have I of frankincense That comes from Sheba, Or fragrant cane from a distant land? Your burnt offerings are not acceptable And your sacrifices are not pleasing to Me.

כ לָמָּה־זֶּה לִי לְבוֹנָה מִשְּׁבָא תָבוֹא וְקָנֶה הַטּוֹב מֵאֶרֶץ מֶרְחָק עֹלוֹתֵיכֶם לֹא לְרָצוֹן וְזִבְחֵיכֶם לֹא־עָרְבוּ לִי:

²¹ Assuredly, thus said *Hashem*: I shall put before this people stumbling blocks Over which they shall stumble – Fathers and children alike, Neighbor and friend shall perish.

כא לָכֵן כֹּה אָמַר יְהֹוָה הִנְנִי נֹתֵן אֶל־הָעָם הַזֶּה מִכְשֹׁלִים וְכָשְׁלוּ בָם אָבוֹת וּבָנִים יַחְדָּו שָׁכֵן וְרֵעוֹ יאבדו [וְאָבָדוּ:]

²² Thus said *Hashem*: See, a people comes from the northland, A great nation is roused From the remotest parts of the earth.

כב כֹּה אָמַר יְהֹוָה הִנֵּה עַם בָּא מֵאֶרֶץ צָפוֹן וְגוֹי גָּדוֹל יֵעוֹר מִיַּרְכְּתֵי־אָרֶץ:

²³ They grasp the bow and javelin; They are cruel, they show no mercy; The sound of them is like the roaring sea. They ride upon horses, Accoutered like a man for battle, Against you, O Fair *Tzion*!

כג קֶשֶׁת וְכִידוֹן יַחֲזִיקוּ אַכְזָרִי הוּא וְלֹא יְרַחֵמוּ קוֹלָם כַּיָּם יֶהֱמֶה וְעַל־סוּסִים יִרְכָּבוּ עָרוּךְ כְּאִישׁ לַמִּלְחָמָה עָלַיִךְ בַּת־צִיּוֹן:

²⁴ "We have heard the report of them, Our hands fail; Pain seizes us, Agony like a woman in childbirth.

כד שָׁמַעְנוּ אֶת־שָׁמְעוֹ רָפוּ יָדֵינוּ צָרָה הֶחֱזִיקַתְנוּ חִיל כַּיּוֹלֵדָה:

²⁵ Do not go out into the country, Do not walk the roads! For the sword of the enemy is there, Terror on every side."

כה אַל־תצאי [תֵּצְאוּ] הַשָּׂדֶה וּבַדֶּרֶךְ אַל־תלכי [תֵּלֵכוּ] כִּי חֶרֶב לְאֹיֵב מָגוֹר מִסָּבִיב:

²⁶ My poor people, Put on sackcloth And strew dust on yourselves! Mourn, as for an only child; Wail bitterly, For suddenly the destroyer Is coming upon us.

כו בַּת־עַמִּי חִגְרִי־שָׂק וְהִתְפַּלְּשִׁי בָאֵפֶר אֵבֶל יָחִיד עֲשִׂי לָךְ מִסְפַּד תַּמְרוּרִים כִּי פִתְאֹם יָבֹא הַשֹּׁדֵד עָלֵינוּ:

²⁷ I have made you an assayer of My people – A refiner – You are to note and assay their ways.

כז בָּחוֹן נְתַתִּיךָ בְעַמִּי מִבְצָר וְתֵדַע וּבָחַנְתָּ אֶת־דַּרְכָּם:

²⁸ They are copper and iron: They are all stubbornly defiant; They deal basely All of them act corruptly.

כח כֻּלָּם סָרֵי סוֹרְרִים הֹלְכֵי רָכִיל נְחֹשֶׁת וּבַרְזֶל כֻּלָּם מַשְׁחִיתִים הֵמָּה:

²⁹ The bellows puff; The lead is consumed by fire. Yet the smelter smelts to no purpose – The dross is not separated out.

כט נָחַר מַפֻּחַ מֵאֵשׁתַּם [מֵאֵשׁ] [תַּם] עֹפָרֶת לַשָּׁוְא צָרַף צָרוֹף וְרָעִים לֹא נִתָּקוּ:

³⁰ They are called "rejected silver," For *Hashem* has rejected them.

ל כֶּסֶף נִמְאָס קָרְאוּ לָהֶם כִּי־מָאַס יְהֹוָה בָּהֶם:

7 ¹ The word which came to *Yirmiyahu* from *Hashem*:

ז א הַדָּבָר אֲשֶׁר הָיָה אֶל־יִרְמְיָהוּ מֵאֵת יְהֹוָה לֵאמֹר:

² Stand at the gate of the House of *Hashem*, and there proclaim this word: Hear the word of *Hashem*, all you of *Yehuda* who enter these gates to worship *Hashem*!

ב עֲמֹד בְּשַׁעַר בֵּית יְהֹוָה וְקָרָאתָ שָּׁם אֶת־הַדָּבָר הַזֶּה וְאָמַרְתָּ שִׁמְעוּ דְבַר־יְהֹוָה כָּל־יְהוּדָה הַבָּאִים בַּשְּׁעָרִים הָאֵלֶּה לְהִשְׁתַּחֲוֹת לַיהֹוָה:

3 Thus said the LORD of Hosts, the God of *Yisrael*: Mend your ways and your actions, and I will let you dwell in this place.

ג כֹּה־אָמַר יְהֹוָה צְבָאוֹת אֱלֹהֵי יִשְׂרָאֵל הֵיטִיבוּ דַרְכֵיכֶם וּמַעַלְלֵיכֶם וַאֲשַׁכְּנָה אֶתְכֶם בַּמָּקוֹם הַזֶּה:

4 Don't put your trust in illusions and say, "The Temple of *Hashem*, the Temple of *Hashem*, the Temple of *Hashem* are these [buildings]."

ד אַל־תִּבְטְחוּ לָכֶם אֶל־דִּבְרֵי הַשֶּׁקֶר לֵאמֹר הֵיכַל יְהֹוָה הֵיכַל יְהֹוָה הֵיכַל יְהֹוָה הֵמָּה:

al tiv-t'-KHU la-KHEM el div-RAY ha-SHE-ker lay-MOR hay-KHAL a-do-NAI hay-KHAL a-do-NAI hay-KHAL a-do-NAI HAY-mah

5 No, if you really mend your ways and your actions; if you execute justice between one man and another;

ה כִּי אִם־הֵיטֵיב תֵּיטִיבוּ אֶת־דַּרְכֵיכֶם וְאֶת־מַעַלְלֵיכֶם אִם־עָשׂוֹ תַעֲשׂוּ מִשְׁפָּט בֵּין אִישׁ וּבֵין רֵעֵהוּ:

6 if you do not oppress the stranger, the orphan, and the widow; if you do not shed the blood of the innocent in this place; if you do not follow other gods, to your own hurt –

ו גֵּר יָתוֹם וְאַלְמָנָה לֹא תַעֲשֹׁקוּ וְדָם נָקִי אַל־תִּשְׁפְּכוּ בַּמָּקוֹם הַזֶּה וְאַחֲרֵי אֱלֹהִים אֲחֵרִים לֹא תֵלְכוּ לְרַע לָכֶם:

7 then only will I let you dwell in this place, in the land that I gave to your fathers for all time.

ז וְשִׁכַּנְתִּי אֶתְכֶם בַּמָּקוֹם הַזֶּה בָּאָרֶץ אֲשֶׁר נָתַתִּי לַאֲבוֹתֵיכֶם לְמִן־עוֹלָם וְעַד־עוֹלָם:

8 See, you are relying on illusions that are of no avail.

ח הִנֵּה אַתֶּם בֹּטְחִים לָכֶם עַל־דִּבְרֵי הַשָּׁקֶר לְבִלְתִּי הוֹעִיל:

9 Will you steal and murder and commit adultery and swear falsely, and sacrifice to Baal, and follow other gods whom you have not experienced,

ט הֲגָנֹב רָצֹחַ וְנָאֹף וְהִשָּׁבֵעַ לַשֶּׁקֶר וְקַטֵּר לַבָּעַל וְהָלֹךְ אַחֲרֵי אֱלֹהִים אֲחֵרִים אֲשֶׁר לֹא־יְדַעְתֶּם:

10 and then come and stand before Me in this House which bears My name and say, "We are safe"? – [Safe] to do all these abhorrent things!

י וּבָאתֶם וַעֲמַדְתֶּם לְפָנַי בַּבַּיִת הַזֶּה אֲשֶׁר נִקְרָא־שְׁמִי עָלָיו וַאֲמַרְתֶּם נִצַּלְנוּ לְמַעַן עֲשׂוֹת אֵת כָּל־הַתּוֹעֵבוֹת הָאֵלֶּה:

11 Do you consider this House, which bears My name, to be a den of thieves? As for Me, I have been watching – declares *Hashem*.

יא הַמְעָרַת פָּרִצִים הָיָה הַבַּיִת הַזֶּה אֲשֶׁר־נִקְרָא־שְׁמִי עָלָיו בְּעֵינֵיכֶם גַּם אָנֹכִי הִנֵּה רָאִיתִי נְאֻם־יְהֹוָה:

12 Just go to My place at *Shilo*, where I had established My name formerly, and see what I did to it because of the wickedness of My people *Yisrael*.

יב כִּי לְכוּ־נָא אֶל־מְקוֹמִי אֲשֶׁר בְּשִׁילוֹ אֲשֶׁר שִׁכַּנְתִּי שְׁמִי שָׁם בָּרִאשׁוֹנָה וּרְאוּ אֵת אֲשֶׁר־עָשִׂיתִי לוֹ מִפְּנֵי רָעַת עַמִּי יִשְׂרָאֵל:

7:4 The Temple of *Hashem* One of *Yirmiyahu's* most famous outcries is uttered in the Temple courtyard. Surrounded by people who came to offer sacrifices, he assails their false sense of security and their belief that as long as the *Beit Hamikdash* stands, *Yerushalayim* can never be overrun. *Yirmiyahu* criticizes their false piety and emphasis on ritual matters while ignoring the needs of others, crying out "the Temple of *Hashem*" three times. Rabbi Samson Raphael Hirsch suggests that the following verses are a continuation of this one, and the meaning is: What is the real "Temple of *Hashem*"? Repentance, justice and charity.

Model of the second *Beit Hamikdash* in *Yerushalayim*

¹³ And now, because you do all these things – declares *Hashem* – and though I spoke to you persistently, you would not listen; and though I called to you, you would not respond –

יג וְעַתָּה יַעַן עֲשׂוֹתְכֶם אֶת־כָּל־הַמַּעֲשִׂים הָאֵלֶּה נְאֻם־יְהֹוָה וָאֲדַבֵּר אֲלֵיכֶם הַשְׁכֵּם וְדַבֵּר וְלֹא שְׁמַעְתֶּם וָאֶקְרָא אֶתְכֶם וְלֹא עֲנִיתֶם:

¹⁴ therefore I will do to the House which bears My name, on which you rely, and to the place which I gave you and your fathers, just what I did to *Shilo*.

יד וְעָשִׂיתִי לַבַּיִת אֲשֶׁר נִקְרָא־שְׁמִי עָלָיו אֲשֶׁר אַתֶּם בֹּטְחִים בּוֹ וְלַמָּקוֹם אֲשֶׁר־נָתַתִּי לָכֶם וְלַאֲבֽוֹתֵיכֶם כַּאֲשֶׁר עָשִׂיתִי לְשִׁלֽוֹ:

¹⁵ And I will cast you out of My presence as I cast out your brothers, the whole brood of *Efraim*.

טו וְהִשְׁלַכְתִּי אֶתְכֶם מֵעַל פָּנָי כַּאֲשֶׁר הִשְׁלַכְתִּי אֶת־כָּל־אֲחֵיכֶם אֵת כָּל־זֶרַע אֶפְרָֽיִם:

¹⁶ As for you, do not pray for this people, do not raise a cry of prayer on their behalf, do not plead with Me; for I will not listen to you.

טז וְאַתָּה אַל־תִּתְפַּלֵּל בְּעַד־הָעָם הַזֶּה וְאַל־תִּשָּׂא בַעֲדָם רִנָּה וּתְפִלָּה וְאַל־תִּפְגַּע־בִּי כִּי־אֵינֶנִּי שֹׁמֵעַ אֹתָֽךְ:

¹⁷ Don't you see what they are doing in the towns of *Yehuda* and in the streets of *Yerushalayim*?

יז הַאֵֽינְךָ רֹאֶה מָה הֵמָּה עֹשִׂים בְּעָרֵי יְהוּדָה וּבְחֻצוֹת יְרוּשָׁלָֽם:

¹⁸ The children gather sticks, the fathers build the fire, and the mothers knead dough, to make cakes for the Queen of Heaven, and they pour libations to other gods, to vex Me.

יח הַבָּנִים מְלַקְּטִים עֵצִים וְהָֽאָבוֹת מְבַעֲרִים אֶת־הָאֵשׁ וְהַנָּשִׁים לָשׁוֹת בָּצֵק לַעֲשׂוֹת כַּוָּנִים לִמְלֶכֶת הַשָּׁמַיִם וְהַסֵּךְ נְסָכִים לֵאלֹהִים אֲחֵרִים לְמַעַן הַכְעִסֵֽנִי:

¹⁹ Is it Me they are vexing? – says *Hashem*. It is rather themselves, to their own disgrace.

יט הַאֹתִי הֵם מַכְעִסִים נְאֻם־יְהֹוָה הֲלוֹא אֹתָם לְמַעַן בֹּשֶׁת פְּנֵיהֶֽם:

²⁰ Assuredly, thus said *Hashem*: My wrath and My fury will be poured out upon this place, on man and on beast, on the trees of the field and the fruit of the soil. It shall burn, with none to quench it.

כ לָכֵן כֹּה־אָמַר אֲדֹנָי יְהֹוִה הִנֵּה אַפִּי וַחֲמָתִי נִתֶּכֶת אֶל־הַמָּקוֹם הַזֶּה עַל־הָאָדָם וְעַל־הַבְּהֵמָה וְעַל־עֵץ הַשָּׂדֶה וְעַל־פְּרִי הָאֲדָמָה וּבָעֲרָה וְלֹא תִכְבֶּֽה:

²¹ Thus said the Lᴏʀᴅ of Hosts, the God of *Yisrael*: Add your burnt offerings to your other sacrifices and eat the meat!

כא כֹּה אָמַר יְהֹוָה צְבָאוֹת אֱלֹהֵי יִשְׂרָאֵל עֹלוֹתֵיכֶם סְפוּ עַל־זִבְחֵיכֶם וְאִכְלוּ בָשָֽׂר:

²² For when I freed your fathers from the land of Egypt, I did not speak with them or command them concerning burnt offerings or sacrifice.

כב כִּי לֹא־דִבַּרְתִּי אֶת־אֲבֽוֹתֵיכֶם וְלֹא צִוִּיתִים בְּיוֹם הוֹצִיא [הוֹצִיאִי] אוֹתָם מֵאֶרֶץ מִצְרָיִם עַל־דִּבְרֵי עוֹלָה וָזָֽבַח:

²³ But this is what I commanded them: Do My bidding, that I may be your God and you may be My people; walk only in the way that I enjoin upon you, that it may go well with you.

כג כִּי אִם־אֶת־הַדָּבָר הַזֶּה צִוִּיתִי אוֹתָם לֵאמֹר שִׁמְעוּ בְקוֹלִי וְהָיִיתִי לָכֶם לֵאלֹהִים וְאַתֶּם תִּהְיוּ־לִי לְעָם וַהֲלַכְתֶּם בְּכָל־הַדֶּרֶךְ אֲשֶׁר אֲצַוֶּה אֶתְכֶם לְמַעַן יִיטַב לָכֶֽם:

²⁴ Yet they did not listen or give ear; they followed their own counsels, the willfulness of their evil hearts. They have gone backward, not forward,

כד וְלֹא שָׁמְעוּ וְלֹא־הִטּוּ אֶת־אָזְנָם וַיֵּלְכוּ בְּמֹעֵצוֹת בִּשְׁרִרוּת לִבָּם הָרָע וַיִּהְיוּ לְאָחוֹר וְלֹא לְפָנִֽים:

²⁵ from the day your fathers left the land of Egypt until today. And though I kept sending all My servants, the *Neviim*, to them daily and persistently,

כה לְמִן־הַיּוֹם אֲשֶׁר יָצְאוּ אֲבוֹתֵיכֶם מֵאֶרֶץ מִצְרַיִם עַד הַיּוֹם הַזֶּה וָאֶשְׁלַח אֲלֵיכֶם אֶת־כָּל־עֲבָדַי הַנְּבִיאִים יוֹם הַשְׁכֵּם וְשָׁלֹחַ:

²⁶ they would not listen to Me or give ear. They stiffened their necks, they acted worse than their fathers.

כו וְלוֹא שָׁמְעוּ אֵלַי וְלֹא הִטּוּ אֶת־אָזְנָם וַיַּקְשׁוּ אֶת־עָרְפָּם הֵרֵעוּ מֵאֲבוֹתָם:

²⁷ You shall say all these things to them, but they will not listen to you; you shall call to them, but they will not respond to you.

כז וְדִבַּרְתָּ אֲלֵיהֶם אֶת־כָּל־הַדְּבָרִים הָאֵלֶּה וְלֹא יִשְׁמְעוּ אֵלֶיךָ וְקָרָאתָ אֲלֵיהֶם וְלֹא יַעֲנוּכָה:

²⁸ Then say to them: This is the nation that would not obey *Hashem* their God, that would not accept rebuke. Faithfulness has perished, vanished from their mouths.

כח וְאָמַרְתָּ אֲלֵיהֶם זֶה הַגּוֹי אֲשֶׁר לוֹא־שָׁמְעוּ בְּקוֹל יְהוָה אֱלֹהָיו וְלֹא לָקְחוּ מוּסָר אָבְדָה הָאֱמוּנָה וְנִכְרְתָה מִפִּיהֶם:

²⁹ Shear your locks and cast them away, Take up a lament on the heights, For *Hashem* has spurned and cast off The brood that provoked His wrath.

כט גָּזִּי נִזְרֵךְ וְהַשְׁלִיכִי וּשְׂאִי עַל־שְׁפָיִם קִינָה כִּי מָאַס יְהוָה וַיִּטֹּשׁ אֶת־דּוֹר עֶבְרָתוֹ:

³⁰ For the people of *Yehuda* have done what displeases Me – declares *Hashem*. They have set up their abominations in the House which is called by My name, and they have defiled it.

ל כִּי־עָשׂוּ בְנֵי־יְהוּדָה הָרַע בְּעֵינַי נְאֻם־ יְהוָה שָׂמוּ שִׁקּוּצֵיהֶם בַּבַּיִת אֲשֶׁר־ נִקְרָא־שְׁמִי עָלָיו לְטַמְּאוֹ:

³¹ And they have built the shrines of Topheth in the Valley of Ben-hinnom to burn their sons and daughters in fire – which I never commanded, which never came to My mind.

לא וּבָנוּ בָּמוֹת הַתֹּפֶת אֲשֶׁר בְּגֵיא בֶן־הִנֹּם לִשְׂרֹף אֶת־בְּנֵיהֶם וְאֶת־בְּנֹתֵיהֶם בָּאֵשׁ אֲשֶׁר לֹא צִוִּיתִי וְלֹא עָלְתָה עַל־לִבִּי:

³² Assuredly, a time is coming – declares *Hashem* – when men shall no longer speak of Topheth or the Valley of Ben-hinnom, but of the Valley of Slaughter; and they shall bury in Topheth until no room is left.

לב לָכֵן הִנֵּה־יָמִים בָּאִים נְאֻם־יְהוָה וְלֹא־ יֵאָמֵר עוֹד הַתֹּפֶת וְגֵיא בֶן־הִנֹּם כִּי אִם־ גֵּיא הַהֲרֵגָה וְקָבְרוּ בְתֹפֶת מֵאֵין מָקוֹם:

³³ The carcasses of this people shall be food for the birds of the sky and the beasts of the earth, with none to frighten them off.

לג וְהָיְתָה נִבְלַת הָעָם הַזֶּה לְמַאֲכָל לְעוֹף הַשָּׁמַיִם וּלְבֶהֱמַת הָאָרֶץ וְאֵין מַחֲרִיד:

³⁴ And I will silence in the towns of *Yehuda* and the streets of *Yerushalayim* the sound of mirth and gladness, the voice of bridegroom and bride. For the whole land shall fall to ruin.

לד וְהִשְׁבַּתִּי מֵעָרֵי יְהוּדָה וּמֵחֻצוֹת יְרוּשָׁלַ͏ִם קוֹל שָׂשׂוֹן וְקוֹל שִׂמְחָה קוֹל חָתָן וְקוֹל כַּלָּה כִּי לְחָרְבָּה תִּהְיֶה הָאָרֶץ:

8 ¹ At that time – declares *Hashem* – the bones of the kings of *Yehuda*, of its officers, of the *Kohanim*, of the *Neviim*, and of the inhabitants of *Yerushalayim* shall be taken out of their graves

ח א בָּעֵת הַהִיא נְאֻם־יְהוָה וְיוֹצִיאוּ [יוֹצִיאוּ] אֶת־עַצְמוֹת מַלְכֵי־יְהוּדָה וְאֶת־עַצְמוֹת־ שָׂרָיו וְאֶת־עַצְמוֹת הַכֹּהֲנִים וְאֵת עַצְמוֹת הַנְּבִיאִים וְאֵת עַצְמוֹת יוֹשְׁבֵי־ יְרוּשָׁלָ͏ִם מִקִּבְרֵיהֶם:

2 and exposed to the sun, the moon, and all the host of heaven which they loved and served and followed, to which they turned and bowed down. They shall not be gathered for reburial; they shall become dung upon the face of the earth.

ב וּשְׁטָחוּם לַשֶּׁמֶשׁ וְלַיָּרֵחַ וּלְכֹל צְבָא הַשָּׁמַיִם אֲשֶׁר אֲהֵבוּם וַאֲשֶׁר עֲבָדוּם וַאֲשֶׁר הָלְכוּ אַחֲרֵיהֶם וַאֲשֶׁר דְּרָשׁוּם וַאֲשֶׁר הִשְׁתַּחֲווּ לָהֶם לֹא יֵאָסְפוּ וְלֹא יִקָּבֵרוּ לְדֹמֶן עַל־פְּנֵי הָאֲדָמָה יִהְיוּ:

3 And death shall be preferable to life for all that are left of this wicked folk, in all the other places to which I shall banish them – declares the LORD of Hosts.

ג וְנִבְחַר מָוֶת מֵחַיִּים לְכֹל הַשְּׁאֵרִית הַנִּשְׁאָרִים מִן־הַמִּשְׁפָּחָה הָרָעָה הַזֹּאת בְּכָל־הַמְּקֹמוֹת הַנִּשְׁאָרִים אֲשֶׁר הִדַּחְתִּים שָׁם נְאֻם יְהוָה צְבָאוֹת:

4 Say to them: Thus said *Hashem*: When men fall, do they not get up again? If they turn aside, do they not turn back?

ד וְאָמַרְתָּ אֲלֵיהֶם כֹּה אָמַר יְהוָה הֲיִפְּלוּ וְלֹא יָקוּמוּ אִם־יָשׁוּב וְלֹא יָשׁוּב:

5 Why is this people – *Yerushalayim* – rebellious With a persistent rebellion? They cling to deceit, They refuse to return.

ה מַדּוּעַ שׁוֹבְבָה הָעָם הַזֶּה יְרוּשָׁלִַם מְשֻׁבָה נִצַּחַת הֶחֱזִיקוּ בַּתַּרְמִית מֵאֲנוּ לָשׁוּב:

6 I have listened and heard: They do not speak honestly. No one regrets his wickedness And says, "What have I done!" They all persist in their wayward course Like a steed dashing forward in the fray.

ו הִקְשַׁבְתִּי וָאֶשְׁמָע לוֹא־כֵן יְדַבֵּרוּ אֵין אִישׁ נִחָם עַל־רָעָתוֹ לֵאמֹר מֶה עָשִׂיתִי כֻּלֹּה שָׁב במרצותם [בִּמְרוּצָתָם] כְּסוּס שׁוֹטֵף בַּמִּלְחָמָה:

7 Even the stork in the sky knows her seasons, And the turtledove, swift, and crane Keep the time of their coming; But My people pay no heed To the law of *Hashem*.

ז גַּם־חֲסִידָה בַשָּׁמַיִם יָדְעָה מוֹעֲדֶיהָ וְתֹר וסיס [וְסוּס] וְעָגוּר שָׁמְרוּ אֶת־עֵת בֹּאָנָה וְעַמִּי לֹא יָדְעוּ אֵת מִשְׁפַּט יְהוָה:

8 How can you say, "We are wise, And we possess the Instruction of *Hashem*"? Assuredly, for naught has the pen labored, For naught the scribes!

ח אֵיכָה תֹאמְרוּ חֲכָמִים אֲנַחְנוּ וְתוֹרַת יְהוָה אִתָּנוּ אָכֵן הִנֵּה לַשֶּׁקֶר עָשָׂה עֵט שֶׁקֶר סֹפְרִים:

9 The wise shall be put to shame, Shall be dismayed and caught; See, they reject the word of *Hashem*, So their wisdom amounts to nothing.

ט הֹבִישׁוּ חֲכָמִים חַתּוּ וַיִּלָּכֵדוּ הִנֵּה בִדְבַר־יְהוָה מָאָסוּ וְחָכְמַת־מֶה לָהֶם:

10 Assuredly, I will give their wives to others, And their fields to dispossessors; For from the smallest to the greatest, They are all greedy for gain; *Kohen* and *Navi* alike, They all act falsely.

י לָכֵן אֶתֵּן אֶת־נְשֵׁיהֶם לַאֲחֵרִים שְׂדוֹתֵיהֶם לְיוֹרְשִׁים כִּי מִקָּטֹן וְעַד־גָּדוֹל כֻּלֹּה בֹּצֵעַ בָּצַע מִנָּבִיא וְעַד־כֹּהֵן כֻּלֹּה עֹשֶׂה שָּׁקֶר:

11 They offer healing offhand For the wounds of My poor people, Saying, "All is well, all is well," When nothing is well.

יא וַיְרַפּוּ אֶת־שֶׁבֶר בַּת־עַמִּי עַל־נְקַלָּה לֵאמֹר שָׁלוֹם שָׁלוֹם וְאֵין שָׁלוֹם:

12 They have acted shamefully; They have done abhorrent things – Yet they do not feel shame, They cannot be made to blush. Assuredly, they shall fall among the falling, They shall stumble at the time of their doom – said *Hashem*.

יב הֹבִשׁוּ כִּי תוֹעֵבָה עָשׂוּ גַּם־בּוֹשׁ לֹא־יֵבֹשׁוּ וְהִכָּלֵם לֹא יָדָעוּ לָכֵן יִפְּלוּ בַנֹּפְלִים בְּעֵת פְּקֻדָּתָם יִכָּשְׁלוּ אָמַר יְהוָה:

13 I will make an end of them – declares *Hashem*: No grapes left on the vine, No figs on the fig tree, The leaves all withered; Whatever I have given them is gone.

יג אָסֹף אֲסִיפֵם נְאֻם־יְהֹוָה אֵין עֲנָבִים בַּגֶּפֶן וְאֵין תְּאֵנִים בַּתְּאֵנָה וְהֶעָלֶה נָבֵל וָאֶתֵּן לָהֶם יַעַבְרוּם:

14 Why are we sitting by? Let us gather into the fortified cities And meet our doom there. For *Hashem* our God has doomed us, He has made us drink a bitter draft, Because we sinned against *Hashem*.

יד עַל־מָה אֲנַחְנוּ יֹשְׁבִים הֵאָסְפוּ וְנָבוֹא אֶל־עָרֵי הַמִּבְצָר וְנִדְּמָה־שָּׁם כִּי יְהֹוָה אֱלֹהֵינוּ הֲדִמָּנוּ וַיַּשְׁקֵנוּ מֵי־רֹאשׁ כִּי חָטָאנוּ לַיהֹוָה:

15 We hoped for good fortune, but no happiness came; For a time of relief – instead there is terror!

טו קַוֵּה לְשָׁלוֹם וְאֵין טוֹב לְעֵת מַרְפֵּה וְהִנֵּה בְעָתָה:

16 The snorting of their horses was heard from *Dan*; At the loud neighing of their steeds The whole land quaked. They came and devoured the land and what was in it, The towns and those who dwelt in them.

טז מִדָּן נִשְׁמַע נַחְרַת סוּסָיו מִקּוֹל מִצְהֲלוֹת אַבִּירָיו רָעֲשָׁה כָּל־הָאָרֶץ וַיָּבוֹאוּ וַיֹּאכְלוּ אֶרֶץ וּמְלוֹאָהּ עִיר וְיֹשְׁבֵי בָהּ:

17 Lo, I will send serpents against you, Adders that cannot be charmed, And they shall bite you – declares *Hashem*.

יז כִּי הִנְנִי מְשַׁלֵּחַ בָּכֶם נְחָשִׁים צִפְעֹנִים אֲשֶׁר אֵין־לָהֶם לָחַשׁ וְנִשְּׁכוּ אֶתְכֶם נְאֻם־יְהֹוָה:

18 When in grief I would seek comfort, My heart is sick within me.

יח מַבְלִיגִיתִי עֲלֵי יָגוֹן עָלַי לִבִּי דַוָּי:

19 "Is not *Hashem* in *Tzion*? Is not her King within her? Why then did they anger Me with their images, With alien futilities?" Hark! The outcry of my poor people From the land far and wide:

יט הִנֵּה־קוֹל שַׁוְעַת בַּת־עַמִּי מֵאֶרֶץ מַרְחַקִּים הַיהֹוָה אֵין בְּצִיּוֹן אִם־מַלְכָּהּ אֵין בָּהּ מַדּוּעַ הִכְעִסוּנִי בִּפְסִלֵיהֶם בְּהַבְלֵי נֵכָר:

20 "Harvest is past, Summer is gone, But we have not been saved."

כ עָבַר קָצִיר כָּלָה קָיִץ וַאֲנַחְנוּ לוֹא נוֹשָׁעְנוּ:

21 Because my people is shattered I am shattered; I am dejected, seized by desolation.

כא עַל־שֶׁבֶר בַּת־עַמִּי הָשְׁבָּרְתִּי קָדַרְתִּי שַׁמָּה הֶחֱזִקָתְנִי:

22 Is there no balm in *Gilad*? Can no physician be found? Why has healing not yet Come to my poor people?

כב הַצֳרִי אֵין בְּגִלְעָד אִם־רֹפֵא אֵין שָׁם כִּי מַדּוּעַ לֹא עָלְתָה אֲרֻכַת בַּת־עַמִּי:

*ha-tzo-REE AYN b'-gil-AD im ro-FAY AYN SHAM KEE
ma-DU-a LO a-l'-TAH a-ru-KHAT bat a-MEE*

8:22 Is there no balm in *Gilad* Yirmiyahu laments the people's suffering. Despite condemning their immorality, impudence and hypocrisy, he nevertheless identifies with their pain. Wistfully, he calls out, "Is there no balm in *Gilad*?" *Gilad* is located on the plains of Jordan, across the river from *Yerushalayim*, and was famous for its medicines. The commentators understand this balm as a metaphor – righteousness and good deeds could have healed the people, but they were too distant.

Sea of Galilee as seen from *Gilad*

23 Oh, that my head were water, My eyes a fount of tears! Then would I weep day and night For the slain of my poor people.

מִי־יִתֵּן רֹאשִׁי מַיִם וְעֵינִי מְקוֹר דִּמְעָה וְאֶבְכֶּה יוֹמָם וָלָיְלָה אֵת חַלְלֵי בַת־עַמִּי: כג

9 1 Oh, to be in the desert, At an encampment for wayfarers! Oh, to leave my people, To go away from them – For they are all adulterers, A band of rogues.

מִי־יִתְּנֵנִי בַמִּדְבָּר מְלוֹן אֹרְחִים וְאֶעֶזְבָה אֶת־עַמִּי וְאֵלְכָה מֵאִתָּם כִּי כֻלָּם מְנָאֲפִים עֲצֶרֶת בֹּגְדִים: א ט

2 They bend their tongues like bows; They are valorous in the land For treachery, not for honesty; They advance from evil to evil. And they do not heed Me – declares *Hashem*.

וַיַּדְרְכוּ אֶת־לְשׁוֹנָם קַשְׁתָּם שֶׁקֶר וְלֹא לֶאֱמוּנָה גָּבְרוּ בָאָרֶץ כִּי מֵרָעָה אֶל־רָעָה יָצָאוּ וְאֹתִי לֹא־יָדָעוּ נְאֻם־יְהוָה: ב

3 Beware, every man of his friend! Trust not even a brother! For every brother takes advantage, Every friend is base in his dealings.

אִישׁ מֵרֵעֵהוּ הִשָּׁמֵרוּ וְעַל־כָּל־אָח אַל־תִּבְטָחוּ כִּי כָל־אָח עָקוֹב יַעְקֹב וְכָל־רֵעַ רָכִיל יַהֲלֹךְ: ג

4 One man cheats the other, They will not speak truth; They have trained their tongues to speak falsely; They wear themselves out working iniquity.

וְאִישׁ בְּרֵעֵהוּ יְהָתֵלּוּ וֶאֱמֶת לֹא יְדַבֵּרוּ לִמְּדוּ לְשׁוֹנָם דַּבֶּר־שֶׁקֶר הַעֲוֵה נִלְאוּ: ד

5 You dwell in the midst of deceit. In their deceit, they refuse to heed Me – declares *Hashem*.

שִׁבְתְּךָ בְּתוֹךְ מִרְמָה בְּמִרְמָה מֵאֲנוּ דַעַת־אוֹתִי נְאֻם־יְהוָה: ה

6 Assuredly, thus said the LORD of Hosts: Lo, I shall smelt and assay them – For what else can I do because of My poor people?

לָכֵן כֹּה אָמַר יְהוָה צְבָאוֹת הִנְנִי צוֹרְפָם וּבְחַנְתִּים כִּי־אֵיךְ אֶעֱשֶׂה מִפְּנֵי בַּת־עַמִּי: ו

7 Their tongue is a sharpened arrow, They use their mouths to deceive. One speaks to his fellow in friendship, But lays an ambush for him in his heart.

חֵץ שׁוֹחֵט [שָׁחוּט] לְשׁוֹנָם מִרְמָה דִבֵּר בְּפִיו שָׁלוֹם אֶת־רֵעֵהוּ יְדַבֵּר וּבְקִרְבּוֹ יָשִׂים אָרְבּוֹ: ז

8 Shall I not punish them for such deeds? – says *Hashem* – Shall I not bring retribution On such a nation as this?

הַעַל־אֵלֶּה לֹא־אֶפְקָד־בָּם נְאֻם־יְהוָה אִם בְּגוֹי אֲשֶׁר־כָּזֶה לֹא תִתְנַקֵּם נַפְשִׁי: ח

9 For the mountains I take up weeping and wailing, For the pastures in the wilderness, a dirge. They are laid waste; no man passes through, And no sound of cattle is heard. Birds of the sky and beasts as well Have fled and are gone.

עַל־הֶהָרִים אֶשָּׂא בְכִי וָנֶהִי וְעַל־נְאוֹת מִדְבָּר קִינָה כִּי נִצְּתוּ מִבְּלִי־אִישׁ עֹבֵר וְלֹא שָׁמְעוּ קוֹל מִקְנֶה מֵעוֹף הַשָּׁמַיִם וְעַד־בְּהֵמָה נָדְדוּ הָלָכוּ: ט

10 I will turn *Yerushalayim* into rubble, Into dens for jackals; And I will make the towns of *Yehuda* A desolation without inhabitants.

וְנָתַתִּי אֶת־יְרוּשָׁלִַם לְגַלִּים מְעוֹן תַּנִּים וְאֶת־עָרֵי יְהוּדָה אֶתֵּן שְׁמָמָה מִבְּלִי יוֹשֵׁב: י

11 What man is so wise That he understands this? To whom has *Hashem*'s mouth spoken, So that he can explain it: Why is the land in ruins, Laid waste like a wilderness, With none passing through?

מִי־הָאִישׁ הֶחָכָם וְיָבֵן אֶת־זֹאת וַאֲשֶׁר דִּבֶּר פִּי־יְהוָה אֵלָיו וְיַגִּדָהּ עַל־מָה אָבְדָה הָאָרֶץ נִצְּתָה כַמִּדְבָּר מִבְּלִי עֹבֵר: יא

12 *Hashem* replied: Because they forsook the Teaching I had set before them. They did not obey Me and they did not follow it,

וַיֹּאמֶר יְהוָה עַל־עָזְבָם אֶת־תּוֹרָתִי אֲשֶׁר נָתַתִּי לִפְנֵיהֶם וְלֹא־שָׁמְעוּ בְקוֹלִי וְלֹא־הָלְכוּ בָהּ: יב

Jeremiah

13 but followed their own willful heart and followed the Baalim, as their fathers had taught them.

יג וַיֵּלְכוּ אַחֲרֵי שְׁרִרוּת לִבָּם וְאַחֲרֵי הַבְּעָלִים אֲשֶׁר לִמְּדוּם אֲבוֹתָם:

14 Assuredly, thus said the LORD of Hosts, the God of *Yisrael*: I am going to feed that people wormwood and make them drink a bitter draft.

יד לָכֵן כֹּה־אָמַר יְהוָה צְבָאוֹת אֱלֹהֵי יִשְׂרָאֵל הִנְנִי מַאֲכִילָם אֶת־הָעָם הַזֶּה לַעֲנָה וְהִשְׁקִיתִים מֵי־רֹאשׁ:

15 I will scatter them among nations which they and their fathers never knew; and I will dispatch the sword after them until I have consumed them.

טו וַהֲפִצוֹתִים בַּגּוֹיִם אֲשֶׁר לֹא יָדְעוּ הֵמָּה וַאֲבוֹתָם וְשִׁלַּחְתִּי אַחֲרֵיהֶם אֶת־הַחֶרֶב עַד כַּלּוֹתִי אוֹתָם:

16 Thus said the LORD of Hosts: Listen! Summon the dirge-singers, let them come; Send for the skilled women, let them come.

טז כֹּה אָמַר יְהוָה צְבָאוֹת הִתְבּוֹנְנוּ וְקִרְאוּ לַמְקוֹנְנוֹת וּתְבוֹאֶינָה וְאֶל־הַחֲכָמוֹת שִׁלְחוּ וְתָבוֹאנָה:

17 Let them quickly start a wailing for us, That our eyes may run with tears, Our pupils flow with water.

יז וּתְמַהֵרְנָה וְתִשֶּׂנָה עָלֵינוּ נֶהִי וְתֵרַדְנָה עֵינֵינוּ דִּמְעָה וְעַפְעַפֵּינוּ יִזְּלוּ־מָיִם:

18 For the sound of wailing Is heard from *Tzion*: How we are despoiled! How greatly we are shamed! Ah, we must leave our land, Abandon our dwellings!

יח כִּי קוֹל נְהִי נִשְׁמַע מִצִּיּוֹן אֵיךְ שֻׁדָּדְנוּ בֹּשְׁנוּ מְאֹד כִּי־עָזַבְנוּ אָרֶץ כִּי הִשְׁלִיכוּ מִשְׁכְּנוֹתֵינוּ:

19 Hear, O women, the word of *Hashem*, Let your ears receive the word of His mouth, And teach your daughters wailing, And one another lamentation.

יט כִּי־שְׁמַעְנָה נָשִׁים דְּבַר־יְהוָה וְתִקַּח אָזְנְכֶם דְּבַר־פִּיו וְלַמֵּדְנָה בְנוֹתֵיכֶם נֶהִי וְאִשָּׁה רְעוּתָהּ קִינָה:

20 For death has climbed through our windows, Has entered our fortresses, To cut off babes from the streets, Young men from the squares.

כ כִּי־עָלָה מָוֶת בְּחַלּוֹנֵינוּ בָּא בְּאַרְמְנוֹתֵינוּ לְהַכְרִית עוֹלָל מִחוּץ בַּחוּרִים מֵרְחֹבוֹת:

21 Speak thus – says *Hashem*: The carcasses of men shall lie Like dung upon the fields, Like sheaves behind the reaper, With none to pick them up.

כא דַּבֵּר כֹּה נְאֻם־יְהוָה וְנָפְלָה נִבְלַת הָאָדָם כְּדֹמֶן עַל־פְּנֵי הַשָּׂדֶה וּכְעָמִיר מֵאַחֲרֵי הַקֹּצֵר וְאֵין מְאַסֵּף:

22 Thus said *Hashem*: Let not the wise man glory in his wisdom; Let not the strong man glory in his strength; Let not the rich man glory in his riches.

כב כֹּה אָמַר יְהוָה אַל־יִתְהַלֵּל חָכָם בְּחָכְמָתוֹ וְאַל־יִתְהַלֵּל הַגִּבּוֹר בִּגְבוּרָתוֹ אַל־יִתְהַלֵּל עָשִׁיר בְּעָשְׁרוֹ:

23 But only in this should one glory: In his earnest devotion to Me. For I *Hashem* act with kindness, Justice, and equity in the world; For in these I delight – declares *Hashem*.

כג כִּי אִם־בְּזֹאת יִתְהַלֵּל הַמִּתְהַלֵּל הַשְׂכֵּל וְיָדֹעַ אוֹתִי כִּי אֲנִי יְהוָה עֹשֶׂה חֶסֶד מִשְׁפָּט וּצְדָקָה בָּאָרֶץ כִּי־בְאֵלֶּה חָפַצְתִּי נְאֻם־יְהוָה:

KEE im b'-ZOT yit-ha-LAYL ha-mit-ha-LAYL has-KAYL v'-ya-DO-a
o-TEE KEE a-NEE a-do-NAI O-seh KHE-sed mish-PAT utz-da-KAH
ba-A-retz kee v'-AY-leh kha-FATZ-tee n'-um a-do-NAI

Rabbi Tuly Weisz delivers *Purim* baskets to Holocaust survivors

9:23 For in these I delight *Yirmiyahu* contrasts two separate ways of living. Some people strive for wisdom, power, and riches, through which they can take pride in themselves. But all this is foolish when compared to *Hashem*, Who has infinite wisdom, power and

²⁴ Lo, days are coming – declares *Hashem* – when I will take note of everyone circumcised in the foreskin:

כד הִנֵּה יָמִים בָּאִים נְאֻם־יְהֹוָה וּפָקַדְתִּי עַל־כׇּל־מוּל בְּעׇרְלָה:

²⁵ of Egypt, *Yehuda*, Edom, the Amonites, Moab, and all the desert dwellers who have the hair of their temples clipped. For all these nations are uncircumcised, but all the House of *Yisrael* are uncircumcised of heart.

כה עַל־מִצְרַיִם וְעַל־יְהוּדָה וְעַל־אֱדוֹם וְעַל־בְּנֵי עַמּוֹן וְעַל־מוֹאָב וְעַל כׇּל־קְצוּצֵי פֵאָה הַיֹּשְׁבִים בַּמִּדְבָּר כִּי כׇל־הַגּוֹיִם עֲרֵלִים וְכׇל־בֵּית יִשְׂרָאֵל עַרְלֵי־לֵב:

10¹ Hear the word which *Hashem* has spoken to you, O House of *Yisrael*!

א שִׁמְעוּ אֶת־הַדָּבָר אֲשֶׁר דִּבֶּר יְהֹוָה עֲלֵיכֶם בֵּית יִשְׂרָאֵל:

² Thus said *Hashem*: Do not learn to go the way of the nations, And do not be dismayed by portents in the sky; Let the nations be dismayed by them!

ב כֹּה אָמַר יְהֹוָה אֶל־דֶּרֶךְ הַגּוֹיִם אַל־תִּלְמָדוּ וּמֵאֹתוֹת הַשָּׁמַיִם אַל־תֵּחָתּוּ כִּי־יֵחַתּוּ הַגּוֹיִם מֵהֵמָּה:

³ For the laws of the nations are delusions: For it is the work of a craftsman's hands. He cuts down a tree in the forest with an ax,

ג כִּי־חֻקּוֹת הָעַמִּים הֶבֶל הוּא כִּי־עֵץ מִיַּעַר כְּרָתוֹ מַעֲשֵׂה יְדֵי־חָרָשׁ בַּמַּעֲצָד:

⁴ He adorns it with silver and gold, He fastens it with nails and hammer, So that it does not totter.

ד בְּכֶסֶף וּבְזָהָב יְיַפֵּהוּ בְּמַסְמְרוֹת וּבְמַקָּבוֹת יְחַזְּקוּם וְלוֹא יָפִיק:

⁵ They are like a scarecrow in a cucumber patch, They cannot speak. They have to be carried, For they cannot walk. Be not afraid of them, for they can do no harm; Nor is it in them to do any good.

ה כְּתֹמֶר מִקְשָׁה הֵמָּה וְלֹא יְדַבֵּרוּ נָשׂוֹא יִנָּשׂוּא כִּי לֹא יִצְעָדוּ אַל־תִּירְאוּ מֵהֶם כִּי־לֹא יָרֵעוּ וְגַם־הֵיטֵיב אֵין אוֹתָם:

⁶ *Hashem*, there is none like You! You are great and Your name is great in power.

ו מֵאֵין כָּמוֹךָ יְהֹוָה גָּדוֹל אַתָּה וְגָדוֹל שִׁמְךָ בִּגְבוּרָה:

⁷ Who would not revere You, O King of the nations? For that is Your due, Since among all the wise of the nations And among all their royalty, There is none like You.

ז מִי לֹא יִרָאֲךָ מֶלֶךְ הַגּוֹיִם כִּי לְךָ יָאָתָה כִּי בְכׇל־חַכְמֵי הַגּוֹיִם וּבְכׇל־מַלְכוּתָם מֵאֵין כָּמוֹךָ:

⁸ But they are both dull and foolish; [Their] doctrine is but delusion; It is a piece of wood,

ח וּבְאַחַת יִבְעֲרוּ וְיִכְסָלוּ מוּסַר הֲבָלִים עֵץ הוּא:

⁹ Silver beaten flat, that is brought from Tarshish, And gold from Uphaz, The work of a craftsman and the goldsmith's hands; Their clothing is blue and purple, All of them are the work of skilled men.

ט כֶּסֶף מְרֻקָּע מִתַּרְשִׁישׁ יוּבָא וְזָהָב מֵאוּפָז מַעֲשֵׂה חָרָשׁ וִידֵי צוֹרֵף תְּכֵלֶת וְאַרְגָּמָן לְבוּשָׁם מַעֲשֵׂה חֲכָמִים כֻּלָּם:

riches. On the other hand, righteous people strive to know and understand God's ways. As *Rambam* writes, this knowledge will motivate the person to seek God's true delights: Loving-kindness, justice, and righteousness. In this way, righteous people will imitate *Hashem*'s ways.

10 But *Hashem* is truly God: He is a living God, The
everlasting King. At His wrath, the earth quakes,
And nations cannot endure His rage.

וַיהוָה אֱלֹהִים אֱמֶת הוּא־אֱלֹהִים חַיִּים
וּמֶלֶךְ עוֹלָם מִקִּצְפּוֹ תִּרְעַשׁ הָאָרֶץ
וְלֹא־יָכִלוּ גוֹיִם זַעְמוֹ:

*va-do-NAI e-lo-HEEM e-MET hu e-lo-HEEM kha-YEEM u-ME-lekh
o-LAM mi-kitz-PO tir-ASH ha-A-retz v'-lo ya-KHI-lu go-YIM za-MO*

11 Thus shall you say to them: Let the gods, who did
not make heaven and earth, perish from the earth
and from under these heavens.

כִּדְנָה תֵּאמְרוּן לְהוֹם אֱלָהַיָּא דִּי־שְׁמַיָּא
וְאַרְקָא לָא עֲבַדוּ יֵאבַדוּ מֵאַרְעָא וּמִן־
תְּחוֹת שְׁמַיָּא אֵלֶּה:

12 He made the earth by His might, Established the
world by His wisdom, And by His understanding
stretched out the skies.

עֹשֵׂה אֶרֶץ בְּכֹחוֹ מֵכִין תֵּבֵל בְּחָכְמָתוֹ
וּבִתְבוּנָתוֹ נָטָה שָׁמָיִם:

13 When He makes His voice heard, There is a
rumbling of water in the skies; He makes vapors
rise from the end of the earth, He makes lightning
for the rain, And brings forth wind from His
treasures.

לְקוֹל תִּתּוֹ הֲמוֹן מַיִם בַּשָּׁמַיִם וַיַּעֲלֶה
נְשִׂאִים מִקְצֵה אֶרֶץ [הָאָרֶץ] בְּרָקִים
לַמָּטָר עָשָׂה וַיּוֹצֵא רוּחַ מֵאֹצְרֹתָיו:

14 Every man is proved dull, without knowledge;
Every goldsmith is put to shame because of the
idol For his molten image is a deceit – There is no
breath in them.

נִבְעַר כָּל־אָדָם מִדַּעַת הֹבִישׁ כָּל־צוֹרֵף
מִפָּסֶל כִּי שֶׁקֶר נִסְכּוֹ וְלֹא־רוּחַ בָּם:

15 They are delusion, a work of mockery; In their hour
of doom, they shall perish.

הֶבֶל הֵמָּה מַעֲשֵׂה תַּעְתֻּעִים בְּעֵת
פְּקֻדָּתָם יֹאבֵדוּ:

16 Not like these is the Portion of *Yaakov*; For it is He
who formed all things, And *Yisrael* is His very own
tribe: LORD of Hosts is His name.

לֹא־כְאֵלֶּה חֵלֶק יַעֲקֹב כִּי־יוֹצֵר הַכֹּל
הוּא וְיִשְׂרָאֵל שֵׁבֶט נַחֲלָתוֹ יְהוָה צְבָאוֹת
שְׁמוֹ:

17 Gather up your bundle from the ground, You who
dwell under siege!

אִסְפִּי מֵאֶרֶץ כִּנְעָתֵךְ ישבתי [יֹשֶׁבֶת]
בַּמָּצוֹר:

18 For thus said *Hashem*: I will fling away the
inhabitants of the land this time: I will harass them
so that they shall feel it.

כִּי־כֹה אָמַר יְהוָה הִנְנִי קוֹלֵעַ אֶת־יוֹשְׁבֵי
הָאָרֶץ בַּפַּעַם הַזֹּאת וַהֲצֵרוֹתִי לָהֶם
לְמַעַן יִמְצָאוּ:

19 Woe unto me for my hurt, My wound is severe! I
thought, "This is but a sickness And I must bear it."

אוֹי לִי עַל־שִׁבְרִי נַחְלָה מַכָּתִי וַאֲנִי
אָמַרְתִּי אַךְ זֶה חֳלִי וְאֶשָּׂאֶנּוּ:

ה'
אלוקים

10:10 But *Hashem* is truly God *Hashem* has
many names in the Bible, each representing a
distinct divine attribute. In his book of sermons,
I Submit, Rabbi David Stavsky explains the difference between the two divine names mentioned in this verse.
Commenting on the words *Hashem Hu Ha-Elokim* (הוא ה'
האלהים) (1 Kings 18:39), 'But *Hashem* is truly God,' Rabbi
Stavsky uncovers a deeper lesson behind the use of these
two names together. "The word *Hashem* (Lord) means

rachamim, 'mercy,' 'kindness,' 'forgiveness.'
The word *Elokim* (God) means *midat hadin*,
'the God of judgement.' At first, judgment
seems harsh, cruel, punishing. But, no, we say
they are together '*Hashem Hu Ha-Elokim*.' In
the *Elokim*, in the judgment, there is, was, and
always will be *Hashem*. He is not just a God of
judgment – for in His judgment is compassion and kindness – may we merit to understand it."

Rabbi David
Stavsky
(1930–2004)

20 My tents are ravaged, All my tent cords are broken. My children have gone forth from me And are no more; No one is left to stretch out my tent And hang my tent cloths.

כ אָהֳלִי שֻׁדָּד וְכָל־מֵיתָרַי נִתָּקוּ בָּנַי יְצָאֻנִי וְאֵינָם אֵין־נֹטֶה עוֹד אָהֳלִי וּמֵקִים יְרִיעוֹתָי:

21 For the shepherds are dull And did not seek *Hashem*; Therefore they have not prospered And all their flock is scattered.

כא כִּי נִבְעֲרוּ הָרֹעִים וְאֶת־יְהֹוָה לֹא דָרָשׁוּ עַל־כֵּן לֹא הִשְׂכִּילוּ וְכָל־מַרְעִיתָם נָפוֹצָה:

22 Hark, a noise! It is coming, A great commotion out of the north, That the towns of *Yehuda* may be made a desolation, A haunt of jackals.

כב קוֹל שְׁמוּעָה הִנֵּה בָאָה וְרַעַשׁ גָּדוֹל מֵאֶרֶץ צָפוֹן לָשׂוּם אֶת־עָרֵי יְהוּדָה שְׁמָמָה מְעוֹן תַּנִּים:

23 I know, *Hashem*, that man's road is not his [to choose], That man, as he walks, cannot direct his own steps.

כג יָדַעְתִּי יְהֹוָה כִּי לֹא לָאָדָם דַּרְכּוֹ לֹא־לְאִישׁ הֹלֵךְ וְהָכִין אֶת־צַעֲדוֹ:

24 Chastise me, *Hashem*, but in measure; Not in Your wrath, lest You reduce me to naught.

כד יַסְּרֵנִי יְהֹוָה אַךְ־בְּמִשְׁפָּט אַל־בְּאַפְּךָ פֶּן־תַּמְעִטֵנִי:

25 Pour out Your wrath on the nations who have not heeded You, Upon the clans that have not invoked Your name. For they have devoured *Yaakov*, Have devoured and consumed him, And have laid desolate his homesteads.

כה שְׁפֹךְ חֲמָתְךָ עַל־הַגּוֹיִם אֲשֶׁר לֹא־יְדָעוּךָ וְעַל מִשְׁפָּחוֹת אֲשֶׁר בְּשִׁמְךָ לֹא קָרָאוּ כִּי־אָכְלוּ אֶת־יַעֲקֹב וַאֲכָלֻהוּ וַיְכַלֻּהוּ וְאֶת־נָוֵהוּ הֵשַׁמּוּ:

*sh'-FOKH kha-ma-t'-KHA al ha-go-YIM a-SHER lo y'-da-U-kha v'-AL
mish-pa-KHOT a-SHER b'-shim-KHA LO ka-RA-u kee a-kh'-LU et
ya-a-KOV va-a-kha-LU-hu vai-kha-LU-hu v'-et na-VAY-hu hay-SHA-mu*

11 1 The word which came to *Yirmiyahu* from *Hashem*:

יא א הַדָּבָר אֲשֶׁר הָיָה אֶל־יִרְמְיָהוּ מֵאֵת יְהֹוָה לֵאמֹר:

2 "Hear the terms of this covenant, and recite them to the men of *Yehuda* and the inhabitants of *Yerushalayim*!

ב שִׁמְעוּ אֶת־דִּבְרֵי הַבְּרִית הַזֹּאת וְדִבַּרְתָּם אֶל־אִישׁ יְהוּדָה וְעַל־יֹשְׁבֵי יְרוּשָׁלָ͏ִם:

3 And say to them, Thus said *Hashem*, the God of *Yisrael*: Cursed be the man who will not obey the terms of this covenant,

ג וְאָמַרְתָּ אֲלֵיהֶם כֹּה־אָמַר יְהֹוָה אֱלֹהֵי יִשְׂרָאֵל אָרוּר הָאִישׁ אֲשֶׁר לֹא יִשְׁמַע אֶת־דִּבְרֵי הַבְּרִית הַזֹּאת:

Passover seder table

10:25 Pour out Your wrath on the nations who have not heeded You In chapter 10, *Yirmiyahu* mocks the futility of idolatry, and describes how the northern country, Babylonia, would turn the land of *Yehuda* into a desolate place that would be home for jackals. He concludes, however, with a plea for justice. If Israel is to be destroyed, then other nations who engaged in evil and violence should also be punished. Their attacks on Israel were motivated by hatred and vindictiveness, and they too should face *Hashem*'s anger. This verse is recited on *Pesach* night during the *Seder* meal, when Jews remember the deliverance from Egypt and pray for the final redemption.

Jeremiah

4 which I enjoined upon your fathers when I freed them from the land of Egypt, the iron crucible, saying, 'Obey Me and observe them, just as I command you, that you may be My people and I may be your God' –

5 in order to fulfill the oath which I swore to your fathers, to give them a land flowing with milk and honey, as is now the case." And I responded, "*Amen, Hashem.*"

6 And *Hashem* said to me, "Proclaim all these things through the towns of *Yehuda* and the streets of *Yerushalayim*: Hear the terms of this covenant, and perform them.

7 For I have repeatedly and persistently warned your fathers from the time I brought them out of Egypt to this day, saying: Obey My commands.

8 But they would not listen or give ear; they all followed the willfulness of their evil hearts. So I have brought upon them all the terms of this covenant, because they did not do what I commanded them to do."

9 *Hashem* said to me, "A conspiracy exists among the men of *Yehuda* and the inhabitants of *Yerushalayim*.

10 They have returned to the iniquities of their fathers of old, who refused to heed My words. They, too, have followed other gods and served them. The House of *Yisrael* and the House of *Yehuda* have broken the covenant that I made with their fathers."

11 Assuredly, thus said *Hashem*: I am going to bring upon them disaster from which they will not be able to escape. Then they will cry out to me, but I will not listen to them.

12 And the townsmen of *Yehuda* and the inhabitants of *Yerushalayim* will go and cry out to the gods to which they sacrifice; but they will not be able to rescue them in their time of disaster.

13 For your gods have become as many as your towns, O *Yehuda*, and you have set up as many altars to Shame as there are streets in *Yerushalayim* – altars for sacrifice to Baal.

14 As for you, do not pray for this people, do not raise a cry of prayer on their behalf; for I will not listen when they call to Me on account of their disaster.

ד אֲשֶׁר צִוִּיתִי אֶת־אֲבוֹתֵיכֶם בְּיוֹם הוֹצִיאִי־אוֹתָם מֵאֶרֶץ־מִצְרַיִם מִכּוּר הַבַּרְזֶל לֵאמֹר שִׁמְעוּ בְקוֹלִי וַעֲשִׂיתֶם אוֹתָם כְּכֹל אֲשֶׁר־אֲצַוֶּה אֶתְכֶם וִהְיִיתֶם לִי לְעָם וְאָנֹכִי אֶהְיֶה לָכֶם לֵאלֹהִים:

ה לְמַעַן הָקִים אֶת־הַשְּׁבוּעָה אֲשֶׁר־ נִשְׁבַּעְתִּי לַאֲבוֹתֵיכֶם לָתֵת לָהֶם אֶרֶץ זָבַת חָלָב וּדְבַשׁ כַּיּוֹם הַזֶּה וָאַעַן וָאֹמַר אָמֵן יְהוָה:

ו וַיֹּאמֶר יְהוָה אֵלַי קְרָא אֶת־כָּל־הַדְּבָרִים הָאֵלֶּה בְּעָרֵי יְהוּדָה וּבְחֻצוֹת יְרוּשָׁלִַם לֵאמֹר שִׁמְעוּ אֶת־דִּבְרֵי הַבְּרִית הַזֹּאת וַעֲשִׂיתֶם אוֹתָם:

ז כִּי הָעֵד הַעִדֹתִי בַּאֲבוֹתֵיכֶם בְּיוֹם הַעֲלוֹתִי אוֹתָם מֵאֶרֶץ מִצְרַיִם וְעַד־ הַיּוֹם הַזֶּה הַשְׁכֵּם וְהָעֵד לֵאמֹר שִׁמְעוּ בְּקוֹלִי:

ח וְלֹא שָׁמְעוּ וְלֹא־הִטּוּ אֶת־אָזְנָם וַיֵּלְכוּ אִישׁ בִּשְׁרִירוּת לִבָּם הָרָע וָאָבִיא עֲלֵיהֶם אֶת־כָּל־דִּבְרֵי הַבְּרִית־הַזֹּאת אֲשֶׁר־צִוִּיתִי לַעֲשׂוֹת וְלֹא עָשׂוּ:

ט וַיֹּאמֶר יְהוָה אֵלָי נִמְצָא־קֶשֶׁר בְּאִישׁ יְהוּדָה וּבְיֹשְׁבֵי יְרוּשָׁלָם:

י שָׁבוּ עַל־עֲוֹנֹת אֲבוֹתָם הָרִאשֹׁנִים אֲשֶׁר מֵאֲנוּ לִשְׁמוֹעַ אֶת־דְּבָרַי וְהֵמָּה הָלְכוּ אַחֲרֵי אֱלֹהִים אֲחֵרִים לְעָבְדָם הֵפֵרוּ בֵית־יִשְׂרָאֵל וּבֵית יְהוּדָה אֶת־בְּרִיתִי אֲשֶׁר כָּרַתִּי אֶת־אֲבוֹתָם:

יא לָכֵן כֹּה אָמַר יְהוָה הִנְנִי מֵבִיא אֲלֵיהֶם רָעָה אֲשֶׁר לֹא־יוּכְלוּ לָצֵאת מִמֶּנָּה וְזָעֲקוּ אֵלַי וְלֹא אֶשְׁמַע אֲלֵיהֶם:

יב וְהָלְכוּ עָרֵי יְהוּדָה וְיֹשְׁבֵי יְרוּשָׁלַם וְזָעֲקוּ אֶל־הָאֱלֹהִים אֲשֶׁר הֵם מְקַטְּרִים לָהֶם וְהוֹשֵׁעַ לֹא־יוֹשִׁיעוּ לָהֶם בְּעֵת רָעָתָם:

יג כִּי מִסְפַּר עָרֶיךָ הָיוּ אֱלֹהֶיךָ יְהוּדָה וּמִסְפַּר חֻצוֹת יְרוּשָׁלַם שַׂמְתֶּם מִזְבְּחוֹת לַבֹּשֶׁת מִזְבְּחוֹת לְקַטֵּר לַבָּעַל:

יד וְאַתָּה אַל־תִּתְפַּלֵּל בְּעַד־הָעָם הַזֶּה וְאַל־תִּשָּׂא בַעֲדָם רִנָּה וּתְפִלָּה כִּי אֵינֶנִּי שֹׁמֵעַ בְּעֵת קָרְאָם אֵלַי בְּעַד רָעָתָם:

15 Why should My beloved be in My House, Who executes so many vile designs? The sacral flesh will pass away from you, For you exult while performing your evil deeds.

טו מֶה לִידִידִי בְּבֵיתִי עֲשׂוֹתָהּ הַמְזִמָּתָה הָרַבִּים וּבְשַׂר־קֹדֶשׁ יַעַבְרוּ מֵעָלָיִךְ כִּי רָעָתֵכִי אָז תַּעֲלֹזִי:

16 *Hashem* named you "Verdant olive tree, Fair, with choice fruit." But with a great roaring sound He has set it on fire, And its boughs are broken.

טז זַיִת רַעֲנָן יְפֵה פְרִי־תֹאַר קָרָא יְהֹוָה שְׁמֵךְ לְקוֹל הֲמוּלָּה גְדֹלָה הִצִּית אֵשׁ עָלֶיהָ וְרָעוּ דָּלִיּוֹתָיו:

ZA-yit ra-a-NAN y'-FAY f'-ree TO-ar ka-RA a-do-NAI sh'-MAYKH l'-KOL ha-mu-LAH g'-do-LAH hi-TZEET AYSH a-LE-ha v'-ra-U da-li-yo-TAV

17 The LORD of Hosts, who planted you, has decreed disaster for you, because of the evil wrought by the House of *Yisrael* and the House of *Yehuda*, who angered Me by sacrificing to Baal.

יז וַיהֹוָה צְבָאוֹת הַנּוֹטֵעַ אוֹתָךְ דִּבֶּר עָלַיִךְ רָעָה בִּגְלַל רָעַת בֵּית־יִשְׂרָאֵל וּבֵית יְהוּדָה אֲשֶׁר עָשׂוּ לָהֶם לְהַכְעִסֵנִי לְקַטֵּר לַבָּעַל:

18 *Hashem* informed me, and I knew – Then You let me see their deeds.

יח וַיהֹוָה הוֹדִיעַנִי וָאֵדָעָה אָז הִרְאִיתַנִי מַעַלְלֵיהֶם:

19 For I was like a docile lamb Led to the slaughter; I did not realize That it was against me They fashioned their plots: "Let us destroy the tree with its fruit, Let us cut him off from the land of the living. That his name be remembered no more!"

יט וַאֲנִי כְּכֶבֶשׂ אַלּוּף יוּבַל לִטְבוֹחַ וְלֹא־יָדַעְתִּי כִּי־עָלַי חָשְׁבוּ מַחֲשָׁבוֹת נַשְׁחִיתָה עֵץ בְּלַחְמוֹ וְנִכְרְתֶנּוּ מֵאֶרֶץ חַיִּים וּשְׁמוֹ לֹא־יִזָּכֵר עוֹד:

20 O LORD of Hosts, O just Judge, Who test the thoughts and the mind, Let me see Your retribution upon them, For I lay my case before You.

כ וַיהֹוָה צְבָאוֹת שֹׁפֵט צֶדֶק בֹּחֵן כְּלָיוֹת וָלֵב אֶרְאֶה נִקְמָתְךָ מֵהֶם כִּי אֵלֶיךָ גִּלִּיתִי אֶת־רִיבִי:

21 Assuredly, thus said the LORD of Hosts concerning the men of *Anatot* who seek your life and say, "You must not prophesy any more in the name of *Hashem*, or you will die by our hand" –

כא לָכֵן כֹּה־אָמַר יְהֹוָה עַל־אַנְשֵׁי עֲנָתוֹת הַמְבַקְשִׁים אֶת־נַפְשְׁךָ לֵאמֹר לֹא תִנָּבֵא בְּשֵׁם יְהֹוָה וְלֹא תָמוּת בְּיָדֵנוּ:

22 Assuredly, thus said the LORD of Hosts: "I am going to deal with them: the young men shall die by the sword, their boys and girls shall die by famine.

כב לָכֵן כֹּה אָמַר יְהֹוָה צְבָאוֹת הִנְנִי פֹקֵד עֲלֵיהֶם הַבַּחוּרִים יָמֻתוּ בַחֶרֶב בְּנֵיהֶם וּבְנוֹתֵיהֶם יָמֻתוּ בָּרָעָב:

23 No remnant shall be left of them, for I will bring disaster on the men of *Anatot*, the year of their doom."

כג וּשְׁאֵרִית לֹא תִהְיֶה לָהֶם כִּי־אָבִיא רָעָה אֶל־אַנְשֵׁי עֲנָתוֹת שְׁנַת פְּקֻדָּתָם:

11:16 Verdant olive tree The first time the olive tree is mentioned in the Bible is when *Noach* checks to see if the flood waters have receded. When the dove returns with an olive branch in its mouth, *Noach* knows that the water has receded sufficiently and life has begun anew (Genesis 8:11, 21). Pure olive oil was also used for the lighting of the golden *menorah* lamp in the *Beit Hamikdash*, as well as to anoint priests and kings as part of their initiation. One lesson we can take from the olive is that just like an olive yields oil only when pressed, so too, as human beings, when we are pressed between the millstones of life, our best selves emerge. Often, we rise to the occasion to meet life's tests only when challenged.

Olives and olive oil at an Israeli market

12 ¹ You will win, *Hashem*, if I make claim against You, Yet I shall present charges against You: Why does the way of the wicked prosper? Why are the workers of treachery at ease?

² You have planted them, and they have taken root, They spread, they even bear fruit. You are present in their mouths, But far from their thoughts.

³ Yet You, *Hashem*, have noted and observed me; You have tested my heart, and found it with You. Drive them out like sheep to the slaughter, Prepare them for the day of slaying!

⁴ How long must the land languish, And the grass of all the countryside dry up? Must beasts and birds perish, Because of the evil of its inhabitants, Who say, "He will not look upon our future"?

⁵ If you race with the foot-runners and they exhaust you, How then can you compete with horses? If you are secure only in a tranquil land, How will you fare in the jungle of the *Yarden*?

⁶ For even your kinsmen and your father's house, Even they are treacherous toward you, They cry after you as a mob. Do not believe them When they speak cordially to you.

⁷ I have abandoned My House, I have deserted My possession, I have given over My dearly beloved Into the hands of her enemies.

⁸ My own people acted toward Me Like a lion in the forest; She raised her voice against Me – Therefore I have rejected her.

⁹ My own people acts toward Me Like a bird of prey [or] a hyena; Let the birds of prey surround her! Go, gather all the wild beasts, Bring them to devour!

¹⁰ Many shepherds have destroyed My vineyard, Have trampled My field, Have made My delightful field A desolate wilderness.

¹¹ They have made her a desolation; Desolate, she pours out grief to Me. The whole land is laid desolate, But no man gives it thought.

¹² Spoilers have come Upon all the bare heights of the wilderness. For a sword of *Hashem* devours From one end of the land to the other; No flesh is safe.

יב א צַדִּיק אַתָּה יְהֹוָה כִּי אָרִיב אֵלֶיךָ אַךְ מִשְׁפָּטִים אֲדַבֵּר אוֹתָךְ מַדּוּעַ דֶּרֶךְ רְשָׁעִים צָלֵחָה שָׁלוּ כׇּל־בֹּגְדֵי בָגֶד:

ב נְטַעְתָּם גַּם־שֹׁרָשׁוּ יֵלְכוּ גַּם־עָשׂוּ פֶרִי קָרוֹב אַתָּה בְּפִיהֶם וְרָחוֹק מִכִּלְיוֹתֵיהֶם:

ג וְאַתָּה יְהֹוָה יְדַעְתָּנִי תִּרְאֵנִי וּבָחַנְתָּ לִבִּי אִתָּךְ הַתִּקֵם כְּצֹאן לְטִבְחָה וְהַקְדִּשֵׁם לְיוֹם הֲרֵגָה:

ד עַד־מָתַי תֶּאֱבַל הָאָרֶץ וְעֵשֶׂב כׇּל־ הַשָּׂדֶה יִיבָשׁ מֵרָעַת יֹשְׁבֵי־בָהּ סָפְתָה בְהֵמוֹת וָעוֹף כִּי אָמְרוּ לֹא יִרְאֶה אֶת־ אַחֲרִיתֵנוּ:

ה כִּי אֶת־רַגְלִים רַצְתָּה וַיַּלְאוּךָ וְאֵיךְ תְּתַחֲרֶה אֶת־הַסּוּסִים וּבְאֶרֶץ שָׁלוֹם אַתָּה בוֹטֵחַ וְאֵיךְ תַּעֲשֶׂה בִּגְאוֹן הַיַּרְדֵּן:

ו כִּי גַם־אַחֶיךָ וּבֵית־אָבִיךָ גַּם־הֵמָּה בָּגְדוּ בָךְ גַּם־הֵמָּה קָרְאוּ אַחֲרֶיךָ מָלֵא אַל־ תַּאֲמֵן בָּם כִּי־יְדַבְּרוּ אֵלֶיךָ טוֹבוֹת:

ז עָזַבְתִּי אֶת־בֵּיתִי נָטַשְׁתִּי אֶת־נַחֲלָתִי נָתַתִּי אֶת־יְדִדוּת נַפְשִׁי בְּכַף אֹיְבֶיהָ:

ח הָיְתָה־לִּי נַחֲלָתִי כְּאַרְיֵה בַיָּעַר נָתְנָה עָלַי בְּקוֹלָהּ עַל־כֵּן שְׂנֵאתִיהָ:

ט הַעַיִט צָבוּעַ נַחֲלָתִי לִי הַעַיִט סָבִיב עָלֶיהָ לְכוּ אִסְפוּ כׇּל־חַיַּת הַשָּׂדֶה הֵתָיוּ לְאׇכְלָה:

י רֹעִים רַבִּים שִׁחֲתוּ כַרְמִי בֹּסְסוּ אֶת־ חֶלְקָתִי נָתְנוּ אֶת־חֶלְקַת חֶמְדָּתִי לְמִדְבַּר שְׁמָמָה:

יא שָׂמָהּ לִשְׁמָמָה אָבְלָה עָלַי שְׁמֵמָה נָשַׁמָּה כׇּל־הָאָרֶץ כִּי אֵין אִישׁ שָׂם עַל־ לֵב:

יב עַל־כׇּל־שְׁפָיִם בַּמִּדְבָּר בָּאוּ שֹׁדְדִים כִּי חֶרֶב לַיהֹוָה אֹכְלָה מִקְצֵה־אֶרֶץ וְעַד־ קְצֵה הָאָרֶץ אֵין שָׁלוֹם לְכׇל־בָּשָׂר:

13 They have sown wheat and reaped thorns, They have endured pain to no avail. Be shamed, then, by your harvest – By the blazing wrath of *Hashem*!

יג זָרְעוּ חִטִּים וְקֹצִים קָצָרוּ נֶחְלוּ לֹא יוֹעִלוּ וּבֹשׁוּ מִתְּבוּאֹתֵיכֶם מֵחֲרוֹן אַף־יְהֹוָה:

14 Thus said *Hashem*: As for My wicked neighbors who encroach on the heritage that I gave to My people *Yisrael* – I am going to uproot them from their soil, and I will uproot the House of *Yehuda* out of the midst of them.

יד כֹּה אָמַר יְהֹוָה עַל־כָּל־שְׁכֵנַי הָרָעִים הַנֹּגְעִים בַּנַּחֲלָה אֲשֶׁר־הִנְחַלְתִּי אֶת־עַמִּי אֶת־יִשְׂרָאֵל הִנְנִי נֹתְשָׁם מֵעַל אַדְמָתָם וְאֶת־בֵּית יְהוּדָה אֶתּוֹשׁ מִתּוֹכָם:

> KOH a-MAR a-do-NAI al kol sh'-khay-NAI ha-ra-EEM ha-no-g'-EEM
> ba-na-kha-LAH a-sher hin-KHAL-tee et a-MEE et yis-ra-AYL hi-n'-NEE
> no-t'-SHAM may-AL ad-ma-TAM v'-et BAYT y'-hu-DAH e-TOSH mi-to-KHAM

15 Then, after I have uprooted them, I will take them back into favor, and restore them each to his own inheritance and his own land.

טו וְהָיָה אַחֲרֵי נָתְשִׁי אוֹתָם אָשׁוּב וְרִחַמְתִּים וַהֲשִׁבֹתִים אִישׁ לְנַחֲלָתוֹ וְאִישׁ לְאַרְצוֹ:

16 And if they learn the ways of My people, to swear by My name – "As *Hashem* lives" – just as they once taught My people to swear by Baal, then they shall be built up in the midst of My people.

טז וְהָיָה אִם־לָמֹד יִלְמְדוּ אֶת־דַּרְכֵי עַמִּי לְהִשָּׁבֵעַ בִּשְׁמִי חַי־יְהֹוָה כַּאֲשֶׁר לִמְּדוּ אֶת־עַמִּי לְהִשָּׁבֵעַ בַּבָּעַל וְנִבְנוּ בְּתוֹךְ עַמִּי:

17 But if they do not give heed, I will tear out that nation, tear it out and destroy it – declares *Hashem*.

יז וְאִם לֹא יִשְׁמָעוּ וְנָתַשְׁתִּי אֶת־הַגּוֹי הַהוּא נָתוֹשׁ וְאַבֵּד נְאֻם־יְהֹוָה:

13 1 Thus *Hashem* said to me: "Go buy yourself a loincloth of linen, and put it around your loins, but do not dip it into water."

יג א כֹּה־אָמַר יְהֹוָה אֵלַי הָלוֹךְ וְקָנִיתָ לְּךָ אֵזוֹר פִּשְׁתִּים וְשַׂמְתּוֹ עַל־מָתְנֶיךָ וּבַמַּיִם לֹא תְבִאֵהוּ:

2 So I bought the loincloth in accordance with *Hashem*'s command, and put it about my loins.

ב וָאֶקְנֶה אֶת־הָאֵזוֹר כִּדְבַר יְהֹוָה וָאָשִׂם עַל־מָתְנָי:

3 And the word of *Hashem* came to me a second time:

ג וַיְהִי דְבַר־יְהֹוָה אֵלַי שֵׁנִית לֵאמֹר:

4 "Take the loincloth which you bought, which is about your loins, and go at once to Perath and cover it up there in a cleft of the rock."

ד קַח אֶת־הָאֵזוֹר אֲשֶׁר קָנִיתָ אֲשֶׁר עַל־מָתְנֶיךָ וְקוּם לֵךְ פְּרָתָה וְטָמְנֵהוּ שָׁם בִּנְקִיק הַסָּלַע:

5 I went and buried it at Perath, as *Hashem* had commanded me.

ה וָאֵלֵךְ וָאֶטְמְנֵהוּ בִּפְרָת כַּאֲשֶׁר צִוָּה יְהֹוָה אוֹתִי:

6 Then, after a long time, *Hashem* said to me, "Go at once to Perath and take there the loincloth which I commanded you to bury there."

ו וַיְהִי מִקֵּץ יָמִים רַבִּים וַיֹּאמֶר יְהֹוָה אֵלַי קוּם לֵךְ פְּרָתָה וְקַח מִשָּׁם אֶת־הָאֵזוֹר אֲשֶׁר צִוִּיתִיךָ לְטָמְנוֹ־שָׁם:

12:14 As for My wicked neighbors Through their actions, the nations have violated the heritage which *Hashem* designated for His people, namely, *Eretz Yisrael*. These evil nations will therefore be uprooted from their land and sent into exile. God will then uproot *Yehuda* from among them, and replant them in safety and security in the Land of Israel. By calling Ammon and Moab "My wicked neighbors," *Hashem* explicitly identifies Himself as one with the People of Israel – their enemies are His enemies.

Airlifting Yeminite Jews to Israel, Operation Magic Carpet

7 So I went to Perath and dug up the loincloth from
the place where I had buried it; and found the
loincloth ruined; it was not good for anything.

ז וָאֵלֵךְ פְּרָתָה וָאֶחְפֹּר וָאֶקַּח אֶת־הָאֵזוֹר
מִן־הַמָּקוֹם אֲשֶׁר־טְמַנְתִּיו שָׁמָּה וְהִנֵּה
נִשְׁחַת הָאֵזוֹר לֹא יִצְלַח לַכֹּל:

8 The word of *Hashem* came to me:

ח וַיְהִי דְבַר־יְהֹוָה אֵלַי לֵאמֹר:

9 Thus said *Hashem*: Even so will I ruin the
overweening pride of *Yehuda* and *Yerushalayim*.

ט כֹּה אָמַר יְהֹוָה כָּכָה אַשְׁחִית אֶת־גְּאוֹן
יְהוּדָה וְאֶת־גְּאוֹן יְרוּשָׁלַ͏ִם הָרָב:

10 This wicked people who refuse to heed My
bidding, who follow the willfulness of their own
hearts, who follow other gods and serve them and
worship them, shall become like that loincloth,
which is not good for anything.

י הָעָם הַזֶּה הָרָע הַמֵּאֲנִים לִשְׁמוֹעַ
אֶת־דְּבָרַי הַהֹלְכִים בִּשְׁרִרוּת לִבָּם
וַיֵּלְכוּ אַחֲרֵי אֱלֹהִים אֲחֵרִים לְעָבְדָם
וּלְהִשְׁתַּחֲוֺת לָהֶם וִיהִי כָּאֵזוֹר הַזֶּה אֲשֶׁר
לֹא־יִצְלַח לַכֹּל:

11 For as the loincloth clings close to the loins of a
man, so I brought close to Me the whole House of
Yisrael and the whole House of *Yehuda* – declares
Hashem – that they might be My people, for fame,
and praise, and splendor. But they would not obey.

יא כִּי כַּאֲשֶׁר יִדְבַּק הָאֵזוֹר אֶל־מָתְנֵי־אִישׁ
כֵּן הִדְבַּקְתִּי אֵלַי אֶת־כָּל־בֵּית יִשְׂרָאֵל
וְאֶת־כָּל־בֵּית יְהוּדָה נְאֻם־יְהֹוָה לִהְיוֹת
לִי לְעָם וּלְשֵׁם וְלִתְהִלָּה וּלְתִפְאָרֶת וְלֹא
שָׁמֵעוּ:

12 And speak this word to them: Thus said *Hashem*,
the God of *Yisrael*: "Every jar should be filled with
wine." And when they say to you, "Don't we know
that every jar should be filled with wine?"

יב וְאָמַרְתָּ אֲלֵיהֶם אֶת־הַדָּבָר הַזֶּה כֹּה־
אָמַר יְהֹוָה אֱלֹהֵי יִשְׂרָאֵל כָּל־נֵבֶל
יִמָּלֵא יָיִן וְאָמְרוּ אֵלֶיךָ הֲיָדֹעַ לֹא נֵדַע
כִּי כָל־נֵבֶל יִמָּלֵא יָיִן:

v'-a-mar-TA a-lay-HEM et ha-da-VAR ha-ZEH koh a-MAR a-do-NAI
e-lo-HAY yis-ra-AYL kol NAY-vel yi-MA-lay YA-yin va'-a-m'-RU ay-LE-kha
ha-ya-DO-a LO nay-DA kee khol NAY-vel yi-MA-lay YA-yin

13 say to them, "Thus said *Hashem*: I am going to fill
with drunkenness all the inhabitants of this land,
and the kings who sit on the throne of *David*,
and the *Kohanim* and the *Neviim*, and all the
inhabitants of *Yerushalayim*.

יג וְאָמַרְתָּ אֲלֵיהֶם כֹּה־אָמַר יְהֹוָה הִנְנִי
מְמַלֵּא אֶת־כָּל־יֹשְׁבֵי הָאָרֶץ הַזֹּאת
וְאֶת־הַמְּלָכִים הַיֹּשְׁבִים לְדָוִד עַל־כִּסְאוֹ
וְאֶת־הַכֹּהֲנִים וְאֶת־הַנְּבִיאִים וְאֵת כָּל־
יֹשְׁבֵי יְרוּשָׁלָ͏ִם שִׁכָּרוֹן:

14 And I will smash them one against the other,
parents and children alike – declares *Hashem*;
no pity, compassion, or mercy will stop Me from
destroying them."

יד וְנִפַּצְתִּים אִישׁ אֶל־אָחִיו וְהָאָבוֹת
וְהַבָּנִים יַחְדָּו נְאֻם־יְהֹוָה לֹא־אֶחְמוֹל
וְלֹא־אָחוּס וְלֹא אֲרַחֵם מֵהַשְׁחִיתָם:

15 Attend and give ear; be not haughty, For *Hashem*
has spoken.

טו שִׁמְעוּ וְהַאֲזִינוּ אַל־תִּגְבָּהוּ כִּי יְהֹוָה
דִּבֵּר:

Jeremiah

13:12 Every jar should be filled with wine
According to *Radak*, the metaphor of the jars
filled with wine symbolizes the Israelites whose
minds will be so preoccupied with the afflictions that will
befall them, it will be as if they are intoxicated. In verse 13,
Yirmiyahu clarifies that no one will be immune from
punishment, and even the leadership of the people –the
kings, princes, and prophets – will be punished. The wine
imagery is particularly poignant, since *Yehuda* is associated with wine; *Yaakov*
blessed his son *Yehuda* that
he should be so rich that he
will wash his garments in
wine (Genesis 49:11). To this
day, the hilly area of *Yehuda*
south of *Yerushalayim* is internationally renowned for
its bountiful vineyards.

Vineyard in *Yehuda*

16 Give honor to *Hashem* your God Before He brings darkness, Before your feet stumble On the mountains in shadow – When you hope for light, And it is turned to darkness And becomes deep gloom.

טז תְּנוּ לַיהוָה אֱלֹהֵיכֶם כָּבוֹד בְּטֶרֶם יַחְשִׁךְ וּבְטֶרֶם יִתְנַגְּפוּ רַגְלֵיכֶם עַל־הָרֵי נָשֶׁף וְקִוִּיתֶם לְאוֹר וְשָׂמָהּ לְצַלְמָוֶת ישית [וְשִׁית] לַעֲרָפֶל:

17 For if you will not give heed, My inmost self must weep, Because of your arrogance; My eye must stream and flow With copious tears, Because the flock of *Hashem* Is taken captive.

יז וְאִם לֹא תִשְׁמָעוּהָ בְּמִסְתָּרִים תִּבְכֶּה־ נַפְשִׁי מִפְּנֵי גֵוָה וְדָמֹעַ תִּדְמַע וְתֵרַד עֵינִי דִּמְעָה כִּי נִשְׁבָּה עֵדֶר יְהוָה:

18 Say to the king and the queen mother, "Sit in a lowly spot; For your diadems are abased, Your glorious crowns."

יח אֱמֹר לַמֶּלֶךְ וְלַגְּבִירָה הַשְׁפִּילוּ שֵׁבוּ כִּי יָרַד מַרְאֲשׁוֹתֵיכֶם עֲטֶרֶת תִּפְאַרְתְּכֶם:

19 The cities of the *Negev* are shut, There is no one to open them; *Yehuda* is exiled completely, All of it exiled.

יט עָרֵי הַנֶּגֶב סֻגְּרוּ וְאֵין פֹּתֵחַ הָגְלָת יְהוּדָה כֻּלָּהּ הָגְלָת שְׁלוֹמִים:

20 Raise your eyes and behold Those who come from the north: Where are the sheep entrusted to you, The flock you took pride in?

כ שְׂאִי [שְׂאוּ] עֵינֵיכֶם וראי [וּרְאוּ] הַבָּאִים מִצָּפוֹן אַיֵּה הָעֵדֶר נִתַּן־לָךְ צֹאן תִּפְאַרְתֵּךְ:

21 What will you say when they appoint as your heads Those among you whom you trained to be tame? Shall not pangs seize you Like a woman in childbirth?

כא מַה־תֹּאמְרִי כִּי־יִפְקֹד עָלַיִךְ וְאַתְּ לִמַּדְתְּ אֹתָם עָלַיִךְ אַלֻּפִים לְרֹאשׁ הֲלוֹא חֲבָלִים יֹאחֱזוּךְ כְּמוֹ אֵשֶׁת לֵדָה:

22 And when you ask yourself, "Why have these things befallen me?" It is because of your great iniquity That your skirts are lifted up, Your limbs exposed.

כב וְכִי תֹאמְרִי בִּלְבָבֵךְ מַדּוּעַ קְרָאֻנִי אֵלֶּה בְּרֹב עֲוֹנֵךְ נִגְלוּ שׁוּלַיִךְ נֶחְמְסוּ עֲקֵבָיִךְ:

23 Can the Cushite change his skin, Or the leopard his spots? Just as much can you do good, Who are practiced in doing evil!

כג הֲיַהֲפֹךְ כּוּשִׁי עוֹרוֹ וְנָמֵר חֲבַרְבֻּרֹתָיו גַּם־ אַתֶּם תּוּכְלוּ לְהֵיטִיב לִמֻּדֵי הָרֵעַ:

24 So I will scatter you like straw that flies Before the desert wind.

כד וַאֲפִיצֵם כְּקַשׁ־עוֹבֵר לְרוּחַ מִדְבָּר:

25 This shall be your lot, Your measured portion from Me – declares *Hashem*. Because you forgot Me And trusted in falsehood,

כה זֶה גוֹרָלֵךְ מְנָת־מִדַּיִךְ מֵאִתִּי נְאֻם־יְהוָה אֲשֶׁר שָׁכַחַתְּ אוֹתִי וַתִּבְטְחִי בַּשָּׁקֶר:

26 I in turn will lift your skirts over your face And your shame shall be seen.

כו וְגַם־אֲנִי חָשַׂפְתִּי שׁוּלַיִךְ עַל־פָּנָיִךְ וְנִרְאָה קְלוֹנֵךְ:

27 I behold your adulteries, Your lustful neighing, Your unbridled depravity, your vile acts On the hills of the countryside. Woe to you, O *Yerushalayim*, Who will not be clean! How much longer shall it be?

כז נִאֻפַיִךְ וּמִצְהֲלוֹתַיִךְ זִמַּת זְנוּתֵךְ עַל־ גְּבָעוֹת בַּשָּׂדֶה רָאִיתִי שִׁקּוּצָיִךְ אוֹי לָךְ יְרוּשָׁלַ͏ִם לֹא תִטְהֲרִי אַחֲרֵי מָתַי עֹד:

14 1 The word of *Hashem* which came to *Yirmiyahu* concerning the droughts.

יד א אֲשֶׁר הָיָה דְבַר־יְהוָה אֶל־יִרְמְיָהוּ עַל־ דִּבְרֵי הַבַּצָּרוֹת:

² *Yehuda* is in mourning, Her settlements languish. Men are bowed to the ground, And the outcry of *Yerushalayim* rises.

ב אָבְלָה יְהוּדָה וּשְׁעָרֶיהָ אֻמְלְלוּ קָדְרוּ לָאָרֶץ וְצִוְחַת יְרוּשָׁלַםִ עָלָתָה:

³ Their nobles sent their servants for water; They came to the cisterns, they found no water. They returned, their vessels empty. They are shamed and humiliated, They cover their heads.

ג וְאַדִּרֵיהֶם שָׁלְחוּ צעוריהם [צְעִירֵיהֶם] לַמָּיִם בָּאוּ עַל־גֵּבִים לֹא־מָצְאוּ מַיִם שָׁבוּ כְלֵיהֶם רֵיקָם בֹּשׁוּ וְהָכְלְמוּ וְחָפוּ רֹאשָׁם:

⁴ Because of the ground there is dismay, For there has been no rain on the earth. The plowmen are shamed, They cover their heads.

ד בַּעֲבוּר הָאֲדָמָה חַתָּה כִּי לֹא־הָיָה גֶשֶׁם בָּאָרֶץ בֹּשׁוּ אִכָּרִים חָפוּ רֹאשָׁם:

⁵ Even the hind in the field Forsakes her new-born fawn, Because there is no grass.

ה כִּי גַם־אַיֶּלֶת בַּשָּׂדֶה יָלְדָה וְעָזוֹב כִּי לֹא־הָיָה דֶּשֶׁא:

⁶ And the wild asses stand on the bare heights, Snuffing the air like jackals; Their eyes pine, Because there is no herbage.

ו וּפְרָאִים עָמְדוּ עַל־שְׁפָיִם שָׁאֲפוּ רוּחַ כַּתַּנִּים כָּלוּ עֵינֵיהֶם כִּי־אֵין עֵשֶׂב:

⁷ Though our iniquities testify against us, Act, *Hashem*, for the sake of Your name; Though our rebellions are many And we have sinned against You.

ז אִם־עֲוֺנֵינוּ עָנוּ בָנוּ יְהֹוָה עֲשֵׂה לְמַעַן שְׁמֶךָ כִּי־רַבּוּ מְשׁוּבֹתֵינוּ לְךָ חָטָאנוּ:

*im a-vo-NAY-nu A-nu VA-nu a-do-NAI a-SAY l'-MA-an sh'-ME-kha
kee ra-BU m'-shu-vo-TAY-nu l'-KHA kha-TA-nu*

⁸ O Hope of *Yisrael*, Its deliverer in time of trouble, Why are You like a stranger in the land, Like a traveler who stops only for the night?

ח מִקְוֵה יִשְׂרָאֵל מוֹשִׁיעוֹ בְּעֵת צָרָה לָמָּה תִהְיֶה כְּגֵר בָּאָרֶץ וּכְאֹרֵחַ נָטָה לָלוּן:

⁹ Why are You like a man who is stunned, Like a warrior who cannot give victory? Yet You are in our midst, *Hashem*, And Your name is attached to us – Do not forsake us!

ט לָמָּה תִהְיֶה כְּאִישׁ נִדְהָם כְּגִבּוֹר לֹא־יוּכַל לְהוֹשִׁיעַ וְאַתָּה בְקִרְבֵּנוּ יְהֹוָה וְשִׁמְךָ עָלֵינוּ נִקְרָא אַל־תַּנִּחֵנוּ:

¹⁰ Thus said *Hashem* concerning this people: "Truly, they love to stray, they have not restrained their feet; so *Hashem* has no pleasure in them. Now He will recall their iniquity and punish their sin."

י כֹּה־אָמַר יְהֹוָה לָעָם הַזֶּה כֵּן אָהֲבוּ לָנוּעַ רַגְלֵיהֶם לֹא חָשָׂכוּ וַיהֹוָה לֹא רָצָם עַתָּה יִזְכֹּר עֲוֺנָם וְיִפְקֹד חַטֹּאתָם:

¹¹ And *Hashem* said to me, "Do not pray for the benefit of this people.

יא וַיֹּאמֶר יְהֹוָה אֵלָי אַל־תִּתְפַּלֵּל בְּעַד־הָעָם הַזֶּה לְטוֹבָה:

14:7 We have sinned against You This chapter contains a prophecy to *Yirmiyahu* "concerning the droughts" (verse 1). Due to lack of water, neither people nor animals have enough to eat or drink, and therefore *Yehuda* is in a state of mourning. Since Israel is a land with few rivers and lakes, it is dependent on rain from Heaven for its subsistence. As such, *Sefer Devarim* (11:11–12) states that *Eretz Yisrael* "soaks up its water from the rains of heaven. It is a land which *Hashem* your God looks after, on which *Hashem* your God always keeps His eye." Because the Israelites are dependent on *Hashem* for their water, the amount of rain that falls is reflective of the relationship between the people and their Creator. Droughts are sent to encourage Israel to repent and to reevaluate their relationship with God. The lack of water at this time is indicative of the fact that the people have sinned against *Hashem*.

A rain storm over the Mediterranean Sea

12 When they fast, I will not listen to their outcry; and when they present burnt offering and meal offering, I will not accept them. I will exterminate them by war, famine, and disease."

יב כִּי יָצֻמוּ אֵינֶנִּי שֹׁמֵעַ אֶל־רִנָּתָם וְכִי יַעֲלוּ עֹלָה וּמִנְחָה אֵינֶנִּי רֹצָם כִּי בַּחֶרֶב וּבָרָעָב וּבַדֶּבֶר אָנֹכִי מְכַלֶּה אוֹתָם:

13 I said, "Ah, *Hashem*! The *Neviim* are saying to them, 'You shall not see the sword, famine shall not come upon you, but I will give you unfailing security in this place.'"

יג וָאֹמַר אֲהָהּ אֲדֹנָי יֱהֹוִה הִנֵּה הַנְּבִאִים אֹמְרִים לָהֶם לֹא־תִרְאוּ חֶרֶב וְרָעָב לֹא־יִהְיֶה לָכֶם כִּי־שְׁלוֹם אֱמֶת אֶתֵּן לָכֶם בַּמָּקוֹם הַזֶּה:

14 *Hashem* replied: It is a lie that the *Neviim* utter in My name. I have not sent them or commanded them. I have not spoken to them. A lying vision, an empty divination, the deceit of their own contriving – that is what they prophesy to you!

יד וַיֹּאמֶר יְהֹוָה אֵלַי שֶׁקֶר הַנְּבִאִים נִבְּאִים בִּשְׁמִי לֹא שְׁלַחְתִּים וְלֹא צִוִּיתִים וְלֹא דִבַּרְתִּי אֲלֵיהֶם חֲזוֹן שֶׁקֶר וְקֶסֶם וֶאֱלוֹל [וֶאֱלִיל] וְתַרְמוּת [וְתַרְמִית] לִבָּם הֵמָּה מִתְנַבְּאִים לָכֶם:

15 Assuredly, thus said *Hashem* concerning the *Neviim* who prophesy in My name though I have not sent them, and who say, "Sword and famine shall not befall this land"; those very *Neviim* shall perish by sword and famine.

טו לָכֵן כֹּה־אָמַר יְהֹוָה עַל־הַנְּבִאִים הַנִּבְּאִים בִּשְׁמִי וַאֲנִי לֹא־שְׁלַחְתִּים וְהֵמָּה אֹמְרִים חֶרֶב וְרָעָב לֹא יִהְיֶה בָּאָרֶץ הַזֹּאת בַּחֶרֶב וּבָרָעָב יִתַּמּוּ הַנְּבִאִים הָהֵמָּה:

16 And the people to whom they prophesy shall be left lying in the streets of *Yerushalayim* because of the famine and the sword, with none to bury them – they, their wives, their sons, and their daughters. I will pour out upon them [the requital of] their wickedness.

טז וְהָעָם אֲשֶׁר־הֵמָּה נִבְּאִים לָהֶם יִהְיוּ מֻשְׁלָכִים בְּחֻצוֹת יְרוּשָׁלִַם מִפְּנֵי הָרָעָב וְהַחֶרֶב וְאֵין מְקַבֵּר לָהֵמָּה הֵמָּה נְשֵׁיהֶם וּבְנֵיהֶם וּבְנֹתֵיהֶם וְשָׁפַכְתִּי עֲלֵיהֶם אֶת־רָעָתָם:

17 And do you speak to them thus: Let my eyes run with tears, Day and night let them not cease, For my hapless people has suffered A grievous injury, a very painful wound.

יז וְאָמַרְתָּ אֲלֵיהֶם אֶת־הַדָּבָר הַזֶּה תֵּרַדְנָה עֵינַי דִּמְעָה לַיְלָה וְיוֹמָם וְאַל־תִּדְמֶינָה כִּי שֶׁבֶר גָּדוֹל נִשְׁבְּרָה בְּתוּלַת בַּת־עַמִּי מַכָּה נַחְלָה מְאֹד:

18 If I go out to the country – Lo, the slain of the sword. If I enter the city – Lo, those who are sick with famine. Both *Kohen* and *Navi* roam the land, They know not where.

יח אִם־יָצָאתִי הַשָּׂדֶה וְהִנֵּה חַלְלֵי־חֶרֶב וְאִם בָּאתִי הָעִיר וְהִנֵּה תַּחֲלוּאֵי רָעָב כִּי־גַם־נָבִיא גַם־כֹּהֵן סָחֲרוּ אֶל־אֶרֶץ וְלֹא יָדָעוּ:

19 Have You, then, rejected *Yehuda*? Have You spurned *Tzion*? Why have You smitten us So that there is no cure? Why do we hope for happiness, But find no good; For a time of healing, And meet terror instead?

יט הֲמָאֹס מָאַסְתָּ אֶת־יְהוּדָה אִם־בְּצִיּוֹן גָּעֲלָה נַפְשֶׁךָ מַדּוּעַ הִכִּיתָנוּ וְאֵין לָנוּ מַרְפֵּא קַוֵּה לְשָׁלוֹם וְאֵין טוֹב וּלְעֵת מַרְפֵּא וְהִנֵּה בְעָתָה:

20 We acknowledge our wickedness, *Hashem* – The iniquity of our fathers – For we have sinned against You.

כ יָדַעְנוּ יְהֹוָה רִשְׁעֵנוּ עֲוֺן אֲבוֹתֵינוּ כִּי חָטָאנוּ לָךְ:

21 For Your name's sake, do not disown us; Do not dishonor Your glorious throne. Remember, do not annul Your covenant with us.

כא אַל־תִּנְאַץ לְמַעַן שִׁמְךָ אַל־תְּנַבֵּל כִּסֵּא כְבוֹדֶךָ זְכֹר אַל־תָּפֵר בְּרִיתְךָ אִתָּנוּ:

²² Can any of the false gods of the nations give rain? Can the skies of themselves give showers? Only You can, *Hashem* our God! So we hope in You, For only You made all these things.

הֲיֵשׁ בְּהַבְלֵי הַגּוֹיִם מַגְשִׁמִים וְאִם־הַשָּׁמַיִם יִתְּנוּ רְבִבִים הֲלֹא אַתָּה־הוּא יְהֹוָה אֱלֹהֵינוּ וּנְקַוֶּה־לָךְ כִּי־אַתָּה עָשִׂיתָ אֶת־כָּל־אֵלֶּה:

טו **א** ¹ *Hashem* said to me, "Even if *Moshe* and *Shmuel* were to intercede with Me, I would not be won over to that people. Dismiss them from My presence, and let them go forth!

וַיֹּאמֶר יְהֹוָה אֵלַי אִם־יַעֲמֹד מֹשֶׁה וּשְׁמוּאֵל לְפָנַי אֵין נַפְשִׁי אֶל־הָעָם הַזֶּה שַׁלַּח מֵעַל־פָּנַי וְיֵצֵאוּ:

va-YO-mer a-do-NAI ay-LAI im ya-a-MOD mo-SHEH ush-mu-AYL l'-fa-NAI AYN naf-SHEE el ha-AM ha-ZEH sha-LAKH may-al pa-NAI v'-yay-TZAY-u

² And if they ask you, 'To what shall we go forth?' answer them, 'Thus said *Hashem*: Those destined for the plague, to the plague; Those destined for the sword, to the sword; Those destined for famine, to famine; Those destined for captivity, to captivity.

ב וְהָיָה כִּי־יֹאמְרוּ אֵלֶיךָ אָנָה נֵצֵא וְאָמַרְתָּ אֲלֵיהֶם כֹּה־אָמַר יְהֹוָה אֲשֶׁר לַמָּוֶת לַמָּוֶת וַאֲשֶׁר לַחֶרֶב לַחֶרֶב וַאֲשֶׁר לָרָעָב לָרָעָב וַאֲשֶׁר לַשְּׁבִי לַשֶּׁבִי:

³ And I will appoint over them four kinds [of punishment] – declares *Hashem* – the sword to slay, the dogs to drag, the birds of the sky, and the beasts of the earth to devour and destroy.

ג וּפָקַדְתִּי עֲלֵיהֶם אַרְבַּע מִשְׁפָּחוֹת נְאֻם־יְהֹוָה אֶת־הַחֶרֶב לַהֲרֹג וְאֶת־הַכְּלָבִים לִסְחֹב וְאֶת־עוֹף הַשָּׁמַיִם וְאֶת־בֶּהֱמַת הָאָרֶץ לֶאֱכֹל וּלְהַשְׁחִית:

⁴ I will make them a horror to all the kingdoms of the earth, on account of King *Menashe* son of *Chizkiyahu* of *Yehuda*, and of what he did in *Yerushalayim*.'"

ד וּנְתַתִּים לְזַעֲוָה [לְזַעֲוָה] לְכֹל מַמְלְכוֹת הָאָרֶץ בִּגְלַל מְנַשֶּׁה בֶן־יְחִזְקִיָּהוּ מֶלֶךְ יְהוּדָה עַל אֲשֶׁר־עָשָׂה בִּירוּשָׁלָ͏ִם:

⁵ But who will pity you, O *Yerushalayim*, Who will console you? Who will turn aside to inquire About your welfare?

ה כִּי מִי־יַחְמֹל עָלַיִךְ יְרוּשָׁלַ͏ִם וּמִי יָנוּד לָךְ וּמִי יָסוּר לִשְׁאֹל לְשָׁלֹם לָךְ:

⁶ You cast Me off – declares *Hashem* – You go ever backward. So I have stretched out My hand to destroy you; I cannot relent.

ו אַתְּ נָטַשְׁתְּ אֹתִי נְאֻם־יְהֹוָה אָחוֹר תֵּלֵכִי וָאַט אֶת־יָדִי עָלַיִךְ וָאַשְׁחִיתֵךְ נִלְאֵיתִי הִנָּחֵם:

⁷ I will scatter them as with a winnowing fork Through the settlements of the earth. I will bereave, I will destroy My people, For they would not turn back from their ways.

ז וָאֶזְרֵם בְּמִזְרֶה בְּשַׁעֲרֵי הָאָרֶץ שִׁכַּלְתִּי אִבַּדְתִּי אֶת־עַמִּי מִדַּרְכֵיהֶם לוֹא־שָׁבוּ:

15:1 Even if *Moshe* and *Shmuel* were to intercede with Me Announcing four causes of destruction that await Israel (death, sword, famine and captivity), *Yirmiyahu* declares that even the prayers of *Moshe* and *Shmuel* would not be able to save the people. *Rashi* explains that both *Moshe* and *Shmuel* were able to induce Israel to repent, before they stood in front of *Hashem* to intercede on the people's behalf and ask for mercy. However, God declares, since *Yirmiyahu* was not successful in influencing the people to change their ways, his prayers are ineffective. Without repentance, even the prayers of *Moshe* and *Shmuel*, which had been accepted in the past, would not be successful at this time.

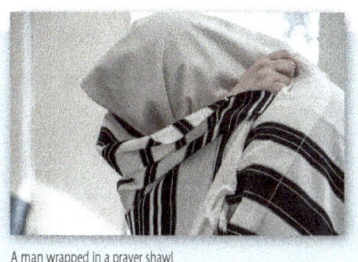

A man wrapped in a prayer shawl

8 Their widows shall be more numerous Than the sands of the seas. I will bring against them – Young men and mothers together – A destroyer at noonday. I will bring down suddenly upon them Alarm and terror.

ח עָצְמוּ־לִי אַלְמְנֹתָו מֵחוֹל יַמִּים הֵבֵאתִי לָהֶם עַל־אֵם בָּחוּר שֹׁדֵד בַּצָּהֳרָיִם הִפַּלְתִּי עָלֶיהָ פִּתְאֹם עִיר וּבֶהָלֽוֹת׃

9 She who bore seven is forlorn, Utterly disconsolate; Her sun has set while it is still day, She is shamed and humiliated. The remnant of them I will deliver to the sword, To the power of their enemies – declares *Hashem*.

ט אֻמְלְלָה יֹלֶדֶת הַשִּׁבְעָה נָפְחָה נַפְשָׁהּ בָּאה [בָּ֣א] שִׁמְשָׁהּ בְּעֹד יוֹמָם בּוֹשָׁה וְחָפֵרָה וּשְׁאֵרִיתָם לַחֶרֶב אֶתֵּן לִפְנֵי אֹיְבֵיהֶם נְאֻם־יְהֹוָֽה׃

10 Woe is me, my mother, that you ever bore me – A man of conflict and strife with all the land! I have not lent, And I have not borrowed; Yet everyone curses me.

י אֽוֹי־לִי אִמִּי כִּי יְלִדְתִּנִי אִישׁ רִיב וְאִישׁ מָדוֹן לְכׇל־הָאָרֶץ לֹא־נָשִׁיתִי וְלֹא־נָשׁוּ־בִי כֻּלֹּה מְקַלְלַֽונִי׃

11 *Hashem* said: Surely, a mere remnant of you Will I spare for a better fate! By the enemy from the north* In a time of distress and a time of disaster, Surely, I will have you struck down!

יא אָמַר יְהֹוָה אִם־לֹא שרותך [שֵֽׁרִיתִךָ֖] לְטוֹב אִם־לוֹא הִפְגַּעְתִּי בְךָ בְּעֵת־רָעָה וּבְעֵת צָרָה אֶת־הָאֹיֵֽב׃

12 Can iron break iron and bronze?

יב הֲיָרֹעַ בַּרְזֶל בַּרְזֶל מִצָּפוֹן וּנְחֹֽשֶׁת׃

13 I will hand over your wealth and your treasures As a spoil, free of charge, Because of all your sins throughout your territory.

יג חֵילְךָ וְאוֹצְרוֹתֶיךָ לָבַז אֶתֵּן לֹא בִמְחִיר וּבְכׇל־חַטֹּאותֶיךָ וּבְכׇל־גְּבוּלֶֽיךָ׃

14 And I will bring your enemies By way of a land you have not known. For a fire has flared in My wrath, It blazes against you.

יד וְהַעֲבַרְתִּי אֶת־אֹיְבֶיךָ בְּאֶרֶץ לֹא יָדָעְתָּ כִּי־אֵשׁ קָדְחָה בְאַפִּי עֲלֵיכֶם תּוּקָֽד׃

15 *Hashem*, you know – Remember me and take thought of me, Avenge me on those who persecute me; Do not yield to Your patience, Do not let me perish! Consider how I have borne insult On Your account.

טו אַתָּה יָדַעְתָּ יְהֹוָה זׇכְרֵנִי וּפׇקְדֵנִי וְהִנָּקֶם לִי מֵרֹדְפַי אַל־לְאֶרֶךְ אַפְּךָ תִּקָּחֵנִי דַּע שְׂאֵתִי עָלֶיךָ חֶרְפָּֽה׃

16 When Your words were offered, I devoured them; Your word brought me the delight and joy Of knowing that Your name is attached to me, *Hashem*, the Lᴏʀᴅ of Hosts.

טז נִמְצְאוּ דְבָרֶיךָ וָאֹכְלֵם וַיְהִי דבריך [דְבָֽרְךָ֙] לִי לְשָׂשׂוֹן וּלְשִׂמְחַת לְבָבִי כִּי־נִקְרָא שִׁמְךָ עָלַי יְהֹוָה אֱלֹהֵי צְבָאֽוֹת׃

17 I have not sat in the company of revelers And made merry! I have sat lonely because of Your hand upon me, For You have filled me with gloom.

יז לֹא־יָשַׁבְתִּי בְסוֹד־מְשַׂחֲקִים וָֽאֶעְלֹז מִפְּנֵי יָֽדְךָ בָּדָד יָשַׁבְתִּי כִּי־זַעַם מִלֵּאתָֽנִי׃

18 Why must my pain be endless, My wound incurable, Resistant to healing? You have been to me like a spring that fails, Like waters that cannot be relied on.

יח לָמָּה הָיָה כְאֵבִי נֶצַח וּמַכָּתִי אֲנוּשָׁה מֵאֲנָה הֵרָפֵא הָיוֹ תִֽהְיֶה לִי כְּמוֹ אַכְזָב מַיִם לֹא נֶאֱמָֽנוּ׃

---

* "from the north" brought up from verse 12 for clarity

¹⁹ Assuredly, thus said *Hashem*: If you turn back, I shall take you back And you shall stand before Me; If you produce what is noble Out of the worthless, You shall be My spokesman. They shall come back to you, Not you to them.

²⁰ Against this people I will make you As a fortified wall of bronze: They will attack you But they shall not overcome you, For I am with you to deliver and save you – declares *Hashem*.

²¹ I will save you from the hands of the wicked And rescue you from the clutches of the violent.

16 ¹ The word of *Hashem* came to me:

² You are not to marry and not to have sons and daughters in this place.

³ For thus said *Hashem* concerning any sons and daughters that may be born in this place, and concerning the mothers who bear them, and concerning the fathers who beget them in this land:

⁴ They shall die gruesome deaths. They shall not be lamented or buried; they shall be like dung on the surface of the ground. They shall be consumed by the sword and by famine, and their corpses shall be food for the birds of the sky and the beasts of the earth.

⁵ For thus said *Hashem*: Do not enter a house of mourning, Do not go to lament and to condole with them; For I have withdrawn My favor from that people – declares *Hashem* – My kindness and compassion.

⁶ Great and small alike shall die in this land, They shall not be buried; men shall not lament them, Nor gash and tonsure themselves for them.

⁷ They shall not break bread for a mourner To comfort him for a bereavement, Nor offer one a cup of consolation For the loss of his father or mother.

⁸ Nor shall you enter a house of feasting, To sit down with them to eat and drink.

⁹ For thus said the Lord of Hosts, the God of *Yisrael*: I am going to banish from this place, in your days and before your eyes, the sound of mirth and gladness, the voice of bridegroom and bride.

יט לָכֵן כֹּה־אָמַר יְהֹוָה אִם־תָּשׁוּב וַאֲשִׁיבְךָ לְפָנַי תַּעֲמֹד וְאִם־תּוֹצִיא יָקָר מִזּוֹלֵל כְּפִי תִהְיֶה יָשֻׁבוּ הֵמָּה אֵלֶיךָ וְאַתָּה לֹא־תָשׁוּב אֲלֵיהֶם:

כ וּנְתַתִּיךָ לָעָם הַזֶּה לְחוֹמַת נְחֹשֶׁת בְּצוּרָה וְנִלְחֲמוּ אֵלֶיךָ וְלֹא־יוּכְלוּ לָךְ כִּי־אִתְּךָ אֲנִי לְהוֹשִׁיעֲךָ וּלְהַצִּילֶךָ נְאֻם־יְהֹוָה:

כא וְהִצַּלְתִּיךָ מִיַּד רָעִים וּפְדִתִיךָ מִכַּף עָרִצִים:

טז א וַיְהִי דְבַר־יְהֹוָה אֵלַי לֵאמֹר:

ב לֹא־תִקַּח לְךָ אִשָּׁה וְלֹא־יִהְיוּ לְךָ בָּנִים וּבָנוֹת בַּמָּקוֹם הַזֶּה:

ג כִּי־כֹה אָמַר יְהֹוָה עַל־הַבָּנִים וְעַל־הַבָּנוֹת הַיִּלּוֹדִים בַּמָּקוֹם הַזֶּה וְעַל־אִמֹּתָם הַיֹּלְדוֹת אוֹתָם וְעַל־אֲבוֹתָם הַמּוֹלִדִים אוֹתָם בָּאָרֶץ הַזֹּאת:

ד מְמוֹתֵי תַחֲלֻאִים יָמֻתוּ לֹא יִסָּפְדוּ וְלֹא יִקָּבֵרוּ לְדֹמֶן עַל־פְּנֵי הָאֲדָמָה יִהְיוּ וּבַחֶרֶב וּבָרָעָב יִכְלוּ וְהָיְתָה נִבְלָתָם לְמַאֲכָל לְעוֹף הַשָּׁמַיִם וּלְבֶהֱמַת הָאָרֶץ:

ה כִּי־כֹה אָמַר יְהֹוָה אַל־תָּבוֹא בֵּית מַרְזֵחַ וְאַל־תֵּלֵךְ לִסְפּוֹד וְאַל־תָּנֹד לָהֶם כִּי־אָסַפְתִּי אֶת־שְׁלוֹמִי מֵאֵת הָעָם־הַזֶּה נְאֻם־יְהֹוָה אֶת־הַחֶסֶד וְאֶת־הָרַחֲמִים:

ו וּמֵתוּ גְדֹלִים וּקְטַנִּים בָּאָרֶץ הַזֹּאת לֹא יִקָּבֵרוּ וְלֹא־יִסְפְּדוּ לָהֶם וְלֹא יִתְגֹּדַד וְלֹא יִקָּרֵחַ לָהֶם:

ז וְלֹא־יִפְרְסוּ לָהֶם עַל־אֵבֶל לְנַחֲמוֹ עַל־מֵת וְלֹא־יַשְׁקוּ אוֹתָם כּוֹס תַּנְחוּמִים עַל־אָבִיו וְעַל־אִמּוֹ:

ח וּבֵית־מִשְׁתֶּה לֹא־תָבוֹא לָשֶׁבֶת אוֹתָם לֶאֱכֹל וְלִשְׁתּוֹת:

ט כִּי כֹה אָמַר יְהֹוָה צְבָאוֹת אֱלֹהֵי יִשְׂרָאֵל הִנְנִי מַשְׁבִּית מִן־הַמָּקוֹם הַזֶּה לְעֵינֵיכֶם וּבִימֵיכֶם קוֹל שָׂשׂוֹן וְקוֹל שִׂמְחָה קוֹל חָתָן וְקוֹל כַּלָּה:

36

10 And when you announce all these things to that people, and they ask you, "Why has *Hashem* decreed upon us all this fearful evil? What is the iniquity and what the sin that we have committed against *Hashem* our God?"

וְהָיָה כִּי תַגִּיד לָעָם הַזֶּה אֵת כָּל־הַדְּבָרִים הָאֵלֶּה וְאָמְרוּ אֵלֶיךָ עַל־מֶה דִבֶּר יְהֹוָה עָלֵינוּ אֵת כָּל־הָרָעָה הַגְּדוֹלָה הַזֹּאת וּמֶה עֲוֺנֵנוּ וּמֶה חַטָּאתֵנוּ אֲשֶׁר חָטָאנוּ לַיהֹוָה אֱלֹהֵינוּ: י

11 say to them, "Because your fathers deserted Me – declares *Hashem* – and followed other gods and served them and worshiped them; they deserted Me and did not keep My Instruction.

וְאָמַרְתָּ אֲלֵיהֶם עַל אֲשֶׁר־עָזְבוּ אֲבוֹתֵיכֶם אוֹתִי נְאֻם־יְהֹוָה וַיֵּלְכוּ אַחֲרֵי אֱלֹהִים אֲחֵרִים וַיַּעַבְדוּם וַיִּשְׁתַּחֲווּ לָהֶם וְאֹתִי עָזָבוּ וְאֶת־תּוֹרָתִי לֹא שָׁמָרוּ: יא

12 And you have acted worse than your fathers, every one of you following the willfulness of his evil heart and paying no heed to Me.

וְאַתֶּם הֲרֵעֹתֶם לַעֲשׂוֹת מֵאֲבוֹתֵיכֶם וְהִנְּכֶם הֹלְכִים אִישׁ אַחֲרֵי שְׁרִרוּת לִבּוֹ־הָרָע לְבִלְתִּי שְׁמֹעַ אֵלָי: יב

13 Therefore I will hurl you out of this land to a land that neither you nor your fathers have known, and there you will serve other gods, day and night; for I will show you no mercy."

וְהֵטַלְתִּי אֶתְכֶם מֵעַל הָאָרֶץ הַזֹּאת עַל־הָאָרֶץ אֲשֶׁר לֹא יְדַעְתֶּם אַתֶּם וַאֲבוֹתֵיכֶם וַעֲבַדְתֶּם שָׁם אֶת־אֱלֹהִים אֲחֵרִים יוֹמָם וָלַיְלָה אֲשֶׁר לֹא־אֶתֵּן לָכֶם חֲנִינָה: יג

14 Assuredly, a time is coming – declares *Hashem* – when it shall no more be said, "As *Hashem* lives who brought the Israelites out of the land of Egypt,"

לָכֵן הִנֵּה־יָמִים בָּאִים נְאֻם־יְהֹוָה וְלֹא־יֵאָמֵר עוֹד חַי־יְהֹוָה אֲשֶׁר הֶעֱלָה אֶת־בְּנֵי יִשְׂרָאֵל מֵאֶרֶץ מִצְרָיִם: יד

15 but rather, "As *Hashem* lives who brought the Israelites out of the northland, and out of all the lands to which He had banished them." For I will bring them back to their land, which I gave to their fathers.

כִּי אִם־חַי־יְהֹוָה אֲשֶׁר הֶעֱלָה אֶת־בְּנֵי יִשְׂרָאֵל מֵאֶרֶץ צָפוֹן וּמִכֹּל הָאֲרָצוֹת אֲשֶׁר הִדִּיחָם שָׁמָּה וַהֲשִׁבֹתִים עַל־אַדְמָתָם אֲשֶׁר נָתַתִּי לַאֲבוֹתָם: טו

KEE im khai a-do-NAI a-SHER he-e-LAH et b'-NAY yis-ra-AYL may-E-retz
tza-FON u-mi-KOL ha-a-ra-TZOT a-SHER hi-dee-KHAM SHA-mah
va-ha-shi-vo-TEEM al ad-ma-TAM a-SHER na-TA-tee la-a-vo-TAM

16 Lo, I am sending for many fishermen – declares *Hashem* – And they shall haul them out; And after that I will send for many hunters, And they shall hunt them Out of every mountain and out of every hill And out of the clefts of the rocks.

הִנְנִי שֹׁלֵחַ לְדַיָּגִים [לְדַיָּגִים] רַבִּים נְאֻם־יְהֹוָה וְדִיגוּם וְאַחֲרֵי־כֵן אֶשְׁלַח לְרַבִּים צַיָּדִים וְצָדוּם מֵעַל כָּל־הַר וּמֵעַל כָּל־גִּבְעָה וּמִנְּקִיקֵי הַסְּלָעִים: טז

A girl sits on a hill overlooking the growing city of Beit Shemesh

16:15 For I will bring them back to their land
Yirmiyahu interrupts a description of death and exile with an uplifting message of consolation, declaring that *Hashem* will bring the Children of Israel back from captivity to their land. He declares that the salvation from the future exile will be so great that it will overshadow the past miracles of the exodus from Egypt. According to *Malbim*, the future redemption will stand out from the first, since it will return the Nation of Israel to the land they had already inherited, occupied and enjoyed. The joy of returning to their land will be even greater in their eyes than the miracles of the redemption from Egypt. This is a powerful message with great relevance in our generation: The miracle of the State of Israel and the extraordinary events we experience today are in fact greater than the exodus.

17 For My eyes are on all their ways, They are not hidden from My presence, Their iniquity is not concealed from My sight.

כִּי עֵינַי עַל־כָּל־דַּרְכֵיהֶם לֹא נִסְתְּרוּ מִלְּפָנָי וְלֹא־נִצְפַּן עֲוֺנָם מִנֶּגֶד עֵינָי: יז

18 I will pay them in full – Nay, doubly for their iniquity and their sins – Because they have defiled My land With the corpses of their abominations, And have filled My own possession With their abhorrent things.

וְשִׁלַּמְתִּי רִאשׁוֹנָה מִשְׁנֵה עֲוֺנָם וְחַטָּאתָם עַל חַלְּלָם אֶת־אַרְצִי בְּנִבְלַת שִׁקּוּצֵיהֶם וְתוֹעֲבֽוֹתֵיהֶם מָלְאוּ אֶת־נַחֲלָתִי: יח

19 *Hashem*, my strength and my stronghold, My refuge in a day of trouble, To You nations shall come From the ends of the earth and say: Our fathers inherited utter delusions, Things that are futile and worthless.

יְהֹוָה עֻזִּי וּמָעֻזִּי וּמְנוּסִי בְּיוֹם צָרָה אֵלֶיךָ גּוֹיִם יָבֹאוּ מֵאַפְסֵי־אָרֶץ וְיֹאמְרוּ אַךְ־שֶׁקֶר נָחֲלוּ אֲבוֹתֵינוּ הֶבֶל וְאֵין־בָּם מוֹעִיל: יט

20 Can a man make gods for himself? No-gods are they!

הֲיַעֲשֶׂה־לּוֹ אָדָם אֱלֹהִים וְהֵמָּה לֹא אֱלֹהִים: כ

21 Assuredly, I will teach them, Once and for all I will teach them My power and My might. And they shall learn that My name is *Hashem*.

לָכֵן הִנְנִי מוֹדִיעָם בַּפַּעַם הַזֹּאת אוֹדִיעֵם אֶת־יָדִי וְאֶת־גְּבוּרָתִי וְיָדְעוּ כִּי־שְׁמִי יְהֹוָה: כא

17 1 The guilt of *Yehuda* is inscribed with a stylus of iron, Engraved with an adamant point On the tablet of their hearts, And on the horns of their altars,

חַטַּאת יְהוּדָה כְּתוּבָה בְּעֵט בַּרְזֶל בְּצִפֹּרֶן שָׁמִיר חֲרוּשָׁה עַל־לוּחַ לִבָּם וּלְקַרְנוֹת מִזְבְּחוֹתֵיכֶם: יז א

2 While their children remember Their altars and sacred posts, By verdant trees, Upon lofty hills.

כִּזְכֹּר בְּנֵיהֶם מִזְבְּחוֹתָם וַאֲשֵׁרֵיהֶם עַל־עֵץ רַעֲנָן עַל גְּבָעוֹת הַגְּבֹהוֹת: ב

3 Because of the sin of your shrines Throughout your borders, I will make your rampart a heap in the field, And all your treasures a spoil.

הֲרָרִי בַּשָּׂדֶה חֵילְךָ כָל־אוֹצְרוֹתֶיךָ לָבַז אֶתֵּן בָּמֹתֶיךָ בְּחַטָּאת בְּכָל־גְּבוּלֶיךָ: ג

4 You will forfeit, by your own act, The inheritance I have given you; I will make you a slave to your enemies In a land you have never known. For you have kindled the flame of My wrath Which shall burn for all time.

וְשָׁמַטְתָּה וּבְךָ מִנַּחֲלָתְךָ אֲשֶׁר נָתַתִּי לָךְ וְהַעֲבַדְתִּיךָ אֶת־אֹיְבֶיךָ בָּאָרֶץ אֲשֶׁר לֹא־יָדָעְתָּ כִּי־אֵשׁ קְדַחְתֶּם בְּאַפִּי עַד־עוֹלָם תּוּקָד: ד

5 Thus said *Hashem*: Cursed is he who trusts in man, Who makes mere flesh his strength, And turns his thoughts from *Hashem*.

כֹּה אָמַר יְהֹוָה אָרוּר הַגֶּבֶר אֲשֶׁר יִבְטַח בָּאָדָם וְשָׂם בָּשָׂר זְרֹעוֹ וּמִן־יְהֹוָה יָסוּר לִבּוֹ: ה

6 He shall be like a bush in the desert, Which does not sense the coming of good: It is set in the scorched places of the wilderness, In a barren land without inhabitant.

וְהָיָה כְּעַרְעָר בָּעֲרָבָה וְלֹא יִרְאֶה כִּי־יָבוֹא טוֹב וְשָׁכַן חֲרֵרִים בַּמִּדְבָּר אֶרֶץ מְלֵחָה וְלֹא תֵשֵׁב: ו

*v'-ha-YAH k'-ar-AR ba-a-ra-VAH v'-LO yir-EH kee ya-VO TOV v'-sha-KHAN
kha-ray-REEM ba-mid-BAR E-retz m'-lay-KHAH v'-LO tay-SHAYV*

 17:6 He shall be like a bush in the desert To illustrate the difference between trusting in *Hashem* and trusting in man, *Yirmiyahu* paints a strong contrast between two vivid images. One who relies on man is compared to a small shrub in the barren and rocky desert. The Hebrew name for this plant is *arar*

Chapter 17

פרק יז

Jeremiah

⁷ Blessed is he who trusts in *Hashem*, Whose trust is *Hashem* alone.

ז בָּר֤וּךְ הַגֶּ֙בֶר֙ אֲשֶׁ֣ר יִבְטַ֣ח בַּֽיהֹוָ֔ה וְהָיָ֥ה יְהֹוָ֖ה מִבְטַחֽוֹ:

⁸ He shall be like a tree planted by waters, Sending forth its roots by a stream: It does not sense the coming of heat, Its leaves are ever fresh; It has no care in a year of drought, It does not cease to yield fruit.

ח וְהָיָ֞ה כְּעֵ֣ץ ׀ שָׁת֣וּל עַל־מַ֗יִם וְעַל־יוּבַל֙ יְשַׁלַּ֣ח שָׁרָשָׁ֔יו וְלֹ֤א יִרְא֙ [יִרְאֶה֙] כִּי־יָ֣בֹא חֹ֔ם וְהָיָ֥ה עָלֵ֖הוּ רַֽעֲנָ֑ן וּבִשְׁנַ֤ת בַּצֹּ֙רֶת֙ לֹ֣א יִדְאָ֔ג וְלֹ֥א יָמִ֖ישׁ מֵֽעֲשׂ֥וֹת פֶּֽרִי:

⁹ Most devious is the heart; It is perverse – who can fathom it?

ט עָקֹ֥ב הַלֵּ֛ב מִכֹּ֖ל וְאָנֻ֣שׁ ה֑וּא מִ֖י יֵֽדָעֶֽנּוּ:

¹⁰ I *Hashem* probe the heart, Search the mind – To repay every man according to his ways, With the proper fruit of his deeds.

י אֲנִ֧י יְהֹוָ֛ה חֹקֵ֥ר לֵ֖ב בֹּחֵ֣ן כְּלָי֑וֹת וְלָתֵ֤ת לְאִישׁ֙ כִּדְרָכֹ֔ו [כִּדְרָכָ֔יו] כִּפְרִ֖י מַֽעֲלָלָֽיו:

¹¹ Like a partridge hatching what she did not lay, So is one who amasses wealth by unjust means; In the middle of his life it will leave him, And in the end he will be proved a fool.

יא קֹרֵ֤א דָגַר֙ וְלֹ֣א יָלָ֔ד עֹ֥שֶׂה עֹ֖שֶׁר וְלֹ֣א בְמִשְׁפָּ֑ט בַּֽחֲצִ֤י יָמֹו֙ [יָמָיו֙] יַֽעַזְבֶ֔נּוּ וּבְאַֽחֲרִיתֹ֖ו יִֽהְיֶ֥ה נָבָֽל:

¹² O Throne of Glory exalted from of old, Our Sacred Shrine!

יב כִּסֵּ֣א כָבֹ֔וד מָר֖וֹם מֵֽרִאשׁ֑וֹן מְק֖וֹם מִקְדָּשֵֽׁנוּ:

¹³ O Hope of *Yisrael*! *Hashem*! All who forsake You shall be put to shame, Those in the land who turn from You Shall be doomed men, For they have forsaken *Hashem*, The Fount of living waters.

יג מִקְוֵ֨ה יִשְׂרָאֵ֤ל יְהֹוָה֙ כָּל־עֹֽזְבֶ֣יךָ יֵבֹ֔שׁוּ יְסוּרַי֙ [וְסוּרַי֙] בָּאָ֣רֶץ יִכָּתֵ֑בוּ כִּ֣י עָֽזְב֗וּ מְק֥וֹר מַֽיִם־חַיִּ֖ים אֶת־יְהֹוָֽה:

¹⁴ Heal me, *Hashem*, and let me be healed; Save me, and let me be saved; For You are my glory.

יד רְפָאֵ֤נִי יְהֹוָה֙ וְאֵ֣רָפֵ֔א הֽוֹשִׁיעֵ֖נִי וְאִוָּשֵׁ֑עָה כִּ֥י תְהִלָּתִ֖י אָֽתָּה:

¹⁵ See, they say to me: "Where is the prediction of *Hashem*? Let it come to pass!"

טו הִנֵּה־הֵ֕מָּה אֹֽמְרִ֖ים אֵלָ֑י אַיֵּ֥ה דְבַר־יְהֹוָ֖ה יָ֥בוֹא נָֽא:

¹⁶ But I have not evaded Being a shepherd in your service, Nor have I longed for the fatal day. You know the utterances of my lips, They were ever before You.

טז וַֽאֲנִ֞י לֹֽא־אַ֣צְתִּי ׀ מֵֽרֹעֶ֣ה אַֽחֲרֶ֗יךָ וְיֹ֥ום אָנ֛וּשׁ לֹ֣א הִתְאַוֵּ֖יתִי אַתָּ֣ה יָדָ֑עְתָּ מֹוצָ֣א שְׂפָתַ֔י נֹ֥כַח פָּנֶ֖יךָ הָיָֽה:

¹⁷ Do not be a cause of dismay to me; You are my refuge in a day of calamity.

יז אַל־תִּֽהְיֵה־לִ֖י לִמְחִתָּ֑ה מַֽחֲסִי־אַ֖תָּה בְּי֥וֹם רָעָֽה:

ערער
ערירי
(עַרְעָר), similar to the Hebrew word for 'childless,' *areeree* (עֲרִירִי), invoking feelings of lifelessness and emptiness. Someone who relies on *Hashem*, however, is likened to a majestic tree with deep roots beside an ever-flowing river, growing tall and whose branches provide shelter from the heat (verse 8). Israel has two choices: They can trust in God and remain secure in their land, flourishing like the tree by the river, or they can cut themselves off from the Divine Presence and choose to be exiled to the wilderness of the *arar*.

Setting sun seen through trees
on the Mediterranean sea

18 Let my persecutors be shamed, And let not me be shamed; Let them be dismayed, And let not me be dismayed. Bring on them the day of disaster, And shatter them with double destruction.

יח יֵבֹ֤שׁוּ רֹדְפַי֙ וְאַל־אֵבֹ֣שָׁה אָ֔נִי יֵחַ֣תּוּ הֵ֔מָּה וְאַל־אֵחַ֣תָּה אָ֑נִי הָבִ֤יא עֲלֵיהֶם֙ י֣וֹם רָעָ֔ה וּמִשְׁנֶ֥ה שִׁבָּר֖וֹן שָׁבְרֵֽם׃

19 Thus said *Hashem* to me: Go and stand in the People's Gate, by which the kings of *Yehuda* enter and by which they go forth, and in all the gates of *Yerushalayim*,

יט כֹּה־אָמַ֨ר יְהֹוָ֜ה אֵלַ֗י הָלֹךְ֙ וְעָמַדְתָּ֙ בְּשַׁ֣עַר בְּנֵֽי־עָ֔ם [הָעָ֔ם] אֲשֶׁ֨ר יָבֹ֤אוּ בוֹ֙ מַלְכֵ֣י יְהוּדָ֔ה וַאֲשֶׁ֖ר יֵ֣צְאוּ ב֑וֹ וּבְכֹ֖ל שַׁעֲרֵ֥י יְרוּשָׁלָֽ͏ִם׃

20 and say to them: Hear the word of *Hashem*, O kings of *Yehuda*, and all *Yehuda*, and all the inhabitants of *Yerushalayim* who enter by these gates!

כ וְאָמַרְתָּ֣ אֲלֵיהֶ֡ם שִׁמְע֣וּ דְבַר־יְהֹוָה֩ מַלְכֵ֨י יְהוּדָ֜ה וְכׇל־יְהוּדָ֗ה וְכֹ֖ל יֹשְׁבֵ֣י יְרוּשָׁלָ֑͏ִם הַבָּאִ֖ים בַּשְּׁעָרִ֥ים הָאֵֽלֶּה׃

21 Thus said *Hashem*: Guard yourselves for your own sake against carrying burdens on the *Shabbat* day, and bringing them through the gates of *Yerushalayim*.

כא כֹּ֚ה אָמַ֣ר יְהֹוָ֔ה הִשָּׁמְר֖וּ בְּנַפְשֽׁוֹתֵיכֶ֑ם וְאַל־תִּשְׂא֤וּ מַשָּׂא֙ בְּי֣וֹם הַשַּׁבָּ֔ת וַהֲבֵאתֶ֖ם בְּשַׁעֲרֵ֥י יְרוּשָׁלָֽ͏ִם׃

22 Nor shall you carry out burdens from your houses on the *Shabbat* day, or do any work, but you shall hallow the *Shabbat* day, as I commanded your fathers.

כב וְלֹא־תוֹצִ֨יאוּ מַשָּׂ֤א מִבָּֽתֵּיכֶם֙ בְּי֣וֹם הַשַּׁבָּ֔ת וְכׇל־מְלָאכָ֖ה לֹ֣א תַעֲשׂ֑וּ וְקִדַּשְׁתֶּם֙ אֶת־י֣וֹם הַשַּׁבָּ֔ת כַּאֲשֶׁ֥ר צִוִּ֖יתִי אֶת־אֲבוֹתֵיכֶֽם׃

23 But they would not listen or turn their ear; they stiffened their necks and would not pay heed or accept discipline.

כג וְלֹ֣א שָֽׁמְע֔וּ וְלֹ֥א הִטּ֖וּ אֶת־אׇזְנָ֑ם וַיַּקְשׁוּ֙ אֶת־עׇרְפָּ֔ם לְבִלְתִּ֣י שׁומע [שְׁמ֔וֹעַ] וּלְבִלְתִּ֖י קַ֥חַת מוּסָֽר׃

24 If you obey Me – declares *Hashem* – and do not bring in burdens through the gates of this city on the *Shabbat* day, but hallow the *Shabbat* day and do no work on it,

כד וְ֠הָיָ֠ה אִם־שָׁמֹ֨עַ תִּשְׁמְע֣וּן אֵלַי֮ נְאֻם־יְהֹוָה֒ לְבִלְתִּ֣י ׀ הָבִ֣יא מַשָּׂ֗א בְּשַׁעֲרֵ֞י הָעִ֤יר הַזֹּאת֙ בְּי֣וֹם הַשַּׁבָּ֔ת וּלְקַדֵּשׁ֙ אֶת־י֣וֹם הַשַּׁבָּ֔ת לְבִלְתִּ֥י עֲשֽׂוֹת־בה [בוֹ֖] כׇּל־מְלָאכָֽה׃

25 then through the gates of this city shall enter kings who sit upon the throne of *David*, with their officers – riding on chariots and horses, they and their officers – and the men of *Yehuda* and the inhabitants of *Yerushalayim*. And this city shall be inhabited for all time.

כה וּבָ֣אוּ בְשַׁעֲרֵ֣י הָעִ֣יר הַזֹּ֡את מְלָכִ֣ים ׀ וְשָׂרִ֡ים יֹשְׁבִים֩ עַל־כִּסֵּ֨א דָוִ֜ד רֹכְבִ֣ים ׀ בָּרֶ֣כֶב וּבַסּוּסִ֗ים הֵ֚מָּה וְשָׂ֣רֵיהֶ֔ם אִ֥ישׁ יְהוּדָ֖ה וְיֹשְׁבֵ֣י יְרוּשָׁלָ֑͏ִם וְיָשְׁבָ֥ה הָעִיר־הַזֹּ֖את לְעוֹלָֽם׃

26 And people shall come from the towns of *Yehuda* and from the environs of *Yerushalayim*, and from the land of *Binyamin*, and from the Shephelah, and from the hill country, and from the *Negev*, bringing burnt offerings and sacrifices, meal offerings and frankincense, and bringing offerings of thanksgiving to the House of *Hashem*.

כו וּבָ֣אוּ מֵעָרֵֽי־יְ֠הוּדָ֠ה וּמִסְּבִיב֨וֹת יְרוּשָׁלַ֜͏ִם וּמֵאֶ֣רֶץ בִּנְיָמִ֗ן וּמִן־הַשְּׁפֵלָ֤ה וּמִן־הָהָר֙ וּמִן־הַנֶּ֔גֶב מְבִאִ֛ים עוֹלָ֥ה וְזֶ֖בַח וּמִנְחָ֣ה וּלְבוֹנָ֑ה וּמְבִאֵ֥י תוֹדָ֖ה בֵּ֥ית יְהֹוָֽה׃

27 But if you do not obey My command to hallow the *Shabbat* day and to carry in no burdens through the gates of *Yerushalayim* on the *Shabbat* day, then I will set fire to its gates; it shall consume the fortresses of *Yerushalayim* and it shall not be extinguished.

כז וְאִם־לֹא תִשְׁמְעוּ אֵלַי לְקַדֵּשׁ אֶת־יוֹם הַשַּׁבָּת וּלְבִלְתִּי שְׂאֵת מַשָּׂא וּבֹא בְּשַׁעֲרֵי יְרוּשָׁלַ͏ִם בְּיוֹם הַשַּׁבָּת וְהִצַּתִּי אֵשׁ בִּשְׁעָרֶיהָ וְאָכְלָה אַרְמְנוֹת יְרוּשָׁלַ͏ִם וְלֹא תִכְבֶּה:

18 1 The word which came to *Yirmiyahu* from *Hashem*:

יח א הַדָּבָר אֲשֶׁר הָיָה אֶל־יִרְמְיָהוּ מֵאֵת יְהֹוָה לֵאמֹר:

2 "Go down to the house of a potter, and there I will impart My words to you."

ב קוּם וְיָרַדְתָּ בֵּית הַיּוֹצֵר וְשָׁמָּה אַשְׁמִיעֲךָ אֶת־דְּבָרָי:

3 So I went down to the house of a potter, and found him working at the wheel.

ג וָאֵרֵד בֵּית הַיּוֹצֵר והנהו [וְהִנֵּה־] [הוּא] עֹשֶׂה מְלָאכָה עַל־הָאָבְנָיִם:

4 And if the vessel he was making was spoiled, as happens to clay in the potter's hands, he would make it into another vessel, such as the potter saw fit to make.

ד וְנִשְׁחַת הַכְּלִי אֲשֶׁר הוּא עֹשֶׂה בַּחֹמֶר בְּיַד הַיּוֹצֵר וְשָׁב וַיַּעֲשֵׂהוּ כְּלִי אַחֵר כַּאֲשֶׁר יָשַׁר בְּעֵינֵי הַיּוֹצֵר לַעֲשׂוֹת:

5 Then the word of *Hashem* came to me:

ה וַיְהִי דְבַר־יְהֹוָה אֵלַי לֵאמוֹר:

6 O House of *Yisrael*, can I not deal with you like this potter? – says *Hashem*. Just like clay in the hands of the potter, so are you in My hands, O House of *Yisrael*!

ו הֲכַיּוֹצֵר הַזֶּה לֹא־אוּכַל לַעֲשׂוֹת לָכֶם בֵּית יִשְׂרָאֵל נְאֻם־יְהֹוָה הִנֵּה כַחֹמֶר בְּיַד הַיּוֹצֵר כֵּן־אַתֶּם בְּיָדִי בֵּית יִשְׂרָאֵל:

7 At one moment I may decree that a nation or a kingdom shall be uprooted and pulled down and destroyed;

ז רֶגַע אֲדַבֵּר עַל־גּוֹי וְעַל־מַמְלָכָה לִנְתוֹשׁ וְלִנְתוֹץ וּלְהַאֲבִיד:

8 but if that nation against which I made the decree turns back from its wickedness, I change My mind concerning the punishment I planned to bring on it.

ח וְשָׁב הַגּוֹי הַהוּא מֵרָעָתוֹ אֲשֶׁר דִּבַּרְתִּי עָלָיו וְנִחַמְתִּי עַל־הָרָעָה אֲשֶׁר חָשַׁבְתִּי לַעֲשׂוֹת לוֹ:

9 At another moment I may decree that a nation or a kingdom shall be built and planted;

ט וְרֶגַע אֲדַבֵּר עַל־גּוֹי וְעַל־מַמְלָכָה לִבְנֹת וְלִנְטֹעַ:

10 but if it does what is displeasing to Me and does not obey Me, then I change My mind concerning the good I planned to bestow upon it.

י וְעָשָׂה הרעה [הָרַע] בְּעֵינַי לְבִלְתִּי שְׁמֹעַ בְּקוֹלִי וְנִחַמְתִּי עַל־הַטּוֹבָה אֲשֶׁר אָמַרְתִּי לְהֵיטִיב אוֹתוֹ:

11 And now, say to the men of *Yehuda* and the inhabitants of *Yerushalayim*: Thus said *Hashem*: I am devising disaster for you and laying plans against you. Turn back, each of you, from your wicked ways, and mend your ways and your actions!

יא וְעַתָּה אֱמָר־נָא אֶל־אִישׁ־יְהוּדָה וְעַל־יוֹשְׁבֵי יְרוּשָׁלַ͏ִם לֵאמֹר כֹּה אָמַר יְהֹוָה הִנֵּה אָנֹכִי יוֹצֵר עֲלֵיכֶם רָעָה וְחֹשֵׁב עֲלֵיכֶם מַחֲשָׁבָה שׁוּבוּ נָא אִישׁ מִדַּרְכּוֹ הָרָעָה וְהֵיטִיבוּ דַרְכֵיכֶם וּמַעַלְלֵיכֶם:

12 But they will say, "It is no use. We will keep on following our own plans; each of us will act in the willfulness of his evil heart."

יב וְאָמְרוּ נוֹאָשׁ כִּי־אַחֲרֵי מַחְשְׁבוֹתֵינוּ נֵלֵךְ וְאִישׁ שְׁרִרוּת לִבּוֹ־הָרָע נַעֲשֶׂה:

Jeremiah

41

¹³ Assuredly, thus said *Hashem*: Inquire among the nations: Who has heard anything like this? Maiden *Yisrael* has done A most horrible thing.

לָכֵן כֹּה אָמַר יְהֹוָה שַׁאֲלוּ־נָא בַּגּוֹיִם מִי שָׁמַע כָּאֵלֶּה שַׁעֲרֻרִת עָשְׂתָה מְאֹד בְּתוּלַת יִשְׂרָאֵל:

¹⁴ Does one forsake Lebanon snow From the mountainous rocks? Does one abandon cool water Flowing from afar?

הֲיַעֲזֹב מִצּוּר שָׂדַי שֶׁלֶג לְבָנוֹן אִם־יִנָּתְשׁוּ מַיִם זָרִים קָרִים נוֹזְלִים:

ha-ya-a-ZOV mi-TZUR sha-DAI SHE-leg l'-va-NON im yi-na-t'-SHU MA-yim za-REEM ka-REEM no-z'-LEEM

¹⁵ Yet My people have forgotten Me: They sacrifice to a delusion: They are made to stumble in their ways – The ancient paths – And to walk instead on byways, On a road not built up.

כִּי־שְׁכֵחֻנִי עַמִּי לַשָּׁוְא יְקַטֵּרוּ וַיַּכְשִׁלוּם בְּדַרְכֵיהֶם שְׁבִילֵי עוֹלָם לָלֶכֶת נְתִיבוֹת דֶּרֶךְ לֹא סְלוּלָה:

¹⁶ So their land will become a desolation, An object of hissing for all time. Every passerby will be appalled And will shake his head.

לָשׂוּם אַרְצָם לְשַׁמָּה שרוקת [שְׁרִיקוֹת] עוֹלָם כֹּל עוֹבֵר עָלֶיהָ יִשֹּׁם וְיָנִיד בְּרֹאשׁוֹ:

¹⁷ Like the east wind, I will scatter them Before the enemy. I will look upon their back, not their face, In their day of disaster.

כְּרוּחַ־קָדִים אֲפִיצֵם לִפְנֵי אוֹיֵב עֹרֶף וְלֹא־פָנִים אֶרְאֵם בְּיוֹם אֵידָם:

¹⁸ They said, "Come let us devise a plot against *Yirmiyahu* – for instruction shall not fail from the *Kohen*, nor counsel from the wise, nor oracle from the *Navi*. Come, let us strike him with the tongue, and we shall no longer have to listen to all those words of his."

וַיֹּאמְרוּ לְכוּ וְנַחְשְׁבָה עַל־יִרְמְיָהוּ מַחֲשָׁבוֹת כִּי לֹא־תֹאבַד תּוֹרָה מִכֹּהֵן וְעֵצָה מֵחָכָם וְדָבָר מִנָּבִיא לְכוּ וְנַכֵּהוּ בַלָּשׁוֹן וְאַל־נַקְשִׁיבָה אֶל־כָּל־דְּבָרָיו:

¹⁹ Listen to me, *Hashem* – And take note of what my enemies say!

הַקְשִׁיבָה יְהֹוָה אֵלָי וּשְׁמַע לְקוֹל יְרִיבָי:

²⁰ Should good be repaid with evil? Yet they have dug a pit for me. Remember how I stood before You To plead in their behalf, To turn Your anger away from them!

הַיְשֻׁלַּם תַּחַת־טוֹבָה רָעָה כִּי־כָרוּ שׁוּחָה לְנַפְשִׁי זְכֹר עָמְדִי לְפָנֶיךָ לְדַבֵּר עֲלֵיהֶם טוֹבָה לְהָשִׁיב אֶת־חֲמָתְךָ מֵהֶם:

²¹ Oh, give their children over to famine, Mow them down by the sword. Let their wives be bereaved Of children and husbands, Let their men be struck down by the plague, And their young men be slain in battle by the sword.

לָכֵן תֵּן אֶת־בְּנֵיהֶם לָרָעָב וְהַגִּרֵם עַל־יְדֵי־חֶרֶב וְתִהְיֶנָה נְשֵׁיהֶם שַׁכֻּלוֹת וְאַלְמָנוֹת וְאַנְשֵׁיהֶם יִהְיוּ הֲרֻגֵי מָוֶת בַּחוּרֵיהֶם מֻכֵּי־חֶרֶב בַּמִּלְחָמָה:

Snow at the Mount *Chermon* ski resort

18:14 Does one forsake Lebanon snow from the mountainous rocks? The prophet contrasts the steadfastness of nature with the inconsistency of the Israelites, who change their ways and stumble from one failure to another, astonishing everyone who sees them. This is unlike the snows in Lebanon to Israel's north. There, the summits consistently remain white. Indeed, the snow would disappear if found anywhere else. So too, the natural place of the Jewish people is with *Hashem* in the Land of Israel, but they refuse to remain with Him, and will therefore be scattered.

²² Let an outcry be heard from their houses When You bring sudden marauders against them; For they have dug a pit to trap me, And laid snares for my feet.

כב תִּשָּׁמַע זְעָקָה מִבָּתֵּיהֶם כִּי־תָבִיא עֲלֵיהֶם גְּדוּד פִּתְאֹם כִּי־כָרוּ שִׁיחה [שׁוּחָה] לְלָכְדֵנִי וּפַחִים טָמְנוּ לְרַגְלָי:

²³ *Hashem*, You know All their plots to kill me. Do not pardon their iniquity, Do not blot out their guilt from Your presence. Let them be made to stumble before You – Act against them in Your hour of wrath!

כג וְאַתָּה יְהֹוָה יָדַעְתָּ אֶת־כָּל־עֲצָתָם עָלַי לַמָּוֶת אַל־תְּכַפֵּר עַל־עֲוֺנָם וְחַטָּאתָם מִלְּפָנֶיךָ אַל־תֶּמְחִי והיו [וְיִהְיוּ] מֻכְשָׁלִים לְפָנֶיךָ בְּעֵת אַפְּךָ עֲשֵׂה בָהֶם:

19 ¹ Thus said *Hashem*: Go buy a jug of potter's ware. And [take] some of the elders of the people and the *Kohanim*,

יט א כֹּה אָמַר יְהֹוָה הָלוֹךְ וְקָנִיתָ בַקְבֻּק יוֹצֵר חָרֶשׂ וּמִזִּקְנֵי הָעָם וּמִזִּקְנֵי הַכֹּהֲנִים:

² and go out to the Valley of Ben-hinnom – at the entrance of the Harsith Gate – and proclaim there the words which I will speak to you.

ב וְיָצָאתָ אֶל־גֵּיא בֶן־הִנֹּם אֲשֶׁר פֶּתַח שַׁעַר הַחרסות [הַחַרְסִית] וְקָרָאתָ שָׁם אֶת־הַדְּבָרִים אֲשֶׁר־אֲדַבֵּר אֵלֶיךָ:

*v'-ya-TZA-ta el GAY ven hi-NOM a-SHER PE-takh SHA-ar ha-khar-SEET
v'-ka-RA-ta SHAM et ha-d'-va-REEM a-SHER a-da-BAYR ay-LE-kha*

³ Say: "Hear the word of *Hashem*, O kings of *Yehuda* and inhabitants of *Yerushalayim*! Thus said the Lord of Hosts, the God of *Yisrael*: I am going to bring such disaster upon this place that the ears of all who hear about it will tingle.

ג וְאָמַרְתָּ שִׁמְעוּ דְבַר־יְהֹוָה מַלְכֵי יְהוּדָה וְיֹשְׁבֵי יְרוּשָׁלָ͏ִם כֹּה־אָמַר יְהֹוָה צְבָאוֹת אֱלֹהֵי יִשְׂרָאֵל הִנְנִי מֵבִיא רָעָה עַל־הַמָּקוֹם הַזֶּה אֲשֶׁר כָּל־שֹׁמְעָהּ תִּצַּלְנָה אָזְנָיו:

⁴ For they and their fathers and the kings of *Yehuda* have forsaken Me, and have made this place alien [to Me]; they have sacrificed in it to other gods whom they have not experienced, and they have filled this place with the blood of the innocent.

ד יַעַן אֲשֶׁר עֲזָבֻנִי וַיְנַכְּרוּ אֶת־הַמָּקוֹם הַזֶּה וַיְקַטְּרוּ־בוֹ לֵאלֹהִים אֲחֵרִים אֲשֶׁר לֹא־יְדָעוּם הֵמָּה וַאֲבוֹתֵיהֶם וּמַלְכֵי יְהוּדָה וּמָלְאוּ אֶת־הַמָּקוֹם הַזֶּה דַּם נְקִיִּם:

⁵ They have built shrines to Baal, to put their children to the fire as burnt offerings to Baal – which I never commanded, never decreed, and which never came to My mind.

ה וּבָנוּ אֶת־בָּמוֹת הַבַּעַל לִשְׂרֹף אֶת־בְּנֵיהֶם בָּאֵשׁ עֹלוֹת לַבָּעַל אֲשֶׁר לֹא־צִוִּיתִי וְלֹא דִבַּרְתִּי וְלֹא עָלְתָה עַל־לִבִּי:

⁶ Assuredly, a time is coming – declares *Hashem* – when this place shall no longer be called Topheth or Valley of Ben-hinnom, but Valley of Slaughter.

ו לָכֵן הִנֵּה־יָמִים בָּאִים נְאֻם־יְהֹוָה וְלֹא־יִקָּרֵא לַמָּקוֹם הַזֶּה עוֹד הַתֹּפֶת וְגֵיא בֶן־הִנֹּם כִּי אִם־גֵּיא הַהֲרֵגָה:

19:2 Go out to the Valley of *Ben-hinnom* *Yirmiyahu* is told to rebuke the people for abandoning *Hashem* and worshipping idols, and to warn them of the harsh punishments that they will suffer as a result. In order to demonstrate to the Israelites the severity of the retribution awaiting them, he is to break a clay flask in front of the elders, their leaders (verse 10). This display was to take place in the valley of Ben-hinnom, outside the gate of Harsith. Since this valley is where the sinful Israelites worship the false god Baal and offer their children to the fire god Molech (see also Jeremiah 7:31 and 32:35), it is an appropriate place for *Yirmiyahu* to deliver this message. The valley is located just below the walls of Jerusalem's Old City.

Valley of Hinnom

7 "And I will frustrate the plans of *Yehuda* and *Yerushalayim* in this place. I will cause them to fall by the sword before their enemies, by the hand of those who seek their lives; and I will give their carcasses as food to the birds of the sky and the beasts of the earth.

ז וּבַקֹּתִי אֶת־עֲצַת יְהוּדָה וִירוּשָׁלִַם בַּמָּקוֹם הַזֶּה וְהִפַּלְתִּים בַּחֶרֶב לִפְנֵי אֹיְבֵיהֶם וּבְיַד מְבַקְשֵׁי נַפְשָׁם וְנָתַתִּי אֶת־נִבְלָתָם לְמַאֲכָל לְעוֹף הַשָּׁמַיִם וּלְבֶהֱמַת הָאָרֶץ:

8 And I will make this city an object of horror and hissing; everyone who passes by it will be appalled and will hiss over all its wounds.

ח וְשַׂמְתִּי אֶת־הָעִיר הַזֹּאת לְשַׁמָּה וְלִשְׁרֵקָה כֹּל עֹבֵר עָלֶיהָ יִשֹּׁם וְיִשְׁרֹק עַל־כָּל־מַכֹּתֶהָ:

9 And I will cause them to eat the flesh of their sons and the flesh of their daughters, and they shall devour one another's flesh – because of the desperate straits to which they will be reduced by their enemies, who seek their life."

ט וְהַאֲכַלְתִּים אֶת־בְּשַׂר בְּנֵיהֶם וְאֵת בְּשַׂר בְּנֹתֵיהֶם וְאִישׁ בְּשַׂר־רֵעֵהוּ יֹאכֵלוּ בְּמָצוֹר וּבְמָצוֹק אֲשֶׁר יָצִיקוּ לָהֶם אֹיְבֵיהֶם וּמְבַקְשֵׁי נַפְשָׁם:

10 Then you shall smash the jug in the sight of the men who go with you,

י וְשָׁבַרְתָּ הַבַּקְבֻּק לְעֵינֵי הָאֲנָשִׁים הַהֹלְכִים אוֹתָךְ:

11 and say to them: "Thus said the LORD of Hosts: So will I smash this people and this city, as one smashes a potter's vessel, which can never be mended. And they shall bury in Topheth until no room is left for burying.

יא וְאָמַרְתָּ אֲלֵיהֶם כֹּה־אָמַר יְהֹוָה צְבָאוֹת כָּכָה אֶשְׁבֹּר אֶת־הָעָם הַזֶּה וְאֶת־הָעִיר הַזֹּאת כַּאֲשֶׁר יִשְׁבֹּר אֶת־כְּלִי הַיּוֹצֵר אֲשֶׁר לֹא־יוּכַל לְהֵרָפֵה עוֹד וּבְתֹפֶת יִקְבְּרוּ מֵאֵין מָקוֹם לִקְבּוֹר:

12 That is what I will do to this place and its inhabitants – declares *Hashem*. I will make this city like Topheth:

יב כֵּן־אֶעֱשֶׂה לַמָּקוֹם הַזֶּה נְאֻם־יְהֹוָה וּלְיוֹשְׁבָיו וְלָתֵת אֶת־הָעִיר הַזֹּאת כְּתֹפֶת:

13 the houses of *Yerushalayim* and the houses of the kings of *Yehuda* shall be unclean, like that place Topheth – all the houses on the roofs of which offerings were made to the whole host of heaven and libations were poured out to other gods."

יג וְהָיוּ בָּתֵּי יְרוּשָׁלִַם וּבָתֵּי מַלְכֵי יְהוּדָה כִּמְקוֹם הַתֹּפֶת הַטְּמֵאִים לְכֹל הַבָּתִּים אֲשֶׁר קִטְּרוּ עַל־גַּגֹּתֵיהֶם לְכֹל צְבָא הַשָּׁמַיִם וְהַסֵּךְ נְסָכִים לֵאלֹהִים אֲחֵרִים:

14 When *Yirmiyahu* returned from Topheth, where *Hashem* had sent him to prophesy, he stood in the court of the House of *Hashem* and said to all the people:

יד וַיָּבֹא יִרְמְיָהוּ מֵהַתֹּפֶת אֲשֶׁר שְׁלָחוֹ יְהֹוָה שָׁם לְהִנָּבֵא וַיַּעֲמֹד בַּחֲצַר בֵּית־יְהֹוָה וַיֹּאמֶר אֶל־כָּל־הָעָם:

15 "Thus said the LORD of Hosts, the God of *Yisrael*: I am going to bring upon this city and upon all its villages all the disaster which I have decreed against it, for they have stiffened their necks and refused to heed My words."

טו כֹּה־אָמַר יְהֹוָה צְבָאוֹת אֱלֹהֵי יִשְׂרָאֵל הִנְנִי מֵבִי [מֵבִיא] אֶל־הָעִיר הַזֹּאת וְעַל־כָּל־עָרֶיהָ אֵת כָּל־הָרָעָה אֲשֶׁר דִּבַּרְתִּי עָלֶיהָ כִּי הִקְשׁוּ אֶת־עָרְפָּם לְבִלְתִּי שְׁמוֹעַ אֶת־דְּבָרָי:

20 1 Pashhur son of Immer, the *Kohen* who was chief officer of the House of *Hashem*, heard *Yirmiyahu* prophesy these things.

כ א וַיִּשְׁמַע פַּשְׁחוּר בֶּן־אִמֵּר הַכֹּהֵן וְהוּא־פָקִיד נָגִיד בְּבֵית יְהֹוָה אֶת־יִרְמְיָהוּ נִבָּא אֶת־הַדְּבָרִים הָאֵלֶּה:

2 Pashhur thereupon had *Yirmiyahu* flogged and put in the cell at the Upper *Binyamin* Gate in the House of *Hashem*.

ב וַיַּכֶּה פַּשְׁחוּר אֵת יִרְמְיָהוּ הַנָּבִיא וַיִּתֵּן אֹתוֹ עַל־הַמַּהְפֶּכֶת אֲשֶׁר בְּשַׁעַר בִּנְיָמִן הָעֶלְיוֹן אֲשֶׁר בְּבֵית יְהֹוָה:

Jeremiah

3 The next day, Pashhur released *Yirmiyahu* from the cell. But *Yirmiyahu* said to him, "*Hashem* has named you not Pashhur, but Magor-missabib.

ג וַיְהִי מִמָּחֳרָת וַיֹּצֵא פַשְׁחוּר אֶת־יִרְמְיָהוּ מִן־הַמַּהְפָּכֶת וַיֹּאמֶר אֵלָיו יִרְמְיָהוּ לֹא פַשְׁחוּר קָרָא יְהֹוָה שְׁמֶךָ כִּי אִם־מָגוֹר מִסָּבִיב:

vai-HEE mi-ma-kho-RAT va-yo-TZAY fash-KHUR et yir-m'-YA-hu min ha-mah-PA-khet va-YO-mer ay-LAV yir-m'-YA-hu LO fash-KHUR ka-RA a-do-NAI sh'-ME-kha KEE im ma-GOR mi-sa-VEEV

4 For thus said *Hashem*: I am going to deliver you and all your friends over to terror: they will fall by the sword of their enemies while you look on. I will deliver all *Yehuda* into the hands of the king of Babylon; he will exile them to Babylon or put them to the sword.

ד כִּי כֹה אָמַר יְהֹוָה הִנְנִי נֹתֶנְךָ לְמָגוֹר לְךָ וּלְכָל־אֹהֲבֶיךָ וְנָפְלוּ בְּחֶרֶב אֹיְבֵיהֶם וְעֵינֶיךָ רֹאוֹת וְאֶת־כָּל־יְהוּדָה אֶתֵּן בְּיַד מֶלֶךְ־בָּבֶל וְהִגְלָם בָּבֶלָה וְהִכָּם בֶּחָרֶב:

5 And I will deliver all the wealth, all the riches, and all the prized possessions of this city, and I will also deliver all the treasures of the kings of *Yehuda* into the hands of their enemies: they shall seize them as plunder and carry them off to Babylon.

ה וְנָתַתִּי אֶת־כָּל־חֹסֶן הָעִיר הַזֹּאת וְאֶת־כָּל־יְגִיעָהּ וְאֶת־כָּל־יְקָרָהּ וְאֵת כָּל־אוֹצְרוֹת מַלְכֵי יְהוּדָה אֶתֵּן בְּיַד אֹיְבֵיהֶם וּבְזָזוּם וּלְקָחוּם וֶהֱבִיאוּם בָּבֶלָה:

6 As for you, Pashhur, and all who live in your house, you shall go into captivity. You shall come to Babylon; there you shall die and there you shall be buried, and so shall all your friends to whom you prophesied falsely."

ו וְאַתָּה פַשְׁחוּר וְכֹל יֹשְׁבֵי בֵיתֶךָ תֵּלְכוּ בַּשֶּׁבִי וּבָבֶל תָּבוֹא וְשָׁם תָּמוּת וְשָׁם תִּקָּבֵר אַתָּה וְכָל־אֹהֲבֶיךָ אֲשֶׁר־נִבֵּאתָ לָהֶם בַּשָּׁקֶר:

7 You enticed me, *Hashem*, and I was enticed; You overpowered me and You prevailed. I have become a constant laughingstock, Everyone jeers at me.

ז פִּתִּיתַנִי יְהֹוָה וָאֶפָּת חֲזַקְתַּנִי וַתּוּכָל הָיִיתִי לִשְׂחוֹק כָּל־הַיּוֹם כֻּלֹּה לֹעֵג לִי:

8 For every time I speak, I must cry out, Must shout, "Lawlessness and rapine!" For the word of *Hashem* causes me Constant disgrace and contempt.

ח כִּי־מִדֵּי אֲדַבֵּר אֶזְעָק חָמָס וָשֹׁד אֶקְרָא כִּי־הָיָה דְבַר־יְהֹוָה לִי לְחֶרְפָּה וּלְקֶלֶס כָּל־הַיּוֹם:

9 I thought, "I will not mention Him, No more will I speak in His name" – But [His word] was like a raging fire in my heart, Shut up in my bones; I could not hold it in, I was helpless.

ט וְאָמַרְתִּי לֹא־אֶזְכְּרֶנּוּ וְלֹא־אֲדַבֵּר עוֹד בִּשְׁמוֹ וְהָיָה בְלִבִּי כְּאֵשׁ בֹּעֶרֶת עָצֻר בְּעַצְמֹתָי וְנִלְאֵיתִי כַּלְכֵל וְלֹא אוּכָל:

Dove, symbol of peace, at the Western Wall

20:3 *Hashem* **has named you not Pashhur, but Magor-missabib** In a failed attempt to silence *Yirmiyahu*, Pashhur, an official in the *Beit Hamikdash*, places the prophet in jail. *Yirmiyahu* is not deterred, and defiantly tells Pashhur that his name is *magor-misaviv* (מגור מסביב), 'terror from all sides' (verse 3). This insult has two layers of meaning. It describes the fate that awaits Pashhur, his family and the entire corrupt bureaucracy as described in this verse. But it also describes the tragedy of the situation. The *Beit Hamikdash* is *Hashem*'s home, where peace and tranquility are to dwell. Yet they have turned it into a place of terror, where disagreement is stifled and people live in fear of offending the authorities.

10 I heard the whispers of the crowd – Terror all around: "Inform! Let us inform against him!" All my [supposed] friends Are waiting for me to stumble: "Perhaps he can be entrapped, And we can prevail against him And take our vengeance on him."

י כִּי שָׁמַעְתִּי דִּבַּת רַבִּים מָגוֹר מִסָּבִיב הַגִּידוּ וְנַגִּידֶנּוּ כֹּל אֱנוֹשׁ שְׁלוֹמִי שֹׁמְרֵי צַלְעִי אוּלַי יְפֻתֶּה וְנוּכְלָה לוֹ וְנִקְחָה נִקְמָתֵנוּ מִמֶּנּוּ:

11 But *Hashem* is with me like a mighty warrior; Therefore my persecutors shall stumble; They shall not prevail and shall not succeed. They shall be utterly shamed With a humiliation for all time, Which shall not be forgotten.

יא וַיהוָה אוֹתִי כְּגִבּוֹר עָרִיץ עַל־כֵּן רֹדְפַי יִכָּשְׁלוּ וְלֹא יֻכָלוּ בֹּשׁוּ מְאֹד כִּי־לֹא הִשְׂכִּילוּ כְּלִמַּת עוֹלָם לֹא תִשָּׁכֵחַ:

12 O Lord of Hosts, You who test the righteous, Who examine the heart and the mind, Let me see Your retribution upon them, For I lay my case before You.

יב וַיהוָה צְבָאוֹת בֹּחֵן צַדִּיק רֹאֶה כְלָיוֹת וָלֵב אֶרְאֶה נִקְמָתְךָ מֵהֶם כִּי אֵלֶיךָ גִּלִּיתִי אֶת־רִיבִי:

13 Sing unto *Hashem*, Praise *Hashem*, For He has rescued the needy From the hands of evildoers!

יג שִׁירוּ לַיהוָה הַלְלוּ אֶת־יְהוָה כִּי הִצִּיל אֶת־נֶפֶשׁ אֶבְיוֹן מִיַּד מְרֵעִים:

14 Accursed be the day That I was born! Let not the day be blessed When my mother bore me!

יד אָרוּר הַיּוֹם אֲשֶׁר יֻלַּדְתִּי בּוֹ יוֹם אֲשֶׁר־יְלָדַתְנִי אִמִּי אַל־יְהִי בָרוּךְ:

15 Accursed be the man Who brought my father the news And said, "A boy Is born to you," And gave him such joy!

טו אָרוּר הָאִישׁ אֲשֶׁר בִּשַּׂר אֶת־אָבִי לֵאמֹר יֻלַּד־לְךָ בֵּן זָכָר שַׂמֵּחַ שִׂמֳּחָהוּ:

16 Let that man become like the cities Which *Hashem* overthrew without relenting! Let him hear shrieks in the morning And battle shouts at noontide –

טז וְהָיָה הָאִישׁ הַהוּא כֶּעָרִים אֲשֶׁר־הָפַךְ יְהוָה וְלֹא נִחָם וְשָׁמַע זְעָקָה בַּבֹּקֶר וּתְרוּעָה בְּעֵת צָהֳרָיִם:

17 Because he did not kill me before birth So that my mother might be my grave, And her womb big [with me] for all time.

יז אֲשֶׁר לֹא־מוֹתְתַנִי מֵרָחֶם וַתְּהִי־לִי אִמִּי קִבְרִי וְרַחְמָה הֲרַת עוֹלָם:

18 Why did I ever issue from the womb, To see misery and woe, To spend all my days in shame!

יח לָמָּה זֶּה מֵרֶחֶם יָצָאתִי לִרְאוֹת עָמָל וְיָגוֹן וַיִּכְלוּ בְּבֹשֶׁת יָמָי:

21 1 The word which came to *Yirmiyahu* from *Hashem*, when King *Tzidkiyahu* sent to him Pashhur son of Malchiah and the *Kohen Tzefanya*, son of Maaseiah, to say,

כא א הַדָּבָר אֲשֶׁר־הָיָה אֶל־יִרְמְיָהוּ מֵאֵת יְהוָה בִּשְׁלֹחַ אֵלָיו הַמֶּלֶךְ צִדְקִיָּהוּ אֶת־פַּשְׁחוּר בֶּן־מַלְכִּיָּה וְאֶת־צְפַנְיָה בֶן־מַעֲשֵׂיָה הַכֹּהֵן לֵאמֹר:

2 "Please inquire of *Hashem* on our behalf, for King Nebuchadrezzar of Babylon is attacking us. Perhaps *Hashem* will act for our sake in accordance with all His wonders, so that [Nebuchadrezzar] will withdraw from us."

ב דְּרָשׁ־נָא בַעֲדֵנוּ אֶת־יְהוָה כִּי נְבוּכַדְרֶאצַּר מֶלֶךְ־בָּבֶל נִלְחָם עָלֵינוּ אוּלַי יַעֲשֶׂה יְהוָה אוֹתָנוּ כְּכָל־נִפְלְאֹתָיו וְיַעֲלֶה מֵעָלֵינוּ:

3 *Yirmiyahu* answered them, "Thus shall you say to *Tzidkiyahu*:

ג וַיֹּאמֶר יִרְמְיָהוּ אֲלֵיהֶם כֹּה תֹאמְרֻן אֶל־צִדְקִיָּהוּ:

Jeremiah

⁴ Thus said *Hashem*, the God of *Yisrael*: I am going to turn around the weapons in your hands with which you are battling outside the wall against those who are besieging you – the king of Babylon and the Chaldeans – and I will take them into the midst of this city;

⁵ and I Myself will battle against you with an outstretched mighty arm, with anger and rage and great wrath.

⁶ I will strike the inhabitants of this city, man and beast: they shall die by a terrible pestilence.

⁷ And then – declares *Hashem* – I will deliver King *Tzidkiyahu* of *Yehuda* and his courtiers and the people – those in this city who survive the pestilence, the sword, and the famine – into the hands of King Nebuchadrezzar of Babylon, into the hands of their enemies, into the hands of those who seek their lives. He will put them to the sword without pity, without compassion, without mercy.

⁸ "And to this people you shall say: Thus said *Hashem*: I set before you the way of life and the way of death.

⁹ Whoever remains in this city shall die by the sword, by famine, and by pestilence; but whoever leaves and goes over to the Chaldeans who are besieging you shall live; he shall at least gain his life.

¹⁰ For I have set My face against this city for evil and not for good – declares *Hashem*. It shall be delivered into the hands of the king of Babylon, who will destroy it by fire."

¹¹ To the House of the king of *Yehuda*: Hear the word of *Hashem*!

¹² O House of *David*, thus said *Hashem*: Render just verdicts Morning by morning; Rescue him who is robbed From him who defrauded him. Else My wrath will break forth like fire And burn, with none to quench it, Because of your wicked acts.

ד כֹּה־אָמַ֞ר יְהוָ֣ה אֱלֹהֵ֣י יִשְׂרָאֵ֗ל הִנְנִ֣י מֵסֵב֮ אֶת־כְּלֵ֣י הַמִּלְחָמָה֮ אֲשֶׁ֣ר בְּיֶדְכֶם֒ אֲשֶׁ֨ר אַתֶּ֜ם נִלְחָמִ֣ים בָּ֗ם אֶת־מֶ֤לֶךְ בָּבֶל֙ וְאֶת־הַכַּשְׂדִּ֔ים הַצָּרִ֥ים עֲלֵיכֶ֖ם מִח֣וּץ לַחוֹמָ֑ה וְאָסַפְתִּ֣י אוֹתָ֔ם אֶל־תּ֖וֹךְ הָעִ֥יר הַזֹּֽאת:

ה וְנִלְחַמְתִּ֤י אֲנִי֙ אִתְּכֶ֔ם בְּיָ֥ד נְטוּיָ֖ה וּבִזְר֣וֹעַ חֲזָקָ֑ה וּבְאַ֥ף וּבְחֵמָ֖ה וּבְקֶ֥צֶף גָּדֽוֹל:

ו וְהִכֵּיתִ֗י אֶת־יֽוֹשְׁבֵי֙ הָעִ֣יר הַזֹּ֔את וְאֶת־הָאָדָ֖ם וְאֶת־הַבְּהֵמָ֑ה בְּדֶ֥בֶר גָּד֖וֹל יָמֻֽתוּ:

ז וְאַחֲרֵי־כֵ֣ן נְאֻם־יְהוָ֡ה אֶתֵּ֣ן אֶת־צִדְקִיָּ֣הוּ מֶֽלֶךְ־יְהוּדָ֣ה וְאֶת־עֲבָדָ֣יו וְאֶת־הָעָ֡ם וְאֶת־הַנִּשְׁאָרִים֩ בָּעִ֨יר הַזֹּ֜את מִן־הַדֶּ֣בֶר מִן־הַחֶ֣רֶב וּמִן־הָֽרָעָ֗ב בְּיַד֙ נְבֽוּכַדְרֶאצַּ֣ר מֶֽלֶךְ־בָּבֶ֔ל וּבְיַד֙ אֹ֣יְבֵיהֶ֔ם וּבְיַ֖ד מְבַקְשֵׁ֣י נַפְשָׁ֑ם וְהִכָּ֣ם לְפִי־חֶ֔רֶב לֹֽא־יָח֣וּס עֲלֵיהֶ֔ם וְלֹ֥א יַחְמֹ֖ל וְלֹ֥א יְרַחֵֽם:

ח וְאֶל־הָעָ֤ם הַזֶּה֙ תֹּאמַ֔ר כֹּ֖ה אָמַ֣ר יְהוָ֑ה הִנְנִ֤י נֹתֵן֙ לִפְנֵיכֶ֔ם אֶת־דֶּ֥רֶךְ הַֽחַיִּ֖ים וְאֶת־דֶּ֥רֶךְ הַמָּֽוֶת:

ט הַיֹּשֵׁב֙ בָּעִ֣יר הַזֹּ֔את יָמ֕וּת בַּחֶ֖רֶב וּבָרָעָ֣ב וּבַדָּ֑בֶר וְהַיּוֹצֵ֞א וְנָפַ֣ל עַל־הַכַּשְׂדִּ֗ים הַצָּרִ֤ים עֲלֵיכֶם֙ [וְחָיָ֔ה] וְהָֽיְתָה־לּ֥וֹ נַפְשׁ֖וֹ לְשָׁלָֽל:

י כִּ֣י שַׂ֣מְתִּי פָ֠נַי בָּעִ֨יר הַזֹּ֧את לְרָעָ֛ה וְלֹ֥א לְטוֹבָ֖ה נְאֻם־יְהוָ֑ה בְּיַד־מֶ֤לֶךְ בָּבֶל֙ תִּנָּתֵ֔ן וּשְׂרָפָ֖הּ בָּאֵֽשׁ:

יא וּלְבֵית֙ מֶ֣לֶךְ יְהוּדָ֔ה שִׁמְע֖וּ דְּבַר־יְהוָֽה:

יב בֵּ֣ית דָּוִ֗ד כֹּ֚ה אָמַ֣ר יְהוָ֔ה דִּ֤ינוּ לַבֹּ֙קֶר֙ מִשְׁפָּ֔ט וְהַצִּ֥ילוּ גָז֖וּל מִיַּ֣ד עוֹשֵׁ֑ק פֶּן־תֵּצֵ֨א כָאֵ֜שׁ חֲמָתִ֗י וּבָֽעֲרָה֙ וְאֵ֣ין מְכַבֶּ֔ה מִפְּנֵ֖י רֹ֥עַ מַעַלְלֵיהֶ֖ם [מַֽעַלְלֵיכֶֽם:]

*BAYT da-VID KOH a-MAR a-do-NAI DEE-nu la-BO-ker mish-PAT
v'-ha-TZEE-lu ga-ZUL mi-YAD o-SHAYK pen tay-TZAY kha-AYSH kha-ma-TEE
u-va-a-RAH v'-AYN m'-kha-BEH mi-p'-NAY RO-a ma-a-l'-lay-KHEM*

21:12 Render just verdicts morning by morning In 598 BCE, the new puppet king of *Yehuda*, *Tzidkiyahu*, asks *Yirmiyahu* if the upcoming destruction can be avoided. *Yirmiyahu's* answer, after threatening destruction, reflects the answer of all the prophets. If there is justice and righteousness in *Eretz Yisrael*, it will be safe from all

יג הִנְנִי אֵלֶיךָ יֹשֶׁבֶת הָעֵמֶק צוּר הַמִּישֹׁר נְאֻם־יְהוָה הָאֹמְרִים מִי־יֵחַת עָלֵינוּ וּמִי יָבוֹא בִּמְעוֹנוֹתֵינוּ:

יד וּפָקַדְתִּי עֲלֵיכֶם כִּפְרִי מַעַלְלֵיכֶם נְאֻם־יְהוָה וְהִצַּתִּי אֵשׁ בְּיַעְרָהּ וְאָכְלָה כָּל־סְבִיבֶיהָ:

22

¹³ I will deal with you, O inhabitants of the valley, O rock of the plain – declares *Hashem* – You who say, "Who can come down against us? Who can get into our lairs?"

¹⁴ I will punish you according to your deeds – declares *Hashem*. I will set fire to its forest; It shall consume all that is around it.

כב א כֹּה אָמַר יְהוָה רֵד בֵּית־מֶלֶךְ יְהוּדָה וְדִבַּרְתָּ שָׁם אֶת־הַדָּבָר הַזֶּה:

ב וְאָמַרְתָּ שְׁמַע דְּבַר־יְהוָה מֶלֶךְ יְהוּדָה הַיֹּשֵׁב עַל־כִּסֵּא דָוִד אַתָּה וַעֲבָדֶיךָ וְעַמְּךָ הַבָּאִים בַּשְּׁעָרִים הָאֵלֶּה:

ג כֹּה אָמַר יְהוָה עֲשׂוּ מִשְׁפָּט וּצְדָקָה וְהַצִּילוּ גָזוּל מִיַּד עָשׁוֹק וְגֵר יָתוֹם וְאַלְמָנָה אַל־תֹּנוּ אַל־תַּחְמֹסוּ וְדָם נָקִי אַל־תִּשְׁפְּכוּ בַּמָּקוֹם הַזֶּה:

ד כִּי אִם־עָשׂוֹ תַּעֲשׂוּ אֶת־הַדָּבָר הַזֶּה וּבָאוּ בְשַׁעֲרֵי הַבַּיִת הַזֶּה מְלָכִים יֹשְׁבִים לְדָוִד עַל־כִּסְאוֹ רֹכְבִים בָּרֶכֶב וּבַסּוּסִים הוּא וַעֲבָדֵו [וַעֲבָדָיו] וְעַמּוֹ:

ה וְאִם לֹא תִשְׁמְעוּ אֶת־הַדְּבָרִים הָאֵלֶּה בִּי נִשְׁבַּעְתִּי נְאֻם־יְהוָה כִּי־לְחָרְבָּה יִהְיֶה הַבַּיִת הַזֶּה:

ו כִּי־כֹה אָמַר יְהוָה עַל־בֵּית מֶלֶךְ יְהוּדָה גִּלְעָד אַתָּה לִי רֹאשׁ הַלְּבָנוֹן אִם־לֹא אֲשִׁיתְךָ מִדְבָּר עָרִים לֹא נוֹשָׁבָה [נוֹשָׁבוּ:]

ז וְקִדַּשְׁתִּי עָלֶיךָ מַשְׁחִתִים אִישׁ וְכֵלָיו וְכָרְתוּ מִבְחַר אֲרָזֶיךָ וְהִפִּילוּ עַל־הָאֵשׁ:

ח וְעָבְרוּ גּוֹיִם רַבִּים עַל הָעִיר הַזֹּאת וְאָמְרוּ אִישׁ אֶל־רֵעֵהוּ עַל־מֶה עָשָׂה יְהוָה כָּכָה לָעִיר הַגְּדוֹלָה הַזֹּאת:

¹ Thus said *Hashem*: Go down to the palace of the king of *Yehuda*, where you shall utter this word.

² Say: "Hear the word of *Hashem*: O king of *Yehuda*, you who sit on the throne of *David*, and your courtiers and your subjects who enter these gates!

³ Thus said *Hashem*: Do what is just and right; rescue from the defrauder him who is robbed; do not wrong the stranger, the fatherless, and the widow; commit no lawless act, and do not shed the blood of the innocent in this place.

⁴ For if you fulfill this command, then through the gates of this palace shall enter kings of *David*'s line who sit upon his throne, riding horse-drawn chariots, with their courtiers and their subjects.

⁵ But if you do not heed these commands, I swear by Myself – declares *Hashem* – that this palace shall become a ruin."

⁶ For thus said *Hashem* concerning the royal palace of *Yehuda*: You are as *Gilad* to Me, As the summit of Lebanon; But I will make you a desert, Uninhabited towns.

⁷ I will appoint destroyers against you, Each with his tools; They shall cut down your choicest cedars And make them fall into the fire.

⁸ And when many nations pass by this city and one man asks another, "Why did *Hashem* do thus to that great city?"

Jeremiah

threats. *Yirmiyahu* emphasizes that this must occur in the morning, since in the ancient world, courts opened at dawn, before the daytime heat became too unbearable. The idea of promoting justice in the land is a theme that appears throughout the Bible. *Hashem* is described as one who "He loves what is right and just" (Psalms 33:5), and it is what He demands of His children as well. It is only through justice and righteousness, therefore, that the People of Israel will merit to remain in the Land of Israel.

The Supreme Court justices with PM Netanyahu and President Rivlin, 2015

9 the reply will be, "Because they forsook the covenant with *Hashem* their God and bowed down to other gods and served them."

ט וְאָמְרוּ עַל אֲשֶׁר עָזְבוּ אֶת־בְּרִית יְהֹוָה אֱלֹהֵיהֶם וַיִּשְׁתַּחֲווּ לֵאלֹהִים אֲחֵרִים וַיַּעַבְדוּם:

10 Do not weep for the dead And do not lament for him; Weep rather for him who is leaving, For he shall never come back To see the land of his birth!

י אַל־תִּבְכּוּ לְמֵת וְאַל־תָּנֻדוּ לוֹ בְּכוּ בָכוֹ לַהֹלֵךְ כִּי לֹא יָשׁוּב עוֹד וְרָאָה אֶת־אֶרֶץ מוֹלַדְתּוֹ:

11 For thus said *Hashem* concerning *Shalum* son of King *Yoshiyahu* of *Yehuda*, who succeeded his father *Yoshiyahu* as king, but who has gone forth from this place: He shall never come back.

יא כִּי כֹה אָמַר־יְהֹוָה אֶל־שַׁלֻּם בֶּן־יֹאשִׁיָּהוּ מֶלֶךְ יְהוּדָה הַמֹּלֵךְ תַּחַת יֹאשִׁיָּהוּ אָבִיו אֲשֶׁר יָצָא מִן־הַמָּקוֹם הַזֶּה לֹא־יָשׁוּב שָׁם עוֹד:

12 He shall die in the place to which he was exiled, and he shall not see this land again.

יב כִּי בִּמְקוֹם אֲשֶׁר־הִגְלוּ אֹתוֹ שָׁם יָמוּת וְאֶת־הָאָרֶץ הַזֹּאת לֹא־יִרְאֶה עוֹד:

13 Ha! he who builds his house with unfairness And his upper chambers with injustice, Who makes his fellow man work without pay And does not give him his wages,

יג הוֹי בֹּנֶה בֵיתוֹ בְּלֹא־צֶדֶק וַעֲלִיּוֹתָיו בְּלֹא מִשְׁפָּט בְּרֵעֵהוּ יַעֲבֹד חִנָּם וּפֹעֲלוֹ לֹא יִתֶּן־לוֹ:

14 Who thinks: I will build me a vast palace With spacious upper chambers, Provided with windows, Paneled in cedar, Painted with vermilion!

יד הָאֹמֵר אֶבְנֶה־לִּי בֵּית מִדּוֹת וַעֲלִיּוֹת מְרֻוָּחִים וְקָרַע לוֹ חַלּוֹנָי וְסָפוּן בָּאָרֶז וּמָשׁוֹחַ בַּשָּׁשַׁר:

15 Do you think you are more a king Because you compete in cedar? Your father ate and drank And dispensed justice and equity – Then all went well with him.

טו הֲתִמְלֹךְ כִּי אַתָּה מְתַחֲרֶה בָאָרֶז אָבִיךָ הֲלוֹא אָכַל וְשָׁתָה וְעָשָׂה מִשְׁפָּט וּצְדָקָה אָז טוֹב לוֹ:

*ha-tim-LOKH KEE a-TAH m'-ta-kha-REH va-A-rez a-VEE-kha ha-LO
a-KHAL v'-sha-TAH v'-a-SAH mish-PAT utz-da-KAH AZ TOV LO*

16 He upheld the rights of the poor and needy – Then all was well. That is truly heeding Me – declares *Hashem*.

טז דָּן דִּין־עָנִי וְאֶבְיוֹן אָז טוֹב הֲלוֹא־הִיא הַדַּעַת אֹתִי נְאֻם־יְהֹוָה:

17 But your eyes and your mind are only On ill-gotten gains, On shedding the blood of the innocent, On committing fraud and violence.

יז כִּי אֵין עֵינֶיךָ וְלִבְּךָ כִּי אִם־עַל־בִּצְעֶךָ וְעַל דַּם־הַנָּקִי לִשְׁפּוֹךְ וְעַל־הָעֹשֶׁק וְעַל־הַמְּרוּצָה לַעֲשׂוֹת:

18 Assuredly, thus said *Hashem* concerning *Yehoyakim* son of *Yoshiyahu*, king of *Yehuda*: They shall not mourn for him, "Ah, brother! Ah, sister!" They shall not mourn for him, "Ah, lord! Ah, his majesty!"

יח לָכֵן כֹּה־אָמַר יְהֹוָה אֶל־יְהוֹיָקִים בֶּן־יֹאשִׁיָּהוּ מֶלֶךְ יְהוּדָה לֹא־יִסְפְּדוּ לוֹ הוֹי אָחִי וְהוֹי אָחוֹת לֹא־יִסְפְּדוּ לוֹ הוֹי אָדוֹן וְהוֹי הֹדֹה:

Rabbi Tuly Weisz delivering food packages to Israel's poor

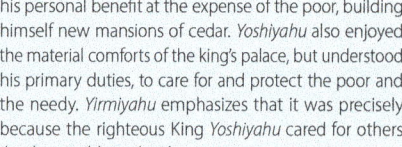

22:15 Your father ate and drank and dispensed justice and equity *Yirmiyahu* wistfully compares the evil king of *Yehuda*, *Yehoyakim*, with his righteous predecessor, his father King *Yoshiyahu*. Ye-hoyakim misused the throne for his personal benefit at the expense of the poor, building himself new mansions of cedar. *Yoshiyahu* also enjoyed the material comforts of the king's palace, but understood his primary duties, to care for and protect the poor and the needy. *Yirmiyahu* emphasizes that it was precisely because the righteous King *Yoshiyahu* cared for others that he was blessed with success.

Jeremiah

19 He shall have the burial of an ass, Dragged out and left lying Outside the gates of *Yerushalayim*.

יט קְבוּרַת חֲמוֹר יִקָּבֵר סָחוֹב וְהַשְׁלֵךְ מֵהָלְאָה לְשַׁעֲרֵי יְרוּשָׁלָָם:

20 Climb Lebanon and cry out, Raise your voice in Bashan, Cry out from Abarim, For all your lovers are crushed.

כ עֲלִי הַלְּבָנוֹן וּצְעָקִי וּבַבָּשָׁן תְּנִי קוֹלֵךְ וְצַעֲקִי מֵעֲבָרִים כִּי נִשְׁבְּרוּ כָּל־מְאַהֲבָיִךְ:

21 I spoke to you when you were prosperous; You said, "I will not listen." That was your way ever since your youth, You would not heed Me.

כא דִּבַּרְתִּי אֵלַיִךְ בְּשַׁלְוֺתַיִךְ אָמַרְתְּ לֹא אֶשְׁמָע זֶה דַרְכֵּךְ מִנְּעוּרַיִךְ כִּי לֹא־שָׁמַעַתְּ בְּקוֹלִי:

22 All your shepherds shall be devoured by the wind, And your lovers shall go into captivity. Then you shall be shamed and humiliated Because of all your depravity.

כב כָּל־רֹעַיִךְ תִּרְעֶה־רוּחַ וּמְאַהֲבַיִךְ בַּשְּׁבִי יֵלֵכוּ כִּי אָז תֵּבֹשִׁי וְנִכְלַמְתְּ מִכֹּל רָעָתֵךְ:

23 You who dwell in Lebanon, Nestled among the cedars, How much grace will you have When pains come upon you, Travail as in childbirth!

כג ישבתי [יֹשַׁבְתְּ] בַּלְּבָנוֹן מקננתי [מְקֻנַּנְתְּ] בָּאֲרָזִים מַה־נֵּחַנְתְּ בְּבֹא־לָךְ חֲבָלִים חִיל כַּיֹּלֵדָה:

24 As I live – declares *Hashem* – if you, O King Coniah, son of *Yehoyakim*, of *Yehuda*, were a signet on my right hand, I would tear you off even from there.

כד חַי־אָנִי נְאֻם־יְהֹוָה כִּי אִם־יִהְיֶה כָּנְיָהוּ בֶן־יְהוֹיָקִים מֶלֶךְ יְהוּדָה חוֹתָם עַל־יַד יְמִינִי כִּי מִשָּׁם אֶתְּקֶנְךָּ:

25 I will deliver you into the hands of those who seek your life, into the hands of those you dread, into the hands of King Nebuchadrezzar of Babylon and into the hands of the Chaldeans.

כה וּנְתַתִּיךָ בְּיַד מְבַקְשֵׁי נַפְשֶׁךָ וּבְיַד אֲשֶׁר־אַתָּה יָגוֹר מִפְּנֵיהֶם וּבְיַד נְבוּכַדְרֶאצַּר מֶלֶךְ־בָּבֶל וּבְיַד הַכַּשְׂדִּים:

26 I will hurl you and the mother who bore you into another land, where you were not born; there you shall both die.

כו וְהֵטַלְתִּי אֹתְךָ וְאֶת־אִמְּךָ אֲשֶׁר יְלָדַתְךָ עַל הָאָרֶץ אַחֶרֶת אֲשֶׁר לֹא־יֻלַּדְתֶּם שָׁם וְשָׁם תָּמוּתוּ:

27 They shall not return to the land that they yearn to come back to.

כז וְעַל־הָאָרֶץ אֲשֶׁר־הֵם מְנַשְּׂאִים אֶת־נַפְשָׁם לָשׁוּב שָׁם שָׁמָּה לֹא יָשׁוּבוּ:

28 Is this man Coniah A wretched broken pot, A vessel no one wants? Why are he and his offspring hurled out, And cast away in a land they knew not?

כח הַעֶצֶב נִבְזֶה נָפוּץ הָאִישׁ הַזֶּה כָּנְיָהוּ אִם־כְּלִי אֵין חֵפֶץ בּוֹ מַדּוּעַ הוּטֲלוּ הוּא וְזַרְעוֹ וְהֻשְׁלְכוּ עַל־הָאָרֶץ אֲשֶׁר לֹא־יָדָעוּ:

29 O land, land, land, Hear the word of *Hashem*!

כט אֶרֶץ אֶרֶץ אָרֶץ שִׁמְעִי דְּבַר־יְהֹוָה:

30 Thus said *Hashem*: Record this man as without succession, One who shall never be found acceptable; For no man of his offspring shall be accepted To sit on the throne of *David* And to rule again in *Yehuda*.

ל כֹּה אָמַר יְהֹוָה כִּתְבוּ אֶת־הָאִישׁ הַזֶּה עֲרִירִי גֶּבֶר לֹא־יִצְלַח בְּיָמָיו כִּי לֹא יִצְלַח מִזַּרְעוֹ אִישׁ יֹשֵׁב עַל־כִּסֵּא דָוִד וּמֹשֵׁל עוֹד בִּיהוּדָה:

23 1 Ah, shepherds who let the flock of My pasture stray and scatter! – declares *Hashem*.

כג א הוֹי רֹעִים מְאַבְּדִים וּמְפִצִים אֶת־צֹאן מַרְעִיתִי נְאֻם־יְהֹוָה:

2 Assuredly, thus said *Hashem*, the God of *Yisrael*, concerning the shepherds who should tend My people: It is you who let My flock scatter and go astray. You gave no thought to them, but I am going to give thought to you, for your wicked acts – declares *Hashem*.

ב לָכֵן כֹּה־אָמַר יְהֹוָה אֱלֹהֵי יִשְׂרָאֵל עַל־הָרֹעִים הָרֹעִים אֶת־עַמִּי אַתֶּם הֲפִצֹתֶם אֶת־צֹאנִי וַתַּדִּחוּם וְלֹא פְקַדְתֶּם אֹתָם הִנְנִי פֹקֵד עֲלֵיכֶם אֶת־רֹעַ מַעַלְלֵיכֶם נְאֻם־יְהֹוָה:

3 And I Myself will gather the remnant of My flock from all the lands to which I have banished them, and I will bring them back to their pasture, where they shall be fertile and increase.

ג וַאֲנִי אֲקַבֵּץ אֶת־שְׁאֵרִית צֹאנִי מִכֹּל הָאֲרָצוֹת אֲשֶׁר־הִדַּחְתִּי אֹתָם שָׁם וַהֲשִׁבֹתִי אֶתְהֶן עַל־נְוֵהֶן וּפָרוּ וְרָבוּ:

4 And I will appoint over them shepherds who will tend them; they shall no longer fear or be dismayed, and none of them shall be missing – declares *Hashem*.

ד וַהֲקִמֹתִי עֲלֵיהֶם רֹעִים וְרָעוּם וְלֹא־יִירְאוּ עוֹד וְלֹא־יֵחַתּוּ וְלֹא יִפָּקֵדוּ נְאֻם־יְהֹוָה:

5 See, a time is coming – declares *Hashem* – when I will raise up a true branch of *David*'s line. He shall reign as king and shall prosper, and he shall do what is just and right in the land.

ה הִנֵּה יָמִים בָּאִים נְאֻם־יְהֹוָה וַהֲקִמֹתִי לְדָוִד צֶמַח צַדִּיק וּמָלַךְ מֶלֶךְ וְהִשְׂכִּיל וְעָשָׂה מִשְׁפָּט וּצְדָקָה בָּאָרֶץ:

6 In his days *Yehuda* shall be delivered and *Yisrael* shall dwell secure. And this is the name by which he shall be called: "*Hashem* is our Vindicator."

ו בְּיָמָיו תִּוָּשַׁע יְהוּדָה וְיִשְׂרָאֵל יִשְׁכֹּן לָבֶטַח וְזֶה־שְּׁמוֹ אֲשֶׁר־יִקְרְאוֹ יְהֹוָה צִדְקֵנוּ:

b'-ya-MAV ti-va-SHA y'-hu-DAH v'-yis-ra-AYL yish-KON la-VE-takh
v'-zeh sh'-MO a-sher yik-r'-Û a-do-NAI tzid-KAY-nu

7 Assuredly, a time is coming – declares *Hashem* – when it shall no more be said, "As *Hashem* lives, who brought the Israelites out of the land of Egypt,"

ז לָכֵן הִנֵּה־יָמִים בָּאִים נְאֻם־יְהֹוָה וְלֹא־יֹאמְרוּ עוֹד חַי־יְהֹוָה אֲשֶׁר הֶעֱלָה אֶת־בְּנֵי יִשְׂרָאֵל מֵאֶרֶץ מִצְרָיִם:

8 but rather, "As *Hashem* lives, who brought out and led the offspring of the House of *Yisrael* from the northland and from all the lands to which I have banished them." And they shall dwell upon their own soil.

ח כִּי אִם־חַי־יְהֹוָה אֲשֶׁר הֶעֱלָה וַאֲשֶׁר הֵבִיא אֶת־זֶרַע בֵּית יִשְׂרָאֵל מֵאֶרֶץ צָפוֹנָה וּמִכֹּל הָאֲרָצוֹת אֲשֶׁר הִדַּחְתִּים שָׁם וְיָשְׁבוּ עַל־אַדְמָתָם:

9 Concerning the *Neviim*. My heart is crushed within me, All my bones are trembling; I have become like a drunken man, Like one overcome by wine – Because of *Hashem* and His holy word.

ט לַנְּבִאִים נִשְׁבַּר לִבִּי בְקִרְבִּי רָחֲפוּ כָּל־עַצְמוֹתַי הָיִיתִי כְּאִישׁ שִׁכּוֹר וּכְגֶבֶר עֲבָרוֹ יָיִן מִפְּנֵי יְהֹוָה וּמִפְּנֵי דִּבְרֵי קָדְשׁוֹ:

השם צדקנו

23:6 He shall be called: "*Hashem* is our Vindicator" After comparing the evil leadership of the people to wicked shepherds that cause the sheep to scatter, *Yirmiyahu* describes the ideal leader, a descendant of *David*. In his days, the exiled northern tribes of the kingdom of *Yisrael* will reunite with the kingdom of *Yehuda* and together they will dwell safely in the Land of Israel. The leader will be given the name *Hashem tzidkaynu* (השם צדקינו), '*Hashem* is our Vindicator.'

The root of the word *tzidkaynu* is *tzedek* (צדק), 'righteousness,' indicating the ideals through which he will lead the nation. *Yirmiyahu* gives the same name to *Yerushalayim* (33:16), representing the values for which the rebuilt city will be known around the world.

Yerushalayim

10 For the land is full of adulterers, The land mourns because of a curse; The pastures of the wilderness are dried up. For they run to do evil, They strain to do wrong.

י כִּי מְנָאֲפִים מָלְאָה הָאָרֶץ כִּי־מִפְּנֵי אָלָה אָבְלָה הָאָרֶץ יָבְשׁוּ נְאוֹת מִדְבָּר וַתְּהִי מְרוּצָתָם רָעָה וּגְבוּרָתָם לֹא־כֵן:

11 For both *Navi* and *Kohen* are godless; Even in My House I find their wickedness – declares *Hashem*.

יא כִּי־גַם־נָבִיא גַם־כֹּהֵן חָנֵפוּ גַּם־בְּבֵיתִי מָצָאתִי רָעָתָם נְאֻם־יְהוָה:

12 Assuredly, Their path shall become Like slippery ground; They shall be thrust into darkness And there they shall fall; For I will bring disaster upon them, The year of their doom – declares *Hashem*.

יב לָכֵן יִהְיֶה דַרְכָּם לָהֶם כַּחֲלַקְלַקּוֹת בָּאֲפֵלָה יִדַּחוּ וְנָפְלוּ בָהּ כִּי־אָבִיא עֲלֵיהֶם רָעָה שְׁנַת פְּקֻדָּתָם נְאֻם־יְהוָה:

13 In the *Neviim* of *Shomron* I saw a repulsive thing: They prophesied by Baal And led My people *Yisrael* astray.

יג וּבִנְבִיאֵי שֹׁמְרוֹן רָאִיתִי תִפְלָה הִנַּבְּאוּ בַבַּעַל וַיַּתְעוּ אֶת־עַמִּי אֶת־יִשְׂרָאֵל:

14 But what I see in the *Neviim* of *Yerushalayim* Is something horrifying: Adultery and false dealing. They encourage evildoers, So that no one turns back from his wickedness. To Me they are all like Sodom, And [all] its inhabitants like Gomorrah.

יד וּבִנְבִאֵי יְרוּשָׁלַם רָאִיתִי שַׁעֲרוּרָה נָאוֹף וְהָלֹךְ בַּשֶּׁקֶר וְחִזְּקוּ יְדֵי מְרֵעִים לְבִלְתִּי־שָׁבוּ אִישׁ מֵרָעָתוֹ הָיוּ־לִי כֻלָּם כִּסְדֹם וְיֹשְׁבֶיהָ כַּעֲמֹרָה:

15 Assuredly, thus said the LORD of Hosts concerning the *Neviim*: I am going to make them eat wormwood And drink a bitter draft; For from the *Neviim* of *Yerushalayim* Godlessness has gone forth to the whole land.

טו לָכֵן כֹּה־אָמַר יְהוָה צְבָאוֹת עַל־הַנְּבִאִים הִנְנִי מַאֲכִיל אוֹתָם לַעֲנָה וְהִשְׁקִתִים מֵי־רֹאשׁ כִּי מֵאֵת נְבִיאֵי יְרוּשָׁלַם יָצְאָה חֲנֻפָּה לְכָל־הָאָרֶץ:

16 Thus said the LORD of Hosts: Do not listen to the words of the *Neviim* Who prophesy to you. They are deluding you, The prophecies they speak are from their own minds, Not from the mouth of *Hashem*.

טז כֹּה־אָמַר יְהוָה צְבָאוֹת אַל־תִּשְׁמְעוּ עַל־דִּבְרֵי הַנְּבִאִים הַנִּבְּאִים לָכֶם מַהְבִּלִים הֵמָּה אֶתְכֶם חֲזוֹן לִבָּם יְדַבֵּרוּ לֹא מִפִּי יְהוָה:

17 They declare to men who despise Me: *Hashem* has said: "All shall be well with you"; And to all who follow their willful hearts they say: "No evil shall befall you."

יז אֹמְרִים אָמוֹר לִמְנַאֲצַי דִּבֶּר יְהוָה שָׁלוֹם יִהְיֶה לָכֶם וְכֹל הֹלֵךְ בִּשְׁרִרוּת לִבּוֹ אָמְרוּ לֹא־תָבוֹא עֲלֵיכֶם רָעָה:

18 But he who has stood in the council of *Hashem*, And seen, and heard His word – He who has listened to His word must obey.

יח כִּי מִי עָמַד בְּסוֹד יְהוָה וְיֵרֶא וְיִשְׁמַע אֶת־דְּבָרוֹ מִי־הִקְשִׁיב דברי [דְּבָרוֹ] וַיִּשְׁמָע:

19 Lo, the storm of *Hashem* goes forth in fury, A whirling storm, It shall whirl down upon the heads of the wicked.

יט הִנֵּה סַעֲרַת יְהוָה חֵמָה יָצְאָה וְסַעַר מִתְחוֹלֵל עַל רֹאשׁ רְשָׁעִים יָחוּל:

20 The anger of *Hashem* shall not turn back Till it has fulfilled and completed His purposes. In the days to come You shall clearly perceive it.

כ לֹא יָשׁוּב אַף־יְהוָה עַד־עֲשֹׂתוֹ וְעַד־הֲקִימוֹ מְזִמּוֹת לִבּוֹ בְּאַחֲרִית הַיָּמִים תִּתְבּוֹנְנוּ בָהּ בִּינָה:

21 I did not send those *Neviim*, But they rushed in; I did not speak to them, Yet they prophesied.

כא לֹא־שָׁלַחְתִּי אֶת־הַנְּבִאִים וְהֵם רָצוּ לֹא־דִבַּרְתִּי אֲלֵיהֶם וְהֵם נִבָּאוּ:

22 If they have stood in My council, Let them announce My words to My people And make them turn back From their evil ways and wicked acts.

כב וְאִם־עָמְדוּ בְּסוֹדִי וְיַשְׁמִעוּ דְבָרַי אֶת־עַמִּי וִישִׁבוּם מִדַּרְכָּם הָרָע וּמֵרֹעַ מַעַלְלֵיהֶם:

23 Am I only a *Hashem* near at hand – says *Hashem* – And not a *Hashem* far away?

כג הַאֱלֹהֵי מִקָּרֹב אָנִי נְאֻם־יְהֹוָה וְלֹא אֱלֹהֵי מֵרָחֹק:

24 If a man enters a hiding place, Do I not see him? – says *Hashem*. For I fill both heaven and earth – declares *Hashem*.

כד אִם־יִסָּתֵר אִישׁ בַּמִּסְתָּרִים וַאֲנִי לֹא־אֶרְאֶנּוּ נְאֻם־יְהֹוָה הֲלוֹא אֶת־הַשָּׁמַיִם וְאֶת־הָאָרֶץ אֲנִי מָלֵא נְאֻם־יְהֹוָה:

25 I have heard what the *Neviim* say, who prophesy falsely in My name: "I had a dream, I had a dream."

כה שָׁמַעְתִּי אֵת אֲשֶׁר־אָמְרוּ הַנְּבִאִים הַנִּבְּאִים בִּשְׁמִי שֶׁקֶר לֵאמֹר חָלַמְתִּי חָלָמְתִּי:

26 How long will there be in the minds of the *Neviim* who prophesy falsehood – the *Neviim* of their own deceitful minds –

כו עַד־מָתַי הֲיֵשׁ בְּלֵב הַנְּבִאִים נִבְּאֵי הַשָּׁקֶר וּנְבִיאֵי תַּרְמִת לִבָּם:

27 the plan to make My people forget My name, by means of the dreams which they tell each other, just as their fathers forgot My name because of Baal?

כז הַחֹשְׁבִים לְהַשְׁכִּיחַ אֶת־עַמִּי שְׁמִי בַּחֲלוֹמֹתָם אֲשֶׁר יְסַפְּרוּ אִישׁ לְרֵעֵהוּ כַּאֲשֶׁר שָׁכְחוּ אֲבוֹתָם אֶת־שְׁמִי בַּבָּעַל:

28 Let the *Navi* who has a dream tell the dream; and let him who has received My word report My word faithfully! How can straw be compared to grain? – says *Hashem*.

כח הַנָּבִיא אֲשֶׁר־אִתּוֹ חֲלוֹם יְסַפֵּר חֲלוֹם וַאֲשֶׁר דְּבָרִי אִתּוֹ יְדַבֵּר דְּבָרִי אֱמֶת מַה־לַתֶּבֶן אֶת־הַבָּר נְאֻם־יְהֹוָה:

29 Behold, My word is like fire – declares *Hashem* – and like a hammer that shatters rock!

כט הֲלוֹא כֹה דְבָרִי כָּאֵשׁ נְאֻם־יְהֹוָה וּכְפַטִּישׁ יְפֹצֵץ סָלַע:

30 Assuredly, I am going to deal with the *Neviim* – declares *Hashem* – who steal My words from one another.

ל לָכֵן הִנְנִי עַל־הַנְּבִאִים נְאֻם־יְהֹוָה מְגַנְּבֵי דְבָרַי אִישׁ מֵאֵת רֵעֵהוּ:

31 I am going to deal with the *Neviim* – declares *Hashem* – who wag their tongues and make oracular utterances.

לא הִנְנִי עַל־הַנְּבִיאִם נְאֻם־יְהֹוָה הַלֹּקְחִים לְשׁוֹנָם וַיִּנְאֲמוּ נְאֻם:

32 I am going to deal with those who prophesy lying dreams – declares *Hashem* – who relate them to lead My people astray with their reckless lies, when I did not send them or command them. They do this people no good – declares *Hashem*.

לב הִנְנִי עַל־נִבְּאֵי חֲלֹמוֹת שֶׁקֶר נְאֻם־יְהֹוָה וַיְסַפְּרוּם וַיַּתְעוּ אֶת־עַמִּי בְּשִׁקְרֵיהֶם וּבְפַחֲזוּתָם וְאָנֹכִי לֹא־שְׁלַחְתִּים וְלֹא צִוִּיתִים וְהוֹעֵיל לֹא־יוֹעִילוּ לָעָם־הַזֶּה נְאֻם־יְהֹוָה:

33 And when this people – or a *Navi* or a *Kohen* – asks you, "What is the burden of *Hashem*?" you shall answer them, "What is the burden? I will cast you oV" – declares *Hashem*.

לג וְכִי־יִשְׁאָלְךָ הָעָם הַזֶּה אוֹ־הַנָּבִיא אוֹ־כֹהֵן לֵאמֹר מַה־מַשָּׂא יְהֹוָה וְאָמַרְתָּ אֲלֵיהֶם אֶת־מַה־מַשָּׂא וְנָטַשְׁתִּי אֶתְכֶם נְאֻם־יְהֹוָה:

34 As for the *Navi* or *Kohen* or layman who shall say "the burden of *Hashem*," I will punish that person and his house.

לד וְהַנָּבִיא וְהַכֹּהֵן וְהָעָם אֲשֶׁר יֹאמַר מַשָּׂא יְהֹוָה וּפָקַדְתִּי עַל־הָאִישׁ הַהוּא וְעַל־בֵּיתוֹ:

Jeremiah

35 Thus you shall speak to each other, every one to his fellow, "What has *Hashem* answered?" or "What has *Hashem* spoken?"

לה כֹּה תֹאמְרוּ אִישׁ עַל־רֵעֵהוּ וְאִישׁ אֶל־אָחִיו מֶה־עָנָה יְהֹוָה וּמַה־דִּבֶּר יְהֹוָה:

36 But do not mention "the burden of *Hashem*" any more. Does a man regard his own word as a "burden," that you pervert the words of the living *Hashem*, the LORD of Hosts, our God?

לו וּמַשָּׂא יְהֹוָה לֹא תִזְכְּרוּ־עוֹד כִּי הַמַּשָּׂא יִהְיֶה לְאִישׁ דְּבָרוֹ וַהֲפַכְתֶּם אֶת־דִּבְרֵי אֱלֹהִים חַיִּים יְהֹוָה צְבָאוֹת אֱלֹהֵינוּ:

37 Thus you shall speak to the *Navi*: "What did *Hashem* answer you?" or "What did *Hashem* speak?"

לז כֹּה תֹאמַר אֶל־הַנָּבִיא מֶה־עָנָךְ יְהֹוָה וּמַה־דִּבֶּר יְהֹוָה:

38 But if you say "the burden of *Hashem*" – assuredly, thus said *Hashem*: Because you said this thing, "the burden of *Hashem*," whereas I sent word to you not to say "the burden of *Hashem*,"

לח וְאִם־מַשָּׂא יְהֹוָה תֹּאמֵרוּ לָכֵן כֹּה אָמַר יְהֹוָה יַעַן אֲמָרְכֶם אֶת־הַדָּבָר הַזֶּה מַשָּׂא יְהֹוָה וָאֶשְׁלַח אֲלֵיכֶם לֵאמֹר לֹא תֹאמְרוּ מַשָּׂא יְהֹוָה:

39 I will utterly forget you and I will cast you away from My presence, together with the city that I gave to you and your fathers.

לט לָכֵן הִנְנִי וְנָשִׁיתִי אֶתְכֶם נָשֹׁא וְנָטַשְׁתִּי אֶתְכֶם וְאֶת־הָעִיר אֲשֶׁר נָתַתִּי לָכֶם וְלַאֲבוֹתֵיכֶם מֵעַל פָּנָי:

40 And I will lay upon you a disgrace for all time, shame for all time, which shall never be forgotten.

מ וְנָתַתִּי עֲלֵיכֶם חֶרְפַּת עוֹלָם וּכְלִמּוּת עוֹלָם אֲשֶׁר לֹא תִשָּׁכֵחַ:

24 1 *Hashem* showed me two baskets of figs, placed in front of the Temple of *Hashem*. This was after King Nebuchadrezzar of Babylon had exiled King *Yechonya* son of *Yehoyakim* of *Yehuda*, and the officials of *Yehuda*, and the craftsmen and smiths, from *Yerushalayim*, and had brought them to Babylon.

כד א הִרְאַנִי יְהֹוָה וְהִנֵּה שְׁנֵי דּוּדָאֵי תְאֵנִים מוּעָדִים לִפְנֵי הֵיכַל יְהֹוָה אַחֲרֵי הַגְלוֹת נְבוּכַדְרֶאצַּר מֶלֶךְ־בָּבֶל אֶת־יְכָנְיָהוּ בֶן־יְהוֹיָקִים מֶלֶךְ־יְהוּדָה וְאֶת־שָׂרֵי יְהוּדָה וְאֶת־הֶחָרָשׁ וְאֶת־הַמַּסְגֵּר מִירוּשָׁלַם וַיְבִאֵם בָּבֶל:

2 One basket contained very good figs, like first-ripened figs, and the other basket contained very bad figs, so bad that they could not be eaten.

ב הַדּוּד אֶחָד תְּאֵנִים טֹבוֹת מְאֹד כִּתְאֵנֵי הַבַּכֻּרוֹת וְהַדּוּד אֶחָד תְּאֵנִים רָעוֹת מְאֹד אֲשֶׁר לֹא־תֵאָכַלְנָה מֵרֹעַ:

ha-DUD e-KHAD t'-ay-NEEM to-VOT m'-OD kit-ay-NAY ha-ba-ku-ROT v'-ha-DUD e-KHAD t'-ay-NEEM ra-OT m'-OD a-SHER lo tay-a-KHAL-nah may-RO-a

Ripe figs at a *Tel Aviv* market

24:2 One basket contained very good figs After the captivity of the ruling classes in 597 BCE, *Yirmiyahu* is shown a vision of two baskets of figs: one basket has good, ripe figs, the other has rotten figs that cannot be eaten. Until this time, exile from the Land of Israel, the source of all goodness and blessing, was considered the worst possible punishment. Those who remained thought they had been spared, while those who were exiled thought that *Hashem* had abandoned them. *Yirmiyahu* explains that in reality, the opposite is true; those in exile will rediscover the ways of God and return (represented in the image by the ripe figs), while those who remain in the land (the bad figs) will eventually be destroyed. The use of the fig, one of the seven agricultural species unique to *Eretz Yisrael*, is significant in this metaphor, as the Bible also uses the image of a fig tree to denote peace and prosperity in the land (see I Kings 5:5).

³ And *Hashem* said to me, "What do you see, *Yirmiyahu*?" I answered, "Figs – the good ones are very good, and the bad ones very bad, so bad that they cannot be eaten."

ג וַיֹּאמֶר יְהֹוָה אֵלַי מָה־אַתָּה רֹאֶה יִרְמְיָהוּ וָאֹמַר תְּאֵנִים הַתְּאֵנִים הַטֹּבוֹת טֹבוֹת מְאֹד וְהָרָעוֹת רָעוֹת מְאֹד אֲשֶׁר לֹא־תֵאָכַלְנָה מֵרֹעַ:

⁴ Then the word of *Hashem* came to me:

ד וַיְהִי דְבַר־יְהֹוָה אֵלַי לֵאמֹר:

⁵ Thus said *Hashem*, the God of *Yisrael*: As with these good figs, so will I single out for good the Judean exiles whom I have driven out from this place to the land of the Chaldeans.

ה כֹּה־אָמַר יְהֹוָה אֱלֹהֵי יִשְׂרָאֵל כַּתְּאֵנִים הַטֹּבוֹת הָאֵלֶּה כֵּן־אַכִּיר אֶת־גָּלוּת יְהוּדָה אֲשֶׁר שִׁלַּחְתִּי מִן־הַמָּקוֹם הַזֶּה אֶרֶץ כַּשְׂדִּים לְטוֹבָה:

⁶ I will look upon them favorably, and I will bring them back to this land; I will build them and not overthrow them; I will plant them and not uproot them.

ו וְשַׂמְתִּי עֵינִי עֲלֵיהֶם לְטוֹבָה וַהֲשִׁבֹתִים עַל־הָאָרֶץ הַזֹּאת וּבְנִיתִים וְלֹא אֶהֱרֹס וּנְטַעְתִּים וְלֹא אֶתּוֹשׁ:

⁷ And I will give them the understanding to acknowledge Me, for I am *Hashem*. And they shall be My people and I will be their God, when they turn back to Me with all their heart.

ז וְנָתַתִּי לָהֶם לֵב לָדַעַת אֹתִי כִּי אֲנִי יְהֹוָה וְהָיוּ־לִי לְעָם וְאָנֹכִי אֶהְיֶה לָהֶם לֵאלֹהִים כִּי־יָשֻׁבוּ אֵלַי בְּכָל־לִבָּם:

⁸ And like the bad figs, which are so bad that they cannot be eaten – thus said *Hashem* – so will I treat King *Tzidkiyahu* of *Yehuda* and his officials and the remnant of *Yerushalayim* that is left in this land, and those who are living in the land of Egypt:

ח וְכַתְּאֵנִים הָרָעוֹת אֲשֶׁר לֹא־תֵאָכַלְנָה מֵרֹעַ כִּי־כֹה אָמַר יְהֹוָה כֵּן אֶתֵּן אֶת־צִדְקִיָּהוּ מֶלֶךְ־יְהוּדָה וְאֶת־שָׂרָיו וְאֵת שְׁאֵרִית יְרוּשָׁלַ͏ִם הַנִּשְׁאָרִים בָּאָרֶץ הַזֹּאת וְהַיֹּשְׁבִים בְּאֶרֶץ מִצְרָיִם:

⁹ I will make them a horror – an evil – to all the kingdoms of the earth, a disgrace and a proverb, a byword and a curse in all the places to which I banish them.

ט וּנְתַתִּים לְזַוְעָה [לְזַעֲוָה] לְרָעָה לְכֹל מַמְלְכוֹת הָאָרֶץ לְחֶרְפָּה וּלְמָשָׁל לִשְׁנִינָה וְלִקְלָלָה בְּכָל־הַמְּקֹמוֹת אֲשֶׁר־אַדִּיחֵם שָׁם:

¹⁰ I will send the sword, famine, and pestilence against them until they are exterminated from the land that I gave to them and their fathers.

י וְשִׁלַּחְתִּי בָם אֶת־הַחֶרֶב אֶת־הָרָעָב וְאֶת־הַדָּבֶר עַד־תֻּמָּם מֵעַל הָאֲדָמָה אֲשֶׁר־נָתַתִּי לָהֶם וְלַאֲבוֹתֵיהֶם:

25 ¹ The word which came to *Yirmiyahu* concerning all the people of *Yehuda*, in the fourth year of King *Yehoyakim* son of *Yoshiyahu* of *Yehuda*, which was the first year of King Nebuchadrezzar of Babylon.

כה א הַדָּבָר אֲשֶׁר־הָיָה עַל־יִרְמְיָהוּ עַל־כָּל־עַם יְהוּדָה בַּשָּׁנָה הָרְבִעִית לִיהוֹיָקִים בֶּן־יֹאשִׁיָּהוּ מֶלֶךְ יְהוּדָה הִיא הַשָּׁנָה הָרִאשֹׁנִית לִנְבוּכַדְרֶאצַּר מֶלֶךְ בָּבֶל:

² This is what the *Navi Yirmiyahu* said to all the people of *Yehuda* and to all the inhabitants of *Yerushalayim*:

ב אֲשֶׁר דִּבֶּר יִרְמְיָהוּ הַנָּבִיא עַל־כָּל־עַם יְהוּדָה וְאֶל כָּל־יֹשְׁבֵי יְרוּשָׁלַ͏ִם לֵאמֹר:

³ From the thirteenth year of King *Yoshiyahu* son of *Amon* of *Yehuda*, to this day – these twenty-three years – the word of *Hashem* has come to me. I have spoken to you persistently, but you would not listen.

ג מִן־שְׁלֹשׁ עֶשְׂרֵה שָׁנָה לְיֹאשִׁיָּהוּ בֶן־אָמוֹן מֶלֶךְ יְהוּדָה וְעַד הַיּוֹם הַזֶּה זֶה שָׁלֹשׁ וְעֶשְׂרִים שָׁנָה הָיָה דְבַר־יְהֹוָה אֵלָי וָאֲדַבֵּר אֲלֵיכֶם אַשְׁכֵּים וְדַבֵּר וְלֹא שְׁמַעְתֶּם:

4 Moreover, *Hashem* constantly sent all his servants the *Neviim* to you, but you would not listen or incline your ears to hear

ד וְשָׁלַח יְהֹוָה אֲלֵיכֶם אֶת־כָּל־עֲבָדָיו הַנְּבִאִים הַשְׁכֵּם וְשָׁלֹחַ וְלֹא שְׁמַעְתֶּם וְלֹא־הִטִּיתֶם אֶת־אָזְנְכֶם לִשְׁמֹעַ:

5 when they said, "Turn back, every one, from your evil ways and your wicked acts, that you may remain throughout the ages on the soil which *Hashem* gave to you and your fathers.

ה לֵאמֹר שׁוּבוּ־נָא אִישׁ מִדַּרְכּוֹ הָרָעָה וּמֵרֹעַ מַעַלְלֵיכֶם וּשְׁבוּ עַל־הָאֲדָמָה אֲשֶׁר נָתַן יְהֹוָה לָכֶם וְלַאֲבוֹתֵיכֶם לְמִן־עוֹלָם וְעַד־עוֹלָם:

6 Do not follow other gods, to serve them and worship them. Do not vex Me with what your own hands have made, and I will not bring disaster upon you."

ו וְאַל־תֵּלְכוּ אַחֲרֵי אֱלֹהִים אֲחֵרִים לְעָבְדָם וּלְהִשְׁתַּחֲוֺת לָהֶם וְלֹא־תַכְעִיסוּ אוֹתִי בְּמַעֲשֵׂה יְדֵיכֶם וְלֹא אָרַע לָכֶם:

7 But you would not listen to Me – declares *Hashem* – but vexed Me with what your hands made, to your own hurt.

ז וְלֹא־שְׁמַעְתֶּם אֵלַי נְאֻם־יְהֹוָה לְמַעַן הכעסוני [הַכְעִיסֵנִי] בְּמַעֲשֵׂה יְדֵיכֶם לְרַע לָכֶם:

8 Assuredly, thus said the LORD of Hosts: Because you would not listen to My words,

ח לָכֵן כֹּה אָמַר יְהֹוָה צְבָאוֹת יַעַן אֲשֶׁר לֹא־שְׁמַעְתֶּם אֶת־דְּבָרָי:

9 I am going to send for all the peoples of the north – declares *Hashem* – and for My servant, King Nebuchadrezzar of Babylon, and bring them against this land and its inhabitants, and against all those nations roundabout. I will exterminate them and make them a desolation, an object of hissing – ruins for all time.

ט הִנְנִי שֹׁלֵחַ וְלָקַחְתִּי אֶת־כָּל־מִשְׁפְּחוֹת צָפוֹן נְאֻם־יְהֹוָה וְאֶל־נְבוּכַדְרֶאצַּר מֶלֶךְ־בָּבֶל עַבְדִּי וַהֲבִאֹתִים עַל־הָאָרֶץ הַזֹּאת וְעַל־יֹשְׁבֶיהָ וְעַל כָּל־הַגּוֹיִם הָאֵלֶּה סָבִיב וְהַחֲרַמְתִּים וְשַׂמְתִּים לְשַׁמָּה וְלִשְׁרֵקָה וּלְחָרְבוֹת עוֹלָם:

10 And I will banish from them the sound of mirth and gladness, the voice of bridegroom and bride, and the sound of the mill and the light of the lamp.

י וְהַאֲבַדְתִּי מֵהֶם קוֹל שָׂשׂוֹן וְקוֹל שִׂמְחָה קוֹל חָתָן וְקוֹל כַּלָּה קוֹל רֵחַיִם וְאוֹר נֵר:

11 This whole land shall be a desolate ruin. And those nations shall serve the king of Babylon seventy years.

יא וְהָיְתָה כָּל־הָאָרֶץ הַזֹּאת לְחָרְבָּה לְשַׁמָּה וְעָבְדוּ הַגּוֹיִם הָאֵלֶּה אֶת־מֶלֶךְ בָּבֶל שִׁבְעִים שָׁנָה:

12 When the seventy years are over, I will punish the king of Babylon and that nation and the land of the Chaldeans for their sins – declares *Hashem* – and I will make it a desolation for all time.

יב וְהָיָה כִמְלֹאות שִׁבְעִים שָׁנָה אֶפְקֹד עַל־מֶלֶךְ־בָּבֶל וְעַל־הַגּוֹי הַהוּא נְאֻם־יְהֹוָה אֶת־עֲוֺנָם וְעַל־אֶרֶץ כַּשְׂדִּים וְשַׂמְתִּי אֹתוֹ לְשִׁמְמוֹת עוֹלָם:

13 And I will bring upon that land all that I have decreed against it, all that is recorded in this book – that which *Yirmiyahu* prophesied against all the nations.

יג והבאתי [וְהֵבֵאתִי] עַל־הָאָרֶץ הַהִיא אֶת־כָּל־דְּבָרַי אֲשֶׁר־דִּבַּרְתִּי עָלֶיהָ אֵת כָּל־הַכָּתוּב בַּסֵּפֶר הַזֶּה אֲשֶׁר־נִבָּא יִרְמְיָהוּ עַל־כָּל־הַגּוֹיִם:

14 For they too shall be enslaved by many nations and great kings; and I will requite them according to their acts and according to their conduct.

יד כִּי עָבְדוּ־בָם גַּם־הֵמָּה גּוֹיִם רַבִּים וּמְלָכִים גְּדוֹלִים וְשִׁלַּמְתִּי לָהֶם כְּפָעֳלָם וּכְמַעֲשֵׂה יְדֵיהֶם:

15 For thus said *Hashem*, the God of *Yisrael*, to me: "Take from My hand this cup of wine – of wrath – and make all the nations to whom I send you drink of it.

טו כִּי כֹה אָמַר יְהֹוָה אֱלֹהֵי יִשְׂרָאֵל אֵלַי קַח אֶת־כּוֹס הַיַּיִן הַחֵמָה הַזֹּאת מִיָּדִי וְהִשְׁקִיתָה אֹתוֹ אֶת־כָּל־הַגּוֹיִם אֲשֶׁר אָנֹכִי שֹׁלֵחַ אוֹתְךָ אֲלֵיהֶם:

16 Let them drink and retch and act crazy, because of the sword that I am sending among them."

טז וְשָׁתוּ וְהִתְגֹּעֲשׁוּ וְהִתְהֹלָלוּ מִפְּנֵי הַחֶרֶב אֲשֶׁר אָנֹכִי שֹׁלֵחַ בֵּינֹתָם:

17 So I took the cup from the hand of *Hashem* and gave drink to all the nations to whom *Hashem* had sent me:

יז וָאֶקַּח אֶת־הַכּוֹס מִיַּד יְהֹוָה וָאַשְׁקֶה אֶת־כָּל־הַגּוֹיִם אֲשֶׁר־שְׁלָחַנִי יְהֹוָה אֲלֵיהֶם:

18 *Yerushalayim* and the towns of *Yehuda*, and its kings and officials, to make them a desolate ruin, an object of hissing and a curse – as is now the case;

יח אֶת־יְרוּשָׁלַם וְאֶת־עָרֵי יְהוּדָה וְאֶת־מְלָכֶיהָ אֶת־שָׂרֶיהָ לָתֵת אֹתָם לְחָרְבָּה לְשַׁמָּה לִשְׁרֵקָה וְלִקְלָלָה כַּיּוֹם הַזֶּה:

19 Pharaoh king of Egypt, his courtiers, his officials, and all his people;

יט אֶת־פַּרְעֹה מֶלֶךְ־מִצְרַיִם וְאֶת־עֲבָדָיו וְאֶת־שָׂרָיו וְאֶת־כָּל־עַמּוֹ:

20 all the mixed peoples; all the kings of the land of *Utz*; all the kings of the land of the Philistines – *Ashkelon, Azza*, Ekron, and what is left of *Ashdod*;

כ וְאֵת כָּל־הָעֶרֶב וְאֵת כָּל־מַלְכֵי אֶרֶץ הָעוּץ וְאֵת כָּל־מַלְכֵי אֶרֶץ פְּלִשְׁתִּים וְאֶת־אַשְׁקְלוֹן וְאֶת־עַזָּה וְאֶת־עֶקְרוֹן וְאֵת שְׁאֵרִית אַשְׁדּוֹד:

21 Edom, Moab, and Ammon;

כא אֶת־אֱדוֹם וְאֶת־מוֹאָב וְאֶת־בְּנֵי עַמּוֹן:

22 all the kings of Tyre and all the kings of Sidon, and all the kings of the coastland across the sea;

כב וְאֵת כָּל־מַלְכֵי־צֹר וְאֵת כָּל־מַלְכֵי צִידוֹן וְאֵת מַלְכֵי הָאִי אֲשֶׁר בְּעֵבֶר הַיָּם:

23 Dedan, Tema, and Buz, and all those who have their hair clipped;

כג וְאֶת־דְּדָן וְאֶת־תֵּימָא וְאֶת־בּוּז וְאֵת כָּל־קְצוּצֵי פֵאָה:

24 all the kings of Arabia, and all the kings of the mixed peoples who live in the desert;

כד וְאֵת כָּל־מַלְכֵי עֲרָב וְאֵת כָּל־מַלְכֵי הָעֶרֶב הַשֹּׁכְנִים בַּמִּדְבָּר:

25 all the kings of Zimri and all the kings of Elam and all the kings of Media;

כה וְאֵת כָּל־מַלְכֵי זִמְרִי וְאֵת כָּל־מַלְכֵי עֵילָם וְאֵת כָּל־מַלְכֵי מָדָי:

26 all the kings of the north, whether far from or close to each other – all the royal lands which are on the earth. And last of all, the king of Sheshach shall drink.

כו וְאֵת כָּל־מַלְכֵי הַצָּפוֹן הַקְּרֹבִים וְהָרְחֹקִים אִישׁ אֶל־אָחִיו וְאֵת כָּל־הַמַּמְלְכוֹת הָאָרֶץ אֲשֶׁר עַל־פְּנֵי הָאֲדָמָה וּמֶלֶךְ שֵׁשַׁךְ יִשְׁתֶּה אַחֲרֵיהֶם:

27 Say to them: "Thus said the LORD of Hosts, the God of *Yisrael*: Drink and get drunk and vomit; fall and never rise again, because of the sword that I send among you."

כז וְאָמַרְתָּ אֲלֵיהֶם כֹּה־אָמַר יְהֹוָה צְבָאוֹת אֱלֹהֵי יִשְׂרָאֵל שְׁתוּ וְשִׁכְרוּ וּקְיוּ וְנִפְלוּ וְלֹא תָקוּמוּ מִפְּנֵי הַחֶרֶב אֲשֶׁר אָנֹכִי שֹׁלֵחַ בֵּינֵיכֶם:

28 And if they refuse to take the cup from your hand and drink, say to them, "Thus said the LORD of Hosts: You must drink!

כח וְהָיָה כִּי יְמָאֲנוּ לָקַחַת־הַכּוֹס מִיָּדְךָ לִשְׁתּוֹת וְאָמַרְתָּ אֲלֵיהֶם כֹּה אָמַר יְהֹוָה צְבָאוֹת שָׁתוֹ תִשְׁתּוּ:

29 If I am bringing the punishment first on the city that bears My name, do you expect to go unpunished? You will not go unpunished, for I am summoning the sword against all the inhabitants of the earth – declares the LORD of Hosts."

כט כִּי הִנֵּה בָעִיר אֲשֶׁר נִקְרָא־שְׁמִי עָלֶיהָ אָנֹכִי מֵחֵל לְהָרַע וְאַתֶּם הִנָּקֵה תִנָּקוּ לֹא תִנָּקוּ כִּי חֶרֶב אֲנִי קֹרֵא עַל־כָּל־יֹשְׁבֵי הָאָרֶץ נְאֻם יְהֹוָה צְבָאוֹת׃

30 You are to prophesy all those things to them, and then say to them: Hashem roars from on high, He makes His voice heard from His holy dwelling; He roars aloud over His [earthly] abode; He utters shouts like the grape-treaders, Against all the dwellers on earth.

ל וְאַתָּה תִּנָּבֵא אֲלֵיהֶם אֵת כָּל־הַדְּבָרִים הָאֵלֶּה וְאָמַרְתָּ אֲלֵיהֶם יְהֹוָה מִמָּרוֹם יִשְׁאָג וּמִמְּעוֹן קָדְשׁוֹ יִתֵּן קוֹלוֹ שָׁאֹג יִשְׁאַג עַל־נָוֵהוּ הֵידָד כְּדֹרְכִים יַעֲנֶה אֶל כָּל־יֹשְׁבֵי הָאָרֶץ׃

*v'-a-TAH ti-na-VAY a-lay-HEM AYT kol ha-d'-va-REEM ha-AY-leh
v'-a-mar-TA a-lay-HEM a-do-NAI mi-ma-ROM yish-AG u-mi-m'-ON
kod-SHO yi-TAYN ko-LO sha-OG yish-AG al na-VAY-hu hay-DAD
k'-do-r'-KHEEM ya-a-NEH EL kol yo-sh'-VAY ha-A-retz*

31 Tumult has reached the ends of the earth, For Hashem has a case against the nations, He contends with all flesh. He delivers the wicked to the sword – declares Hashem.

לא בָּא שָׁאוֹן עַד־קְצֵה הָאָרֶץ כִּי רִיב לַיהֹוָה בַּגּוֹיִם נִשְׁפָּט הוּא לְכָל־בָּשָׂר הָרְשָׁעִים נְתָנָם לַחֶרֶב נְאֻם־יְהֹוָה׃

32 Thus said the LORD of Hosts: Disaster goes forth From nation to nation; A great storm is unleashed From the remotest parts of earth.

לב כֹּה אָמַר יְהֹוָה צְבָאוֹת הִנֵּה רָעָה יֹצֵאת מִגּוֹי אֶל־גּוֹי וְסַעַר גָּדוֹל יֵעוֹר מִיַּרְכְּתֵי־אָרֶץ׃

33 In that day, the earth shall be strewn with the slain of Hashem from one end to the other. They shall not be mourned, or gathered and buried; they shall become dung upon the face of the earth.

לג וְהָיוּ חַלְלֵי יְהֹוָה בַּיּוֹם הַהוּא מִקְצֵה הָאָרֶץ וְעַד־קְצֵה הָאָרֶץ לֹא יִסָּפְדוּ וְלֹא יֵאָסְפוּ וְלֹא יִקָּבֵרוּ לְדֹמֶן עַל־פְּנֵי הָאֲדָמָה יִהְיוּ׃

34 Howl, you shepherds, and yell, Strew [dust] on yourselves, you lords of the flock! For the day of your slaughter draws near. I will break you in pieces, And you shall fall like a precious vessel.

לד הֵילִילוּ הָרֹעִים וְזַעֲקוּ וְהִתְפַּלְּשׁוּ אַדִּירֵי הַצֹּאן כִּי־מָלְאוּ יְמֵיכֶם לִטְבוֹחַ וּתְפוֹצוֹתִיכֶם וּנְפַלְתֶּם כִּכְלִי חֶמְדָּה׃

35 Flight shall fail the shepherds, And escape, the lords of the flock.

לה וְאָבַד מָנוֹס מִן־הָרֹעִים וּפְלֵיטָה מֵאַדִּירֵי הַצֹּאן׃

36 Hark, the outcry of the shepherds, And the howls of the lords of the flock! For Hashem is ravaging their pasture.

לו קוֹל צַעֲקַת הָרֹעִים וִילְלַת אַדִּירֵי הַצֹּאן כִּי־שֹׁדֵד יְהֹוָה אֶת־מַרְעִיתָם׃

A lion at the Ramat Gan safari

25:30 Hashem roars from on high The prophecy in this chapter was uttered in the year 605 BCE, a pivotal time for Yirmiyahu. At the great battle of Carchemish, Babylonia decisively defeated Assyria and Egypt, becoming the sole dominant power in the ancient world. Those nations, like Yehuda, who had sided with the losers would soon face Babylonia's wrath. Yirmiyahu assures the people that this dark period is temporary; the Babylonians will fall to the Persians seventy years later. And though the Beit Hamikdash will be destroyed, ultimately Hashem will hold all the nations accountable for this outrage. Roaring like a lion, His wrath will go forth and exact retribution for the violence done to the Children of Israel and to His land.

37 The peaceful meadows shall be wiped out By the fierce wrath of *Hashem*.

לז וְנָדַמּוּ נְאוֹת הַשָּׁלוֹם מִפְּנֵי חֲרוֹן אַף־יְהוָה:

38 Like a lion, He has gone forth from His lair; The land has become a desolation, Because of the oppressive wrath, Because of His fierce anger.

לח עָזַב כַּכְּפִיר סֻכּוֹ כִּי־הָיְתָה אַרְצָם לְשַׁמָּה מִפְּנֵי חֲרוֹן הַיּוֹנָה וּמִפְּנֵי חֲרוֹן אַפּוֹ:

26 1 At the beginning of the reign of King *Yehoyakim* son of *Yoshiyahu* of *Yehuda*, this word came from *Hashem*:

כו א בְּרֵאשִׁית מַמְלְכוּת יְהוֹיָקִים בֶּן־יֹאשִׁיָּהוּ מֶלֶךְ יְהוּדָה הָיָה הַדָּבָר הַזֶּה מֵאֵת יְהוָה לֵאמֹר:

2 "Thus said *Hashem*: Stand in the court of the House of *Hashem*, and speak to [the men of] all the towns of *Yehuda*, who are coming to worship in the House of *Hashem*, all the words which I command you to speak to them. Do not omit anything.

ב כֹּה אָמַר יְהוָה עֲמֹד בַּחֲצַר בֵּית־יְהוָה וְדִבַּרְתָּ עַל־כָּל־עָרֵי יְהוּדָה הַבָּאִים לְהִשְׁתַּחֲוֹת בֵּית־יְהוָה אֵת כָּל־הַדְּבָרִים אֲשֶׁר צִוִּיתִיךָ לְדַבֵּר אֲלֵיהֶם אַל־תִּגְרַע דָּבָר:

3 Perhaps they will listen and turn back, each from his evil way, that I may renounce the punishment I am planning to bring upon them for their wicked acts.

ג אוּלַי יִשְׁמְעוּ וְיָשֻׁבוּ אִישׁ מִדַּרְכּוֹ הָרָעָה וְנִחַמְתִּי אֶל־הָרָעָה אֲשֶׁר אָנֹכִי חֹשֵׁב לַעֲשׂוֹת לָהֶם מִפְּנֵי רֹעַ מַעַלְלֵיהֶם:

4 "Say to them: Thus said *Hashem*: If you do not obey Me, abiding by the Teaching that I have set before you,

ד וְאָמַרְתָּ אֲלֵיהֶם כֹּה אָמַר יְהוָה אִם־לֹא תִשְׁמְעוּ אֵלַי לָלֶכֶת בְּתוֹרָתִי אֲשֶׁר נָתַתִּי לִפְנֵיכֶם:

5 heeding the words of My servants the *Neviim* whom I have been sending to you persistently – but you have not heeded –

ה לִשְׁמֹעַ עַל־דִּבְרֵי עֲבָדַי הַנְּבִאִים אֲשֶׁר אָנֹכִי שֹׁלֵחַ אֲלֵיכֶם וְהַשְׁכֵּם וְשָׁלֹחַ וְלֹא שְׁמַעְתֶּם:

6 then I will make this House like *Shilo*, and I will make this city a curse for all the nations of earth."

ו וְנָתַתִּי אֶת־הַבַּיִת הַזֶּה כְּשִׁלֹה וְאֶת־הָעִיר הַזֹּאתָה [הַזֹּאת] אֶתֵּן לִקְלָלָה לְכֹל גּוֹיֵי הָאָרֶץ:

7 The *Kohanim* and *Neviim* and all the people heard *Yirmiyahu* speaking these words in the House of *Hashem*.

ז וַיִּשְׁמְעוּ הַכֹּהֲנִים וְהַנְּבִאִים וְכָל־הָעָם אֶת־יִרְמְיָהוּ מְדַבֵּר אֶת־הַדְּבָרִים הָאֵלֶּה בְּבֵית יְהוָה:

8 And when *Yirmiyahu* finished speaking all that *Hashem* had commanded him to speak to all the people, the *Kohanim* and the *Neviim* and all the people seized him, shouting, "You shall die!"

ח וַיְהִי כְּכַלּוֹת יִרְמְיָהוּ לְדַבֵּר אֵת כָּל־אֲשֶׁר־צִוָּה יְהוָה לְדַבֵּר אֶל־כָּל־הָעָם וַיִּתְפְּשׂוּ אֹתוֹ הַכֹּהֲנִים וְהַנְּבִאִים וְכָל־הָעָם לֵאמֹר מוֹת תָּמוּת:

9 How dare you prophesy in the name of *Hashem* that this House shall become like *Shilo* and this city be made desolate, without inhabitants?" And all the people crowded about *Yirmiyahu* in the House of *Hashem*.

ט מַדּוּעַ נִבֵּיתָ בְשֵׁם־יְהוָה לֵאמֹר כְּשִׁלוֹ יִהְיֶה הַבַּיִת הַזֶּה וְהָעִיר הַזֹּאת תֶּחֱרַב מֵאֵין יוֹשֵׁב וַיִּקָּהֵל כָּל־הָעָם אֶל־יִרְמְיָהוּ בְּבֵית יְהוָה:

10 When the officials of *Yehuda* heard about this, they went up from the king's palace to the House of *Hashem* and held a session at the entrance of the New Gate of the House of *Hashem*.

י וַיִּשְׁמְעוּ שָׂרֵי יְהוּדָה אֵת הַדְּבָרִים הָאֵלֶּה וַיַּעֲלוּ מִבֵּית־הַמֶּלֶךְ בֵּית יְהוָה וַיֵּשְׁבוּ בְּפֶתַח שַׁעַר־יְהוָה הֶחָדָשׁ:

11 The *Kohanim* and *Neviim* said to the officials and to all the people, "This man deserves the death penalty, for he has prophesied against this city, as you yourselves have heard."

יא וַיֹּאמְרוּ הַכֹּהֲנִים וְהַנְּבִיאִים אֶל־הַשָּׂרִים וְאֶל־כָּל־הָעָם לֵאמֹר מִשְׁפַּט־מָוֶת לָאִישׁ הַזֶּה כִּי נִבָּא אֶל־הָעִיר הַזֹּאת כַּאֲשֶׁר שְׁמַעְתֶּם בְּאָזְנֵיכֶם:

12 *Yirmiyahu* said to the officials and to all the people, "It was *Hashem* who sent me to prophesy against this House and this city all the words you heard.

יב וַיֹּאמֶר יִרְמְיָהוּ אֶל־כָּל־הַשָּׂרִים וְאֶל־כָּל־הָעָם לֵאמֹר יְהוָה שְׁלָחַנִי לְהִנָּבֵא אֶל־הַבַּיִת הַזֶּה וְאֶל־הָעִיר הַזֹּאת אֵת כָּל־הַדְּבָרִים אֲשֶׁר שְׁמַעְתֶּם:

13 Therefore mend your ways and your acts, and heed *Hashem* your God, that *Hashem* may renounce the punishment He has decreed for you.

יג וְעַתָּה הֵיטִיבוּ דַרְכֵיכֶם וּמַעַלְלֵיכֶם וְשִׁמְעוּ בְּקוֹל יְהוָה אֱלֹהֵיכֶם וְיִנָּחֵם יְהוָה אֶל־הָרָעָה אֲשֶׁר דִּבֶּר עֲלֵיכֶם:

14 As for me, I am in your hands: do to me what seems good and right to you.

יד וַאֲנִי הִנְנִי בְיֶדְכֶם עֲשׂוּ־לִי כַּטּוֹב וְכַיָּשָׁר בְּעֵינֵיכֶם:

15 But know that if you put me to death, you and this city and its inhabitants will be guilty of shedding the blood of an innocent man. For in truth *Hashem* has sent me to you, to speak all these words to you."

טו אַךְ יָדֹעַ תֵּדְעוּ כִּי אִם־מְמִתִים אַתֶּם אֹתִי כִּי־דָם נָקִי אַתֶּם נֹתְנִים עֲלֵיכֶם וְאֶל־הָעִיר הַזֹּאת וְאֶל־יֹשְׁבֶיהָ כִּי בֶאֱמֶת שְׁלָחַנִי יְהוָה עֲלֵיכֶם לְדַבֵּר בְּאָזְנֵיכֶם אֵת כָּל־הַדְּבָרִים הָאֵלֶּה:

16 Then the officials and all the people said to the *Kohanim* and *Neviim*, "This man does not deserve the death penalty, for he spoke to us in the name of *Hashem* our God."

טז וַיֹּאמְרוּ הַשָּׂרִים וְכָל־הָעָם אֶל־הַכֹּהֲנִים וְאֶל־הַנְּבִיאִים אֵין־לָאִישׁ הַזֶּה מִשְׁפַּט־מָוֶת כִּי בְּשֵׁם יְהוָה אֱלֹהֵינוּ דִּבֶּר אֵלֵינוּ:

17 And some of the elders of the land arose and said to the entire assemblage of the people,

יז וַיָּקֻמוּ אֲנָשִׁים מִזִּקְנֵי הָאָרֶץ וַיֹּאמְרוּ אֶל־כָּל־קְהַל הָעָם לֵאמֹר:

18 "*Micha* the Morashtite, who prophesied in the days of King *Chizkiyahu* of *Yehuda*, said to all the people of *Yehuda*: 'Thus said the LORD of Hosts: *Tzion* shall be plowed as a field, *Yerushalayim* shall become heaps of ruins And the *Har Habayit* a shrine in the woods.'

יח מיכיה [מִיכָה] הַמּוֹרַשְׁתִּי הָיָה נִבָּא בִּימֵי חִזְקִיָּהוּ מֶלֶךְ־יְהוּדָה וַיֹּאמֶר אֶל־כָּל־עַם יְהוּדָה לֵאמֹר כֹּה־אָמַר יְהוָה צְבָאוֹת צִיּוֹן שָׂדֶה תֵחָרֵשׁ וִירוּשָׁלַיִם עִיִּים תִּהְיֶה וְהַר הַבַּיִת לְבָמוֹת יָעַר:

19 "Did King *Chizkiyahu* of *Yehuda*, and all *Yehuda*, put him to death? Did he not rather fear *Hashem* and implore *Hashem*, so that *Hashem* renounced the punishment He had decreed against them? We are about to do great injury to ourselves!"

יט הֶהָמֵת הֱמִתֻהוּ חִזְקִיָּהוּ מֶלֶךְ־יְהוּדָה וְכָל־יְהוּדָה הֲלֹא יָרֵא אֶת־יְהוָה וַיְחַל אֶת־פְּנֵי יְהוָה וַיִּנָּחֶם יְהוָה אֶל־הָרָעָה אֲשֶׁר־דִּבֶּר עֲלֵיהֶם וַאֲנַחְנוּ עֹשִׂים רָעָה גְדוֹלָה עַל־נַפְשׁוֹתֵינוּ:

he-ha-MAYT he-mi-TU-hu khiz-ki-YA-hu me-lekh y'-hu-DAH v'-khol y'-hu-DAH ha-LO ya-RAY et a-do-NAI vai-KHAL et p'-NAY a-do-NAI va-yi-na-KHEM a-do-NAI el ha-ra-AH a-sher di-BER a-lay-HEM va-a-NAKH-nu o-SEEM ra-AH g'-do-LAH al naf-sho-TAY-nu

---

26:19 Did King *Chizkiyahu* of *Yehuda*, and all *Yehuda*, put him to death? *Yirmiyahu* is arrested by the officers and placed on trial as a false prophet. They claim that *Yirmi*-yahu's prophecies of destruction and exile contradict the eternal bond between *Hashem* and His people. However, the elders of Israel come to *Yirmiyahu's* defense. A century

Jeremiah

20 There was also a man prophesying in the name of *Hashem*, Uriya son of *Shemaya* from *Kiryat Ye'arim*, who prophesied against this city and this land the same things as *Yirmiyahu*.

כ וְגַם־אִישׁ הָיָה מִתְנַבֵּא בְּשֵׁם יְהֹוָה אוּרִיָּהוּ בֶּן־שְׁמַעְיָהוּ מִקִּרְיַת הַיְּעָרִים וַיִּנָּבֵא עַל־הָעִיר הַזֹּאת וְעַל־הָאָרֶץ הַזֹּאת כְּכֹל דִּבְרֵי יִרְמְיָהוּ:

21 King *Yehoyakim* and all his warriors and all the officials heard about his address, and the king wanted to put him to death. *Uriya* heard of this and fled in fear, and came to Egypt.

כא וַיִּשְׁמַע הַמֶּלֶךְ־יְהוֹיָקִים וְכָל־גִּבּוֹרָיו וְכָל־הַשָּׂרִים אֶת־דְּבָרָיו וַיְבַקֵּשׁ הַמֶּלֶךְ הֲמִיתוֹ וַיִּשְׁמַע אוּרִיָּהוּ וַיִּרָא וַיִּבְרַח וַיָּבֹא מִצְרָיִם:

22 But King *Yehoyakim* sent men to Egypt, Elnathan son of Achbor and men with him to Egypt.

כב וַיִּשְׁלַח הַמֶּלֶךְ יְהוֹיָקִים אֲנָשִׁים מִצְרָיִם אֵת אֶלְנָתָן בֶּן־עַכְבּוֹר וַאֲנָשִׁים אִתּוֹ אֶל־מִצְרָיִם:

23 They took *Uriya* out of Egypt and brought him to King *Yehoyakim*, who had him put to the sword and his body thrown into the burial place of the common people.

כג וַיּוֹצִיאוּ אֶת־אוּרִיָּהוּ מִמִּצְרַיִם וַיְבִאֻהוּ אֶל־הַמֶּלֶךְ יְהוֹיָקִים וַיַּכֵּהוּ בֶּחָרֶב וַיַּשְׁלֵךְ אֶת־נִבְלָתוֹ אֶל־קִבְרֵי בְּנֵי הָעָם:

24 However, *Achikam* son of *Shafan* protected *Yirmiyahu*, so that he was not handed over to the people for execution.

כד אַךְ יַד אֲחִיקָם בֶּן־שָׁפָן הָיְתָה אֶת־יִרְמְיָהוּ לְבִלְתִּי תֵּת־אֹתוֹ בְיַד־הָעָם לַהֲמִיתוֹ:

27 1 At the beginning of the reign of King *Yehoyakim* son of *Yoshiyahu* of *Yehuda*, this word came to *Yirmiyahu* from *Hashem*:

כז א בְּרֵאשִׁית מַמְלֶכֶת יְהוֹיָקִם בֶּן־יֹאושִׁיָּהוּ מֶלֶךְ יְהוּדָה הָיָה הַדָּבָר הַזֶּה אֶל־יִרְמְיָה מֵאֵת יְהֹוָה לֵאמֹר:

2 Thus said *Hashem* to me: Make for yourself thongs and bars of a yoke, and put them on your neck.

ב כֹּה־אָמַר יְהֹוָה אֵלַי עֲשֵׂה לְךָ מוֹסֵרוֹת וּמֹטוֹת וּנְתַתָּם עַל־צַוָּארֶךָ:

koh a-MAR a-do-NAI ay-LAI a-SAY l'-KHA mo-say-ROT
u-mo-TOT un-ta-TAM al tza-va-RE-kha

3 And send them to the king of Edom, the king of Moab, the king of the Amonites, the king of Tyre, and the king of Sidon, by envoys who have come to King *Tzidkiyahu* of *Yehuda* in *Yerushalayim*;

ג וְשִׁלַּחְתָּם אֶל־מֶלֶךְ אֱדוֹם וְאֶל־מֶלֶךְ מוֹאָב וְאֶל־מֶלֶךְ בְּנֵי עַמּוֹן וְאֶל־מֶלֶךְ צֹר וְאֶל־מֶלֶךְ צִידוֹן בְּיַד מַלְאָכִים הַבָּאִים יְרוּשָׁלַםִ אֶל־צִדְקִיָּהוּ מֶלֶךְ יְהוּדָה:

4 and give them this charge to their masters: Thus said the LORD of Hosts, the God of *Yisrael*: Say this to your masters:

ד וְצִוִּיתָ אֹתָם אֶל־אֲדֹנֵיהֶם לֵאמֹר כֹּה־אָמַר יְהֹוָה צְבָאוֹת אֱלֹהֵי יִשְׂרָאֵל כֹּה תֹאמְרוּ אֶל־אֲדֹנֵיכֶם:

A yoke used for oxen

earlier, at the time of the Assyrian invasion, the prophet *Micha* had also spoken against the city. Rather than feeling threatened, the righteous king *Chizkiyahu* had led the people in repentance, and God saved the people. *Yirmiyahu* is hoping that the people of his generation will have a similar response to his prophecies, that they will return to *Hashem* and be spared. The message is true for all time, as it says in *Yechezkel* 33:11: "As I live – declares *Hashem* – it is not My desire that the wicked shall die, but that the wicked [one] turn from his [evil] ways and live."

27:2 Put them on your neck In the year 593 BCE, *Tzidkiyahu* leads a confederation of neighboring states in planning a rebellion against Babylonia. *Yirmiyahu* warns them against this folly by means of a highly visual symbol. He walks through the streets wearing a yoke, normally used to harness oxen while plowing, on his neck. When onlookers ask him about his strange behavior, he answers that this was the divine message: Accept the yoke of Babylonia and submit peacefully in order to live. Had the people listened, they would have avoided the destruction of the *Beit Hamikdash* and exile from their land.

5 "It is I who made the earth, and the men and beasts who are on the earth, by My great might and My outstretched arm; and I give it to whomever I deem proper.

ה אָנֹכִי עָשִׂיתִי אֶת־הָאָרֶץ אֶת־הָאָדָם וְאֶת־הַבְּהֵמָה אֲשֶׁר עַל־פְּנֵי הָאָרֶץ בְּכֹחִי הַגָּדוֹל וּבִזְרוֹעִי הַנְּטוּיָה וּנְתַתִּיהָ לַאֲשֶׁר יָשַׁר בְּעֵינָי:

6 I herewith deliver all these lands to My servant, King Nebuchadnezzar of Babylon; I even give him the wild beasts to serve him.

ו וְעַתָּה אָנֹכִי נָתַתִּי אֶת־כָּל־הָאֲרָצוֹת הָאֵלֶּה בְּיַד נְבוּכַדְנֶאצַּר מֶלֶךְ־בָּבֶל עַבְדִּי וְגַם אֶת־חַיַּת הַשָּׂדֶה נָתַתִּי לוֹ לְעָבְדוֹ:

7 All nations shall serve him, his son and his grandson – until the turn of his own land comes, when many nations and great kings shall subjugate him.

ז וְעָבְדוּ אֹתוֹ כָּל־הַגּוֹיִם וְאֶת־בְּנוֹ וְאֶת־בֶּן־ בְּנוֹ עַד בֹּא־עֵת אַרְצוֹ גַּם־הוּא וְעָבְדוּ בוֹ גּוֹיִם רַבִּים וּמְלָכִים גְּדֹלִים:

8 The nation or kingdom that does not serve him – King Nebuchadnezzar of Babylon – and does not put its neck under the yoke of the king of Babylon, that nation I will visit – declares *Hashem* – with sword, famine, and pestilence, until I have destroyed it by his hands.

ח וְהָיָה הַגּוֹי וְהַמַּמְלָכָה אֲשֶׁר לֹא־יַעַבְדוּ אֹתוֹ אֶת־נְבוּכַדְנֶאצַּר מֶלֶךְ־בָּבֶל וְאֵת אֲשֶׁר לֹא־יִתֵּן אֶת־צַוָּארוֹ בְּעֹל מֶלֶךְ בָּבֶל בַּחֶרֶב וּבָרָעָב וּבַדֶּבֶר אֶפְקֹד עַל־הַגּוֹי הַהוּא נְאֻם־יְהֹוָה עַד־תֻּמִּי אֹתָם בְּיָדוֹ:

9 As for you, give no heed to your *Neviim*, augurs, dreamers, diviners, and sorcerers, who say to you, 'Do not serve the king of Babylon.'

ט וְאַתֶּם אַל־תִּשְׁמְעוּ אֶל־נְבִיאֵיכֶם וְאֶל־ קֹסְמֵיכֶם וְאֶל חֲלֹמֹתֵיכֶם וְאֶל־עֹנְנֵיכֶם וְאֶל־כַּשָּׁפֵיכֶם אֲשֶׁר־הֵם אֹמְרִים אֲלֵיכֶם לֵאמֹר לֹא תַעַבְדוּ אֶת־מֶלֶךְ בָּבֶל:

10 For they prophesy falsely to you – with the result that you shall be banished from your land; I will drive you out and you shall perish.

י כִּי שֶׁקֶר הֵם נִבְּאִים לָכֶם לְמַעַן הַרְחִיק אֶתְכֶם מֵעַל אַדְמַתְכֶם וְהִדַּחְתִּי אֶתְכֶם וַאֲבַדְתֶּם:

11 But the nation that puts its neck under the yoke of the king of Babylon, and serves him, will be left by Me on its own soil – declares *Hashem* – to till it and dwell on it."

יא וְהַגּוֹי אֲשֶׁר יָבִיא אֶת־צַוָּארוֹ בְּעֹל מֶלֶךְ־ בָּבֶל וַעֲבָדוֹ וְהִנַּחְתִּיו עַל־אַדְמָתוֹ נְאֻם־ יְהֹוָה וַעֲבָדָהּ וְיָשַׁב בָּהּ:

12 I also spoke to King *Tzidkiyahu* of *Yehuda* in just the same way: "Put your necks under the yoke of the king of Babylon; serve him and his people, and live!

יב וְאֶל־צִדְקִיָּה מֶלֶךְ־יְהוּדָה דִּבַּרְתִּי כְּכָל־ הַדְּבָרִים הָאֵלֶּה לֵאמֹר הָבִיאוּ אֶת־ צַוְּארֵיכֶם בְּעֹל מֶלֶךְ־בָּבֶל וְעִבְדוּ אֹתוֹ וְעַמּוֹ וִחְיוּ:

13 Otherwise you will die together with your people, by sword, famine, and pestilence, as *Hashem* has decreed against any nation that does not serve the king of Babylon.

יג לָמָּה תָמוּתוּ אַתָּה וְעַמֶּךָ בַּחֶרֶב בָּרָעָב וּבַדָּבֶר כַּאֲשֶׁר דִּבֶּר יְהֹוָה אֶל־הַגּוֹי אֲשֶׁר לֹא־יַעֲבֹד אֶת־מֶלֶךְ בָּבֶל:

14 Give no heed to the words of the *Neviim* who say to you, 'Do not serve the king of Babylon,' for they prophesy falsely to you.

יד וְאַל־תִּשְׁמְעוּ אֶל־דִּבְרֵי הַנְּבִאִים הָאֹמְרִים אֲלֵיכֶם לֵאמֹר לֹא תַעַבְדוּ אֶת־מֶלֶךְ בָּבֶל כִּי שֶׁקֶר הֵם נִבְּאִים לָכֶם:

15 I have not sent them – declares *Hashem* – and they prophesy falsely in My name, with the result that I will drive you out and you shall perish, together with the *Neviim* who prophesy to you."

טו כִּי לֹא שְׁלַחְתִּים נְאֻם־יְהֹוָה וְהֵם נִבְּאִים בִּשְׁמִי לַשָּׁקֶר לְמַעַן הַדִּיחִי אֶתְכֶם וַאֲבַדְתֶּם אַתֶּם וְהַנְּבִאִים הַנִּבְּאִים לָכֶם:

16 And to the *Kohanim* and to all that people I said: "Thus said *Hashem*: Give no heed to the words of the *Neviim* who prophesy to you, 'The vessels of the House of *Hashem* shall shortly be brought back from Babylon,' for they prophesy falsely to you.

טז וְאֶל־הַכֹּהֲנִים וְאֶל־כָּל־הָעָם הַזֶּה דִּבַּרְתִּי לֵאמֹר כֹּה אָמַר יְהֹוָה אַל־תִּשְׁמְעוּ אֶל־דִּבְרֵי נְבִיאֵיכֶם הַנִּבְּאִים לָכֶם לֵאמֹר הִנֵּה כְלֵי בֵית־יְהֹוָה מוּשָׁבִים מִבָּבֶלָה עַתָּה מְהֵרָה כִּי שֶׁקֶר הֵמָּה נִבְּאִים לָכֶם:

17 Give them no heed. Serve the king of Babylon, and live! Otherwise this city shall become a ruin.

יז אַל־תִּשְׁמְעוּ אֲלֵיהֶם עִבְדוּ אֶת־מֶלֶךְ־בָּבֶל וִחְיוּ לָמָּה תִהְיֶה הָעִיר הַזֹּאת חָרְבָּה:

18 If they are really *Neviim* and the word of *Hashem* is with them, let them intercede with the LORD of Hosts not to let the vessels remaining in the House of *Hashem*, in the royal palace of *Yehuda*, and in *Yerushalayim*, go to Babylon!

יח וְאִם־נְבִאִים הֵם וְאִם־יֵשׁ דְּבַר־יְהֹוָה אִתָּם יִפְגְּעוּ־נָא בַּיהֹוָה צְבָאוֹת לְבִלְתִּי־בֹאוּ הַכֵּלִים הַנּוֹתָרִים בְּבֵית־יְהֹוָה וּבֵית מֶלֶךְ יְהוּדָה וּבִירוּשָׁלַ͏ִם בָּבֶלָה:

19 "For thus said the LORD of Hosts concerning the columns, the tank, the stands, and the rest of the vessels remaining in this city,

יט כִּי כֹה אָמַר יְהֹוָה צְבָאוֹת אֶל־הָעַמֻּדִים וְעַל־הַיָּם וְעַל־הַמְּכֹנוֹת וְעַל יֶתֶר הַכֵּלִים הַנּוֹתָרִים בָּעִיר הַזֹּאת:

20 which King Nebuchadnezzar of Babylon did not take when he exiled King *Yechonya* son of *Yehoyakim* of *Yehuda*, from *Yerushalayim* to Babylon, with all the nobles of *Yehuda* and *Yerushalayim*;

כ אֲשֶׁר לֹא־לְקָחָם נְבוּכַדְנֶאצַּר מֶלֶךְ בָּבֶל בַּגְלוֹתוֹ אֶת־יְכָנְיָה בֶן־יְהוֹיָקִים מֶלֶךְ־יְהוּדָה מִירוּשָׁלַ͏ִם בָּבֶלָה וְאֵת כָּל־חֹרֵי יְהוּדָה וִירוּשָׁלָ͏ִם:

21 for thus said the LORD of Hosts, the God of *Yisrael*, concerning the vessels remaining in the House of *Hashem*, in the royal palace of *Yehuda*, and in *Yerushalayim*:

כא כִּי כֹה אָמַר יְהֹוָה צְבָאוֹת אֱלֹהֵי יִשְׂרָאֵל עַל־הַכֵּלִים הַנּוֹתָרִים בֵּית יְהֹוָה וּבֵית מֶלֶךְ־יְהוּדָה וִירוּשָׁלָ͏ִם:

22 They shall be brought to Babylon, and there they shall remain, until I take note of them – declares the LORD of Hosts – and bring them up and restore them to this place."

כב בָּבֶלָה יוּבָאוּ וְשָׁמָּה יִהְיוּ עַד יוֹם פָּקְדִי אֹתָם נְאֻם־יְהֹוָה וְהַעֲלִיתִים וַהֲשִׁיבֹתִים אֶל־הַמָּקוֹם הַזֶּה:

28 1 That year, early in the reign of King *Tzidkiyahu* of *Yehuda*, in the fifth month of the fourth year, the *Navi Chananya* son of Azzur, who was from *Givon*, spoke to me in the House of *Hashem*, in the presence of the *Kohanim* and all the people. He said:

כח א וַיְהִי בַּשָּׁנָה הַהִיא בְּרֵאשִׁית מַמְלֶכֶת צִדְקִיָּה מֶלֶךְ־יְהוּדָה בשנת [בַּשָּׁנָה] הָרְבִעִית בַּחֹדֶשׁ הַחֲמִישִׁי אָמַר אֵלַי חֲנַנְיָה בֶן־עַזּוּר הַנָּבִיא אֲשֶׁר מִגִּבְעוֹן בְּבֵית יְהֹוָה לְעֵינֵי הַכֹּהֲנִים וְכָל־הָעָם לֵאמֹר:

2 "Thus said the LORD of Hosts, the God of *Yisrael*: I hereby break the yoke of the king of Babylon.

ב כֹּה־אָמַר יְהֹוָה צְבָאוֹת אֱלֹהֵי יִשְׂרָאֵל לֵאמֹר שָׁבַרְתִּי אֶת־עֹל מֶלֶךְ בָּבֶל:

Jeremiah

³ In two years, I will restore to this place all the vessels of the House of *Hashem* which King Nebuchadnezzar of Babylon took from this place and brought to Babylon.

ג בְּעוֹד שְׁנָתַיִם יָמִים אֲנִי מֵשִׁיב אֶל־הַמָּקוֹם הַזֶּה אֶת־כָּל־כְּלֵי בֵּית יְהֹוָה אֲשֶׁר לָקַח נְבוּכַדְנֶאצַּר מֶלֶךְ־בָּבֶל מִן־הַמָּקוֹם הַזֶּה וַיְבִיאֵם בָּבֶל:

⁴ And I will bring back to this place King *Yechonya* son of *Yehoyakim* of *Yehuda*, and all the Judean exiles who went to Babylon – declares *Hashem*. Yes, I will break the yoke of the king of Babylon."

ד וְאֶת־יְכָנְיָה בֶן־יְהוֹיָקִים מֶלֶךְ־יְהוּדָה וְאֶת־כָּל־גָּלוּת יְהוּדָה הַבָּאִים בָּבֶלָה אֲנִי מֵשִׁיב אֶל־הַמָּקוֹם הַזֶּה נְאֻם־יְהֹוָה כִּי אֶשְׁבֹּר אֶת־עֹל מֶלֶךְ בָּבֶל:

⁵ Then the *Navi Yirmiyahu* answered the *Navi Chananya* in the presence of the *Kohanim* and of all the people who were standing in the House of *Hashem*.

ה וַיֹּאמֶר יִרְמְיָה הַנָּבִיא אֶל־חֲנַנְיָה הַנָּבִיא לְעֵינֵי הַכֹּהֲנִים וּלְעֵינֵי כָל־הָעָם הָעֹמְדִים בְּבֵית יְהֹוָה:

⁶ The *Navi Yirmiyahu* said: "*Amen*! May *Hashem* do so! May *Hashem* fulfill what you have prophesied and bring back from Babylon to this place the vessels of the House of *Hashem* and all the exiles!

ו וַיֹּאמֶר יִרְמְיָה הַנָּבִיא אָמֵן כֵּן יַעֲשֶׂה יְהֹוָה יָקֵם יְהֹוָה אֶת־דְּבָרֶיךָ אֲשֶׁר וּבֵאתָ לְהָשִׁיב כְּלֵי בֵית־יְהֹוָה וְכָל־הַגּוֹלָה מִבָּבֶל אֶל־הַמָּקוֹם הַזֶּה:

⁷ But just listen to this word which I address to you and to all the people:

ז אַךְ־שְׁמַע־נָא הַדָּבָר הַזֶּה אֲשֶׁר אָנֹכִי דֹּבֵר בְּאָזְנֶיךָ וּבְאָזְנֵי כָּל־הָעָם:

⁸ The *Neviim* who lived before you and me from ancient times prophesied war, disaster, and pestilence against many lands and great kingdoms.

ח הַנְּבִיאִים אֲשֶׁר הָיוּ לְפָנַי וּלְפָנֶיךָ מִן־הָעוֹלָם וַיִּנָּבְאוּ אֶל־אֲרָצוֹת רַבּוֹת וְעַל־מַמְלָכוֹת גְּדֹלוֹת לְמִלְחָמָה וּלְרָעָה וּלְדָבֶר:

ha-n'-vee-EEM a-SHER ha-YU l'-fa-NAI ul-fa-NE-kha min ha-o-LAM va-yi-na-v'-U el a-ra-TZOT ra-BOT v'-al mam-la-KHOT g'-do-LOT l'-mil-kha-MAH ul-ra-AH ul-DA-ver

⁹ So if a *Navi* prophesies good fortune, then only when the word of the *Navi* comes true can it be known that *Hashem* really sent him."

ט הַנָּבִיא אֲשֶׁר יִנָּבֵא לְשָׁלוֹם בְּבֹא דְּבַר הַנָּבִיא יִוָּדַע הַנָּבִיא אֲשֶׁר־שְׁלָחוֹ יְהֹוָה בֶּאֱמֶת:

¹⁰ But the *Navi Chananya* removed the bar from the neck of the *Navi Yirmiyahu*, and broke it;

י וַיִּקַּח חֲנַנְיָה הַנָּבִיא אֶת־הַמּוֹטָה מֵעַל צַוַּאר יִרְמְיָה הַנָּבִיא וַיִּשְׁבְּרֵהוּ:

¹¹ and *Chananya* said in the presence of all the people, "Thus said *Hashem*: So will I break the yoke of King Nebuchadnezzar of Babylon from off the necks of all the nations, in two years." And the *Navi Yirmiyahu* went on his way.

יא וַיֹּאמֶר חֲנַנְיָה לְעֵינֵי כָל־הָעָם לֵאמֹר כֹּה אָמַר יְהֹוָה כָּכָה אֶשְׁבֹּר אֶת־עֹל נְבֻכַדְנֶאצַּר מֶלֶךְ־בָּבֶל בְּעוֹד שְׁנָתַיִם יָמִים מֵעַל צַוַּאר כָּל־הַגּוֹיִם וַיֵּלֶךְ יִרְמְיָה הַנָּבִיא לְדַרְכּוֹ:

28:8 Prophesied war, disaster, and pestilence against many lands *Chananya* dramatically breaks *Yirmiyahu's* symbolic yoke, claiming that the Babylonian empire will be overthrown in two years. *Yirmiyahu* argues that while this is a more reassuring message, it is false. It is easy to ingratiate oneself with the masses by telling them what they want to hear, but telling them the truth requires courage and the willingness to speak out and become unpopular. The great prophets of Israel uttered their prophecies fearlessly, conveying the divine message without hesitation or fear. Everyone is a messenger of God in this world. One must never hesitate to stand up for God, His people and His land, *Eretz Yisrael*, even when it seems like an unpopular message.

Canada's Conservatives support Israel at the UJA Federation Walk with Israel in Toronto, May 2018

12 After the *Navi Chananya* had broken the bar from off the neck of the *Navi Yirmiyahu*, the word of *Hashem* came to *Yirmiyahu*:

יב וַיְהִי דְבַר־יְהֹוָה אֶל־יִרְמְיָה אַחֲרֵי שְׁבוֹר חֲנַנְיָה הַנָּבִיא אֶת־הַמּוֹטָה מֵעַל צַוַּאר יִרְמְיָה הַנָּבִיא לֵאמֹר:

13 "Go say to *Chananya*: Thus said *Hashem*: You broke bars of wood, but you shall make bars of iron instead.

יג הָלוֹךְ וְאָמַרְתָּ אֶל־חֲנַנְיָה לֵאמֹר כֹּה אָמַר יְהֹוָה מוֹטֹת עֵץ שָׁבָרְתָּ וְעָשִׂיתָ תַחְתֵּיהֶן מֹטוֹת בַּרְזֶל:

14 For thus said the Lord of Hosts, the God of *Yisrael*: I have put an iron yoke upon the necks of all those nations, that they may serve King Nebuchadnezzar of Babylon – and serve him they shall! I have even given the wild beasts to him."

יד כִּי כֹה־אָמַר יְהֹוָה צְבָאוֹת אֱלֹהֵי יִשְׂרָאֵל עֹל בַּרְזֶל נָתַתִּי עַל־צַוַּאר כָּל־הַגּוֹיִם הָאֵלֶּה לַעֲבֹד אֶת־נְבֻכַדְנֶאצַּר מֶלֶךְ־בָּבֶל וַעֲבָדֻהוּ וְגַם אֶת־חַיַּת הַשָּׂדֶה נָתַתִּי לוֹ:

15 And the *Navi Yirmiyahu* said to the *Navi Chananya*, "Listen, *Chananya*! *Hashem* did not send you, and you have given this people lying assurances.

טו וַיֹּאמֶר יִרְמְיָה הַנָּבִיא אֶל־חֲנַנְיָה הַנָּבִיא שְׁמַע־נָא חֲנַנְיָה לֹא־שְׁלָחֲךָ יְהֹוָה וְאַתָּה הִבְטַחְתָּ אֶת־הָעָם הַזֶּה עַל־שָׁקֶר:

16 Assuredly, thus said *Hashem*: I am going to banish you from off the earth. This year you shall die, for you have urged disloyalty to *Hashem*."

טז לָכֵן כֹּה אָמַר יְהֹוָה הִנְנִי מְשַׁלֵּחֲךָ מֵעַל פְּנֵי הָאֲדָמָה הַשָּׁנָה אַתָּה מֵת כִּי־סָרָה דִבַּרְתָּ אֶל־יְהֹוָה:

17 And the *Navi Chananya* died that year, in the seventh month.

יז וַיָּמָת חֲנַנְיָה הַנָּבִיא בַּשָּׁנָה הַהִיא בַּחֹדֶשׁ הַשְּׁבִיעִי:

29 1 This is the text of the letter which the *Navi Yirmiyahu* sent from *Yerushalayim* to the *Kohanim*, the *Neviim*, the rest of the elders of the exile community, and to all the people whom Nebuchadnezzar had exiled from *Yerushalayim* to Babylon –

כט א וְאֵלֶּה דִּבְרֵי הַסֵּפֶר אֲשֶׁר שָׁלַח יִרְמְיָה הַנָּבִיא מִירוּשָׁלָ͏ִם אֶל־יֶתֶר זִקְנֵי הַגּוֹלָה וְאֶל־הַכֹּהֲנִים וְאֶל־הַנְּבִיאִים וְאֶל־כָּל־הָעָם אֲשֶׁר הֶגְלָה נְבוּכַדְנֶאצַּר מִירוּשָׁלַ͏ִם בָּבֶלָה:

2 after King *Yechonya*, the queen mother, the eunuchs, the officials of *Yehuda* and *Yerushalayim*, and the craftsmen and smiths had left *Yerushalayim*.

ב אַחֲרֵי צֵאת יְכָנְיָה־הַמֶּלֶךְ וְהַגְּבִירָה וְהַסָּרִיסִים שָׂרֵי יְהוּדָה וִירוּשָׁלַ͏ִם וְהֶחָרָשׁ וְהַמַּסְגֵּר מִירוּשָׁלָ͏ִם:

3 [The letter was sent] through Elasah son of *Shafan* and Gemariah son of *Chilkiyahu*, whom King *Tzidkiyahu* of *Yehuda* had dispatched to Babylon, to King Nebuchadnezzar of Babylon.

ג בְּיַד אֶלְעָשָׂה בֶן־שָׁפָן וּגְמַרְיָה בֶּן־חִלְקִיָּה אֲשֶׁר שָׁלַח צִדְקִיָּה מֶלֶךְ־יְהוּדָה אֶל־נְבוּכַדְנֶאצַּר מֶלֶךְ בָּבֶל בָּבֶלָה לֵאמֹר:

4 Thus said the Lord of Hosts, the God of *Yisrael*, to the whole community which I exiled from *Yerushalayim* to Babylon:

ד כֹּה אָמַר יְהֹוָה צְבָאוֹת אֱלֹהֵי יִשְׂרָאֵל לְכָל־הַגּוֹלָה אֲשֶׁר־הִגְלֵיתִי מִירוּשָׁלַ͏ִם בָּבֶלָה:

5 Build houses and live in them, plant gardens and eat their fruit.

ה בְּנוּ בָתִּים וְשֵׁבוּ וְנִטְעוּ גַנּוֹת וְאִכְלוּ אֶת־פִּרְיָן:

6 Take wives and beget sons and daughters; and take wives for your sons, and give your daughters to husbands, that they may bear sons and daughters. Multiply there, do not decrease.

ו קְחוּ נָשִׁים וְהוֹלִידוּ בָּנִים וּבָנוֹת וּקְחוּ לִבְנֵיכֶם נָשִׁים וְאֶת־בְּנוֹתֵיכֶם תְּנוּ לַאֲנָשִׁים וְתֵלַדְנָה בָּנִים וּבָנוֹת וּרְבוּ־שָׁם וְאַל־תִּמְעָטוּ:

7 And seek the welfare of the city to which I have exiled you and pray to *Hashem* in its behalf; for in its prosperity you shall prosper.

ז וְדִרְשׁוּ אֶת־שְׁלוֹם הָעִיר אֲשֶׁר הִגְלֵיתִי אֶתְכֶם שָׁמָּה וְהִתְפַּלְלוּ בַעֲדָהּ אֶל־יְהֹוָה כִּי בִשְׁלוֹמָהּ יִהְיֶה לָכֶם שָׁלוֹם:

8 For thus said the LORD of Hosts, the God of *Yisrael*: Let not the *Neviim* and diviners in your midst deceive you, and pay no heed to the dreams they dream.

ח כִּי כֹה אָמַר יְהֹוָה צְבָאוֹת אֱלֹהֵי יִשְׂרָאֵל אַל־יַשִּׁיאוּ לָכֶם נְבִיאֵיכֶם אֲשֶׁר־בְּקִרְבְּכֶם וְקֹסְמֵיכֶם וְאַל־תִּשְׁמְעוּ אֶל־חֲלֹמֹתֵיכֶם אֲשֶׁר אַתֶּם מַחְלְמִים:

9 For they prophesy to you in My name falsely; I did not send them – declares *Hashem*.

ט כִּי בְשֶׁקֶר הֵם נִבְּאִים לָכֶם בִּשְׁמִי לֹא שְׁלַחְתִּים נְאֻם־יְהֹוָה:

10 For thus said *Hashem*: When Babylon's seventy years are over, I will take note of you, and I will fulfill to you My promise of favor – to bring you back to this place.

י כִּי־כֹה אָמַר יְהֹוָה כִּי לְפִי מְלֹאת לְבָבֶל שִׁבְעִים שָׁנָה אֶפְקֹד אֶתְכֶם וַהֲקִמֹתִי עֲלֵיכֶם אֶת־דְּבָרִי הַטּוֹב לְהָשִׁיב אֶתְכֶם אֶל־הַמָּקוֹם הַזֶּה:

11 For I am mindful of the plans I have made concerning you – declares *Hashem* – plans for your welfare, not for disaster, to give you a hopeful future.

יא כִּי אָנֹכִי יָדַעְתִּי אֶת־הַמַּחֲשָׁבֹת אֲשֶׁר אָנֹכִי חֹשֵׁב עֲלֵיכֶם נְאֻם־יְהֹוָה מַחְשְׁבוֹת שָׁלוֹם וְלֹא לְרָעָה לָתֵת לָכֶם אַחֲרִית וְתִקְוָה:

12 When you call Me, and come and pray to Me, I will give heed to you.

יב וּקְרָאתֶם אֹתִי וַהֲלַכְתֶּם וְהִתְפַּלַּלְתֶּם אֵלָי וְשָׁמַעְתִּי אֲלֵיכֶם:

13 You will search for Me and find Me, if only you seek Me wholeheartedly.

יג וּבִקַּשְׁתֶּם אֹתִי וּמְצָאתֶם כִּי תִדְרְשֻׁנִי בְּכָל־לְבַבְכֶם:

u-vi-kash-TEM o-TEE um-tza-TEM KEE tid-r'-SHU-nee b'-khol l'-vav-KHEM

14 I will be at hand for you – declares *Hashem* – and I will restore your fortunes. And I will gather you from all the nations and from all the places to which I have banished you – declares *Hashem* – and I will bring you back to the place from which I have exiled you.

יד וְנִמְצֵאתִי לָכֶם נְאֻם־יְהֹוָה וְשַׁבְתִּי אֶת־שביתכם [שְׁבוּתְכֶם] וְקִבַּצְתִּי אֶתְכֶם מִכָּל־הַגּוֹיִם וּמִכָּל־הַמְּקוֹמוֹת אֲשֶׁר הִדַּחְתִּי אֶתְכֶם שָׁם נְאֻם־יְהֹוָה וַהֲשִׁבֹתִי אֶתְכֶם אֶל־הַמָּקוֹם אֲשֶׁר־הִגְלֵיתִי אֶתְכֶם מִשָּׁם:

15 But you say, "*Hashem* has raised up *Neviim* for us in Babylon."

טו כִּי אֲמַרְתֶּם הֵקִים לָנוּ יְהֹוָה נְבִאִים בָּבֶלָה:

16 Thus said *Hashem* concerning the king who sits on the throne of *David*, and concerning all the people who dwell in this city, your brothers who did not go out with you into exile –

טז כִּי־כֹה אָמַר יְהֹוָה אֶל־הַמֶּלֶךְ הַיּוֹשֵׁב אֶל־כִּסֵּא דָוִד וְאֶל־כָּל־הָעָם הַיּוֹשֵׁב בָּעִיר הַזֹּאת אֲחֵיכֶם אֲשֶׁר לֹא־יָצְאוּ אִתְּכֶם בַּגּוֹלָה:

29:13 You will search for Me and find Me *Yirmiyahu* pens a letter to the exiles in Babylonia. He tells them to disregard the false prophecies, according to which they will return to Israel soon. Instead, they are to settle in Babylonia and raise families there, as they will remain there for seventy years, and only after that will they be permitted to return to Israel. However, only those who truly desire to return to their homeland will be given divine assistance to do so. In his work, *The Kuzari*, medieval philosopher Rabbi Yehuda Halevi lists the people's lack of desire to return to their homeland as Israel's greatest historic failing. This serves as a reminder to Jews in today's generation not to take Israel for granted.

Holocaust survivors yearning for Israel

17 thus said the LORD of Hosts: I am going to let loose sword, famine, and pestilence against them and I will treat them as loathsome figs, so bad that they cannot be eaten.

יז כֹּה אָמַר יְהֹוָה צְבָאוֹת הִנְנִי מְשַׁלֵּחַ בָּם אֶת־הַחֶרֶב אֶת־הָרָעָב וְאֶת־הַדָּבֶר וְנָתַתִּי אוֹתָם כַּתְּאֵנִים הַשֹּׁעָרִים אֲשֶׁר לֹא־תֵאָכַלְנָה מֵרֹעַ:

18 I will pursue them with the sword, with famine, and with pestilence; and I will make them a horror to all the kingdoms of the earth, a curse and an object of horror and hissing and scorn among all the nations to which I shall banish them,

יח וְרָדַפְתִּי אַחֲרֵיהֶם בַּחֶרֶב בָּרָעָב וּבַדָּבֶר וּנְתַתִּים לְזֹעָה [לְזַעֲוָה] לְכֹל מַמְלְכוֹת הָאָרֶץ לְאָלָה וּלְשַׁמָּה וְלִשְׁרֵקָה וּלְחֶרְפָּה בְּכָל־הַגּוֹיִם אֲשֶׁר־הִדַּחְתִּים שָׁם:

19 because they did not heed My words – declares *Hashem* – when I persistently sent to them My servants, the *Neviim*, and they did not heed – declares *Hashem*.

יט תַּחַת אֲשֶׁר־לֹא־שָׁמְעוּ אֶל־דְּבָרַי נְאֻם־יְהֹוָה אֲשֶׁר שָׁלַחְתִּי אֲלֵיהֶם אֶת־עֲבָדַי הַנְּבִאִים הַשְׁכֵּם וְשָׁלֹחַ וְלֹא שְׁמַעְתֶּם נְאֻם־יְהֹוָה:

20 But you, the whole exile community which I banished from *Yerushalayim* to Babylon, hear the word of *Hashem*!

כ וְאַתֶּם שִׁמְעוּ דְבַר־יְהֹוָה כָּל־הַגּוֹלָה אֲשֶׁר־שִׁלַּחְתִּי מִירוּשָׁלַם בָּבֶלָה:

21 Thus said the LORD of Hosts, the God of *Yisrael*, concerning *Achav* son of Kolaiah and *Tzidkiyahu* son of Maaseiah, who prophesy falsely to you in My name: I am going to deliver them into the hands of King Nebuchadrezzar of Babylon, and he shall put them to death before your eyes.

כא כֹּה־אָמַר יְהֹוָה צְבָאוֹת אֱלֹהֵי יִשְׂרָאֵל אֶל־אַחְאָב בֶּן־קוֹלָיָה וְאֶל־צִדְקִיָּהוּ בֶן־מַעֲשֵׂיָה הַנִּבְּאִים לָכֶם בִּשְׁמִי שָׁקֶר הִנְנִי נֹתֵן אֹתָם בְּיַד נְבוּכַדְרֶאצַּר מֶלֶךְ־בָּבֶל וְהִכָּם לְעֵינֵיכֶם:

22 And the whole community of *Yehuda* in Babylonia shall use a curse derived from their fate: "May *Hashem* make you like *Tzidkiyahu* and *Achav*, whom the king of Babylon consigned to the flames!" –

כב וְלֻקַּח מֵהֶם קְלָלָה לְכֹל גָּלוּת יְהוּדָה אֲשֶׁר בְּבָבֶל לֵאמֹר יְשִׂמְךָ יְהֹוָה כְּצִדְקִיָּהוּ וּכְאֶחָב אֲשֶׁר־קָלָם מֶלֶךְ־בָּבֶל בָּאֵשׁ:

23 because they did vile things in *Yisrael*, committing adultery with the wives of their fellows and speaking in My name false words which I had not commanded them. I am He who knows and bears witness – declares *Hashem*.

כג יַעַן אֲשֶׁר עָשׂוּ נְבָלָה בְּיִשְׂרָאֵל וַיְנַאֲפוּ אֶת־נְשֵׁי רֵעֵיהֶם וַיְדַבְּרוּ דָבָר בִּשְׁמִי שֶׁקֶר אֲשֶׁר לוֹא צִוִּיתִם וְאָנֹכִי הוֹידֵעַ [הַיּוֹדֵעַ] וָעֵד נְאֻם־יְהֹוָה:

24 Concerning *Shemaya* the Nehelamite you shall say:

כד וְאֶל־שְׁמַעְיָהוּ הַנֶּחֱלָמִי תֹּאמַר לֵאמֹר:

25 Thus said the LORD of Hosts, the God of *Yisrael*: Because you sent letters in your own name to all the people in *Yerushalayim*, to *Tzefanya* son of Maaseiah and to the rest of the *Kohanim*, as follows,

כה כֹּה־אָמַר יְהֹוָה צְבָאוֹת אֱלֹהֵי יִשְׂרָאֵל לֵאמֹר יַעַן אֲשֶׁר אַתָּה שָׁלַחְתָּ בְשִׁמְכָה סְפָרִים אֶל־כָּל־הָעָם אֲשֶׁר בִּירוּשָׁלַם וְאֶל־צְפַנְיָה בֶן־מַעֲשֵׂיָה הַכֹּהֵן וְאֶל כָּל־הַכֹּהֲנִים לֵאמֹר:

26 "*Hashem* appointed you *Kohen* in place of the *Kohen Yehoyada*, to exercise authority in the House of *Hashem* over every madman who wants to play the *Navi*, to put him into the stocks and into the pillory.

כו יְהֹוָה נְתָנְךָ כֹהֵן תַּחַת יְהוֹיָדָע הַכֹּהֵן לִהְיוֹת פְּקִדִים בֵּית יְהֹוָה לְכָל־אִישׁ מְשֻׁגָּע וּמִתְנַבֵּא וְנָתַתָּה אֹתוֹ אֶל־הַמַּהְפֶּכֶת וְאֶל־הַצִּינֹק:

Jeremiah

Jeremiah

27 Now why have you not rebuked *Yirmiyahu* the Anatotite, who plays the *Navi* among you?

כז וְעַתָּה לָמָּה לֹא גָעַרְתָּ בְּיִרְמְיָהוּ הָעֲנְּתֹתִי הַמִּתְנַבֵּא לָכֶם:

28 For he has actually sent a message to us in Babylon to this effect: It will be a long time. Build houses and live in them, plant gardens and enjoy their fruit." –

כח כִּי עַל־כֵּן שָׁלַח אֵלֵינוּ בָּבֶל לֵאמֹר אֲרֻכָּה הִיא בְּנוּ בָתִּים וְשֵׁבוּ וְנִטְעוּ גַנּוֹת וְאִכְלוּ אֶת־פְּרִיהֶן:

29 When the *Kohen Tzefanya* read this letter in the hearing of the *Navi Yirmiyahu*,

כט וַיִּקְרָא צְפַנְיָה הַכֹּהֵן אֶת־הַסֵּפֶר הַזֶּה בְּאָזְנֵי יִרְמְיָהוּ הַנָּבִיא:

30 the word of *Hashem* came to *Yirmiyahu*:

ל וַיְהִי דְּבַר־יְהֹוָה אֶל־יִרְמְיָהוּ לֵאמֹר:

31 Send a message to the entire exile community: "Thus said *Hashem* concerning *Shemaya* the Nehelamite: Because *Shemaya* prophesied to you, though I did not send him, and made you false promises,

לא שְׁלַח עַל־כָּל־הַגּוֹלָה לֵאמֹר כֹּה אָמַר יְהֹוָה אֶל־שְׁמַעְיָה הַנֶּחֱלָמִי יַעַן אֲשֶׁר נִבָּא לָכֶם שְׁמַעְיָה וַאֲנִי לֹא שְׁלַחְתִּיו וַיַּבְטַח אֶתְכֶם עַל־שָׁקֶר:

32 assuredly, thus said *Hashem*: I am going to punish *Shemaya* the Nehelamite and his offspring. There shall be no man of his line dwelling among this people or seeing the good things I am going to do for My people – declares *Hashem* – for he has urged disloyalty toward *Hashem*."

לב לָכֵן כֹּה־אָמַר יְהֹוָה הִנְנִי פֹקֵד עַל־שְׁמַעְיָה הַנֶּחֱלָמִי וְעַל־זַרְעוֹ לֹא־יִהְיֶה לוֹ אִישׁ יוֹשֵׁב בְּתוֹךְ־הָעָם הַזֶּה וְלֹא־יִרְאֶה בַטּוֹב אֲשֶׁר־אֲנִי עֹשֶׂה־לְעַמִּי נְאֻם־יְהֹוָה כִּי־סָרָה דִבֶּר עַל־יְהֹוָה:

30 1 The word which came to *Yirmiyahu* from *Hashem*:

ל א הַדָּבָר אֲשֶׁר הָיָה אֶל־יִרְמְיָהוּ מֵאֵת יְהֹוָה לֵאמֹר:

2 Thus said *Hashem*, the God of *Yisrael*: Write down in a scroll all the words that I have spoken to you.

ב כֹּה־אָמַר יְהֹוָה אֱלֹהֵי יִשְׂרָאֵל לֵאמֹר כְּתָב־לְךָ אֵת כָּל־הַדְּבָרִים אֲשֶׁר־דִּבַּרְתִּי אֵלֶיךָ אֶל־סֵפֶר:

3 For days are coming – declares *Hashem* – when I will restore the fortunes of My people *Yisrael* and *Yehuda*, said *Hashem*; and I will bring them back to the land that I gave their fathers, and they shall possess it.

ג כִּי הִנֵּה יָמִים בָּאִים נְאֻם־יְהֹוָה וְשַׁבְתִּי אֶת־שְׁבוּת עַמִּי יִשְׂרָאֵל וִיהוּדָה אָמַר יְהֹוָה וַהֲשִׁבֹתִים אֶל־הָאָרֶץ אֲשֶׁר־נָתַתִּי לַאֲבוֹתָם וִירֵשׁוּהָ:

KEE hi-NAY ya-MEEM ba-EEM n'-um a-do-NAI v'-shav-TEE et sh'-VUT a-MEE yis-ra-AYL vee-hu-DAH a-MAR a-do-NAI va-ha-shi-vo-TEEM el ha-A-retz a-sher na-TA-tee la-a-vo-TAM vee-ray-SHU-ha

4 And these are the words that *Hashem* spoke concerning *Yisrael* and *Yehuda*:

ד וְאֵלֶּה הַדְּבָרִים אֲשֶׁר דִּבֶּר יְהֹוָה אֶל־יִשְׂרָאֵל וְאֶל־יְהוּדָה:

5 Thus said *Hashem*: We have heard cries of panic, Terror without relief.

ה כִּי־כֹה אָמַר יְהֹוָה קוֹל חֲרָדָה שָׁמָעְנוּ פַּחַד וְאֵין שָׁלוֹם:

30:3 I will bring them back to the land that I gave their fathers The return of the Jewish People to the Land of Israel has great significance to all. The legendary first Chief Rabbi of Israel, Abraham Isaac Kook, wrote that "The building of the Israeli nation means the building of the land, the government, the army, the people and the spirit together… the rebirth of the nation is the foundation of the 'Great *Teshuva*' ('Return') – the 'Great *Teshuva*' of the Jewish nation and the *teshuva* of the entire world which comes in its wake."

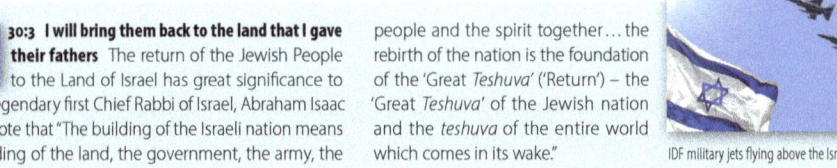

IDF military jets flying above the Israeli flag

6 Ask and see: Surely males do not bear young! Why
then do I see every man With his hands on his loins
Like a woman in labor? Why have all faces turned
pale?

ו שַׁאֲלוּ־נָ֣א וּרְא֔וּ אִם־יֹלֵ֖ד זָכָ֑ר מַדּ֩וּעַ֩
רָאִ֨יתִי כָל־גֶּ֜בֶר יָדָ֤יו עַל־חֲלָצָיו֙ כַּיּ֣וֹלֵדָ֔ה
וְנֶהֶפְכ֥וּ כָל־פָּנִ֖ים לְיֵרָקֽוֹן׃

7 Ah, that day is awesome; There is none like it! It is a
time of trouble for *Yaakov*, But he shall be delivered
from it.

ז ה֗וֹי כִּ֥י גָד֛וֹל הַיּ֥וֹם הַה֖וּא מֵאַ֣יִן כָּמֹ֑הוּ
וְעֵת־צָרָ֥ה הִיא֙ לְיַֽעֲקֹ֔ב וּמִמֶּ֖נָּה יִוָּשֵֽׁעַ׃

8 In that day – declares the LORD of Hosts – I will
break the yoke from off your neck and I will rip off
your bonds. Strangers shall no longer make slaves
of them;

ח וְהָיָה֩ בַיּ֨וֹם הַה֜וּא נְאֻ֣ם יְהֹוָ֣ה צְבָא֗וֹת
אֶשְׁבֹּ֤ר עֻלּוֹ֙ מֵעַ֣ל צַוָּארֶ֔ךָ וּמֽוֹסְרוֹתֶ֖יךָ
אֲנַתֵּ֑ק וְלֹא־יַֽעַבְדוּ־ב֥וֹ ע֖וֹד זָרִֽים׃

9 instead, they shall serve *Hashem* their God and
David, the king whom I will raise up for them.

ט וְעָ֣בְד֔וּ אֵ֖ת יְהֹוָ֣ה אֱלֹֽהֵיהֶ֑ם וְאֵת֙ דָּוִ֣ד
מַלְכָּ֔ם אֲשֶׁ֖ר אָקִ֥ים לָהֶֽם׃

10 But you, Have no fear, My servant *Yaakov* –
declares *Hashem* – Be not dismayed, O *Yisrael*! I
will deliver you from far away, Your folk from their
land of captivity. And *Yaakov* shall again have calm
And quiet with none to trouble him;

י וְאַתָּ֡ה אַל־תִּירָא֩ עַבְדִּ֨י יַֽעֲקֹ֤ב נְאֻם־יְהֹוָה֙
וְאַל־תֵּחַ֣ת יִשְׂרָאֵ֔ל כִּ֠י הִנְנִ֤י מֽוֹשִֽׁיעֲךָ֙
מֵֽרָח֔וֹק וְאֶֽת־זַרְעֲךָ֖ מֵאֶ֣רֶץ שִׁבְיָ֑ם וְשָׁ֧ב
יַֽעֲקֹ֛ב וְשָׁקַ֥ט וְשַׁאֲנַ֖ן וְאֵ֥ין מַֽחֲרִֽיד׃

11 For I am with you to deliver you – declares
Hashem. I will make an end of all the nations
Among which I have dispersed you; But I will
not make an end of you! I will not leave you
unpunished, But will chastise you in measure.

יא כִּֽי־אִתְּךָ֥ אֲנִ֛י נְאֻם־יְהֹוָ֖ה לְהֽוֹשִׁיעֶ֑ךָ כִּי֩
אֶֽעֱשֶׂ֨ה כָלָ֜ה בְּכָֽל־הַגּוֹיִ֣ם ׀ אֲשֶׁ֧ר הֲפִֽצוֹתִ֣יךָ
שָּׁ֗ם אַ֤ךְ אֹֽתְךָ֙ לֹֽא־אֶֽעֱשֶׂ֣ה כָלָ֔ה וְיִסַּרְתִּ֙יךָ֙
לַמִּשְׁפָּ֔ט וְנַקֵּ֖ה לֹ֥א אֲנַקֶּֽךָּ׃

12 For thus said *Hashem*: Your injury is incurable,
Your wound severe;

יב כִּ֣י כֹ֤ה אָמַ֣ר יְהֹוָ֔ה אָנ֖וּשׁ לְשִׁבְרֵ֑ךְ נַחְלָ֖ה
מַכָּתֵֽךְ׃

13 No one pleads for the healing of your sickness,
There is no remedy, no recovery for you.

יג אֵֽין־דָּ֥ן דִּינֵ֖ךְ לְמָז֑וֹר רְפֻא֥וֹת תְּעָלָ֖ה אֵ֥ין
לָֽךְ׃

14 All your lovers have forgotten you, They do not
seek you out; For I have struck you as an enemy
strikes, With cruel chastisement, Because your
iniquity was so great And your sins so many.

יד כָּל־מְאַֽהֲבַ֣יִךְ שְׁכֵח֔וּךְ אוֹתָ֖ךְ לֹ֣א יִדְרֹ֑שׁוּ
כִּי֩ מַכַּ֨ת אוֹיֵ֤ב הִכִּיתִ֙יךְ֙ מוּסַ֣ר אַכְזָרִ֔י עַ֚ל
רֹ֣ב עֲוֹנֵ֔ךְ עָֽצְמ֖וּ חַטֹּאתָֽיִךְ׃

15 Why cry out over your injury, That your wound is
incurable? I did these things to you Because your
iniquity was so great And your sins so many.

טו מַה־תִּזְעַק֙ עַל־שִׁבְרֵ֔ךְ אָנ֖וּשׁ מַכְאֹבֵ֑ךְ
עַ֣ל ׀ רֹ֣ב עֲוֹנֵ֗ךְ עָֽצְמוּ֙ חַטֹּאתַ֔יִךְ עָשִׂ֥יתִי
אֵ֖לֶּה לָֽךְ׃

16 Assuredly, All who wanted to devour you shall
be devoured, And every one of your foes shall go
into captivity; Those who despoiled you shall be
despoiled, And all who pillaged you I will give up
to pillage.

טז לָכֵ֞ן כָּל־אֹֽכְלַ֙יִךְ֙ יֵֽאָכֵ֔לוּ וְכָל־צָרַ֥יִךְ כֻּלָּ֖ם
בַּשְּׁבִ֣י יֵלֵ֑כוּ וְהָי֤וּ שֹׁאסַ֙יִךְ֙ לִמְשִׁסָּ֔ה וְכָל־
בֹּֽזְזַ֖יִךְ אֶתֵּ֥ן לָבַֽז׃

17 But I will bring healing to you And cure you of your wounds – declares *Hashem*. Though they called you "Outcast, That *Tzion* whom no one seeks out,"

יז כִּי אַעֲלֶה אֲרֻכָה לָךְ וּמִמַּכּוֹתַיִךְ אֶרְפָּאֵךְ נְאֻם־יְהֹוָה כִּי נִדָּחָה קָרְאוּ לָךְ צִיּוֹן הִיא דֹּרֵשׁ אֵין לָהּ:

18 Thus said *Hashem*: I will restore the fortunes of *Yaakov*'s tents And have compassion upon his dwellings. The city shall be rebuilt on its mound, And the fortress in its proper place.

יח כֹּה אָמַר יְהֹוָה הִנְנִי־שָׁב שְׁבוּת אָהֳלֵי יַעֲקוֹב וּמִשְׁכְּנֹתָיו אֲרַחֵם וְנִבְנְתָה עִיר עַל־תִּלָּהּ וְאַרְמוֹן עַל־מִשְׁפָּטוֹ יֵשֵׁב:

19 From them shall issue thanksgiving And the sound of dancers. I will multiply them, And they shall not be few; I will make them honored, And they shall not be humbled.

יט וְיָצָא מֵהֶם תּוֹדָה וְקוֹל מְשַׂחֲקִים וְהִרְבִּתִים וְלֹא יִמְעָטוּ וְהִכְבַּדְתִּים וְלֹא יִצְעָרוּ:

20 His children shall be as of old, And his community shall be established by My grace; And I will deal with all his oppressors.

כ וְהָיוּ בָנָיו כְּקֶדֶם וַעֲדָתוֹ לְפָנַי תִּכּוֹן וּפָקַדְתִּי עַל כָּל־לֹחֲצָיו:

21 His chieftain shall be one of his own, His ruler shall come from his midst; I will bring him near, that he may approach Me – declares *Hashem* – For who would otherwise dare approach Me?

כא וְהָיָה אַדִּירוֹ מִמֶּנּוּ וּמשְׁלוֹ מִקִּרְבּוֹ יֵצֵא וְהִקְרַבְתִּיו וְנִגַּשׁ אֵלָי כִּי מִי הוּא־זֶה עָרַב אֶת־לִבּוֹ לָגֶשֶׁת אֵלַי נְאֻם־יְהֹוָה:

22 You shall be My people, And I will be your God.

כב וִהְיִיתֶם לִי לְעָם וְאָנֹכִי אֶהְיֶה לָכֶם לֵאלֹהִים:

23 Lo, the storm of *Hashem* goes forth in fury, A raging tempest; It shall whirl down upon the head of the wicked.

כג הִנֵּה סַעֲרַת יְהֹוָה חֵמָה יָצְאָה סַעַר מִתְגּוֹרֵר עַל רֹאשׁ רְשָׁעִים יָחוּל:

24 The anger of *Hashem* shall not turn back Till it has fulfilled and completed His purposes. In the days to come You shall perceive it.

כד לֹא יָשׁוּב חֲרוֹן אַף־יְהֹוָה עַד־עֲשׂתוֹ וְעַד־הֲקִימוֹ מְזִמּוֹת לִבּוֹ בְּאַחֲרִית הַיָּמִים תִּתְבּוֹנְנוּ בָהּ:

25 At that time – declares *Hashem* – I will be God to all the clans of *Yisrael*, and they shall be My people.

כה בָּעֵת הַהִיא נְאֻם־יְהֹוָה אֶהְיֶה לֵאלֹהִים לְכֹל מִשְׁפְּחוֹת יִשְׂרָאֵל וְהֵמָּה יִהְיוּ־לִי לְעָם:

31 1 Thus said *Hashem*: The people escaped from the sword, Found favor in the wilderness; When *Yisrael* was marching homeward

לא א כֹּה אָמַר יְהֹוָה מָצָא חֵן בַּמִּדְבָּר עַם שְׂרִידֵי חָרֶב הָלוֹךְ לְהַרְגִּיעוֹ יִשְׂרָאֵל:

2 *Hashem* revealed Himself to me of old. Eternal love I conceived for you then; Therefore I continue My grace to you.

ב מֵרָחוֹק יְהֹוָה נִרְאָה לִי וְאַהֲבַת עוֹלָם אֲהַבְתִּיךְ עַל־כֵּן מְשַׁכְתִּיךְ חָסֶד:

3 I will build you firmly again, O Maiden *Yisrael*! Again you shall take up your timbrels And go forth to the rhythm of the dancers.

ג עוֹד אֶבְנֵךְ וְנִבְנֵית בְּתוּלַת יִשְׂרָאֵל עוֹד תַּעְדִּי תֻפַּיִךְ וְיָצָאת בִּמְחוֹל מְשַׂחֲקִים:

Jeremiah

4 Again you shall plant vineyards On the hills of *Shomron*; Men shall plant and live to enjoy them.

ד עוֹד תִּטְּעִי כְרָמִים בְּהָרֵי שֹׁמְרוֹן נָטְעוּ נֹטְעִים וְחִלֵּלוּ:

OD ti-t'-EE kh'-ra-MEEM b'-ha-RAY sho-m'-RON na-t'-U no-t'-EEM v'-khi-LAY-lu

5 For the day is coming when watchmen Shall proclaim on the heights of *Efraim*: Come, let us go up to *Tzion*, To *Hashem* our God!

ה כִּי יֶשׁ־יוֹם קָרְאוּ נֹצְרִים בְּהַר אֶפְרָיִם קוּמוּ וְנַעֲלֶה צִיּוֹן אֶל־יְהֹוָה אֱלֹהֵינוּ:

6 For thus said *Hashem*: Cry out in joy for *Yaakov*, Shout at the crossroads of the nations! Sing aloud in praise, and say: Save, *Hashem*, Your people, The remnant of *Yisrael*.

ו כִּי־כֹה אָמַר יְהֹוָה רָנּוּ לְיַעֲקֹב שִׂמְחָה וְצַהֲלוּ בְּרֹאשׁ הַגּוֹיִם הַשְׁמִיעוּ הַלְלוּ וְאִמְרוּ הוֹשַׁע יְהֹוָה אֶת־עַמְּךָ אֵת שְׁאֵרִית יִשְׂרָאֵל:

7 I will bring them in from the northland, Gather them from the ends of the earth – The blind and the lame among them, Those with child and those in labor – In a vast throng they shall return here.

ז הִנְנִי מֵבִיא אוֹתָם מֵאֶרֶץ צָפוֹן וְקִבַּצְתִּים מִיַּרְכְּתֵי־אָרֶץ בָּם עִוֵּר וּפִסֵּחַ הָרָה וְיֹלֶדֶת יַחְדָּו קָהָל גָּדוֹל יָשׁוּבוּ הֵנָּה:

8 They shall come with weeping, And with compassion will I guide them. I will lead them to streams of water, By a level road where they will not stumble. For I am ever a Father to *Yisrael*, *Efraim* is My first-born.

ח בִּבְכִי יָבֹאוּ וּבְתַחֲנוּנִים אוֹבִילֵם אֱלֹיכֵם אֶל־נַחֲלֵי מַיִם בְּדֶרֶךְ יָשָׁר לֹא יִכָּשְׁלוּ בָּהּ כִּי־הָיִיתִי לְיִשְׂרָאֵל לְאָב וְאֶפְרַיִם בְּכֹרִי הוּא:

9 Hear the word of *Hashem*, O nations, And tell it in the isles afar. Say: He who scattered *Yisrael* will gather them, And will guard them as a shepherd his flock.

ט שִׁמְעוּ דְבַר־יְהֹוָה גּוֹיִם וְהַגִּידוּ בָאִיִּים מִמֶּרְחָק וְאִמְרוּ מְזָרֵה יִשְׂרָאֵל יְקַבְּצֶנּוּ וּשְׁמָרוֹ כְּרֹעֶה עֶדְרוֹ:

10 For *Hashem* will ransom *Yaakov*, Redeem him from one too strong for him.

י כִּי־פָדָה יְהֹוָה אֶת־יַעֲקֹב וּגְאָלוֹ מִיַּד חָזָק מִמֶּנּוּ:

11 They shall come and shout on the heights of *Tzion*, Radiant over the bounty of *Hashem* – Over new grain and wine and oil, And over sheep and cattle. They shall fare like a watered garden, They shall never languish again.

יא וּבָאוּ וְרִנְּנוּ בִמְרוֹם־צִיּוֹן וְנָהֲרוּ אֶל־טוּב יְהֹוָה עַל־דָּגָן וְעַל־תִּירֹשׁ וְעַל־יִצְהָר וְעַל־בְּנֵי־צֹאן וּבָקָר וְהָיְתָה נַפְשָׁם כְּגַן רָוֶה וְלֹא־יוֹסִיפוּ לְדַאֲבָה עוֹד:

12 Then shall maidens dance gaily, Young men and old alike. I will turn their mourning to joy, I will comfort them and cheer them in their grief.

יב אָז תִּשְׂמַח בְּתוּלָה בְּמָחוֹל וּבַחֻרִים וּזְקֵנִים יַחְדָּו וְהָפַכְתִּי אֶבְלָם לְשָׂשׂוֹן וְנִחַמְתִּים וְשִׂמַּחְתִּים מִיגוֹנָם:

31:4 Again you shall plant vineyards on the hills of *Shomron* Return of life to the Holy Land is symbolized by the rejuvenation of vineyards in Samaria, a miracle taking place today. Grapes and vineyards play a prominent role throughout *Tanakh*. The first cultivated plants mentioned in the Bible were grapevines: "*Noach*, the tiller of soil, was the first to plant a vineyard" (Genesis 9:20). Grapes are mentioned more than any other fruit in the entire *Tanakh*. When *Moshe* sent the 12 spies to scout out *Eretz Yisrael*, the book of *Bamidbar* (13:23) records that they returned with a sample of grapes that was so large it had to be carried on poles by strong men, an image used as the logo of Israel's Ministry of Tourism. This honored fruit aslo plays a prominent role in Judaism, as *Shabbat* and Holiday meals begin with a blessing over a cup of wine.

Logo for Israel's Ministry of Tourism

¹³ I will give the *Kohanim* their fill of fatness, And My people shall enjoy My full bounty – declares *Hashem*.

יג וְרִוֵּיתִי נֶפֶשׁ הַכֹּהֲנִים דָּשֶׁן וְעַמִּי אֶת־טוּבִי יִשְׂבָּעוּ נְאֻם־יְהֹוָה:

¹⁴ Thus said *Hashem*: A cry is heard in *Rama* – Wailing, bitter weeping – *Rachel* weeping for her children. She refuses to be comforted For her children, who are gone.

יד כֹּה אָמַר יְהֹוָה קוֹל בְּרָמָה נִשְׁמָע נְהִי בְּכִי תַמְרוּרִים רָחֵל מְבַכָּה עַל־בָּנֶיהָ מֵאֲנָה לְהִנָּחֵם עַל־בָּנֶיהָ כִּי אֵינֶנּוּ:

¹⁵ Thus said *Hashem*: Restrain your voice from weeping, Your eyes from shedding tears; For there is a reward for your labor – declares *Hashem*: They shall return from the enemy's land.

טו כֹּה אָמַר יְהֹוָה מִנְעִי קוֹלֵךְ מִבֶּכִי וְעֵינַיִךְ מִדִּמְעָה כִּי יֵשׁ שָׂכָר לִפְעֻלָּתֵךְ נְאֻם־יְהֹוָה וְשָׁבוּ מֵאֶרֶץ אוֹיֵב:

¹⁶ And there is hope for your future – declares *Hashem*: Your children shall return to their country.

טז וְיֵשׁ־תִּקְוָה לְאַחֲרִיתֵךְ נְאֻם־יְהֹוָה וְשָׁבוּ בָנִים לִגְבוּלָם:

v'-yaysh tik-VAH l'-a-kha-ree-TAYKH n'-um a-do-NAI
v'-SHA-vu va-NEEM lig-vu-LAM

¹⁷ I can hear *Efraim* lamenting: You have chastised me, and I am chastised Like a calf that has not been broken. Receive me back, let me return, For You, *Hashem*, are my God.

יז שָׁמוֹעַ שָׁמַעְתִּי אֶפְרַיִם מִתְנוֹדֵד יִסַּרְתַּנִי וָאִוָּסֵר כְּעֵגֶל לֹא לֻמָּד הֲשִׁיבֵנִי וְאָשׁוּבָה כִּי אַתָּה יְהֹוָה אֱלֹהָי:

¹⁸ Now that I have turned back, I am filled with remorse; Now that I am made aware, I strike my thigh. I am ashamed and humiliated, For I bear the disgrace of my youth.

יח כִּי־אַחֲרֵי שׁוּבִי נִחַמְתִּי וְאַחֲרֵי הִוָּדְעִי סָפַקְתִּי עַל־יָרֵךְ בֹּשְׁתִּי וְגַם־נִכְלַמְתִּי כִּי נָשָׂאתִי חֶרְפַּת נְעוּרָי:

¹⁹ Truly, *Efraim* is a dear son to Me, A child that is dandled! Whenever I have turned against him, My thoughts would dwell on him still. That is why My heart yearns for him; I will receive him back in love – declares *Hashem*.

יט הֲבֵן יַקִּיר לִי אֶפְרַיִם אִם יֶלֶד שַׁעֲשֻׁעִים כִּי־מִדֵּי דַבְּרִי בּוֹ זָכֹר אֶזְכְּרֶנּוּ עוֹד עַל־כֵּן הָמוּ מֵעַי לוֹ רַחֵם אֲרַחֲמֶנּוּ נְאֻם־יְהֹוָה:

²⁰ Erect markers, Set up signposts; Keep in mind the highway, The road that you traveled. Return, Maiden *Yisrael*! Return to these towns of yours!

כ הַצִּיבִי לָךְ צִיֻּנִים שִׂמִי לָךְ תַּמְרוּרִים שִׁתִי לִבֵּךְ לַמְסִלָּה דֶּרֶךְ הָלָכְתִּי [הָלָכְתְּ] שׁוּבִי בְּתוּלַת יִשְׂרָאֵל שֻׁבִי אֶל־עָרַיִךְ אֵלֶּה:

²¹ How long will you waver, O rebellious daughter? (For *Hashem* has created something new on earth: A woman courts a man.)

כא עַד־מָתַי תִּתְחַמָּקִין הַבַּת הַשּׁוֹבֵבָה כִּי־בָרָא יְהֹוָה חֲדָשָׁה בָּאָרֶץ נְקֵבָה תְּסוֹבֵב גָּבֶר:

31:16 Your children shall return to their country In this moving passage, God speaks directly to the matriarch *Rachel*, who is known in Jewish tradition as having a special role in the redemption of her children, the Jewish people, and their return to Israel. According to Jewish tradition, when her father Laban gave her sister *Leah* to *Yaakov* in marriage in her stead, *Rachel* revealed to *Leah* a secret sign she had made with *Yaakov* in order to spare *Leah* from embarrassment. Because of *Rachel's* unparalleled selflessness and love for her sister, it is *Rachel's* prayers, tears and cries for compassion to her children that are heard by God more than any other biblical figure. God promises *Rachel* that those tears are not for naught, but rather "There is a reward for your labor" (verse 16) and "your children shall return to their country." In a moving example of symbolism, this verse is often sung with emotion at Ben Gurion Airport as new Jewish immigrants arrive in Israel.

Greeting new immigrants with "your children shall return to their country"

Jeremiah

22 Thus said the Lord of Hosts, the God of *Yisrael*:
They shall again say this in the land of *Yehuda*
and in its towns, when I restore their fortunes:
"*Hashem* bless you, Abode of righteousness, O holy
mountain!"

23 *Yehuda* and all its towns alike shall be inhabited by
the farmers and such as move about with the flocks.

24 For I will give the thirsty abundant drink, and
satisfy all who languish.

25 At this I awoke and looked about, and my sleep had
been pleasant to me.

26 See, a time is coming – declares *Hashem* – when
I will sow the House of *Yisrael* and the House of
Yehuda with seed of men and seed of cattle;

27 and just as I was watchful over them to uproot and
to pull down, to overthrow and to destroy and to
bring disaster, so I will be watchful over them to
build and to plant – declares *Hashem*.

28 In those days, they shall no longer say, "Parents have
eaten sour grapes and children's teeth are blunted."

29 But every one shall die for his own sins: whosoever
eats sour grapes, his teeth shall be blunted.

30 See, a time is coming – declares *Hashem* – when
I will make a new covenant with the House of
Yisrael and the House of *Yehuda*.

כב כֹּה־אָמַר יְהֹוָה צְבָאוֹת אֱלֹהֵי יִשְׂרָאֵל
עוֹד יֹאמְרוּ אֶת־הַדָּבָר הַזֶּה בְּאֶרֶץ
יְהוּדָה וּבְעָרָיו בְּשׁוּבִי אֶת־שְׁבוּתָם
יְבָרֶכְךָ יְהֹוָה נְוֵה־צֶדֶק הַר הַקֹּדֶשׁ:

כג וְיָשְׁבוּ בָהּ יְהוּדָה וְכָל־עָרָיו יַחְדָּו אִכָּרִים
וְנָסְעוּ בַּעֵדֶר:

כד כִּי הִרְוֵיתִי נֶפֶשׁ עֲיֵפָה וְכָל־נֶפֶשׁ דָּאֲבָה
מִלֵּאתִי:

כה עַל־זֹאת הֱקִיצֹתִי וָאֶרְאֶה וּשְׁנָתִי עָרְבָה
לִי:

כו הִנֵּה יָמִים בָּאִים נְאֻם־יְהֹוָה וְזָרַעְתִּי
אֶת־בֵּית יִשְׂרָאֵל וְאֶת־בֵּית יְהוּדָה זֶרַע
אָדָם וְזֶרַע בְּהֵמָה:

כז וְהָיָה כַּאֲשֶׁר שָׁקַדְתִּי עֲלֵיהֶם לִנְתוֹשׁ
וְלִנְתוֹץ וְלַהֲרֹס וּלְהַאֲבִיד וּלְהָרֵעַ כֵּן
אֶשְׁקֹד עֲלֵיהֶם לִבְנוֹת וְלִנְטוֹעַ נְאֻם־
יְהֹוָה:

כח בַּיָּמִים הָהֵם לֹא־יֹאמְרוּ עוֹד אָבוֹת
אָכְלוּ בֹסֶר וְשִׁנֵּי בָנִים תִּקְהֶינָה:

כט כִּי אִם־אִישׁ בַּעֲוֹנוֹ יָמוּת כָּל־הָאָדָם
הָאֹכֵל הַבֹּסֶר תִּקְהֶינָה שִׁנָּיו:

ל הִנֵּה יָמִים בָּאִים נְאֻם־יְהֹוָה וְכָרַתִּי אֶת־
בֵּית יִשְׂרָאֵל וְאֶת־בֵּית יְהוּדָה בְּרִית
חֲדָשָׁה:

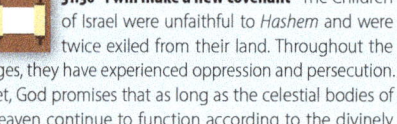
hi-NAY ya-MEEM ba-EEM n'-UM a-do-NAI v'-kha-ra-TEE et BAYT
yis-ra-AYL v'-et BAYT y'-du-DAH b'-REET kha-da-SHAH

31 It will not be like the covenant I made with their
fathers, when I took them by the hand to lead them
out of the land of Egypt, a covenant which they
broke, though I espoused them – declares *Hashem*.

32 But such is the covenant I will make with the
House of *Yisrael* after these days – declares *Hashem*:
I will put My Teaching into their inmost being and
inscribe it upon their hearts. Then I will be their
God, and they shall be My people.

לא לֹא כַבְּרִית אֲשֶׁר כָּרַתִּי אֶת־אֲבוֹתָם
בְּיוֹם הֶחֱזִיקִי בְיָדָם לְהוֹצִיאָם מֵאֶרֶץ
מִצְרָיִם אֲשֶׁר־הֵמָּה הֵפֵרוּ אֶת־בְּרִיתִי
וְאָנֹכִי בָּעַלְתִּי בָם נְאֻם־יְהֹוָה:

לב כִּי זֹאת הַבְּרִית אֲשֶׁר אֶכְרֹת אֶת־בֵּית
יִשְׂרָאֵל אַחֲרֵי הַיָּמִים הָהֵם נְאֻם־יְהֹוָה
נָתַתִּי אֶת־תּוֹרָתִי בְּקִרְבָּם וְעַל־לִבָּם
אֶכְתֲּבֶנָּה וְהָיִיתִי לָהֶם לֵאלֹהִים וְהֵמָּה
יִהְיוּ־לִי לְעָם:

Full moon over an aqueduct in Ceasarea

31:30 I will make a new covenant The Children of Israel were unfaithful to *Hashem* and were twice exiled from their land. Throughout the ages, they have experienced oppression and persecution. Yet, God promises that as long as the celestial bodies of heaven continue to function according to the divinely ordained laws of nature, Israel will continue to be His chosen people (verses 34–35). This verse confirms that God has not abandoned or replaced His people; the Nation of Israel will never be cast away from *Hashem*.

Jeremiah

33 No longer will they need to teach one another and say to one another, "Heed *Hashem*"; for all of them, from the least of them to the greatest, shall heed Me – declares *Hashem*. For I will forgive their iniquities, And remember their sins no more.

לג וְלֹא יְלַמְּדוּ עוֹד אִישׁ אֶת־רֵעֵהוּ וְאִישׁ אֶת־אָחִיו לֵאמֹר דְּעוּ אֶת־יְהֹוָה כִּי־כוּלָּם יֵדְעוּ אוֹתִי לְמִקְטַנָּם וְעַד־גְּדוֹלָם נְאֻם־יְהֹוָה כִּי אֶסְלַח לַעֲוֹנָם וּלְחַטָּאתָם לֹא אֶזְכָּר־עוֹד:

34 Thus said *Hashem*, Who established the sun for light by day, The laws of moon and stars for light by night, Who stirs up the sea into roaring waves, Whose name is LORD of Hosts:

לד כֹּה אָמַר יְהֹוָה נֹתֵן שֶׁמֶשׁ לְאוֹר יוֹמָם חֻקֹּת יָרֵחַ וְכוֹכָבִים לְאוֹר לָיְלָה רֹגַע הַיָּם וַיֶּהֱמוּ גַּלָּיו יְהֹוָה צְבָאוֹת שְׁמוֹ:

35 If these laws should ever be annulled by Me – declares *Hashem* – Only then would the offspring of *Yisrael* cease To be a nation before Me for all time.

לה אִם־יָמֻשׁוּ הַחֻקִּים הָאֵלֶּה מִלְּפָנַי נְאֻם־יְהֹוָה גַּם זֶרַע יִשְׂרָאֵל יִשְׁבְּתוּ מִהְיוֹת גּוֹי לְפָנַי כָּל־הַיָּמִים:

36 Thus said *Hashem*: If the heavens above could be measured, and the foundations of the earth below could be fathomed, only then would I reject all the offspring of *Yisrael* for all that they have done – declares *Hashem*.

לו כֹּה אָמַר יְהֹוָה אִם־יִמַּדּוּ שָׁמַיִם מִלְמַעְלָה וְיֵחָקְרוּ מוֹסְדֵי־אֶרֶץ לְמָטָּה גַּם־אֲנִי אֶמְאַס בְּכָל־זֶרַע יִשְׂרָאֵל עַל־כָּל־אֲשֶׁר עָשׂוּ נְאֻם־יְהֹוָה:

37 See, a time is coming – declares *Hashem* – when the city shall be rebuilt for *Hashem* from the Tower of Hananel to the Corner Gate;

לז הִנֵּה יָמִים [בָּאִים] נְאֻם־יְהֹוָה וְנִבְנְתָה הָעִיר לַיהֹוָה מִמִּגְדַּל חֲנַנְאֵל שַׁעַר הַפִּנָּה:

38 and the measuring line shall go straight out to the Gareb Hill, and then turn toward Goah.

לח וְיָצָא עוֹד קָוֵה [קָו] הַמִּדָּה נֶגְדּוֹ עַל גִּבְעַת גָּרֵב וְנָסַב גֹּעָתָה:

39 And the entire Valley of the Corpses and Ashes, and all the fields as far as the Wadi Kidron, and the corner of the Horse Gate on the east, shall be holy to *Hashem*. They shall never again be uprooted or overthrown.

לט וְכָל־הָעֵמֶק הַפְּגָרִים וְהַדֶּשֶׁן וְכָל־הַשְּׁרֵמוֹת [הַשְּׁדֵמוֹת] עַד־נַחַל קִדְרוֹן עַד־פִּנַּת שַׁעַר הַסּוּסִים מִזְרָחָה קֹדֶשׁ לַיהֹוָה לֹא־יִנָּתֵשׁ וְלֹא־יֵהָרֵס עוֹד לְעוֹלָם:

32 1 The word which came to *Yirmiyahu* from *Hashem* in the tenth year of King *Tzidkiyahu* of *Yehuda*, which was the eighteenth year of Nebuchadrezzar.

לב א הַדָּבָר אֲשֶׁר־הָיָה אֶל־יִרְמְיָהוּ מֵאֵת יְהֹוָה בשנת [בַּשָּׁנָה] הָעֲשִׂרִית לְצִדְקִיָּהוּ מֶלֶךְ יְהוּדָה הִיא הַשָּׁנָה שְׁמֹנֶה־עֶשְׂרֵה שָׁנָה לִנְבוּכַדְרֶאצַּר:

2 At that time the army of the king of Babylon was besieging *Yerushalayim*, and the *Navi Yirmiyahu* was confined in the prison compound attached to the palace of the king of *Yehuda*.

ב וְאָז חֵיל מֶלֶךְ בָּבֶל צָרִים עַל־יְרוּשָׁלָ͏ִם וְיִרְמְיָהוּ הַנָּבִיא הָיָה כָלוּא בַּחֲצַר הַמַּטָּרָה אֲשֶׁר בֵּית־מֶלֶךְ יְהוּדָה:

3 For King *Tzidkiyahu* of *Yehuda* had confined him, saying, "How dare you prophesy: 'Thus said *Hashem*: I am delivering this city into the hands of the king of Babylon, and he shall capture it.

ג אֲשֶׁר כְּלָאוֹ צִדְקִיָּהוּ מֶלֶךְ־יְהוּדָה לֵאמֹר מַדּוּעַ אַתָּה נִבָּא לֵאמֹר כֹּה אָמַר יְהֹוָה הִנְנִי נֹתֵן אֶת־הָעִיר הַזֹּאת בְּיַד מֶלֶךְ־בָּבֶל וּלְכָדָהּ:

4 And King *Tzidkiyahu* of *Yehuda* shall not escape from the Chaldeans; he shall be delivered into the hands of the king of Babylon, and he shall speak to him face to face and see him in person.

ד וְצִדְקִיָּהוּ מֶלֶךְ יְהוּדָה לֹא יִמָּלֵט מִיַּד הַכַּשְׂדִּים כִּי הִנָּתֹן יִנָּתֵן בְּיַד מֶלֶךְ־בָּבֶל וְדִבֶּר־פִּיו עִם־פִּיו וְעֵינָיו אֶת־עֵינֵו [עֵינָיו] תִּרְאֶינָה:

5 And *Tzidkiyahu* shall be brought to Babylon, there to remain until I take note of him – declares *Hashem*. When you wage war against the Chaldeans, you shall not be successful.'"

ה וּבָבֶל יוֹלִךְ אֶת־צִדְקִיָּהוּ וְשָׁם יִהְיֶה עַד־פָּקְדִי אֹתוֹ נְאֻם־יְהֹוָה כִּי תִלָּחֲמוּ אֶת־הַכַּשְׂדִּים לֹא תַצְלִיחוּ:

6 *Yirmiyahu* said: The word of *Hashem* came to me:

ו וַיֹּאמֶר יִרְמְיָהוּ הָיָה דְּבַר־יְהֹוָה אֵלַי לֵאמֹר:

7 *Chanamel*, the son of your uncle *Shalum*, will come to you and say, "Buy my land in *Anatot*, for you are next in succession to redeem it by purchase."

ז הִנֵּה חֲנַמְאֵל בֶּן־שַׁלֻּם דֹּדְךָ בָּא אֵלֶיךָ לֵאמֹר קְנֵה לְךָ אֶת־שָׂדִי אֲשֶׁר בַּעֲנָתוֹת כִּי לְךָ מִשְׁפַּט הַגְּאֻלָּה לִקְנוֹת:

hi-NAY kha-nam-AYL ben sha-LUM do-d'-KHA BA ay-LE-kha lay-MOR k'-NAY l'-KHA et sa-DEE a-SHER ba-a-na-TOT KEE l'-KHA mish-PAT ha-g'-u-LAH lik-NOT

8 And just as *Hashem* had said, my cousin *Chanamel* came to me in the prison compound and said to me, "Please buy my land in *Anatot*, in the territory of *Binyamin*; for the right of succession is yours, and you have the duty of redemption. Buy it." Then I knew that it was indeed the word of *Hashem*.

ח וַיָּבֹא אֵלַי חֲנַמְאֵל בֶּן־דֹּדִי כִּדְבַר יְהֹוָה אֶל־חֲצַר הַמַּטָּרָה וַיֹּאמֶר אֵלַי קְנֵה נָא אֶת־שָׂדִי אֲשֶׁר־בַּעֲנָתוֹת אֲשֶׁר בְּאֶרֶץ בִּנְיָמִין כִּי־לְךָ מִשְׁפַּט הַיְרֻשָּׁה וּלְךָ הַגְּאֻלָּה קְנֵה־לָךְ וָאֵדַע כִּי דְבַר־יְהֹוָה הוּא:

9 So I bought the land in *Anatot* from my cousin *Chanamel*. I weighed out the money to him, seventeen *shekalim* of silver.

ט וָאֶקְנֶה אֶת־הַשָּׂדֶה מֵאֵת חֲנַמְאֵל בֶּן־דֹּדִי אֲשֶׁר בַּעֲנָתוֹת וָאֶשְׁקֲלָה־לּוֹ אֶת־הַכֶּסֶף שִׁבְעָה שְׁקָלִים וַעֲשָׂרָה הַכָּסֶף:

10 I wrote a deed, sealed it, and had it witnessed; and I weighed out the silver on a balance.

י וָאֶכְתֹּב בַּסֵּפֶר וָאֶחְתֹּם וָאָעֵד עֵדִים וָאֶשְׁקֹל הַכֶּסֶף בְּמֹאזְנָיִם:

11 I took the deed of purchase, the sealed text and the open one according to rule and law,

יא וָאֶקַּח אֶת־סֵפֶר הַמִּקְנָה אֶת־הֶחָתוּם הַמִּצְוָה וְהַחֻקִּים וְאֶת־הַגָּלוּי:

12 and gave the deed to *Baruch* son of *Nerya* son of *Machseya* in the presence of my kinsman *Chanamel*, of the witnesses who were named in the deed, and all the Judeans who were sitting in the prison compound.

יב וָאֶתֵּן אֶת־הַסֵּפֶר הַמִּקְנָה אֶל־בָּרוּךְ בֶּן־נֵרִיָּה בֶּן־מַחְסֵיָה לְעֵינֵי חֲנַמְאֵל דֹּדִי וּלְעֵינֵי הָעֵדִים הַכֹּתְבִים בְּסֵפֶר הַמִּקְנָה לְעֵינֵי כָּל־הַיְּהוּדִים הַיֹּשְׁבִים בַּחֲצַר הַמַּטָּרָה:

13 In their presence I charged *Baruch* as follows:

יג וָאֲצַוֶּה אֶת־בָּרוּךְ לְעֵינֵיהֶם לֵאמֹר:

14 Thus said the LORD of Hosts, the God of *Yisrael*: "Take these documents, this deed of purchase, the sealed text and the open one, and put them into an earthen jar, so that they may last a long time."

יד כֹּה־אָמַר יְהֹוָה צְבָאוֹת אֱלֹהֵי יִשְׂרָאֵל לָקוֹחַ אֶת־הַסְּפָרִים הָאֵלֶּה אֵת סֵפֶר הַמִּקְנָה הַזֶּה וְאֵת הֶחָתוּם וְאֵת סֵפֶר הַגָּלוּי הַזֶּה וּנְתַתָּם בִּכְלִי־חָרֶשׂ לְמַעַן יַעַמְדוּ יָמִים רַבִּים:

The modern town of Anatot

32:7 Buy my land in *Anatot* At a time of impending destruction, *Yirmiyahu* is told to redeem his family's property. This symbolic purchase reflects not only the biblical law that land could be redeemed by relatives (see Leviticus 25, Ruth 4), but it also demonstrates *Yirmiyahu's* total faith that even though the exile to Babylonia is quickly approaching, it will in fact be only temporary. The sale also demonstrates, with poetic words and symbolic action, the eternal connection between the Jewish people and the land. Though currently on the brink of exile, they remain attached to their land, with the deed preserved in an earthenware vessel.

15 For thus said the Lord of Hosts, the God of *Yisrael*: "Houses, fields, and vineyards shall again be purchased in this land."

טו כִּי כֹה אָמַר יְהֹוָה צְבָאוֹת אֱלֹהֵי יִשְׂרָאֵל עוֹד יִקָּנוּ בָתִּים וְשָׂדוֹת וּכְרָמִים בָּאָרֶץ הַזֹּאת:

16 But after I had given the deed to *Baruch* son of *Nerya*, I prayed to *Hashem*:

טז וָאֶתְפַּלֵּל אֶל־יְהֹוָה אַחֲרֵי תִתִּי אֶת־סֵפֶר הַמִּקְנָה אֶל־בָּרוּךְ בֶּן־נֵרִיָּה לֵאמֹר:

17 "Ah, *Hashem*! You made heaven and earth with Your great might and outstretched arm. Nothing is too wondrous for You!

יז אֲהָהּ אֲדֹנָי יֱהֹוִה הִנֵּה אַתָּה עָשִׂיתָ אֶת־הַשָּׁמַיִם וְאֶת־הָאָרֶץ בְּכֹחֲךָ הַגָּדוֹל וּבִזְרֹעֲךָ הַנְּטוּיָה לֹא־יִפָּלֵא מִמְּךָ כָּל־דָּבָר:

18 You show kindness to the thousandth generation, but visit the guilt of the fathers upon their children after them. O great and mighty *Hashem* whose name is Lord of Hosts,

יח עֹשֶׂה חֶסֶד לַאֲלָפִים וּמְשַׁלֵּם עֲוֹן אָבוֹת אֶל־חֵיק בְּנֵיהֶם אַחֲרֵיהֶם הָאֵל הַגָּדוֹל הַגִּבּוֹר יְהֹוָה צְבָאוֹת שְׁמוֹ:

19 wondrous in purpose and mighty in deed, whose eyes observe all the ways of men, so as to repay every man according to his ways, and with the proper fruit of his deeds!

יט גְּדֹל הָעֵצָה וְרַב הָעֲלִילִיָּה אֲשֶׁר־עֵינֶיךָ פְקֻחוֹת עַל־כָּל־דַּרְכֵי בְּנֵי אָדָם לָתֵת לְאִישׁ כִּדְרָכָיו וְכִפְרִי מַעֲלָלָיו:

20 You displayed signs and marvels in the land of Egypt with lasting effect, and won renown in *Yisrael* and among mankind to this very day.

כ אֲשֶׁר־שַׂמְתָּ אֹתוֹת וּמֹפְתִים בְּאֶרֶץ־מִצְרַיִם עַד־הַיּוֹם הַזֶּה וּבְיִשְׂרָאֵל וּבָאָדָם וַתַּעֲשֶׂה־לְּךָ שֵׁם כַּיּוֹם הַזֶּה:

21 You freed Your people *Yisrael* from the land of Egypt with signs and marvels, with a strong hand and an outstretched arm, and with great terror.

כא וַתֹּצֵא אֶת־עַמְּךָ אֶת־יִשְׂרָאֵל מֵאֶרֶץ מִצְרָיִם בְּאֹתוֹת וּבְמוֹפְתִים וּבְיָד חֲזָקָה וּבְאֶזְרוֹעַ נְטוּיָה וּבְמוֹרָא גָּדוֹל:

22 You gave them this land that You had sworn to their fathers to give them, a land flowing with milk and honey,

כב וַתִּתֵּן לָהֶם אֶת־הָאָרֶץ הַזֹּאת אֲשֶׁר־נִשְׁבַּעְתָּ לַאֲבוֹתָם לָתֵת לָהֶם אֶרֶץ זָבַת חָלָב וּדְבָשׁ:

23 and they came and took possession of it. But they did not listen to You or follow Your Teaching; they did nothing of what You commanded them to do. Therefore you have caused all this misfortune to befall them.

כג וַיָּבֹאוּ וַיִּרְשׁוּ אֹתָהּ וְלֹא־שָׁמְעוּ בְקוֹלֶךָ וּבְתֹרֹתְךָ [וּבְתוֹרָתְךָ] לֹא־הָלָכוּ אֵת כָּל־אֲשֶׁר צִוִּיתָה לָהֶם לַעֲשׂוֹת לֹא עָשׂוּ וַתַּקְרֵא אֹתָם אֵת כָּל־הָרָעָה הַזֹּאת:

24 Here are the siegemounds, raised against the city to storm it; and the city, because of sword and famine and pestilence, is at the mercy of the Chaldeans who are attacking it. What You threatened has come to pass – as You see.

כד הִנֵּה הַסֹּלְלוֹת בָּאוּ הָעִיר לְלָכְדָהּ וְהָעִיר נִתְּנָה בְּיַד הַכַּשְׂדִּים הַנִּלְחָמִים עָלֶיהָ מִפְּנֵי הַחֶרֶב וְהָרָעָב וְהַדָּבֶר וַאֲשֶׁר דִּבַּרְתָּ הָיָה וְהִנְּךָ רֹאֶה:

25 Yet You, *Hashem*, said to me: Buy the land for money and call in witnesses – when the city is at the mercy of the Chaldeans!"

כה וְאַתָּה אָמַרְתָּ אֵלַי אֲדֹנָי יֱהֹוִה קְנֵה־לְךָ הַשָּׂדֶה בַּכֶּסֶף וְהָעֵד עֵדִים וְהָעִיר נִתְּנָה בְּיַד הַכַּשְׂדִּים:

26 Then the word of *Hashem* came to *Yirmiyahu*:

כו וַיְהִי דְּבַר־יְהֹוָה אֶל־יִרְמְיָהוּ לֵאמֹר:

27 "Behold I am *Hashem*, the God of all flesh. Is anything too wondrous for Me?

כז הִנֵּה אֲנִי יְהֹוָה אֱלֹהֵי כָּל־בָּשָׂר הֲמִמֶּנִּי יִפָּלֵא כָּל־דָּבָר:

28 Assuredly, thus said *Hashem*: I am delivering this city into the hands of the Chaldeans and of King Nebuchadrezzar of Babylon, and he shall capture it.

29 And the Chaldeans who have been attacking this city shall come and set this city on fire and burn it down – with the houses on whose roofs they made offerings to Baal and poured out libations to other gods, so as to vex Me.

30 For the people of *Yisrael* and *Yehuda* have done nothing but evil in My sight since their youth; the people of *Yisrael* have done nothing but vex Me by their conduct – declares *Hashem*.

31 This city has aroused My anger and My wrath from the day it was built until this day; so that it must be removed from My sight

32 because of all the wickedness of the people of *Yisrael* and *Yehuda* who have so acted as to vex Me – they, their kings, their officials, their *Kohanim* and *Neviim*, and the men of *Yehuda* and the inhabitants of *Yerushalayim*.

33 They turned their backs to Me, not their faces; though I have taught them persistently, they do not give heed or accept rebuke.

34 They placed their abominations in the House which bears My name and defiled it;

35 and they built the shrines of Baal which are in the Valley of Ben-hinnom, where they offered up their sons and daughters to Molech – when I had never commanded, or even thought [of commanding], that they should do such an abominable thing, and so bring guilt on *Yehuda*.

36 But now, assuredly, thus said *Hashem*, the God of *Yisrael*, concerning this city of which you say, "It is being delivered into the hands of the king of Babylon through the sword, through famine, and through pestilence":

37 See, I will gather them from all the lands to which I have banished them in My anger and wrath, and in great rage; and I will bring them back to this place and let them dwell secure.

38 They shall be My people, and I will be their God.

כח לָכֵן כֹּה אָמַר יְהוָה הִנְנִי נֹתֵן אֶת־הָעִיר הַזֹּאת בְּיַד הַכַּשְׂדִּים וּבְיַד נְבוּכַדְרֶאצַּר מֶלֶךְ־בָּבֶל וּלְכָדָהּ:

כט וּבָאוּ הַכַּשְׂדִּים הַנִּלְחָמִים עַל־הָעִיר הַזֹּאת וְהִצִּיתוּ אֶת־הָעִיר הַזֹּאת בָּאֵשׁ וּשְׂרָפוּהָ וְאֵת הַבָּתִּים אֲשֶׁר קִטְּרוּ עַל־גַּגּוֹתֵיהֶם לַבַּעַל וְהִסִּכוּ נְסָכִים לֵאלֹהִים אֲחֵרִים לְמַעַן הַכְעִסֵנִי:

ל כִּי־הָיוּ בְנֵי־יִשְׂרָאֵל וּבְנֵי יְהוּדָה אַךְ עֹשִׂים הָרַע בְּעֵינַי מִנְּעֻרֹתֵיהֶם כִּי בְנֵי־יִשְׂרָאֵל אַךְ מַכְעִסִים אֹתִי בְּמַעֲשֵׂה יְדֵיהֶם נְאֻם־יְהוָה:

לא כִּי עַל־אַפִּי וְעַל־חֲמָתִי הָיְתָה לִּי הָעִיר הַזֹּאת לְמִן־הַיּוֹם אֲשֶׁר בָּנוּ אוֹתָהּ וְעַד הַיּוֹם הַזֶּה לַהֲסִירָהּ מֵעַל פָּנָי:

לב עַל כָּל־רָעַת בְּנֵי־יִשְׂרָאֵל וּבְנֵי יְהוּדָה אֲשֶׁר עָשׂוּ לְהַכְעִסֵנִי הֵמָּה מַלְכֵיהֶם שָׂרֵיהֶם כֹּהֲנֵיהֶם וּנְבִיאֵיהֶם וְאִישׁ יְהוּדָה וְיֹשְׁבֵי יְרוּשָׁלָ͏ִם:

לג וַיִּפְנוּ אֵלַי עֹרֶף וְלֹא פָנִים וְלַמֵּד אֹתָם הַשְׁכֵּם וְלַמֵּד וְאֵינָם שֹׁמְעִים לָקַחַת מוּסָר:

לד וַיָּשִׂימוּ שִׁקּוּצֵיהֶם בַּבַּיִת אֲשֶׁר־נִקְרָא־שְׁמִי עָלָיו לְטַמְּאוֹ:

לה וַיִּבְנוּ אֶת־בָּמוֹת הַבַּעַל אֲשֶׁר בְּגֵיא בֶן־הִנֹּם לְהַעֲבִיר אֶת־בְּנֵיהֶם וְאֶת־בְּנוֹתֵיהֶם לַמֹּלֶךְ אֲשֶׁר לֹא־צִוִּיתִים וְלֹא עָלְתָה עַל־לִבִּי לַעֲשׂוֹת הַתּוֹעֵבָה הַזֹּאת לְמַעַן הַחֲטִי [הַחֲטִיא] אֶת־יְהוּדָה:

לו וְעַתָּה לָכֵן כֹּה־אָמַר יְהוָה אֱלֹהֵי יִשְׂרָאֵל אֶל־הָעִיר הַזֹּאת אֲשֶׁר אַתֶּם אֹמְרִים נִתְּנָה בְּיַד מֶלֶךְ־בָּבֶל בַּחֶרֶב וּבָרָעָב וּבַדָּבֶר:

לז הִנְנִי מְקַבְּצָם מִכָּל־הָאֲרָצוֹת אֲשֶׁר הִדַּחְתִּים שָׁם בְּאַפִּי וּבַחֲמָתִי וּבְקֶצֶף גָּדוֹל וַהֲשִׁבֹתִים אֶל־הַמָּקוֹם הַזֶּה וְהֹשַׁבְתִּים לָבֶטַח:

לח וְהָיוּ לִי לְעָם וַאֲנִי אֶהְיֶה לָהֶם לֵאלֹהִים:

Jeremiah

39 I will give them a single heart and a single nature to revere Me for all time, and it shall be well with them and their children after them.

לט וְנָתַתִּי לָהֶם לֵב אֶחָד וְדֶרֶךְ אֶחָד לְיִרְאָה אוֹתִי כָּל־הַיָּמִים לְטוֹב לָהֶם וְלִבְנֵיהֶם אַחֲרֵיהֶם:

40 And I will make an everlasting covenant with them that I will not turn away from them and that I will treat them graciously; and I will put into their hearts reverence for Me, so that they do not turn away from Me.

מ וְכָרַתִּי לָהֶם בְּרִית עוֹלָם אֲשֶׁר לֹא־אָשׁוּב מֵאַחֲרֵיהֶם לְהֵיטִיבִי אוֹתָם וְאֶת־יִרְאָתִי אֶתֵּן בִּלְבָבָם לְבִלְתִּי סוּר מֵעָלָי:

41 I will delight in treating them graciously, and I will plant them in this land faithfully, with all My heart and soul.

מא וְשַׂשְׂתִּי עֲלֵיהֶם לְהֵטִיב אוֹתָם וּנְטַעְתִּים בָּאָרֶץ הַזֹּאת בֶּאֱמֶת בְּכָל־לִבִּי וּבְכָל־נַפְשִׁי:

42 For thus said *Hashem*: As I have brought this terrible disaster upon this people, so I am going to bring upon them the vast good fortune which I have promised for them.

מב כִּי־כֹה אָמַר יְהֹוָה כַּאֲשֶׁר הֵבֵאתִי אֶל־הָעָם הַזֶּה אֵת כָּל־הָרָעָה הַגְּדוֹלָה הַזֹּאת כֵּן אָנֹכִי מֵבִיא עֲלֵיהֶם אֶת־כָּל־הַטּוֹבָה אֲשֶׁר אָנֹכִי דֹּבֵר עֲלֵיהֶם:

43 And fields shall again be purchased in this land of which you say, "It is a desolation, without man or beast; it is delivered into the hands of the Chaldeans."

מג וְנִקְנָה הַשָּׂדֶה בָּאָרֶץ הַזֹּאת אֲשֶׁר אַתֶּם אֹמְרִים שְׁמָמָה הִיא מֵאֵין אָדָם וּבְהֵמָה נִתְּנָה בְּיַד הַכַּשְׂדִּים:

44 Fields shall be purchased, and deeds written and sealed, and witnesses called in the land of *Binyamin* and in the environs of *Yerushalayim*, and in the towns of *Yehuda*; the towns of the hill country, the towns of the Shephelah, and the towns of the *Negev*. For I will restore their fortunes – declares *Hashem*.

מד שָׂדוֹת בַּכֶּסֶף יִקְנוּ וְכָתוֹב בַּסֵּפֶר וְחָתוֹם וְהָעֵד עֵדִים בְּאֶרֶץ בִּנְיָמִן וּבִסְבִיבֵי יְרוּשָׁלִַם וּבְעָרֵי יְהוּדָה וּבְעָרֵי הָהָר וּבְעָרֵי הַשְּׁפֵלָה וּבְעָרֵי הַנֶּגֶב כִּי־אָשִׁיב אֶת־שְׁבוּתָם נְאֻם־יְהֹוָה:

33 1 The word of *Hashem* came to *Yirmiyahu* a second time, while he was still confined in the prison compound, as follows:

לג א וַיְהִי דְבַר־יְהֹוָה אֶל־יִרְמְיָהוּ שֵׁנִית וְהוּא עוֹדֶנּוּ עָצוּר בַּחֲצַר הַמַּטָּרָה לֵאמֹר:

2 Thus said *Hashem* who is planning it, *Hashem* who is shaping it to bring it about, Whose name is *Hashem*:

ב כֹּה־אָמַר יְהֹוָה עֹשָׂהּ יְהֹוָה יוֹצֵר אוֹתָהּ לַהֲכִינָהּ יְהֹוָה שְׁמוֹ:

3 Call to Me, and I will answer you, And I will tell you wondrous things, Secrets you have not known.

ג קְרָא אֵלַי וְאֶעֱנֶךָּ וְאַגִּידָה לְּךָ גְּדֹלוֹת וּבְצֻרוֹת לֹא יְדַעְתָּם:

4 For thus said *Hashem*, the God of *Yisrael*, concerning the houses of this city and the palaces of the kings of *Yehuda* that were torn down for [defense] against the siegemounds and against the sword,

ד כִּי כֹה אָמַר יְהֹוָה אֱלֹהֵי יִשְׂרָאֵל עַל־בָּתֵּי הָעִיר הַזֹּאת וְעַל־בָּתֵּי מַלְכֵי יְהוּדָה הַנְּתֻצִים אֶל־הַסֹּלְלוֹת וְאֶל־הֶחָרֶב:

5 and were filled by those who went to fight the Chaldeans, – with the corpses of the men whom I struck down in My anger and rage, hiding My face from this city because of all their wickedness:

ה בָּאִים לְהִלָּחֵם אֶת־הַכַּשְׂדִּים וּלְמַלְאָם אֶת־פִּגְרֵי הָאָדָם אֲשֶׁר־הִכֵּיתִי בְאַפִּי וּבַחֲמָתִי וַאֲשֶׁר הִסְתַּרְתִּי פָנַי מֵהָעִיר הַזֹּאת עַל כָּל־רָעָתָם:

Jeremiah

6 I am going to bring her relief and healing. I will heal them and reveal to them abundance of true favor.

7 And I will restore the fortunes of *Yehuda* and *Yisrael*, and I will rebuild them as of old.

8 And I will purge them of all the sins which they committed against Me, and I will pardon all the sins which they committed against Me, by which they rebelled against Me.

9 And she shall gain through Me renown, joy, fame, and glory above all the nations on earth, when they hear of all the good fortune I provide for them. They will thrill and quiver because of all the good fortune and all the prosperity that I provide for her.

10 Thus said *Hashem*: Again there shall be heard in this place, which you say is ruined, without man or beast – in the towns of *Yehuda* and the streets of *Yerushalayim* that are desolate, without man, without inhabitants, without beast –

11 the sound of mirth and gladness, the voice of bridegroom and bride, the voice of those who cry, "Give thanks to the Lord of Hosts, for *Hashem* is good, for His kindness is everlasting!" as they bring thanksgiving offerings to the House of *Hashem*. For I will restore the fortunes of the land as of old – said *Hashem*.

ו הִנְנִי מַעֲלֶה־לָּהּ אֲרֻכָה וּמַרְפֵּא וּרְפָאתִים וְגִלֵּיתִי לָהֶם עֲתֶרֶת שָׁלוֹם וֶאֱמֶת:

ז וַהֲשִׁבֹתִי אֶת־שְׁבוּת יְהוּדָה וְאֵת שְׁבוּת יִשְׂרָאֵל וּבְנִתִים כְּבָרִאשֹׁנָה:

ח וְטִהַרְתִּים מִכָּל־עֲוֺנָם אֲשֶׁר חָטְאוּ־לִי וְסָלַחְתִּי לכול־[לְכָל־] עֲוֺנוֹתֵיהֶם אֲשֶׁר חָטְאוּ־לִי וַאֲשֶׁר פָּשְׁעוּ בִי:

ט וְהָיְתָה לִי לְשֵׁם שָׂשׂוֹן לִתְהִלָּה וּלְתִפְאֶרֶת לְכֹל גּוֹיֵי הָאָרֶץ אֲשֶׁר יִשְׁמְעוּ אֶת־כָּל־הַטּוֹבָה אֲשֶׁר אָנֹכִי עֹשֶׂה אֹתָם וּפָחֲדוּ וְרָגְזוּ עַל כָּל־הַטּוֹבָה וְעַל כָּל־הַשָּׁלוֹם אֲשֶׁר אָנֹכִי עֹשֶׂה לָּהּ:

י כֹּה אָמַר יְהוָה עוֹד יִשָּׁמַע בַּמָּקוֹם־הַזֶּה אֲשֶׁר אַתֶּם אֹמְרִים חָרֵב הוּא מֵאֵין אָדָם וּמֵאֵין בְּהֵמָה בְּעָרֵי יְהוּדָה וּבְחֻצוֹת יְרוּשָׁלַיִם הַנְשַׁמּוֹת מֵאֵין אָדָם וּמֵאֵין יוֹשֵׁב וּמֵאֵין בְּהֵמָה:

יא קוֹל שָׂשׂוֹן וְקוֹל שִׂמְחָה קוֹל חָתָן וְקוֹל כַּלָּה קוֹל אֹמְרִים הוֹדוּ אֶת־יְהוָה צְבָאוֹת כִּי־טוֹב יְהוָה כִּי־לְעוֹלָם חַסְדּוֹ מְבִאִים תּוֹדָה בֵּית יְהוָה כִּי־אָשִׁיב אֶת־שְׁבוּת־הָאָרֶץ כְּבָרִאשֹׁנָה אָמַר יְהוָה:

KOL sa-SON v'-KOL sim-KHAH KOL kha-TAN v'-KOL ka-LAH
KOL o-m'-REEM ho-DU et a-do-NAI tz'-va-OT kee TOV a-do-NAI
kee l'-o-LAM khas-DO m'-vee-EEM to-DAH BAYT a-do-NAI kee
a-SHEEV et sh'-vut ha-A-retz k'-va-ree-sho-NAH a-MAR a-do-NAI

12 Thus said the Lord of Hosts: In this ruined place, without man and beast, and in all its towns, there shall again be a pasture for shepherds, where they can rest their flocks.

יב כֹּה־אָמַר יְהוָה צְבָאוֹת עוֹד יִהְיֶה בַּמָּקוֹם הַזֶּה הֶחָרֵב מֵאֵין־אָדָם וְעַד־בְּהֵמָה וּבְכָל־עָרָיו נְוֵה רֹעִים מַרְבִּצִים צֹאן:

שָׂשׂוֹן
שִׂמְחָה

א **33:11 The sound of mirth and gladness** The *Torah* never uses extraneous words and every Hebrew letter of the *Tanakh* has infinite meaning. If so, why does this verse use two different expressions to connote happiness: *Sasson* (שָׂשׂוֹן), 'mirth,' and *simcha* (שִׂמְחָה), 'gladness'? According to Rabbi Mordechai Willig, *sasson* is the enduring happy feeling of satisfaction and fulfillment. *Simcha*, on the other hand, refers to an exuberant but temporary experience of joy, felt on special occasions. The feeling of *simcha* is more intense but short lived, while *sasson* is less powerful but persists endlessly.

Yirmiyahu promises that one day the Land of Israel will be filled with the sweet sounds of both *sas-son* and *simcha*. Not only will there be intense gladness over the redemption, but the people will experience the long-lasting joy of dwelling permanently in *Eretz Yisrael* in the presence of God.

Jubilant residents celebrating the UN decision on the partition of Palestine, *Tel Aviv*, 1947

13 In the towns of the hill country, in the towns of
the Shephelah, and in the towns of the *Negev*,
in the land of *Binyamin* and in the environs of
Yerushalayim and in the towns of *Yehuda*, sheep
shall pass again under the hands of one who counts
them – said *Hashem*.

יג בְּעָרֵי הָהָר בְּעָרֵי הַשְּׁפֵלָה וּבְעָרֵי הַנֶּגֶב
וּבְאֶרֶץ בִּנְיָמִן וּבִסְבִיבֵי יְרוּשָׁלַ͏ִם וּבְעָרֵי
יְהוּדָה עֹד תַּעֲבֹרְנָה הַצֹּאן עַל־יְדֵי מוֹנֶה
אָמַר יְהוָֹה:

14 See, days are coming – declares *Hashem* – when I
will fulfill the promise that I made concerning the
House of *Yisrael* and the House of *Yehuda*.

יד הִנֵּה יָמִים בָּאִים נְאֻם־יְהוָֹה וַהֲקִמֹתִי
אֶת־הַדָּבָר הַטּוֹב אֲשֶׁר דִּבַּרְתִּי אֶל־בֵּית
יִשְׂרָאֵל וְעַל־בֵּית יְהוּדָה:

15 In those days and at that time, I will raise up a true
branch of *David*'s line, and he shall do what is just
and right in the land.

טו בַּיָּמִים הָהֵם וּבָעֵת הַהִיא אַצְמִיחַ לְדָוִד
צֶמַח צְדָקָה וְעָשָׂה מִשְׁפָּט וּצְדָקָה
בָּאָרֶץ:

16 In those days *Yehuda* shall be delivered and *Yisrael*
shall dwell secure. And this is what she shall be
called: "*Hashem* is our Vindicator."

טז בַּיָּמִים הָהֵם תִּוָּשַׁע יְהוּדָה וִירוּשָׁלַ͏ִם
תִּשְׁכּוֹן לָבֶטַח וְזֶה אֲשֶׁר־יִקְרָא־לָהּ יְהוָֹה
צִדְקֵנוּ:

17 For thus said *Hashem*: There shall never be an end
to men of *David*'s line who sit upon the throne of
the House of *Yisrael*.

יז כִּי־כֹה אָמַר יְהוָֹה לֹא־יִכָּרֵת לְדָוִד אִישׁ
יֹשֵׁב עַל־כִּסֵּא בֵית־יִשְׂרָאֵל:

18 Nor shall there ever be an end to the line of the
levitical *Kohanim* before Me, of those who present
burnt offerings and turn the meal offering to smoke
and perform sacrifices.

יח וְלַכֹּהֲנִים הַלְוִיִּם לֹא־יִכָּרֵת אִישׁ מִלְּפָנָי
מַעֲלֶה עוֹלָה וּמַקְטִיר מִנְחָה וְעֹשֶׂה־זֶּבַח
כָּל־הַיָּמִים:

19 The word of *Hashem* came to *Yirmiyahu*:

יט וַיְהִי דְּבַר־יְהוָֹה אֶל־יִרְמְיָהוּ לֵאמוֹר:

20 Thus said *Hashem*: If you could break My covenant
with the day and My covenant with the night, so
that day and night should not come at their proper
time,

כ כֹּה אָמַר יְהוָֹה אִם־תָּפֵרוּ אֶת־בְּרִיתִי
הַיּוֹם וְאֶת־בְּרִיתִי הַלָּיְלָה וּלְבִלְתִּי הֱיוֹת
יוֹמָם־וָלַיְלָה בְּעִתָּם:

21 only then could My covenant with My servant
David be broken – so that he would not have a
descendant reigning upon his throne – or with My
ministrants, the levitical *Kohanim*.

כא גַּם־בְּרִיתִי תֻפַר אֶת־דָּוִד עַבְדִּי מִהְיוֹת־
לוֹ בֵן מֹלֵךְ עַל־כִּסְאוֹ וְאֶת־הַלְוִיִּם
הַכֹּהֲנִים מְשָׁרְתָי:

22 Like the host of heaven which cannot be counted,
and the sand of the sea which cannot be measured,
so will I multiply the offspring of My servant
David, and of the *Leviim* who minister to Me.

כב אֲשֶׁר לֹא־יִסָּפֵר צְבָא הַשָּׁמַיִם וְלֹא יִמַּד
חוֹל הַיָּם כֵּן אַרְבֶּה אֶת־זֶרַע דָּוִד עַבְדִּי
וְאֶת־הַלְוִיִּם מְשָׁרְתֵי אֹתִי:

23 The word of *Hashem* came to *Yirmiyahu*:

כג וַיְהִי דְּבַר־יְהוָֹה אֶל־יִרְמְיָהוּ לֵאמֹר:

24 You see what this people said: "The two families
which *Hashem* chose have now been rejected by
Him." Thus they despise My people, and regard
them as no longer a nation.

כד הֲלוֹא רָאִיתָ מָה־הָעָם הַזֶּה דִּבְּרוּ לֵאמֹר
שְׁתֵּי הַמִּשְׁפָּחוֹת אֲשֶׁר בָּחַר יְהוָֹה בָּהֶם
וַיִּמְאָסֵם וְאֶת־עַמִּי יִנְאָצוּן מִהְיוֹת עוֹד
גּוֹי לִפְנֵיהֶם:

25 Thus said *Hashem*: As surely as I have established
My covenant with day and night – the laws of
heaven and earth –

כה כֹּה אָמַר יְהוָֹה אִם־לֹא בְרִיתִי יוֹמָם
וָלָיְלָה חֻקּוֹת שָׁמַיִם וָאָרֶץ לֹא־שָׂמְתִּי:

26 so I will never reject the offspring of *Yaakov* and My servant *David*; I will never fail to take from his offspring rulers for the descendants of *Avraham*, *Yitzchak*, and *Yaakov*. Indeed, I will restore their fortunes and take them back in love.

כו גַּם־זֶרַע יַעֲקוֹב וְדָוִד עַבְדִּי אֶמְאַס מִקַּחַת מִזַּרְעוֹ מֹשְׁלִים אֶל־זֶרַע אַבְרָהָם יִשְׂחָק וְיַעֲקֹב כִּי־[אָשׁוּב] אָשִׁיב אֶת־שְׁבוּתָם וְרִחַמְתִּים:

34 1 The word which came to *Yirmiyahu* from *Hashem*, when King Nebuchadrezzar of Babylon and all his army, and all the kingdoms of the earth and all the peoples under his sway, were waging war against *Yerushalayim* and all its towns:

לד א הַדָּבָר אֲשֶׁר־הָיָה אֶל־יִרְמְיָהוּ מֵאֵת יְהֹוָה וּנְבוּכַדְרֶאצַּר מֶלֶךְ־בָּבֶל וְכָל־חֵילוֹ וְכָל־מַמְלְכוֹת אֶרֶץ מֶמְשֶׁלֶת יָדוֹ וְכָל־הָעַמִּים נִלְחָמִים עַל־יְרוּשָׁלַ͏ִם וְעַל־כָּל־עָרֶיהָ לֵאמֹר:

2 Thus said *Hashem*, the God of *Yisrael*: Go speak to King *Tzidkiyahu* of *Yehuda*, and say to him: "Thus said *Hashem*: I am going to deliver this city into the hands of the king of Babylon, and he will destroy it by fire.

ב כֹּה־אָמַר יְהֹוָה אֱלֹהֵי יִשְׂרָאֵל הָלֹךְ וְאָמַרְתָּ אֶל־צִדְקִיָּהוּ מֶלֶךְ יְהוּדָה וְאָמַרְתָּ אֵלָיו כֹּה אָמַר יְהֹוָה הִנְנִי נֹתֵן אֶת־הָעִיר הַזֹּאת בְּיַד מֶלֶךְ־בָּבֶל וּשְׂרָפָהּ בָּאֵשׁ:

3 And you will not escape from him; you will be captured and handed over to him. And you will see the king of Babylon face to face and speak to him in person; and you will be brought to Babylon.

ג וְאַתָּה לֹא תִמָּלֵט מִיָּדוֹ כִּי תָּפֹשׂ תִּתָּפֵשׂ וּבְיָדוֹ תִּנָּתֵן וְעֵינֶיךָ אֶת־עֵינֵי מֶלֶךְ־בָּבֶל תִּרְאֶינָה וּפִיהוּ אֶת־פִּיךָ יְדַבֵּר וּבָבֶל תָּבוֹא:

4 But hear the word of *Hashem*, O King *Tzidkiyahu* of *Yehuda*! Thus said *Hashem* concerning you: You will not die by the sword.

ד אַךְ שְׁמַע דְּבַר־יְהֹוָה צִדְקִיָּהוּ מֶלֶךְ יְהוּדָה כֹּה־אָמַר יְהֹוָה עָלֶיךָ לֹא תָמוּת בֶּחָרֶב:

5 You will die a peaceful death; and as incense was burned for your ancestors, the earlier kings who preceded you, so they will burn incense for you, and they will lament for you 'Ah, lord!' For I Myself have made the promise – declares *Hashem*."

ה בְּשָׁלוֹם תָּמוּת וּכְמִשְׂרְפוֹת אֲבוֹתֶיךָ הַמְּלָכִים הָרִאשֹׁנִים אֲשֶׁר־הָיוּ לְפָנֶיךָ כֵּן יִשְׂרְפוּ־לָךְ וְהוֹי אָדוֹן יִסְפְּדוּ־לָךְ כִּי־דָבָר אֲנִי־דִבַּרְתִּי נְאֻם־יְהֹוָה:

6 The *Navi Yirmiyahu* spoke all these words to King *Tzidkiyahu* of *Yehuda* in *Yerushalayim*,

ו וַיְדַבֵּר יִרְמְיָהוּ הַנָּבִיא אֶל־צִדְקִיָּהוּ מֶלֶךְ יְהוּדָה אֵת כָּל־הַדְּבָרִים הָאֵלֶּה בִּירוּשָׁלָ͏ִם:

7 when the army of the king of Babylon was waging war against *Yerushalayim* and against the remaining towns of *Yehuda* – against *Lachish* and *Azeika*, for they were the only fortified towns of *Yehuda* that were left.

ז וְחֵיל מֶלֶךְ־בָּבֶל נִלְחָמִים עַל־יְרוּשָׁלַ͏ִם וְעַל כָּל־עָרֵי יְהוּדָה הַנּוֹתָרוֹת אֶל־לָכִישׁ וְאֶל־עֲזֵקָה כִּי הֵנָּה נִשְׁאֲרוּ בְּעָרֵי יְהוּדָה עָרֵי מִבְצָר:

8 The word which came to *Yirmiyahu* from *Hashem* after King *Tzidkiyahu* had made a covenant with all the people in *Yerushalayim* to proclaim a release among them –

ח הַדָּבָר אֲשֶׁר־הָיָה אֶל־יִרְמְיָהוּ מֵאֵת יְהֹוָה אַחֲרֵי כְּרֹת הַמֶּלֶךְ צִדְקִיָּהוּ בְּרִית אֶת־כָּל־הָעָם אֲשֶׁר בִּירוּשָׁלַ͏ִם לִקְרֹא לָהֶם דְּרוֹר:

9 that everyone should set free his Hebrew slaves, both male and female, and that no one should keep his fellow Judean enslaved.

ט לְשַׁלַּח אִישׁ אֶת־עַבְדּוֹ וְאִישׁ אֶת־שִׁפְחָתוֹ הָעִבְרִי וְהָעִבְרִיָּה חָפְשִׁים לְבִלְתִּי עֲבָד־בָּם בִּיהוּדִי אָחִיהוּ אִישׁ:

10 Everyone, officials and people, who had entered into the covenant agreed to set their male and female slaves free and not keep them enslaved any longer; they complied and let them go.

וַיִּשְׁמְעוּ כָל־הַשָּׂרִים וְכָל־הָעָם אֲשֶׁר־בָּאוּ בַבְּרִית לְשַׁלַּח אִישׁ אֶת־עַבְדּוֹ וְאִישׁ אֶת־שִׁפְחָתוֹ חָפְשִׁים לְבִלְתִּי עֲבָד־בָּם עוֹד וַיִּשְׁמְעוּ וַיְשַׁלֵּחוּ: י

11 But afterward they turned about and brought back the men and women they had set free, and forced them into slavery again.

וַיָּשׁוּבוּ אַחֲרֵי־כֵן וַיָּשִׁבוּ אֶת־הָעֲבָדִים וְאֶת־הַשְּׁפָחוֹת אֲשֶׁר שִׁלְּחוּ חָפְשִׁים ויכבישום [וַיִּכְבְּשׁוּם] לַעֲבָדִים וְלִשְׁפָחוֹת: יא

12 Then it was that the word of *Hashem* came to *Yirmiyahu* from *Hashem*:

וַיְהִי דְבַר־יְהֹוָה אֶל־יִרְמְיָהוּ מֵאֵת יְהֹוָה לֵאמֹר: יב

13 Thus said *Hashem*, the God of *Yisrael*: I made a covenant with your fathers when I brought them out of the land of Egypt, the house of bondage, saying:

כֹּה־אָמַר יְהֹוָה אֱלֹהֵי יִשְׂרָאֵל אָנֹכִי כָּרַתִּי בְרִית אֶת־אֲבוֹתֵיכֶם בְּיוֹם הוֹצִאִי אוֹתָם מֵאֶרֶץ מִצְרַיִם מִבֵּית עֲבָדִים לֵאמֹר: יג

14 "In the seventh year each of you must let go any fellow Hebrew who may be sold to you; when he has served you six years, you must set him free." But your fathers would not obey Me or give ear.

מִקֵּץ שֶׁבַע שָׁנִים תְּשַׁלְּחוּ אִישׁ אֶת־אָחִיו הָעִבְרִי אֲשֶׁר־יִמָּכֵר לְךָ וַעֲבָדְךָ שֵׁשׁ שָׁנִים וְשִׁלַּחְתּוֹ חָפְשִׁי מֵעִמָּךְ וְלֹא־שָׁמְעוּ אֲבוֹתֵיכֶם אֵלַי וְלֹא הִטּוּ אֶת־אָזְנָם: יד

15 Lately you turned about and did what is proper in My sight, and each of you proclaimed a release to his countrymen; and you made a covenant accordingly before Me in the House which bears My name.

וַתָּשֻׁבוּ אַתֶּם הַיּוֹם וַתַּעֲשׂוּ אֶת־הַיָּשָׁר בְּעֵינַי לִקְרֹא דְרוֹר אִישׁ לְרֵעֵהוּ וַתִּכְרְתוּ בְרִית לְפָנַי בַּבַּיִת אֲשֶׁר־נִקְרָא שְׁמִי עָלָיו: טו

16 But now you have turned back and have profaned My name; each of you has brought back the men and women whom you had given their freedom, and forced them to be your slaves again.

וַתָּשֻׁבוּ וַתְּחַלְּלוּ אֶת־שְׁמִי וַתָּשִׁבוּ אִישׁ אֶת־עַבְדּוֹ וְאִישׁ אֶת־שִׁפְחָתוֹ אֲשֶׁר־שִׁלַּחְתֶּם חָפְשִׁים לְנַפְשָׁם וַתִּכְבְּשׁוּ אֹתָם לִהְיוֹת לָכֶם לַעֲבָדִים וְלִשְׁפָחוֹת: טז

17 Assuredly, thus said *Hashem*: You would not obey Me and proclaim a release, each to his kinsman and countryman. Lo! I proclaim your release – declares *Hashem* – to the sword, to pestilence, and to famine; and I will make you a horror to all the kingdoms of the earth.

לָכֵן כֹּה־אָמַר יְהֹוָה אַתֶּם לֹא־שְׁמַעְתֶּם אֵלַי לִקְרֹא דְרוֹר אִישׁ לְאָחִיו וְאִישׁ לְרֵעֵהוּ הִנְנִי קֹרֵא לָכֶם דְּרוֹר נְאֻם־יְהֹוָה אֶל־הַחֶרֶב אֶל־הַדֶּבֶר וְאֶל־הָרָעָב וְנָתַתִּי אֶתְכֶם לזועה [לְזַעֲוָה] לְכֹל מַמְלְכוֹת הָאָרֶץ: יז

la-KHAYN koh a-MAR a-do-NAI a-TEM lo sh'-ma-TEM ay-LAI lik-RO
d'-ROR EESH l'-a-KHEEV v'-EESH l'-ray-AY-hu hi-n'-NEE ko-RAY
la-KHEM d'-ROR n'-um a-do-NAI el ha-KHE-rev el ha-DE-ver v'-el ha-ra-AV
v'-na-ta-TEE et-KHEM l'-za-a-VAH l'-KHOL mam-l'-KHOT ha-A-retz

Jeremiah

34:17 You would not obey Me and proclaim a release With the Babylonian onslaught, the nobility and landowners made a covenant with the people to release all the slaves and workers from their servitude. Once the threat receded temporarily, they reneged on their promise and re-enslaved the poor workers. God declares this

18 I will make the men who violated My covenant, who did not fulfill the terms of the covenant which they made before Me, [like] the calf which they cut in two so as to pass between the halves:

יח וְנָתַתִּי אֶת־הָאֲנָשִׁים הָעֹבְרִים אֶת־בְּרִתִי אֲשֶׁר לֹא־הֵקִימוּ אֶת־דִּבְרֵי הַבְּרִית אֲשֶׁר כָּרְתוּ לְפָנָי הָעֵגֶל אֲשֶׁר כָּרְתוּ לִשְׁנַיִם וַיַּעַבְרוּ בֵּין בְּתָרָיו:

19 The officers of *Yehuda* and *Yerushalayim*, the officials, the *Kohanim*, and all the people of the land who passed between the halves of the calf

יט שָׂרֵי יְהוּדָה וְשָׂרֵי יְרוּשָׁלַם הַסָּרִסִים וְהַכֹּהֲנִים וְכֹל עַם הָאָרֶץ הָעֹבְרִים בֵּין בְּתָרֵי הָעֵגֶל:

20 shall be handed over to their enemies, to those who seek to kill them. Their carcasses shall become food for the birds of the sky and the beasts of the earth.

כ וְנָתַתִּי אוֹתָם בְּיַד אֹיְבֵיהֶם וּבְיַד מְבַקְשֵׁי נַפְשָׁם וְהָיְתָה נִבְלָתָם לְמַאֲכָל לְעוֹף הַשָּׁמַיִם וּלְבֶהֱמַת הָאָרֶץ:

21 I will hand over King *Tzidkiyahu* of *Yehuda* and his officers to their enemies, who seek to kill them – to the army of the king of Babylon which has withdrawn from you.

כא וְאֶת־צִדְקִיָּהוּ מֶלֶךְ־יְהוּדָה וְאֶת־שָׂרָיו אֶתֵּן בְּיַד אֹיְבֵיהֶם וּבְיַד מְבַקְשֵׁי נַפְשָׁם וּבְיַד חֵיל מֶלֶךְ בָּבֶל הָעֹלִים מֵעֲלֵיכֶם:

22 I hereby give the command – declares *Hashem* – by which I will bring them back against this city. They shall attack it and capture it, and burn it down. I will make the towns of *Yehuda* a desolation, without inhabitant.

כב הִנְנִי מְצַוֶּה נְאֻם־יְהוָה וַהֲשִׁבֹתִים אֶל־הָעִיר הַזֹּאת וְנִלְחֲמוּ עָלֶיהָ וּלְכָדוּהָ וּשְׂרָפֻהָ בָאֵשׁ וְאֶת־עָרֵי יְהוּדָה אֶתֵּן שְׁמָמָה מֵאֵין יֹשֵׁב:

35 **1** The word which came to *Yirmiyahu* from *Hashem* in the days of King *Yehoyakim* son of *Yoshiyahu* of *Yehuda*:

לה א הַדָּבָר אֲשֶׁר־הָיָה אֶל־יִרְמְיָהוּ מֵאֵת יְהוָה בִּימֵי יְהוֹיָקִים בֶּן־יֹאשִׁיָּהוּ מֶלֶךְ יְהוּדָה לֵאמֹר:

2 Go to the house of the Rechabites and speak to them, and bring them to the House of *Hashem*, to one of the chambers, and give them wine to drink.

ב הָלוֹךְ אֶל־בֵּית הָרֵכָבִים וְדִבַּרְתָּ אוֹתָם וַהֲבִאוֹתָם בֵּית יְהוָה אֶל־אַחַת הַלְּשָׁכוֹת וְהִשְׁקִיתָ אוֹתָם יָיִן:

ha-LOKH el BAYT ha-ray-kha-VEEM v'-di-bar-TA o-TAM va-ha-vi-o-TAM BAYT a-do-NAI el a-KHAT ha-l'-sha-KHOT v'-hish-kee-TA o-TAM YA-yin

3 So I took Jaazaniah son of *Yirmiyahu* son of Habazziniah, and his brothers, all his sons, and the whole household of the Rechabites;

ג וָאֶקַּח אֶת־יַאֲזַנְיָה בֶן־יִרְמְיָהוּ בֶּן־חֲבַצִּנְיָה וְאֶת־אֶחָיו וְאֶת־כָּל־בָּנָיו וְאֵת כָּל־בֵּית הָרֵכָבִים:

An Israeli vineyard at sunset

injustice intolerable. He freed the Jewish people from Egyptian servitude so that they would dwell as a free nation in the Land of Israel, living up to the highest standards of ethics and morality. However, should they begin to enslave others or engage in other unscrupulous or deceptive behavior, *Hashem* will give the nations of the world the freedom to strike, and they will once again become slaves to foreigners.

35:2 Go to the house of the Rechabites *Yirmiyahu* wishes to demonstrate the meaning of true fidelity and loyalty. He brings the tribe of the Rechabites, descendants of Jethro, into the *Beit Hamikdash* and offers them wine. They refuse, explaining that they live by a set of laws passed down from generation to generation, including prohibitions against planting vineyards or drinking wine. Their loyal behavior offers a subtle rebuke to the wayward People of Israel.

4 and I brought them to the House of *Hashem*, to the
chamber of the sons of Hanan son of Igdaliah, the
man of *Hashem*, which is next to the chamber of
the officials and above the chamber of Maaseiah
son of *Shalum*, the guardian of the threshold.

ד וָאָבִא אֹתָם בֵּית יְהֹוָה אֶל־לִשְׁכַּת בְּנֵי
חָנָן בֶּן־יִגְדַּלְיָהוּ אִישׁ הָאֱלֹהִים אֲשֶׁר־
אֵצֶל לִשְׁכַּת הַשָּׂרִים אֲשֶׁר מִמַּעַל
לְלִשְׁכַּת מַעֲשֵׂיָהוּ בֶן־שַׁלֻּם שֹׁמֵר הַסַּף:

5 I set bowls full of wine and cups before the men
of the house of the Rechabites, and said to them,
"Have some wine."

ה וָאֶתֵּן לִפְנֵי בְּנֵי בֵית־הָרֵכָבִים גְּבִעִים
מְלֵאִים יַיִן וְכֹסוֹת וָאֹמַר אֲלֵיהֶם שְׁתוּ־
יָיִן:

6 They replied, "We will not drink wine, for our
ancestor, *Yonadav* son of Rechab, commanded
us: 'You shall never drink wine, either you or your
children.

ו וַיֹּאמְרוּ לֹא נִשְׁתֶּה־יָּיִן כִּי יוֹנָדָב בֶּן־רֵכָב
אָבִינוּ צִוָּה עָלֵינוּ לֵאמֹר לֹא תִשְׁתּוּ־יַיִן
אַתֶּם וּבְנֵיכֶם עַד־עוֹלָם:

7 Nor shall you build houses or sow fields or plant
vineyards, nor shall you own such things; but you
shall live in tents all your days, so that you may live
long upon the land where you sojourn.'

ז וּבַיִת לֹא־תִבְנוּ וְזֶרַע לֹא־תִזְרָעוּ וְכֶרֶם
לֹא־תִטָּעוּ וְלֹא יִהְיֶה לָכֶם כִּי בָּאֳהָלִים
תֵּשְׁבוּ כָּל־יְמֵיכֶם לְמַעַן תִּחְיוּ יָמִים
רַבִּים עַל־פְּנֵי הָאֲדָמָה אֲשֶׁר אַתֶּם גָּרִים
שָׁם:

8 And we have obeyed our ancestor *Yonadav* son
of Rechab in all that he commanded us: we never
drink wine, neither we nor our wives nor our sons
and daughters.

ח וַנִּשְׁמַע בְּקוֹל יְהוֹנָדָב בֶּן־רֵכָב אָבִינוּ
לְכֹל אֲשֶׁר צִוָּנוּ לְבִלְתִּי שְׁתוֹת־יַיִן כָּל־
יָמֵינוּ אֲנַחְנוּ נָשֵׁינוּ בָּנֵינוּ וּבְנֹתֵינוּ:

9 Nor do we build houses to live in, and we do not
own vineyards or fields for sowing;

ט וּלְבִלְתִּי בְּנוֹת בָּתִּים לְשִׁבְתֵּנוּ וְכֶרֶם
וְשָׂדֶה וָזֶרַע לֹא יִהְיֶה־לָּנוּ:

10 but we live in tents. We have obeyed and done all
that our ancestor *Yonadav* commanded us.

י וַנֵּשֶׁב בָּאֳהָלִים וַנִּשְׁמַע וַנַּעַשׂ כְּכֹל
אֲשֶׁר־צִוָּנוּ יוֹנָדָב אָבִינוּ:

11 But when King Nebuchadrezzar of Babylon
invaded the country, we said, 'Come, let us go into
Yerushalayim because of the army of the Chaldeans
and the army of Aram.' And so we are living in
Yerushalayim."

יא וַיְהִי בַּעֲלוֹת נְבוּכַדְרֶאצַּר מֶלֶךְ־בָּבֶל אֶל־
הָאָרֶץ וַנֹּאמֶר בֹּאוּ וְנָבוֹא יְרוּשָׁלַםִ מִפְּנֵי
חֵיל הַכַּשְׂדִּים וּמִפְּנֵי חֵיל אֲרָם וַנֵּשֶׁב
בִּירוּשָׁלָםִ:

12 Then the word of *Hashem* came to *Yirmiyahu*:

יב וַיְהִי דְּבַר־יְהֹוָה אֶל־יִרְמְיָהוּ לֵאמֹר:

13 Thus said the LORD of Hosts, the God of *Yisrael*:
Go say to the men of *Yehuda* and the inhabitants of
Yerushalayim: "You can learn a lesson [here] about
obeying My commands – declares *Hashem*.

יג כֹּה־אָמַר יְהֹוָה צְבָאוֹת אֱלֹהֵי יִשְׂרָאֵל
הָלֹךְ וְאָמַרְתָּ לְאִישׁ יְהוּדָה וּלְיוֹשְׁבֵי
יְרוּשָׁלָםִ הֲלוֹא תִקְחוּ מוּסָר לִשְׁמֹעַ אֶל־
דְּבָרַי נְאֻם־יְהֹוָה:

14 The commands of *Yonadav* son of Rechab have
been fulfilled: he charged his children not to
drink wine, and to this day they have not drunk,
in obedience to the charge of their ancestor. But I
spoke to you persistently, and you did not listen to
Me.

יד הוּקַם אֶת־דִּבְרֵי יְהוֹנָדָב בֶּן־רֵכָב אֲשֶׁר־
צִוָּה אֶת־בָּנָיו לְבִלְתִּי שְׁתוֹת־יַיִן וְלֹא
שָׁתוּ עַד־הַיּוֹם הַזֶּה כִּי שָׁמְעוּ אֵת
מִצְוַת אֲבִיהֶם וְאָנֹכִי דִּבַּרְתִּי אֲלֵיכֶם
הַשְׁכֵּם וְדַבֵּר וְלֹא שְׁמַעְתֶּם אֵלָי:

¹⁵ I persistently sent you all My servants, the *Neviim*, to say: 'Turn back, every one of you, from your wicked ways and mend your deeds; do not follow other gods or serve them. Then you may remain on the land that I gave to you and your fathers.' But you did not give ear or listen to Me.

טו וָאֶשְׁלַח אֲלֵיכֶם אֶת־כָּל־עֲבָדַי הַנְּבִאִים הַשְׁכֵּים וְשָׁלֹחַ לֵאמֹר שֻׁבוּ־נָא אִישׁ מִדַּרְכּוֹ הָרָעָה וְהֵיטִיבוּ מַעַלְלֵיכֶם וְאַל־תֵּלְכוּ אַחֲרֵי אֱלֹהִים אֲחֵרִים לְעָבְדָם וּשְׁבוּ אֶל־הָאֲדָמָה אֲשֶׁר־נָתַתִּי לָכֶם וְלַאֲבֹתֵיכֶם וְלֹא הִטִּיתֶם אֶת־אָזְנְכֶם וְלֹא שְׁמַעְתֶּם אֵלָי:

¹⁶ The family of *Yonadav* son of *Rechab* have indeed fulfilled the charge which their ancestor gave them; but this people has not listened to Me.

טז כִּי הֵקִימוּ בְּנֵי יְהוֹנָדָב בֶּן־רֵכָב אֶת־מִצְוַת אֲבִיהֶם אֲשֶׁר צִוָּם וְהָעָם הַזֶּה לֹא שָׁמְעוּ אֵלָי:

¹⁷ Assuredly, thus said *Hashem*, the the Lord of Hosts, the God of *Yisrael*: I am going to bring upon *Yehuda* and upon all the inhabitants of *Yerushalayim* all the disaster with which I have threatened them; for I spoke to them, but they would not listen; I called to them, but they would not respond."

יז לָכֵן כֹּה־אָמַר יְהֹוָה אֱלֹהֵי צְבָאוֹת אֱלֹהֵי יִשְׂרָאֵל הִנְנִי מֵבִיא אֶל־יְהוּדָה וְאֶל כָּל־יוֹשְׁבֵי יְרוּשָׁלַם אֵת כָּל־הָרָעָה אֲשֶׁר דִּבַּרְתִּי עֲלֵיהֶם יַעַן דִּבַּרְתִּי אֲלֵיהֶם וְלֹא שָׁמֵעוּ וָאֶקְרָא לָהֶם וְלֹא עָנוּ:

¹⁸ And to the family of the Rechabites *Yirmiyahu* said: "Thus said the Lord of Hosts, the God of *Yisrael*: Because you have obeyed the charge of your ancestor *Yonadav* and kept all his commandments, and done all that he enjoined upon you,

יח וּלְבֵית הָרֵכָבִים אָמַר יִרְמְיָהוּ כֹּה־אָמַר יְהֹוָה צְבָאוֹת אֱלֹהֵי יִשְׂרָאֵל יַעַן אֲשֶׁר שְׁמַעְתֶּם עַל־מִצְוַת יְהוֹנָדָב אֲבִיכֶם וַתִּשְׁמְרוּ אֶת־כָּל־מִצְוֹתָיו וַתַּעֲשׂוּ כְּכֹל אֲשֶׁר־צִוָּה אֶתְכֶם:

¹⁹ assuredly, thus said the Lord of Hosts, the God of *Yisrael*: There shall never cease to be a man of the line of *Yonadav* son of *Rechab* standing before Me."

יט לָכֵן כֹּה אָמַר יְהֹוָה צְבָאוֹת אֱלֹהֵי יִשְׂרָאֵל לֹא־יִכָּרֵת אִישׁ לְיוֹנָדָב בֶּן־רֵכָב עֹמֵד לְפָנַי כָּל־הַיָּמִים:

36 ¹ In the fourth year of King *Yehoyakim* son of *Yoshiyahu* of *Yehuda*, this word came to *Yirmiyahu* from *Hashem*:

לו א וַיְהִי בַּשָּׁנָה הָרְבִיעִת לִיהוֹיָקִים בֶּן־יֹאשִׁיָּהוּ מֶלֶךְ יְהוּדָה הָיָה הַדָּבָר הַזֶּה אֶל־יִרְמְיָהוּ מֵאֵת יְהֹוָה לֵאמֹר:

² Get a scroll and write upon it all the words that I have spoken to you – concerning *Yisrael* and *Yehuda* and all the nations – from the time I first spoke to you in the days of *Yoshiyahu* to this day.

ב קַח־לְךָ מְגִלַּת־סֵפֶר וְכָתַבְתָּ אֵלֶיהָ אֵת כָּל־הַדְּבָרִים אֲשֶׁר־דִּבַּרְתִּי אֵלֶיךָ עַל־יִשְׂרָאֵל וְעַל־יְהוּדָה וְעַל־כָּל־הַגּוֹיִם מִיּוֹם דִּבַּרְתִּי אֵלֶיךָ מִימֵי יֹאשִׁיָּהוּ וְעַד הַיּוֹם הַזֶּה:

³ Perhaps when the House of *Yehuda* hear of all the disasters I intend to bring upon them, they will turn back from their wicked ways, and I will pardon their iniquity and their sin.

ג אוּלַי יִשְׁמְעוּ בֵּית יְהוּדָה אֵת כָּל־הָרָעָה אֲשֶׁר אָנֹכִי חֹשֵׁב לַעֲשׂוֹת לָהֶם לְמַעַן יָשׁוּבוּ אִישׁ מִדַּרְכּוֹ הָרָעָה וְסָלַחְתִּי לַעֲוֺנָם וּלְחַטָּאתָם:

⁴ So *Yirmiyahu* called *Baruch* son of *Nerya*; and *Baruch* wrote down in the scroll, at *Yirmiyahu*'s dictation, all the words which *Hashem* had spoken to him.

ד וַיִּקְרָא יִרְמְיָהוּ אֶת־בָּרוּךְ בֶּן־נֵרִיָּה וַיִּכְתֹּב בָּרוּךְ מִפִּי יִרְמְיָהוּ אֵת כָּל־דִּבְרֵי יְהֹוָה אֲשֶׁר־דִּבֶּר אֵלָיו עַל־מְגִלַּת־סֵפֶר:

⁵ *Yirmiyahu* instructed *Baruch*, "I am in hiding; I cannot go to the House of *Hashem*.

ה וַיְצַוֶּה יִרְמְיָהוּ אֶת־בָּרוּךְ לֵאמֹר אֲנִי עָצוּר לֹא אוּכַל לָבוֹא בֵּית יְהֹוָה:

6 But you go and read aloud the words of *Hashem* from the scroll which you wrote at my dictation, to all the people in the House of *Hashem* on a fast day; thus you will also be reading them to all the Judeans who come in from the towns.

7 Perhaps their entreaty will be accepted by *Hashem*, if they turn back from their wicked ways. For great is the anger and wrath with which *Hashem* has threatened this people."

8 *Baruch* son of *Nerya* did just as the *Navi Yirmiyahu* had instructed him, about reading the words of *Hashem* from the scroll in the House of *Hashem*.

9 In the ninth month of the fifth year of King *Yehoyakim* son of *Yoshiyahu* of *Yehuda*, all the people in *Yerushalayim* and all the people coming from *Yehuda* proclaimed a fast before *Hashem* in *Yerushalayim*.

10 It was then that *Baruch* – in the chamber of Gemariah son of *Shafan* the scribe, in the upper court, near the new gateway of the House of *Hashem* – read the words of *Yirmiyahu* from the scroll to all the people in the House of *Hashem*.

11 *Michaihu* son of Gemariah son of *Shafan* heard all the words of *Hashem* [read] from the scroll,

12 and he went down to the king's palace, to the chamber of the scribe. There he found all the officials in session: Elishama the scribe, Delaiah son of *Shemaya*, Elnathan son of *Achbor*, Gemariah son of *Shafan*, Tzidkiyahu son of *Chananya*, and all the other officials.

13 And *Michaihu* told them all that he had heard as *Baruch* read from the scroll in the hearing of the people.

14 Then all the officials sent Jehudi son of Nethaniah son of Shelemiah son of *Kushi* to say to *Baruch*, "Take that scroll from which you read to the people, and come along!" And *Baruch* took the scroll and came to them.

15 They said, "Sit down and read it to us." And *Baruch* read it to them.

16 When they heard all these words, they turned to each other in fear; and they said to *Baruch*, "We must report all this to the king."

ו וּבָאתָ֣ אַתָּ֡ה וְקָרָ֣אתָ בַמְּגִלָּ֣ה אֲשֶׁר־כָּתַ֣בְתָּ מִפִּי֩ אֶת־דִּבְרֵ֨י יְהֹוָ֜ה בְּאׇזְנֵ֥י הָעָ֛ם בֵּ֥ית יְהֹוָ֖ה בְּי֣וֹם צ֑וֹם וְגַ֨ם בְּאׇזְנֵ֧י כׇל־יְהוּדָ֛ה הַבָּאִ֥ים מֵעָרֵיהֶ֖ם תִּקְרָאֵֽם׃

ז אוּלַ֞י תִּפֹּ֤ל תְּחִנָּתָם֙ לִפְנֵ֣י יְהֹוָ֔ה וְיָשֻׁ֕בוּ אִ֖ישׁ מִדַּרְכּ֣וֹ הָרָעָ֑ה כִּֽי־גָד֤וֹל הָאַף֙ וְהַ֣חֵמָ֔ה אֲשֶׁר־דִּבֶּ֥ר יְהֹוָ֖ה אֶל־הָעָ֥ם הַזֶּֽה׃

ח וַיַּ֗עַשׂ בָּר֙וּךְ֙ בֶּן־נֵ֣רִיָּ֔ה כְּכֹ֥ל אֲשֶׁר־צִוָּ֖הוּ יִרְמְיָ֣הוּ הַנָּבִ֑יא לִקְרֹ֥א בַסֵּ֛פֶר דִּבְרֵ֥י יְהֹוָ֖ה בֵּ֥ית יְהֹוָֽה׃

ט וַיְהִ֣י בַשָּׁנָ֣ה הַ֠חֲמִשִׁ֠ית לִיהוֹיָקִ֨ים בֶּן־יֹֽאשִׁיָּ֤הוּ מֶֽלֶךְ־יְהוּדָה֙ בַּחֹ֣דֶשׁ הַתְּשִׁעִ֔י קָרְא֨וּ צ֜וֹם לִפְנֵ֤י יְהֹוָה֙ כׇּל־הָעָ֣ם בִּירֽוּשָׁלָ֔͏ִם וְכׇל־הָעָ֗ם הַבָּאִ֛ים מֵעָרֵ֥י יְהוּדָ֖ה בִּירוּשָׁלָֽ͏ִם׃

י וַיִּקְרָ֨א בָר֜וּךְ בַּסֵּ֗פֶר אֶת־דִּבְרֵ֣י יִרְמְיָ֘הוּ֮ בֵּ֣ית יְהֹוָה֒ בְּלִשְׁכַּ֡ת גְּמַרְיָ֩הוּ֩ בֶן־שָׁפָ֨ן הַסֹּפֵ֜ר בֶּחָצֵ֣ר הָעֶלְי֗וֹן פֶּ֜תַח שַׁ֤עַר בֵּית־יְהֹוָה֙ הֶֽחָדָ֔שׁ בְּאׇזְנֵ֖י כׇל־הָעָֽם׃

יא וַ֠יִּשְׁמַ֠ע מִכָ֨יְהוּ בֶן־גְּמַרְיָ֧הוּ בֶן־שָׁפָ֛ן אֶת־כׇּל־דִּבְרֵ֥י יְהֹוָ֖ה מֵעַ֥ל הַסֵּֽפֶר׃

יב וַיֵּ֤רֶד בֵּית־הַמֶּ֙לֶךְ֙ עַל־לִשְׁכַּ֣ת הַסֹּפֵ֔ר וְהִ֨נֵּה־שָׁ֔ם כׇּל־הַשָּׂרִ֖ים יֽוֹשְׁבִ֑ים אֱלִישָׁמָ֣ע הַסֹּפֵ֡ר וּדְלָיָ֣הוּ בֶן־שְׁ֠מַעְיָ֠הוּ וְאֶלְנָתָ֨ן בֶּן־עַכְבּ֜וֹר וּגְמַרְיָ֧הוּ בֶן־שָׁפָ֛ן וְצִדְקִיָּ֥הוּ בֶן־חֲנַנְיָ֖הוּ וְכׇל־הַשָּׂרִֽים׃

יג וַיַּגֵּ֤ד לָהֶם֙ מִכָ֔יְהוּ אֵ֥ת כׇּל־הַדְּבָרִ֖ים אֲשֶׁ֣ר שָׁמֵ֑עַ בִּקְרֹ֥א בָר֛וּךְ בַּסֵּ֖פֶר בְּאׇזְנֵ֥י הָעָֽם׃

יד וַיִּשְׁלְח֨וּ כׇל־הַשָּׂרִ֜ים אֶל־בָּר֗וּךְ אֶת־יְהוּדִ֡י בֶּן־נְ֠תַנְיָ֠הוּ בֶּן־שֶׁלֶמְיָ֣הוּ בֶן־כּוּשִׁי֮ לֵאמֹר֒ הַמְּגִלָּ֗ה אֲשֶׁ֨ר קָרָ֤אתָ בָּהּ֙ בְּאׇזְנֵ֣י הָעָ֔ם קָחֶ֥נָּה בְיָדְךָ֖ וָלֵ֑ךְ וַ֠יִּקַּ֠ח בָּר֨וּךְ בֶּן־נֵרִיָּ֤הוּ אֶת־הַמְּגִלָּה֙ בְּיָד֔וֹ וַיָּבֹ֖א אֲלֵיהֶֽם׃

טו וַיֹּאמְר֣וּ אֵלָ֔יו שֵׁ֣ב נָ֔א וּקְרָאֶ֖נָּה בְּאׇזְנֵ֑ינוּ וַיִּקְרָ֥א בָר֖וּךְ בְּאׇזְנֵיהֶֽם׃

טז וַיְהִ֗י כְּשׇׁמְעָם֙ אֶת־כׇּל־הַדְּבָרִ֔ים פָּחֲד֖וּ אִ֣ישׁ אֶל־רֵעֵ֑הוּ וַיֹּֽאמְרוּ֙ אֶל־בָּר֔וּךְ הַגֵּ֤יד נַגִּיד֙ לַמֶּ֔לֶךְ אֵ֥ת כׇּל־הַדְּבָרִ֖ים הָאֵֽלֶּה׃

Jeremiah

17 And they questioned *Baruch* further, "Tell us how you wrote down all these words that he spoke."

וְאֶת־בָּרוּךְ שָׁאֲלוּ לֵאמֹר הַגֶּד־נָא לָנוּ אֵיךְ כָּתַבְתָּ אֶת־כָּל־הַדְּבָרִים הָאֵלֶּה מִפִּיו:

18 He answered them, "He himself recited all those words to me, and I would write them down in the scroll in ink."

וַיֹּאמֶר לָהֶם בָּרוּךְ מִפִּיו יִקְרָא אֵלַי אֵת כָּל־הַדְּבָרִים הָאֵלֶּה וַאֲנִי כֹּתֵב עַל־הַסֵּפֶר בַּדְּיוֹ:

19 The officials said to *Baruch*, "Go into hiding, you and *Yirmiyahu*. Let no man know where you are!"

וַיֹּאמְרוּ הַשָּׂרִים אֶל־בָּרוּךְ לֵךְ הִסָּתֵר אַתָּה וְיִרְמְיָהוּ וְאִישׁ אַל־יֵדַע אֵיפֹה אַתֶּם:

20 And they went to the king in the court, after leaving the scroll in the chamber of the scribe Elishama. And they reported all these matters to the king.

וַיָּבֹאוּ אֶל־הַמֶּלֶךְ חָצֵרָה וְאֶת־הַמְּגִלָּה הִפְקִדוּ בְּלִשְׁכַּת אֱלִישָׁמָע הַסֹּפֵר וַיַּגִּידוּ בְּאָזְנֵי הַמֶּלֶךְ אֵת כָּל־הַדְּבָרִים:

21 The king sent Jehudi to get the scroll and he fetched it from the chamber of the scribe Elishama. Jehudi read it to the king and to all the officials who were in attendance on the king.

וַיִּשְׁלַח הַמֶּלֶךְ אֶת־יְהוּדִי לָקַחַת אֶת־הַמְּגִלָּה וַיִּקָּחֶהָ מִלִּשְׁכַּת אֱלִישָׁמָע הַסֹּפֵר וַיִּקְרָאֶהָ יְהוּדִי בְּאָזְנֵי הַמֶּלֶךְ וּבְאָזְנֵי כָּל־הַשָּׂרִים הָעֹמְדִים מֵעַל הַמֶּלֶךְ:

22 Since it was the ninth month, the king was sitting in the winter house, with a fire burning in the brazier before him.

וְהַמֶּלֶךְ יוֹשֵׁב בֵּית הַחֹרֶף בַּחֹדֶשׁ הַתְּשִׁיעִי וְאֶת־הָאָח לְפָנָיו מְבֹעָרֶת:

v'-ha-ME-lekh yo-SHAYV BAYT ha-KHO-ref ba-KHO-desh ha-t'-shee-EE v'-et ha-AKH l'-fa-NAV m'-vo-A-ret

23 And every time Jehudi read three or four columns, [the king] would cut it up with a scribe's knife and throw it into the fire in the brazier, until the entire scroll was consumed by the fire in the brazier.

וַיְהִי כִּקְרוֹא יְהוּדִי שָׁלֹשׁ דְּלָתוֹת וְאַרְבָּעָה יִקְרָעֶהָ בְּתַעַר הַסֹּפֵר וְהַשְׁלֵךְ אֶל־הָאֵשׁ אֲשֶׁר אֶל־הָאָח עַד־תֹּם כָּל־הַמְּגִלָּה עַל־הָאֵשׁ אֲשֶׁר עַל־הָאָח:

24 Yet the king and all his courtiers who heard all these words showed no fear and did not tear their garments;

וְלֹא פָחֲדוּ וְלֹא קָרְעוּ אֶת־בִּגְדֵיהֶם הַמֶּלֶךְ וְכָל־עֲבָדָיו הַשֹּׁמְעִים אֵת כָּל־הַדְּבָרִים הָאֵלֶּה:

25 moreover, Elnathan, Delaiah, and Gemariah begged the king not to burn the scroll, but he would not listen to them.

וְגַם אֶלְנָתָן וּדְלָיָהוּ וּגְמַרְיָהוּ הִפְגִּעוּ בַמֶּלֶךְ לְבִלְתִּי שְׂרֹף אֶת־הַמְּגִלָּה וְלֹא שָׁמַע אֲלֵיהֶם:

36:22 The king was sitting in the winter house The dramatic showdown between the word of God, as dictated to *Baruch* by *Yirmiyahu*, and the unrepentant *Yehoyakim*, takes place in the king's winter palace. The ninth month on the Hebrew calendar, the month of *Kislev*, occurs in the dead of winter. *Kislev* can be a cold, bitter month, with fierce rains and snow. The aristocracy and the wealthy class could afford to build winter homes heated by coal stoves. In this fire *Yehoyakim* mockingly burns *Yirmiyahu's* scroll, sealing his own fate. Ruins of a palace found in *Ramat Rachel*, in south-east Jerusalem, have been identified as the winter palace of *Yehoyakim*.

Palace in Ramat Rachel

26 The king ordered Jerahmeel, the king's son, and *Seraya* son of Azriel, and Shelemiah son of Abdeel to arrest the scribe *Baruch* and the *Navi Yirmiyahu*. But *Hashem* hid them.

כו וַיְצַוֶּה הַמֶּלֶךְ אֶת־יְרַחְמְאֵל בֶּן־הַמֶּלֶךְ וְאֶת־שְׂרָיָהוּ בֶּן־עַזְרִיאֵל וְאֶת־שֶׁלֶמְיָהוּ בֶּן־עַבְדְּאֵל לָקַחַת אֶת־בָּרוּךְ הַסֹּפֵר וְאֵת יִרְמְיָהוּ הַנָּבִיא וַיַּסְתִּרֵם יְהֹוָה:

27 The word of *Hashem* came to *Yirmiyahu* after the king had burned the scroll containing the words that *Baruch* had written at *Yirmiyahu*'s dictation:

כז וַיְהִי דְבַר־יְהֹוָה אֶל־יִרְמְיָהוּ אַחֲרֵי שְׂרֹף הַמֶּלֶךְ אֶת־הַמְּגִלָּה וְאֶת־הַדְּבָרִים אֲשֶׁר כָּתַב בָּרוּךְ מִפִּי יִרְמְיָהוּ לֵאמֹר:

28 Get yourself another scroll, and write upon it the same words that were in the first scroll that was burned by King *Yehoyakim* of *Yehuda*.

כח שׁוּב קַח־לְךָ מְגִלָּה אַחֶרֶת וּכְתֹב עָלֶיהָ אֵת כָּל־הַדְּבָרִים הָרִאשֹׁנִים אֲשֶׁר הָיוּ עַל־הַמְּגִלָּה הָרִאשֹׁנָה אֲשֶׁר שָׂרַף יְהוֹיָקִים מֶלֶךְ־יְהוּדָה:

29 And concerning King *Yehoyakim* of *Yehuda* you shall say: Thus said *Hashem*: You burned that scroll, saying, "How dare you write in it that the king of Babylon will come and destroy this land and cause man and beast to cease from it?"

כט וְעַל־יְהוֹיָקִים מֶלֶךְ־יְהוּדָה תֹאמַר כֹּה אָמַר יְהֹוָה אַתָּה שָׂרַפְתָּ אֶת־הַמְּגִלָּה הַזֹּאת לֵאמֹר מַדּוּעַ כָּתַבְתָּ עָלֶיהָ לֵאמֹר בֹּא־יָבוֹא מֶלֶךְ־בָּבֶל וְהִשְׁחִית אֶת־הָאָרֶץ הַזֹּאת וְהִשְׁבִּית מִמֶּנָּה אָדָם וּבְהֵמָה:

30 Assuredly, thus said *Hashem* concerning King *Yehoyakim* of *Yehuda*: He shall not have any of his line sitting on the throne of *David*; and his own corpse shall be left exposed to the heat by day and the cold by night.

ל לָכֵן כֹּה־אָמַר יְהֹוָה עַל־יְהוֹיָקִים מֶלֶךְ יְהוּדָה לֹא־יִהְיֶה־לּוֹ יוֹשֵׁב עַל־כִּסֵּא דָוִד וְנִבְלָתוֹ תִּהְיֶה מֻשְׁלֶכֶת לַחֹרֶב בַּיּוֹם וְלַקֶּרַח בַּלָּיְלָה:

31 And I will punish him and his offspring and his courtiers for their iniquity; I will bring on them and on the inhabitants of *Yerushalayim* and on all the men of *Yehuda* all the disasters of which I have warned them – but they would not listen.

לא וּפָקַדְתִּי עָלָיו וְעַל־זַרְעוֹ וְעַל־עֲבָדָיו אֶת־עֲוֹנָם וְהֵבֵאתִי עֲלֵיהֶם וְעַל־יֹשְׁבֵי יְרוּשָׁלִַם וְאֶל־אִישׁ יְהוּדָה אֵת כָּל־הָרָעָה אֲשֶׁר־דִּבַּרְתִּי אֲלֵיהֶם וְלֹא שָׁמֵעוּ:

32 So *Yirmiyahu* got another scroll and gave it to the scribe *Baruch* son of *Nerya*. And at *Yirmiyahu*'s dictation, he wrote in it the whole text of the scroll that King *Yehoyakim* of *Yehuda* had burned; and more of the like was added.

לב וְיִרְמְיָהוּ לָקַח מְגִלָּה אַחֶרֶת וַיִּתְּנָהּ אֶל־בָּרוּךְ בֶּן־נֵרִיָּהוּ הַסֹּפֵר וַיִּכְתֹּב עָלֶיהָ מִפִּי יִרְמְיָהוּ אֵת כָּל־דִּבְרֵי הַסֵּפֶר אֲשֶׁר שָׂרַף יְהוֹיָקִים מֶלֶךְ־יְהוּדָה בָּאֵשׁ וְעוֹד נוֹסַף עֲלֵיהֶם דְּבָרִים רַבִּים כָּהֵמָּה:

37 1 *Tzidkiyahu* son of *Yoshiyahu* became king instead of *Coniah* son of *Yehoyakim*, for King Nebuchadrezzar of Babylon set him up as king over the land of *Yehuda*.

לז א וַיִּמְלָךְ־מֶלֶךְ צִדְקִיָּהוּ בֶּן־יֹאשִׁיָּהוּ תַּחַת כָּנְיָהוּ בֶּן־יְהוֹיָקִים אֲשֶׁר הִמְלִיךְ נְבוּכַדְרֶאצַּר מֶלֶךְ־בָּבֶל בְּאֶרֶץ יְהוּדָה:

2 Neither he nor his courtiers nor the people of the land gave heed to the words which *Hashem* spoke through the *Navi Yirmiyahu*.

ב וְלֹא שָׁמַע הוּא וַעֲבָדָיו וְעַם הָאָרֶץ אֶל־דִּבְרֵי יְהֹוָה אֲשֶׁר דִּבֶּר בְּיַד יִרְמְיָהוּ הַנָּבִיא:

3 Yet King *Tzidkiyahu* sent Jehucal son of Shelemiah and *Tzefanya* son of the *Kohen* Maaseiah to the *Navi Yirmiyahu*, to say, "Please pray on our behalf to *Hashem* our God."

ג וַיִּשְׁלַח הַמֶּלֶךְ צִדְקִיָּהוּ אֶת־יְהוּכַל בֶּן־שֶׁלֶמְיָה וְאֶת־צְפַנְיָהוּ בֶן־מַעֲשֵׂיָה הַכֹּהֵן אֶל־יִרְמְיָהוּ הַנָּבִיא לֵאמֹר הִתְפַּלֶּל־נָא בַעֲדֵנוּ אֶל־יְהֹוָה אֱלֹהֵינוּ:

4 (*Yirmiyahu* could still go in and out among the people, for they had not yet put him in prison.

ד וְיִרְמְיָהוּ בָּא וְיֹצֵא בְּתוֹךְ הָעָם וְלֹא־נָתְנוּ אֹתוֹ בֵּית הַכְּלִיא [הַכְּלוּא]:

5 The army of Pharaoh had set out from Egypt; and when the Chaldeans who were besieging *Yerushalayim* heard the report, they raised the siege of *Yerushalayim*.)

ה וְחֵיל פַּרְעֹה יָצָא מִמִּצְרָיִם וַיִּשְׁמְעוּ הַכַּשְׂדִּים הַצָּרִים עַל־יְרוּשָׁלַ͏ִם אֶת־שִׁמְעָם וַיֵּעָלוּ מֵעַל יְרוּשָׁלָ͏ִם:

6 Then the word of *Hashem* came to the *Navi Yirmiyahu*:

ו וַיְהִי דְּבַר־יְהֹוָה אֶל־יִרְמְיָהוּ הַנָּבִיא לֵאמֹר:

7 Thus said *Hashem*, the God of *Yisrael*: Thus shall you say to the king of *Yehuda* who sent you to Me to inquire of Me: "The army of Pharaoh, which set out to help you, will return to its own land, to Egypt.

ז כֹּה־אָמַר יְהֹוָה אֱלֹהֵי יִשְׂרָאֵל כֹּה תֹאמְרוּ אֶל־מֶלֶךְ יְהוּדָה הַשֹּׁלֵחַ אֶתְכֶם אֵלַי לְדָרְשֵׁנִי הִנֵּה חֵיל פַּרְעֹה הַיֹּצֵא לָכֶם לְעֶזְרָה שָׁב לְאַרְצוֹ מִצְרָיִם:

8 And the Chaldeans will come back and attack this city and they will capture it and destroy it by fire."

ח וְשָׁבוּ הַכַּשְׂדִּים וְנִלְחֲמוּ עַל־הָעִיר הַזֹּאת וּלְכָדֻהָ וּשְׂרָפֻהָ בָאֵשׁ:

9 Thus said *Hashem*: Do not delude yourselves into thinking, "The Chaldeans will go away from us." They will not.

ט כֹּה אָמַר יְהֹוָה אַל־תַּשִּׁאוּ נַפְשֹׁתֵיכֶם לֵאמֹר הָלֹךְ יֵלְכוּ מֵעָלֵינוּ הַכַּשְׂדִּים כִּי־לֹא יֵלֵכוּ:

10 Even if you defeated the whole army of the Chaldeans that are fighting against you, and only wounded men were left lying in their tents, they would get up and burn this city down!

י כִּי אִם־הִכִּיתֶם כָּל־חֵיל כַּשְׂדִּים הַנִּלְחָמִים אִתְּכֶם וְנִשְׁאֲרוּ בָם אֲנָשִׁים מְדֻקָּרִים אִישׁ בְּאׇהֳלוֹ יָקוּמוּ וְשָׂרְפוּ אֶת־הָעִיר הַזֹּאת בָּאֵשׁ:

11 When the army of the Chaldeans raised the siege of *Yerushalayim* on account of the army of Pharaoh,

יא וְהָיָה בְּהֵעָלוֹת חֵיל הַכַּשְׂדִּים מֵעַל יְרוּשָׁלָ͏ִם מִפְּנֵי חֵיל פַּרְעֹה:

12 *Yirmiyahu* was going to leave *Yerushalayim* and go to the territory of *Binyamin* to share in some property there among the people.

יב וַיֵּצֵא יִרְמְיָהוּ מִירוּשָׁלַ͏ִם לָלֶכֶת אֶרֶץ בִּנְיָמִן לַחֲלִק מִשָּׁם בְּתוֹךְ הָעָם:

va-yay-TZAY yir-m'-YA-hu mee-ru-sha-LA-im la-LE-khet E-retz bin-ya-MIN la-kha-LIK mi-SHAM b'-TOKH ha-AM

13 When he got to the *Binyamin* Gate, there was a guard officer there named Irijah son of Shelemiah son of *Chananya*; and he arrested the *Navi Yirmiyahu*, saying, "You are defecting to the Chaldeans!"

יג וַיְהִי־הוּא בְּשַׁעַר בִּנְיָמִן וְשָׁם בַּעַל פְּקִדֻת וּשְׁמוֹ יִרְאִיָּיה בֶּן־שֶׁלֶמְיָה בֶּן־חֲנַנְיָה וַיִּתְפֹּשׂ אֶת־יִרְמְיָהוּ הַנָּבִיא לֵאמֹר אֶל־הַכַּשְׂדִּים אַתָּה נֹפֵל:

Kfar Adumim in the mountains of Binyamin

37:12 And go to the territory of *Binyamin* The Egyptians manage to temporarily repulse the Babylonian invaders, thus ending the siege of *Yerushalayim*. With the siege lifted, *Yirmiyahu* leaves the capital for the tribal land of *Binyamin*, to inherit a portion of land. The area of *Binyamin* encompasses the mountain ridges found to the immediate north of *Yerushalayim*, and included *Yirmiyahu's* hometown, the priestly city *Anatot*. This has been identified with the contemporary Arab village of Anata, which is now a neighborhood of Jerusalem.

14 *Yirmiyahu* answered, "That's a lie! I'm not defecting to the Chaldeans!" But Irijah would not listen to him; he arrested *Yirmiyahu* and brought him to the officials.

יד וַיֹּאמֶר יִרְמְיָהוּ שֶׁקֶר אֵינֶנִּי נֹפֵל עַל־הַכַּשְׂדִּים וְלֹא שָׁמַע אֵלָיו וַיִּתְפֹּשׂ יִרְאִיָּיה בְּיִרְמְיָהוּ וַיְבִאֵהוּ אֶל־הַשָּׂרִים:

15 The officials were furious with *Yirmiyahu*; they beat him and put him into prison, in the house of the scribe *Yehonatan* – for it had been made into a jail.

טו וַיִּקְצְפוּ הַשָּׂרִים עַל־יִרְמְיָהוּ וְהִכּוּ אֹתוֹ וְנָתְנוּ אוֹתוֹ בֵּית הָאֵסוּר בֵּית יְהוֹנָתָן הַסֹּפֵר כִּי־אֹתוֹ עָשׂוּ לְבֵית הַכֶּלֶא:

16 Thus *Yirmiyahu* came to the pit and the cells, and *Yirmiyahu* remained there a long time.

טז כִּי בָא יִרְמְיָהוּ אֶל־בֵּית הַבּוֹר וְאֶל־הַחֲנוּיֹת וַיֵּשֶׁב־שָׁם יִרְמְיָהוּ יָמִים רַבִּים:

17 Then King *Tzidkiyahu* sent for him, and the king questioned him secretly in his palace. He asked, "Is there any word from *Hashem*?" "There is!" *Yirmiyahu* answered, and he continued, "You will be delivered into the hands of the king of Babylon."

יז וַיִּשְׁלַח הַמֶּלֶךְ צִדְקִיָּהוּ וַיִּקָּחֵהוּ וַיִּשְׁאָלֵהוּ הַמֶּלֶךְ בְּבֵיתוֹ בַּסֵּתֶר וַיֹּאמֶר הֲיֵשׁ דָּבָר מֵאֵת יְהוָה וַיֹּאמֶר יִרְמְיָהוּ יֵשׁ וַיֹּאמֶר בְּיַד מֶלֶךְ־בָּבֶל תִּנָּתֵן:

18 And *Yirmiyahu* said to King *Tzidkiyahu*, "What wrong have I done to you, to your courtiers, and to this people, that you have put me in jail?

יח וַיֹּאמֶר יִרְמְיָהוּ אֶל־הַמֶּלֶךְ צִדְקִיָּהוּ מֶה חָטָאתִי לְךָ וְלַעֲבָדֶיךָ וְלָעָם הַזֶּה כִּי־נְתַתֶּם אוֹתִי אֶל־בֵּית הַכֶּלֶא:

19 And where are those *Neviim* of yours who prophesied to you that the king of Babylon would never move against you and against this land?"

יט וְאַיֵּה [וְאַיֵּה] נְבִיאֵיכֶם אֲשֶׁר־נִבְּאוּ לָכֶם לֵאמֹר לֹא־יָבֹא מֶלֶךְ־בָּבֶל עֲלֵיכֶם וְעַל הָאָרֶץ הַזֹּאת:

20 Now, please hear me, O lord king, and grant my plea: Don't send me back to the house of the scribe *Yehonatan* to die there."

כ וְעַתָּה שְׁמַע־נָא אֲדֹנִי הַמֶּלֶךְ תִּפָּל־נָא תְחִנָּתִי לְפָנֶיךָ וְאַל־תְּשִׁבֵנִי בֵּית יְהוֹנָתָן הַסֹּפֵר וְלֹא אָמוּת שָׁם:

21 So King *Tzidkiyahu* gave instructions to lodge *Yirmiyahu* in the prison compound and to supply him daily with a loaf of bread from the Bakers' Street – until all the bread in the city was gone. *Yirmiyahu* remained in the prison compound.

כא וַיְצַוֶּה הַמֶּלֶךְ צִדְקִיָּהוּ וַיַּפְקִדוּ אֶת־יִרְמְיָהוּ בַּחֲצַר הַמַּטָּרָה וְנָתֹן לוֹ כִכַּר־לֶחֶם לַיּוֹם מִחוּץ הָאֹפִים עַד־תֹּם כָּל־הַלֶּחֶם מִן־הָעִיר וַיֵּשֶׁב יִרְמְיָהוּ בַּחֲצַר הַמַּטָּרָה:

38 1 Shephatiah son of Mattan, Gedaliah son of Pashhur, Jucal son of Shelemiah, and Pashhur son of Malchiah heard what *Yirmiyahu* was saying to all the people:

לח א וַיִּשְׁמַע שְׁפַטְיָה בֶן־מַתָּן וּגְדַלְיָהוּ בֶּן־פַּשְׁחוּר וְיוּכַל בֶּן־שֶׁלֶמְיָהוּ וּפַשְׁחוּר בֶּן־מַלְכִּיָּה אֶת־הַדְּבָרִים אֲשֶׁר יִרְמְיָהוּ מְדַבֵּר אֶל־כָּל־הָעָם לֵאמֹר:

2 "Thus said *Hashem*: Whoever remains in this city shall die by the sword, by famine, and by pestilence; but whoever surrenders to the Chaldeans shall live; he shall at least gain his life and shall live.

ב כֹּה אָמַר יְהוָה הַיֹּשֵׁב בָּעִיר הַזֹּאת יָמוּת בַּחֶרֶב בָּרָעָב וּבַדָּבֶר וְהַיֹּצֵא אֶל־הַכַּשְׂדִּים יִחְיֶה [וְחָיָה] וְהָיְתָה־לּוֹ נַפְשׁוֹ לְשָׁלָל וָחָי:

3 Thus said *Hashem*: This city shall be delivered into the hands of the king of Babylon's army, and he shall capture it."

ג כֹּה אָמַר יְהוָה הִנָּתֹן תִּנָּתֵן הָעִיר הַזֹּאת בְּיַד חֵיל מֶלֶךְ־בָּבֶל וּלְכָדָהּ:

Jeremiah

4 Then the officials said to the king, "Let that man be put to death, for he disheartens the soldiers, and all the people who are left in this city, by speaking such things to them. That man is not seeking the welfare of this people, but their harm!"

ד וַיֹּאמְר֤וּ הַשָּׂרִים֙ אֶל־הַמֶּ֔לֶךְ י֣וּמַת נָ֣א אֶת־הָאִ֣ישׁ הַזֶּ֗ה כִּֽי־עַל־כֵּ֡ן הֽוּא־מְרַפֵּ֣א אֶת־יְדֵי֩ אַנְשֵׁ֨י הַמִּלְחָמָ֜ה הַנִּשְׁאָרִ֣ים ׀ בָּעִ֣יר הַזֹּ֗את וְאֵת֙ יְדֵ֣י כָל־הָעָ֔ם לְדַבֵּ֣ר אֲלֵיהֶ֔ם כַּדְּבָרִ֖ים הָאֵ֑לֶּה כִּ֣י ׀ הָאִ֣ישׁ הַזֶּ֗ה אֵינֶ֨נּוּ דֹרֵ֧שׁ לְשָׁל֛וֹם לָעָ֥ם הַזֶּ֖ה כִּ֥י אִם־לְרָעָֽה׃

5 King *Tzidkiyahu* replied, "He is in your hands; the king cannot oppose you in anything!"

ה וַיֹּ֙אמֶר֙ הַמֶּ֣לֶךְ צִדְקִיָּ֔הוּ הִנֵּה־ה֖וּא בְּיֶדְכֶ֑ם כִּֽי־אֵ֣ין הַמֶּ֔לֶךְ יוּכַ֥ל אֶתְכֶ֖ם דָּבָֽר׃

va-YO-mer ha-ME-lekh tzid-ki-YA-hu hi-nay HU b'-yed-KHEM
kee AYN ha-ME-lekh yu-KHAL et-KHEM da-VAR

6 So they took *Yirmiyahu* and put him down in the pit of Malchiah, the king's son, which was in the prison compound; they let *Yirmiyahu* down by ropes. There was no water in the pit, only mud, and *Yirmiyahu* sank into the mud.

ו וַיִּקְח֣וּ אֶֽת־יִרְמְיָ֗הוּ וַיַּשְׁלִ֨כוּ אֹת֜וֹ אֶל־הַבּ֣וֹר ׀ מַלְכִּיָּ֣הוּ בֶן־הַמֶּ֗לֶךְ אֲשֶׁר֙ בַּחֲצַ֣ר הַמַּטָּרָ֔ה וַיְשַׁלְּח֥וּ אֶֽת־יִרְמְיָ֖הוּ בַּחֲבָלִ֑ים וּבַבּ֤וֹר אֵֽין־מַ֙יִם֙ כִּ֣י אִם־טִ֔יט וַיִּטְבַּ֥ע יִרְמְיָ֖הוּ בַּטִּֽיט׃

7 *Eved Melech* the Cushite, a eunuch who was in the king's palace, heard that they had put *Yirmiyahu* in the pit. The king was then sitting at the *Binyamin* Gate;

ז וַיִּשְׁמַ֡ע עֶֽבֶד־מֶ֨לֶךְ הַכּוּשִׁ֜י אִ֣ישׁ סָרִ֗יס וְהוּא֙ בְּבֵ֣ית הַמֶּ֔לֶךְ כִּֽי־נָתְנ֥וּ אֶֽת־יִרְמְיָ֖הוּ אֶל־הַבּ֑וֹר וְהַמֶּ֥לֶךְ יוֹשֵׁ֖ב בְּשַׁ֥עַר בִּנְיָמִֽן׃

8 so *Eved Melech* left the king's palace, and spoke to the king:

ח וַיֵּצֵ֥א עֶֽבֶד־מֶ֖לֶךְ מִבֵּ֣ית הַמֶּ֑לֶךְ וַיְדַבֵּ֥ר אֶל־הַמֶּ֖לֶךְ לֵאמֹֽר׃

9 "O lord king, those men have acted wickedly in all they did to the *Navi Yirmiyahu*; they have put him down in the pit, to die there of hunger." For there was no more bread in the city.

ט אֲדֹנִ֣י הַמֶּ֗לֶךְ הֵרֵ֜עוּ הָאֲנָשִׁ֤ים הָאֵ֙לֶּה֙ אֵ֣ת כָּל־אֲשֶׁ֤ר עָשׂוּ֙ לְיִרְמְיָ֣הוּ הַנָּבִ֔יא אֵ֥ת אֲשֶׁר־הִשְׁלִ֖יכוּ אֶל־הַבּ֑וֹר וַיָּ֤מׇת תַּחְתָּיו֙ מִפְּנֵ֣י הָֽרָעָ֔ב כִּ֣י אֵ֥ין הַלֶּ֛חֶם ע֖וֹד בָּעִֽיר׃

10 Then the king instructed *Eved Melech* the Cushite, "Take with you thirty men from here, and pull the *Navi Yirmiyahu* up from the pit before he dies."

י וַיְצַוֶּ֣ה הַמֶּ֗לֶךְ אֵ֚ת עֶֽבֶד־מֶ֣לֶךְ הַכּוּשִׁ֔י לֵאמֹ֕ר קַ֥ח בְּיָדְךָ֖ מִזֶּ֣ה שְׁלֹשִׁ֣ים אֲנָשִׁ֑ים וְֽהַעֲלִ֜יתָ אֶֽת־יִרְמְיָ֧הוּ הַנָּבִ֛יא מִן־הַבּ֖וֹר בְּטֶ֥רֶם יָמֽוּת׃

11 So *Eved Melech* took the men with him, and went to the king's palace, to a place below the treasury. There they got worn cloths and rags, which they let down to *Yirmiyahu* in the pit by ropes.

יא וַיִּקַּ֣ח ׀ עֶֽבֶד־מֶ֨לֶךְ אֶת־הָאֲנָשִׁ֜ים בְּיָד֗וֹ וַיָּבֹ֤א בֵית־הַמֶּ֙לֶךְ֙ אֶל־תַּ֣חַת הָאוֹצָ֔ר וַיִּקַּ֤ח מִשָּׁם֙ בְּלוֹיֵ֣ הַסְּחָב֔וֹת [סְחָבוֹת] וּבְלוֹיֵ֖ מְלָחִ֑ים וַיְשַׁלְּחֵ֧ם אֶֽל־יִרְמְיָ֛הוּ אֶל־הַבּ֖וֹר בַּחֲבָלִֽים׃

צדק

38:5 The king cannot oppose you in anything Among the tragedies of Israel's downfall is the reign of the final king of *David's* dynasty, *Tzidkiyahu*. Unlike his predecessors who were genuinely wicked, *Tzidkiyahu* is good at heart, as suggested by his name *Tzidkiyahu*, which comes from the word *tzedek* (צדק), 'righteousness.' He secretly tries to support *Yirmiyahu* (see Jeremiah 37:21) and repeatedly inquires of the word of *Hashem* (21:2; 37:17; 38:14). However, *Tzidkiyahu* does not heed *Yirmiyahu's* plea to submit to Babylonia, as he is weak and unable to oppose his officers. They desire to kill *Yirmiyahu* for preaching against Israel, and argue that his words weaken the resolve of the people to keep fighting. By listening to his officers instead of the prophet, his fate and that of the people are sealed. Had *Tzidkiyahu* repented and led the people to follow God's word, they would have been able to avert the disaster and remain in Israel, God's Land.

The Garden of the Righteous at Yad Vashem

Jeremiah

12 And *Eved Melech* the Cushite called to *Yirmiyahu*, "Put the worn cloths and rags under your armpits, inside the ropes." *Yirmiyahu* did so,

יב וַיֹּאמֶר עֶבֶד־מֶלֶךְ הַכּוּשִׁי אֶל־יִרְמְיָהוּ שִׂים נָא בְּלוֹאֵי הַסְּחָבוֹת וְהַמְּלָחִים תַּחַת אַצִּלוֹת יָדֶיךָ מִתַּחַת לַחֲבָלִים וַיַּעַשׂ יִרְמְיָהוּ כֵּן:

13 and they pulled *Yirmiyahu* up by the ropes and got him out of the pit. And *Yirmiyahu* remained in the prison compound.

יג וַיִּמְשְׁכוּ אֶת־יִרְמְיָהוּ בַּחֲבָלִים וַיַּעֲלוּ אֹתוֹ מִן־הַבּוֹר וַיֵּשֶׁב יִרְמְיָהוּ בַּחֲצַר הַמַּטָּרָה:

14 King *Tzidkiyahu* sent for the *Navi Yirmiyahu*, and had him brought to him at the third entrance of the House of *Hashem*. And the king said to *Yirmiyahu*, "I want to ask you something; don't conceal anything from me."

יד וַיִּשְׁלַח הַמֶּלֶךְ צִדְקִיָּהוּ וַיִּקַּח אֶת־יִרְמְיָהוּ הַנָּבִיא אֵלָיו אֶל־מָבוֹא הַשְּׁלִישִׁי אֲשֶׁר בְּבֵית יְהֹוָה וַיֹּאמֶר הַמֶּלֶךְ אֶל־יִרְמְיָהוּ שֹׁאֵל אֲנִי אֹתְךָ דָּבָר אַל־תְּכַחֵד מִמֶּנִּי דָּבָר:

15 *Yirmiyahu* answered the king, "If I tell you, you'll surely kill me; and if I give you advice, you won't listen to me."

טו וַיֹּאמֶר יִרְמְיָהוּ אֶל־צִדְקִיָּהוּ כִּי אַגִּיד לְךָ הֲלוֹא הָמֵת תְּמִיתֵנִי וְכִי אִיעָצְךָ לֹא תִשְׁמַע אֵלָי:

16 Thereupon King *Tzidkiyahu* secretly promised *Yirmiyahu* on oath: "As *Hashem* lives who has given us this life, I will not put you to death or leave you in the hands of those men who seek your life."

טז וַיִּשָּׁבַע הַמֶּלֶךְ צִדְקִיָּהוּ אֶל־יִרְמְיָהוּ בַּסֵּתֶר לֵאמֹר חַי־יְהֹוָה אֵת אֲשֶׁר עָשָׂה־לָנוּ אֶת־הַנֶּפֶשׁ הַזֹּאת אִם־אֲמִיתֶךָ וְאִם־אֶתֶּנְךָ בְּיַד הָאֲנָשִׁים הָאֵלֶּה אֲשֶׁר מְבַקְשִׁים אֶת־נַפְשֶׁךָ:

17 Then *Yirmiyahu* said to *Tzidkiyahu*, "Thus said *Hashem*, the the LORD of Hosts, the God of *Yisrael*: If you surrender to the officers of the king of Babylon, your life will be spared and this city will not be burned down. You and your household will live.

יז וַיֹּאמֶר יִרְמְיָהוּ אֶל־צִדְקִיָּהוּ כֹּה־אָמַר יְהֹוָה אֱלֹהֵי צְבָאוֹת אֱלֹהֵי יִשְׂרָאֵל אִם־יָצֹא תֵצֵא אֶל־שָׂרֵי מֶלֶךְ־בָּבֶל וְחָיְתָה נַפְשֶׁךָ וְהָעִיר הַזֹּאת לֹא תִשָּׂרֵף בָּאֵשׁ וְחָיִתָה אַתָּה וּבֵיתֶךָ:

18 But if you do not surrender to the officers of the king of Babylon, this city will be delivered into the hands of the Chaldeans, who will burn it down; and you will not escape from them."

יח וְאִם לֹא־תֵצֵא אֶל־שָׂרֵי מֶלֶךְ בָּבֶל וְנִתְּנָה הָעִיר הַזֹּאת בְּיַד הַכַּשְׂדִּים וּשְׂרָפוּהָ בָּאֵשׁ וְאַתָּה לֹא־תִמָּלֵט מִיָּדָם:

19 King *Tzidkiyahu* said to *Yirmiyahu*, "I am worried about the Judeans who have defected to the Chaldeans; that they [the Chaldeans] might hand me over to them to abuse me."

יט וַיֹּאמֶר הַמֶּלֶךְ צִדְקִיָּהוּ אֶל־יִרְמְיָהוּ אֲנִי דֹאֵג אֶת־הַיְּהוּדִים אֲשֶׁר נָפְלוּ אֶל־הַכַּשְׂדִּים פֶּן־יִתְּנוּ אֹתִי בְּיָדָם וְהִתְעַלְּלוּ־בִי:

20 "They will not hand you over," *Yirmiyahu* replied. "Listen to the voice of *Hashem*, to what I tell you, that it may go well with you and your life be spared.

כ וַיֹּאמֶר יִרְמְיָהוּ לֹא יִתֵּנוּ שְׁמַע־נָא בְּקוֹל יְהֹוָה לַאֲשֶׁר אֲנִי דֹּבֵר אֵלֶיךָ וְיִיטַב לְךָ וּתְחִי נַפְשֶׁךָ:

21 For this is what *Hashem* has shown me if you refuse to surrender:

כא וְאִם־מָאֵן אַתָּה לָצֵאת זֶה הַדָּבָר אֲשֶׁר הִרְאַנִי יְהֹוָה:

Jeremiah

92

22 All the women who are left in the palace of the
king of *Yehuda* shall be brought out to the officers
of the king of Babylon; and they shall say: The
men who were your friends Have seduced you and
vanquished you. Now that your feet are sunk in the
mire, They have turned their backs [on you].

כב וְהִנֵּה כָל־הַנָּשִׁים אֲשֶׁר נִשְׁאֲרוּ בְּבֵית
מֶלֶךְ־יְהוּדָה מוּצָאוֹת אֶל־שָׂרֵי מֶלֶךְ בָּבֶל
וְהֵנָּה אֹמְרוֹת הִסִּיתוּךָ וְיָכְלוּ לְךָ אַנְשֵׁי
שְׁלֹמֶךָ הָטְבְּעוּ בַבֹּץ רַגְלֶךָ נָסֹגוּ אָחוֹר:

23 They will bring out all your wives and children to
the Chaldeans, and you yourself will not escape
from them. You will be captured by the king of
Babylon, and this city shall be burned down."

כג וְאֶת־כָּל־נָשֶׁיךָ וְאֶת־בָּנֶיךָ מוֹצִאִים אֶל־
הַכַּשְׂדִּים וְאַתָּה לֹא־תִמָּלֵט מִיָּדָם כִּי
בְיַד מֶלֶךְ־בָּבֶל תִּתָּפֵשׂ וְאֶת־הָעִיר הַזֹּאת
תִּשְׂרֹף בָּאֵשׁ:

24 *Tzidkiyahu* said to *Yirmiyahu*, "Don't let anyone
know about this conversation, or you will die.

כד וַיֹּאמֶר צִדְקִיָּהוּ אֶל־יִרְמְיָהוּ אִישׁ אַל־
יֵדַע בַּדְּבָרִים־הָאֵלֶּה וְלֹא תָמוּת:

25 If the officials should hear that I have spoken with
you, and they should come and say to you, 'Tell us
what you said to the king; hide nothing from us, or
we'll kill you. And what did the king say to you?'

כה וְכִי־יִשְׁמְעוּ הַשָּׂרִים כִּי־דִבַּרְתִּי אִתָּךְ
וּבָאוּ אֵלֶיךָ וְאָמְרוּ אֵלֶיךָ הַגִּידָה־נָּא לָנוּ
מַה־דִּבַּרְתָּ אֶל־הַמֶּלֶךְ אַל־תְּכַחֵד מִמֶּנּוּ
וְלֹא נְמִיתֶךָ וּמַה־דִּבֶּר אֵלֶיךָ הַמֶּלֶךְ:

26 say to them, 'I was presenting my petition to the
king not to send me back to the house of *Yehonatan*
to die there.'"

כו וְאָמַרְתָּ אֲלֵיהֶם מַפִּיל־אֲנִי תְחִנָּתִי לִפְנֵי
הַמֶּלֶךְ לְבִלְתִּי הֲשִׁיבֵנִי בֵּית יְהוֹנָתָן
לָמוּת שָׁם:

27 All the officials did come to *Yirmiyahu* to question
him; and he replied to them just as the king had
instructed him. So they stopped questioning him,
for the conversation had not been overheard.

כז וַיָּבֹאוּ כָל־הַשָּׂרִים אֶל־יִרְמְיָהוּ וַיִּשְׁאֲלוּ
אֹתוֹ וַיַּגֵּד לָהֶם כְּכָל־הַדְּבָרִים הָאֵלֶּה
אֲשֶׁר צִוָּה הַמֶּלֶךְ וַיַּחֲרִשׁוּ מִמֶּנּוּ כִּי לֹא־
נִשְׁמַע הַדָּבָר:

28 *Yirmiyahu* remained in the prison compound
until the day *Yerushalayim* was captured. When
Yerushalayim was captured…

כח וַיֵּשֶׁב יִרְמְיָהוּ בַּחֲצַר הַמַּטָּרָה עַד־יוֹם
אֲשֶׁר־נִלְכְּדָה יְרוּשָׁלָ͏ִם וְהָיָה כַּאֲשֶׁר
נִלְכְּדָה יְרוּשָׁלָ͏ִם:

39 ¹ In the ninth year of King *Tzidkiyahu* of *Yehuda*, in
the tenth month, King Nebuchadrezzar of Babylon
moved against *Yerushalayim* with his whole army,
and they laid siege to it.

לט א בַּשָּׁנָה הַתְּשִׁעִית לְצִדְקִיָּהוּ מֶלֶךְ־יְהוּדָה
בַּחֹדֶשׁ הָעֲשִׂרִי בָּא נְבוּכַדְרֶאצַּר מֶלֶךְ־
בָּבֶל וְכָל־חֵילוֹ אֶל־יְרוּשָׁלַ͏ִם וַיָּצֻרוּ
עָלֶיהָ:

² And in the eleventh year of *Tzidkiyahu*, on the
ninth day of the fourth month, the [walls of] the
city were breached.

ב בְּעַשְׁתֵּי־עֶשְׂרֵה שָׁנָה לְצִדְקִיָּהוּ בַּחֹדֶשׁ
הָרְבִיעִי בְּתִשְׁעָה לַחֹדֶשׁ הָבְקְעָה הָעִיר:

³ All the officers of the king of Babylon entered,
and took up quarters at the middle gate – Nergal-
sarezer, Samgar-nebo, Sarsechim the Rab-saris,
Nergal-sarezer the Rab-mag, and all the rest of the
officers of the king of Babylon.

ג וַיָּבֹאוּ כֹל שָׂרֵי מֶלֶךְ־בָּבֶל וַיֵּשְׁבוּ בְּשַׁעַר
הַתָּוֶךְ נֵרְגַל שַׂרְאֶצֶר סַמְגַּר־נְבוּ שַׂר־
סְכִים רַב־סָרִיס נֵרְגַל שַׂרְאֶצֶר רַב־מָג
וְכָל־שְׁאֵרִית שָׂרֵי מֶלֶךְ בָּבֶל:

⁴ When King *Tzidkiyahu* of *Yehuda* saw them, he and
all the soldiers fled. They left the city at night, by
way of the king's garden, through the gate between
the double walls; and he set out toward the Arabah.

ד וַיְהִי כַּאֲשֶׁר רָאָם צִדְקִיָּהוּ מֶלֶךְ־יְהוּדָה
וְכֹל אַנְשֵׁי הַמִּלְחָמָה וַיִּבְרְחוּ וַיֵּצְאוּ
לַיְלָה מִן־הָעִיר דֶּרֶךְ גַּן הַמֶּלֶךְ בְּשַׁעַר בֵּין
הַחֹמֹתָיִם וַיֵּצֵא דֶּרֶךְ הָעֲרָבָה:

5 But the Chaldean troops pursued them, and they overtake *Tzidkiyahu* in the steppes of *Yericho*. They captured him and brought him before King Nebuchadrezzar of Babylon at Riblah in the region of Hamath; and he put him on trial.

ה וַיִּרְדְּפוּ חֵיל־כַּשְׂדִּים אַחֲרֵיהֶם וַיַּשִּׂגוּ אֶת־צִדְקִיָּהוּ בְּעַרְבוֹת יְרֵחוֹ וַיִּקְחוּ אֹתוֹ וַיַּעֲלֻהוּ אֶל־נְבוּכַדְרֶאצַּר מֶלֶךְ־בָּבֶל רִבְלָתָה בְּאֶרֶץ חֲמָת וַיְדַבֵּר אִתּוֹ מִשְׁפָּטִים:

va-yir-d'-FU khayl kas-DEEM a-kha-ray-HEM va-ya-SEE-gu et tzid-ki-YA-hu b'-ar-VOT y'-ray-KHO va-yik-KHU o-TO va-ya-a-LU-hu el n'-vu-khad-RE-tzar me-lekh ba-VEL riv-LA-tah b'-E-retz kha-MAT vai-da-BAYR i-TO mish-pa-TEEM

6 The king of Babylon had *Tzidkiyahu*'s children slaughtered at Riblah before his eyes; the king of Babylon had all the nobles of *Yehuda* slaughtered.

ו וַיִּשְׁחַט מֶלֶךְ בָּבֶל אֶת־בְּנֵי צִדְקִיָּהוּ בְּרִבְלָה לְעֵינָיו וְאֵת כָּל־חֹרֵי יְהוּדָה שָׁחַט מֶלֶךְ בָּבֶל:

7 Then the eyes of *Tzidkiyahu* were put out and he was chained in bronze fetters, that he might be brought to Babylon.

ז וְאֶת־עֵינֵי צִדְקִיָּהוּ עִוֵּר וַיַּאַסְרֵהוּ בַּנְחֻשְׁתַּיִם לָבִיא אֹתוֹ בָּבֶלָה:

8 The Chaldeans burned down the king's palace and the houses of the people by fire, and they tore down the walls of *Yerushalayim*.

ח וְאֶת־בֵּית הַמֶּלֶךְ וְאֶת־בֵּית הָעָם שָׂרְפוּ הַכַּשְׂדִּים בָּאֵשׁ וְאֶת־חֹמוֹת יְרוּשָׁלִַם נָתָצוּ:

9 The remnant of the people that was left in the city, and the defectors who had gone over to him – the remnant of the people that was left – were exiled by Nebuzaradan, the chief of the guards, to Babylon.

ט וְאֵת יֶתֶר הָעָם הַנִּשְׁאָרִים בָּעִיר וְאֶת־הַנֹּפְלִים אֲשֶׁר נָפְלוּ עָלָיו וְאֵת יֶתֶר הָעָם הַנִּשְׁאָרִים הֶגְלָה נְבוּזַר־אֲדָן רַב־טַבָּחִים בָּבֶל:

10 But some of the poorest people who owned nothing were left in the land of *Yehuda* by Nebuzaradan, the chief of the guards, and he gave them vineyards and fields at that time.

י וּמִן־הָעָם הַדַּלִּים אֲשֶׁר אֵין־לָהֶם מְאוּמָה הִשְׁאִיר נְבוּזַרְאֲדָן רַב־טַבָּחִים בְּאֶרֶץ יְהוּדָה וַיִּתֵּן לָהֶם כְּרָמִים וִיגֵבִים בַּיּוֹם הַהוּא:

11 King Nebuchadrezzar of Babylon had given orders to Nebuzaradan, the chief of the guards, concerning *Yirmiyahu*:

יא וַיְצַו נְבוּכַדְרֶאצַּר מֶלֶךְ־בָּבֶל עַל־יִרְמְיָהוּ בְּיַד נְבוּזַרְאֲדָן רַב־טַבָּחִים לֵאמֹר:

12 "Take him and look after him; do him no harm, but grant whatever he asks of you."

יב קָחֶנּוּ וְעֵינֶיךָ שִׂים עָלָיו וְאַל־תַּעַשׂ לוֹ מְאוּמָה רָע כִּי אִם כַּאֲשֶׁר יְדַבֵּר אֵלֶיךָ כֵּן עֲשֵׂה עִמּוֹ:

13 So Nebuzaradan, the chief of the guards, and Nebushazban the Rab-saris, and Nergal-sarezer the Rab-mag, and all the commanders of the king of Babylon sent

יג וַיִּשְׁלַח נְבוּזַרְאֲדָן רַב־טַבָּחִים וּנְבוּשַׁזְבָּן רַב־סָרִיס וְנֵרְגַל שַׂר־אֶצֶר רַב־מָג וְכֹל רַבֵּי מֶלֶךְ־בָּבֶל:

39:5 And they overtook *Tzidkiyahu* in the steppes of *Yericho* Chapter 39 describes the tragic, final downfall of *Yerushalayim*. *Tzidki-yahu* attempts to flee, but is caught just miles away from the *Yarden* river, in *Yericho*. *Rashi* elaborates that "a cave went from his house until the plains of *Yericho*, and he fled through the cave. The Holy One, Blessed be He, ordained a deer walking on the roof of the cave. The Chaldeans pursued the deer, and when they reached the entrance of the cave in the plains of *Yericho*, they saw him and captured him." This is what *Yechezkel* said about him, (12:13) "I will spread My net over him, and he shall be caught in My snare." No matter what plans a person makes, God's plan prevails.

The plains of *Yericho*

Jeremiah

¹⁴ and had *Yirmiyahu* brought from the prison compound. They committed him to the care of *Gedalya* son of *Achikam* son of *Shafan*, that he might be left at liberty in a house. So he dwelt among the people.

יד וַיִּשְׁלְחוּ וַיִּקְחוּ אֶת־יִרְמְיָהוּ מֵחֲצַר הַמַּטָּרָה וַיִּתְּנוּ אֹתוֹ אֶל־גְּדַלְיָהוּ בֶן־אֲחִיקָם בֶּן־שָׁפָן לְהוֹצִאֵהוּ אֶל־הַבָּיִת וַיֵּשֶׁב בְּתוֹךְ הָעָם:

¹⁵ The word of *Hashem* had come to *Yirmiyahu* while he was still confined in the prison compound:

טו וְאֶל־יִרְמְיָהוּ הָיָה דְבַר־יְהֹוָה בִּהְיֹתוֹ עָצוּר בַּחֲצַר הַמַּטָּרָה לֵאמֹר:

¹⁶ Go and say to *Eved Melech* the Ethiopian: "Thus said the Lᴏʀᴅ of Hosts, the God of *Yisrael*: I am going to fulfill My words concerning this city – for disaster, not for good – and they shall come true on that day in your presence.

טז הָלוֹךְ וְאָמַרְתָּ לְעֶבֶד־מֶלֶךְ הַכּוּשִׁי לֵאמֹר כֹּה־אָמַר יְהֹוָה צְבָאוֹת אֱלֹהֵי יִשְׂרָאֵל הִנְנִי מֵבִי [מֵבִיא] אֶת־דְּבָרַי אֶל־הָעִיר הַזֹּאת לְרָעָה וְלֹא לְטוֹבָה וְהָיוּ לְפָנֶיךָ בַּיּוֹם הַהוּא:

¹⁷ But I will save you on that day – declares *Hashem*; you shall not be delivered into the hands of the men you dread.

יז וְהִצַּלְתִּיךָ בַיּוֹם־הַהוּא נְאֻם־יְהֹוָה וְלֹא תִנָּתֵן בְּיַד הָאֲנָשִׁים אֲשֶׁר־אַתָּה יָגוֹר מִפְּנֵיהֶם:

¹⁸ I will rescue you, and you shall not fall by the sword. You shall escape with your life, because you trusted Me – declares *Hashem*."

יח כִּי מַלֵּט אֲמַלֶּטְךָ וּבַחֶרֶב לֹא תִפֹּל וְהָיְתָה לְךָ נַפְשְׁךָ לְשָׁלָל כִּי־בָטַחְתָּ בִּי נְאֻם־יְהֹוָה:

40 ¹ The word that came to *Yirmiyahu* from *Hashem*, after Nebuzaradan, the chief of the guards, set him free at *Rama*, to which he had taken him, chained in fetters, among those from *Yerushalayim* and *Yehuda* who were being exiled to Babylon.

מ א הַדָּבָר אֲשֶׁר־הָיָה אֶל־יִרְמְיָהוּ מֵאֵת יְהֹוָה אַחַר שַׁלַּח אֹתוֹ נְבוּזַרְאֲדָן רַב־טַבָּחִים מִן־הָרָמָה בְּקַחְתּוֹ אֹתוֹ וְהוּא־אָסוּר בָּאזִקִּים בְּתוֹךְ כָּל־גָּלוּת יְרוּשָׁלַ͏ִם וִיהוּדָה הַמֻּגְלִים בָּבֶלָה:

> ha-da-VAR a-SHER ha-YAH el yir-m'-YA-hu may-AYT a-do-NAI
> a-KHAR sha-LAKH o-TO n'-vu-zar-a-DAN rav ta-ba-KHEEM min
> ha-ra-MAH b'-kakh-TO o-TO v'-hu a-SUR ba-zi-KEEM b'-TOKH kol
> ga-LUT y'-ru-sha-LA-im vee-hu-DAH ha-mug-LEEM ba-VE-lah

² The chief of the guards took charge of *Yirmiyahu*, and he said to him, "*Hashem* your God threatened this place with this disaster;

ב וַיִּקַּח רַב־טַבָּחִים לְיִרְמְיָהוּ וַיֹּאמֶר אֵלָיו יְהֹוָה אֱלֹהֶיךָ דִּבֶּר אֶת־הָרָעָה הַזֹּאת אֶל־הַמָּקוֹם הַזֶּה:

³ and now *Hashem* has brought it about. He has acted as He threatened, because you sinned against *Hashem* and did not obey Him. That is why this has happened to you.

ג וַיָּבֵא וַיַּעַשׂ יְהֹוָה כַּאֲשֶׁר דִּבֵּר כִּי־חֲטָאתֶם לַיהֹוָה וְלֹא־שְׁמַעְתֶּם בְּקוֹלוֹ וְהָיָה לָכֶם דבר [הַדָּבָר] הַזֶּה:

40:1 Set him free at *Rama* Although King Nebuchadnezzar of Babylon orders his soldiers to treat *Yirmiyahu* with respect and consideration, only when the convoy reaches *Rama*, about nine kilometers north of *Yerushalayim*, does the Babylonian captain release him from his chains. According to *Rashi*, *Yirmiyahu* voluntarily fettered himself to the chains leading the exiles away from Israel in order to demonstrate his complete identification with his people and their suffering. Such is the characteristic of a true leader. Though mistreated and abused by them, *Yirmiyahu* still identifies with, and cares for, his people.

Site of the biblical city of *Rama* in *Binyamin*

4 Now, I release you this day from the fetters which
were on your hands. If you would like to go with
me to Babylon, come, and I will look after you.
And if you don't want to come with me to Babylon,
you need not. See, the whole land is before you: go
wherever seems good and right to you." –

ד וְעַתָּה הִנֵּה פִתַּחְתִּיךָ הַיּוֹם מִן־הָאזִקִּים
אֲשֶׁר עַל־יָדֶךָ אִם־טוֹב בְּעֵינֶיךָ לָבוֹא
אִתִּי בָבֶל בֹּא וְאָשִׂים אֶת־עֵינִי עָלֶיךָ
וְאִם־רַע בְּעֵינֶיךָ לָבוֹא־אִתִּי בָבֶל חֲדָל
רְאֵה כָּל־הָאָרֶץ לְפָנֶיךָ אֶל־טוֹב וְאֶל־
הַיָּשָׁר בְּעֵינֶיךָ לָלֶכֶת שָׁמָּה לֵךְ:

5 But [*Yirmiyahu*] still did not turn back. – "Or go to
Gedalya son of *Achikam* son of *Shafan*, whom the
king of Babylon has put in charge of the towns of
Yehuda, and stay with him among the people, or go
wherever you want to go." The chief of the guards
gave him an allowance of food, and dismissed him.

ה וְעוֹדֶנּוּ לֹא־יָשׁוּב וְשֻׁבָה אֶל־גְּדַלְיָה בֶן־
אֲחִיקָם בֶּן־שָׁפָן אֲשֶׁר הִפְקִיד מֶלֶךְ־בָּבֶל
בְּעָרֵי יְהוּדָה וְשֵׁב אִתּוֹ בְּתוֹךְ הָעָם אוֹ
אֶל־כָּל־הַיָּשָׁר בְּעֵינֶיךָ לָלֶכֶת לֵךְ וַיִּתֶּן־לוֹ
רַב־טַבָּחִים אֲרֻחָה וּמַשְׂאֵת וַיְשַׁלְּחֵהוּ:

6 So *Yirmiyahu* came to *Gedalya* son of *Achikam* at
Mitzpa, and stayed with him among the people
who were left in the land.

ו וַיָּבֹא יִרְמְיָהוּ אֶל־גְּדַלְיָה בֶן־אֲחִיקָם
הַמִּצְפָּתָה וַיֵּשֶׁב אִתּוֹ בְּתוֹךְ הָעָם
הַנִּשְׁאָרִים בָּאָרֶץ:

7 The officers of the troops in the open country,
and their men with them, heard that the king of
Babylon had put *Gedalya* son of *Achikam* in charge
of the region, and that he had put in his charge the
men, women, and children – of the poorest in the
land – those who had not been exiled to Babylon.

ז וַיִּשְׁמְעוּ כָל־שָׂרֵי הַחֲיָלִים אֲשֶׁר בַּשָּׂדֶה
הֵמָּה וְאַנְשֵׁיהֶם כִּי־הִפְקִיד מֶלֶךְ־בָּבֶל
אֶת־גְּדַלְיָהוּ בֶן־אֲחִיקָם בָּאָרֶץ וְכִי
הִפְקִיד אִתּוֹ אֲנָשִׁים וְנָשִׁים וָטָף וּמִדַּלַּת
הָאָרֶץ מֵאֲשֶׁר לֹא־הָגְלוּ בָּבֶלָה:

8 So they with their men came to *Gedalya* at
Mitzpa – Ishmael son of Nethaniah; *Yochanan*
and *Yonatan* the sons of Kareah; *Seraya* son of
Tanhumeth; the sons of Ephai the Netophathite;
and Jezaniah son of the Maacathite.

ח וַיָּבֹאוּ אֶל־גְּדַלְיָה הַמִּצְפָּתָה וְיִשְׁמָעֵאל
בֶּן־נְתַנְיָהוּ וְיוֹחָנָן וְיוֹנָתָן בְּנֵי־קָרֵחַ
וּשְׂרָיָה בֶן־תַּנְחֻמֶת וּבְנֵי עֵיפַי [עוֹפַי]
הַנְּטֹפָתִי וִיזַנְיָהוּ בֶּן־הַמַּעֲכָתִי הֵמָּה
וְאַנְשֵׁיהֶם:

9 *Gedalya* son of *Achikam* son of *Shafan* reassured
them and their men, saying, "Do not be afraid to
serve the Chaldeans. Stay in the land and serve the
king of Babylon, and it will go well with you.

ט וַיִּשָּׁבַע לָהֶם גְּדַלְיָהוּ בֶן־אֲחִיקָם בֶּן־שָׁפָן
וּלְאַנְשֵׁיהֶם לֵאמֹר אַל־תִּירְאוּ מֵעֲבוֹד
הַכַּשְׂדִּים שְׁבוּ בָאָרֶץ וְעִבְדוּ אֶת־מֶלֶךְ
בָּבֶל וְיִיטַב לָכֶם:

10 I am going to stay in *Mitzpa* to attend upon the
Chaldeans who will come to us. But you may
gather wine and figs and oil and put them in your
own vessels, and settle in the towns you have
occupied."

י וַאֲנִי הִנְנִי יֹשֵׁב בַּמִּצְפָּה לַעֲמֹד לִפְנֵי
הַכַּשְׂדִּים אֲשֶׁר יָבֹאוּ אֵלֵינוּ וְאַתֶּם
אִסְפוּ יַיִן וְקַיִץ וְשֶׁמֶן וְשִׂמוּ בִּכְלֵיכֶם
וּשְׁבוּ בְּעָרֵיכֶם אֲשֶׁר־תְּפַשְׂתֶּם:

11 Likewise, all the Judeans who were in Moab,
Ammon, and Edom, or who were in other lands,
heard that the king of Babylon had let a remnant
stay in *Yehuda*, and that he had put *Gedalya* son of
Achikam son of *Shafan* in charge of them.

יא וְגַם כָּל־הַיְּהוּדִים אֲשֶׁר־בְּמוֹאָב וּבִבְנֵי־
עַמּוֹן וּבֶאֱדוֹם וַאֲשֶׁר בְּכָל־הָאֲרָצוֹת
שָׁמְעוּ כִּי־נָתַן מֶלֶךְ־בָּבֶל שְׁאֵרִית
לִיהוּדָה וְכִי הִפְקִיד עֲלֵיהֶם אֶת־גְּדַלְיָהוּ
בֶן־אֲחִיקָם בֶּן־שָׁפָן:

12 All these Judeans returned from all the places to
which they had scattered. They came to the land
of *Yehuda*, to *Gedalya* at *Mitzpa*, and they gathered
large quantities of wine and figs.

יב וַיָּשֻׁבוּ כָל־הַיְּהוּדִים מִכָּל־הַמְּקֹמוֹת
אֲשֶׁר נִדְּחוּ־שָׁם וַיָּבֹאוּ אֶרֶץ־יְהוּדָה
אֶל־גְּדַלְיָהוּ הַמִּצְפָּתָה וַיַּאַסְפוּ יַיִן וָקַיִץ
הַרְבֵּה מְאֹד:

13 *Yochanan* son of Kareah, and all the officers of the troops in the open country, came to *Gedalya* at *Mitzpa*

14 and said to him, "Do you know that King Baalis of Ammon has sent Ishmael son of Nethaniah to kill you?" But *Gedalya* son of *Achikam* would not believe them.

15 *Yochanan* son of Kareah also said secretly to *Gedalya* at *Mitzpa*, "Let me go and strike down Ishmael son of Nethaniah before anyone knows about it; otherwise he will kill you, and all the Judeans who have gathered about you will be dispersed, and the remnant of *Yehuda* will perish!"

16 But *Gedalya* son of *Achikam* answered *Yochanan* son of Kareah, "Do not do such a thing: what you are saying about Ishmael is not true!"

41 1 In the seventh month, Ishmael son of Nethaniah son of Elishama, who was of royal descent and one of the king's commanders, came with ten men to *Gedalya* son of *Achikam* at *Mitzpa*; and they ate together there at *Mitzpa*.

2 Then Ishmael son of Nethaniah and the ten men who were with him arose and struck down *Gedalya* son of *Achikam* son of *Shafan* with the sword and killed him, because the king of Babylon had put him in charge of the land.

*va-YA-kom yish-ma-AYL ben n'-tan-YAH va-a-SE-ret ha-a-na-SHEEM
a-sher ha-YU i-TO va-ya-KU et g'-dal-YA-hu ven a-khee-KAM ben sha-FAN
ba-KHE-rev va-YA-met o-TO a-sher hif-KEED me-lekh ba-VEL ba-A-retz*

3 Ishmael also killed all the Judeans who were with him – with *Gedalya* in *Mitzpa* – and the Chaldean soldiers who were stationed there.

יג וְיוֹחָנָן בֶּן־קָרֵחַ וְכָל־שָׂרֵי הַחֲיָלִים אֲשֶׁר בַּשָּׂדֶה בָּאוּ אֶל־גְּדַלְיָהוּ הַמִּצְפָּתָה׃

יד וַיֹּאמְרוּ אֵלָיו הֲיָדֹעַ תֵּדַע כִּי בַּעֲלִיס מֶלֶךְ בְּנֵי־עַמּוֹן שָׁלַח אֶת־יִשְׁמָעֵאל בֶּן־נְתַנְיָה לְהַכֹּתְךָ נָפֶשׁ וְלֹא־הֶאֱמִין לָהֶם גְּדַלְיָהוּ בֶּן־אֲחִיקָם׃

טו וְיוֹחָנָן בֶּן־קָרֵחַ אָמַר אֶל־גְּדַלְיָהוּ בַסֵּתֶר בַּמִּצְפָּה לֵאמֹר אֵלְכָה נָּא וְאַכֶּה אֶת־יִשְׁמָעֵאל בֶּן־נְתַנְיָה וְאִישׁ לֹא יֵדָע לָמָּה יַכֶּכָה נֶּפֶשׁ וְנָפֹצוּ כָּל־יְהוּדָה הַנִּקְבָּצִים אֵלֶיךָ וְאָבְדָה שְׁאֵרִית יְהוּדָה׃

טז וַיֹּאמֶר גְּדַלְיָהוּ בֶן־אֲחִיקָם אֶל־יוֹחָנָן בֶּן־קָרֵחַ אַל־תַּעַשׂ [תַּעֲשֵׂה] אֶת־הַדָּבָר הַזֶּה כִּי־שֶׁקֶר אַתָּה דֹבֵר אֶל־יִשְׁמָעֵאל׃

מא א וַיְהִי בַּחֹדֶשׁ הַשְּׁבִיעִי בָּא יִשְׁמָעֵאל בֶּן־נְתַנְיָה בֶן־אֱלִישָׁמָע מִזֶּרַע הַמְּלוּכָה וְרַבֵּי הַמֶּלֶךְ וַעֲשָׂרָה אֲנָשִׁים אִתּוֹ אֶל־גְּדַלְיָהוּ בֶן־אֲחִיקָם הַמִּצְפָּתָה וַיֹּאכְלוּ שָׁם לֶחֶם יַחְדָּו בַּמִּצְפָּה׃

ב וַיָּקָם יִשְׁמָעֵאל בֶּן־נְתַנְיָה וַעֲשֶׂרֶת הָאֲנָשִׁים אֲשֶׁר־הָיוּ אִתּוֹ וַיַּכּוּ אֶת־גְּדַלְיָהוּ בֶן־אֲחִיקָם בֶּן־שָׁפָן בַּחֶרֶב וַיָּמֶת אֹתוֹ אֲשֶׁר־הִפְקִיד מֶלֶךְ־בָּבֶל בָּאָרֶץ׃

ג וְאֵת כָּל־הַיְּהוּדִים אֲשֶׁר־הָיוּ אִתּוֹ אֶת־גְּדַלְיָהוּ בַּמִּצְפָּה וְאֶת־הַכַּשְׂדִּים אֲשֶׁר נִמְצְאוּ־שָׁם אֵת אַנְשֵׁי הַמִּלְחָמָה הִכָּה יִשְׁמָעֵאל׃

41:2 And struck down Gedalya *Gedalya* son of *Achikam* is appointed by the Babylonians as governor of *Yehuda* after the destruction of *Yerushalayim*. A small band of Jewish fanatics, led by Ishmael the son of Nethaniah, take advantage of *Gedalya's* hospitality and assassinate him on *Rosh Hashana*, the Jewish new year. As a result, the few Jews remaining in Israel flee to Egypt to avoid the vengeance of the Babylonian army, ridding the Holy Land of a Jewish presence for the remainder of the Babylonian exile. The death of the last

Rabbi Tuly Weisz celebrating Chanukkah with Holocaust survivors

Jewish leader in Israel marked the end of the First Israelite Commonwealth. Since then, for over two thousand years, Jews have fasted in commemoration of *Gedalyah's* death on the day after *Rosh Hashana*, to remind them how hatred and zealousness cost them their sovereignty in the Land of Israel. Rabbi Abraham Isaac Kook taught that since *Yerushalayim* was destroyed on account of hatred and factionalism (*Yoma* 9b), it is through love and kindness that the Jews will return to the land and the *Beit Hamikdash* will be rebuilt.

4 The second day after *Gedalya* was killed, when no one yet knew about it,

ד וַיְהִי בַּיּוֹם הַשֵּׁנִי לְהָמִית אֶת־גְּדַלְיָהוּ וְאִישׁ לֹא יָדָע:

5 eighty men came from *Shechem*, *Shilo*, and *Shomron*, their beards shaved, their garments torn, and their bodies gashed, carrying meal offerings and frankincense to present at the House of *Hashem*.

ה וַיָּבֹאוּ אֲנָשִׁים מִשְּׁכֶם מִשִּׁלוֹ וּמִשֹּׁמְרוֹן שְׁמֹנִים אִישׁ מְגֻלְּחֵי זָקָן וּקְרֻעֵי בְגָדִים וּמִתְגֹּדְדִים וּמִנְחָה וּלְבוֹנָה בְּיָדָם לְהָבִיא בֵּית יְהוָה:

6 Ishmael son of Nethaniah went out from *Mitzpa* to meet them, weeping as he walked. As he met them, he said to them, "Come to *Gedalya* son of *Achikam*."

ו וַיֵּצֵא יִשְׁמָעֵאל בֶּן־נְתַנְיָה לִקְרָאתָם מִן־הַמִּצְפָּה הֹלֵךְ הָלֹךְ וּבֹכֶה וַיְהִי כִּפְגֹשׁ אֹתָם וַיֹּאמֶר אֲלֵיהֶם בֹּאוּ אֶל־גְּדַלְיָהוּ בֶּן־אֲחִיקָם:

7 When they came inside the town, Ishmael son of Nethaniah and the men who were with him slaughtered them [and threw their bodies] into a cistern.

ז וַיְהִי כְּבוֹאָם אֶל־תּוֹךְ הָעִיר וַיִּשְׁחָטֵם יִשְׁמָעֵאל בֶּן־נְתַנְיָה אֶל־תּוֹךְ הַבּוֹר הוּא וְהָאֲנָשִׁים אֲשֶׁר־אִתּוֹ:

8 But there were ten men among them who said to Ishmael, "Don't kill us! We have stores hidden in a field – wheat, barley, oil, and honey." So he stopped, and did not kill them along with their fellows. –

ח וַעֲשָׂרָה אֲנָשִׁים נִמְצְאוּ־בָם וַיֹּאמְרוּ אֶל־יִשְׁמָעֵאל אַל־תְּמִתֵנוּ כִּי־יֶשׁ־לָנוּ מַטְמֹנִים בַּשָּׂדֶה חִטִּים וּשְׂעֹרִים וְשֶׁמֶן וּדְבָשׁ וַיֶּחְדַּל וְלֹא הֱמִיתָם בְּתוֹךְ אֲחֵיהֶם:

9 The cistern into which Ishmael threw all the corpses of the men he had killed in the affair of *Gedalya* was the one that King *Asa* had constructed on account of King *Basha* of *Yisrael*. That was the one which Ishmael son of Nethaniah filled with corpses. –

ט וְהַבּוֹר אֲשֶׁר הִשְׁלִיךְ שָׁם יִשְׁמָעֵאל אֵת כָּל־פִּגְרֵי הָאֲנָשִׁים אֲשֶׁר הִכָּה בְיַד־גְּדַלְיָהוּ הוּא אֲשֶׁר עָשָׂה הַמֶּלֶךְ אָסָא מִפְּנֵי בַּעְשָׁא מֶלֶךְ־יִשְׂרָאֵל אֹתוֹ מִלֵּא יִשְׁמָעֵאל בֶּן־נְתַנְיָהוּ חֲלָלִים:

10 Ishmael carried off all the rest of the people who were in *Mitzpa*, including the daughters of the king – all the people left in *Mitzpa*, over whom Nebuzaradan, the chief of the guards, had appointed *Gedalya* son of *Achikam*. Ishmael son of Nethaniah carried them off, and set out to cross over to the Amonites.

י וַיִּשְׁבְּ יִשְׁמָעֵאל אֶת־כָּל־שְׁאֵרִית הָעָם אֲשֶׁר בַּמִּצְפָּה אֶת־בְּנוֹת הַמֶּלֶךְ וְאֶת־כָּל־הָעָם הַנִּשְׁאָרִים בַּמִּצְפָּה אֲשֶׁר הִפְקִיד נְבוּזַרְאֲדָן רַב־טַבָּחִים אֶת־גְּדַלְיָהוּ בֶּן־אֲחִיקָם וַיִּשְׁבֵּם יִשְׁמָעֵאל בֶּן־נְתַנְיָה וַיֵּלֶךְ לַעֲבֹר אֶל־בְּנֵי עַמּוֹן:

11 *Yochanan* son of Kareah, and all the army officers with him, heard of all the crimes committed by Ishmael son of Nethaniah.

יא וַיִּשְׁמַע יוֹחָנָן בֶּן־קָרֵחַ וְכָל־שָׂרֵי הַחֲיָלִים אֲשֶׁר אִתּוֹ אֵת כָּל־הָרָעָה אֲשֶׁר עָשָׂה יִשְׁמָעֵאל בֶּן־נְתַנְיָה:

12 They took all their men and went to fight against Ishmael son of Nethaniah; and they encountered him by the great pool in *Givon*.

יב וַיִּקְחוּ אֶת־כָּל־הָאֲנָשִׁים וַיֵּלְכוּ לְהִלָּחֵם עִם־יִשְׁמָעֵאל בֶּן־נְתַנְיָה וַיִּמְצְאוּ אֹתוֹ אֶל־מַיִם רַבִּים אֲשֶׁר בְּגִבְעוֹן:

13 When all the people held by Ishmael saw *Yochanan* son of Kareah and all the army officers with him, they were glad;

יג וַיְהִי כִּרְאוֹת כָּל־הָעָם אֲשֶׁר אֶת־יִשְׁמָעֵאל אֶת־יוֹחָנָן בֶּן־קָרֵחַ וְאֵת כָּל־שָׂרֵי הַחֲיָלִים אֲשֶׁר אִתּוֹ וַיִּשְׂמָחוּ:

Jeremiah

14 all the people whom Ishmael had carried off from
Mitzpa turned back and went over to *Yochanan* son
of Kareah.

יד וַיָּסֹבּוּ כָּל־הָעָם אֲשֶׁר־שָׁבָה יִשְׁמָעֵאל
מִן־הַמִּצְפָּה וַיָּשֻׁבוּ וַיֵּלְכוּ אֶל־יוֹחָנָן בֶּן־
קָרֵחַ:

15 But Ishmael son of Nethaniah escaped from
Yochanan with eight men, and went to the
Amonites.

טו וְיִשְׁמָעֵאל בֶּן־נְתַנְיָה נִמְלַט בִּשְׁמֹנָה
אֲנָשִׁים מִפְּנֵי יוֹחָנָן וַיֵּלֶךְ אֶל־בְּנֵי עַמּוֹן:

16 *Yochanan* son of Kareah and all the army officers
with him took all the rest of the people whom he
had rescued from Ishmael son of Nethaniah from
Mitzpa after he had murdered *Gedalya* son of
Achikam – the men, soldiers, women, children, and
eunuchs whom [*Yochanan*] had brought back from
Givon.

טז וַיִּקַּח יוֹחָנָן בֶּן־קָרֵחַ וְכָל־שָׂרֵי הַחֲיָלִים
אֲשֶׁר־אִתּוֹ אֵת כָּל־שְׁאֵרִית הָעָם
אֲשֶׁר הֵשִׁיב מֵאֵת יִשְׁמָעֵאל בֶּן־נְתַנְיָה
מִן־הַמִּצְפָּה אַחַר הִכָּה אֶת־גְּדַלְיָה בֶּן־
אֲחִיקָם גְּבָרִים אַנְשֵׁי הַמִּלְחָמָה וְנָשִׁים
וְטַף וְסָרִסִים אֲשֶׁר הֵשִׁיב מִגִּבְעוֹן:

17 They set out, and they stopped at Geruth
Chimham, near *Beit Lechem*, on their way to go to
Egypt

יז וַיֵּלְכוּ וַיֵּשְׁבוּ בְּגֵרוּת כמוהם [כִּמְהָם]
אֲשֶׁר־אֵצֶל בֵּית לָחֶם לָלֶכֶת לָבוֹא
מִצְרָיִם:

18 because of the Chaldeans. For they were afraid
of them, because Ishmael son of Nethaniah had
killed *Gedalya* son of *Achikam*, whom the king of
Babylon had put in charge of the land.

יח מִפְּנֵי הַכַּשְׂדִּים כִּי יָרְאוּ מִפְּנֵיהֶם כִּי־
הִכָּה יִשְׁמָעֵאל בֶּן־נְתַנְיָה אֶת־גְּדַלְיָהוּ
בֶּן־אֲחִיקָם אֲשֶׁר־הִפְקִיד מֶלֶךְ־בָּבֶל
בָּאָרֶץ:

42 1 Then all the army officers, with *Yochanan* son of
Kareah, Jezaniah son of Hoshaiah, and all the rest
of the people, great and small, approached

מב א וַיִּגְּשׁוּ כָּל־שָׂרֵי הַחֲיָלִים וְיוֹחָנָן בֶּן־קָרֵחַ
וִיזַנְיָה בֶּן־הוֹשַׁעְיָה וְכָל־הָעָם מִקָּטֹן
וְעַד־גָּדוֹל:

2 the *Navi Yirmiyahu* and said, "Grant our plea,
and pray for us to *Hashem* your God, for all this
remnant! For we remain but a few out of many, as
you can see.

ב וַיֹּאמְרוּ אֶל־יִרְמְיָהוּ הַנָּבִיא תִּפָּל־נָא
תְחִנָּתֵנוּ לְפָנֶיךָ וְהִתְפַּלֵּל בַּעֲדֵנוּ אֶל־
יְהוָה אֱלֹהֶיךָ בְּעַד כָּל־הַשְּׁאֵרִית הַזֹּאת
כִּי־נִשְׁאַרְנוּ מְעַט מֵהַרְבֵּה כַּאֲשֶׁר עֵינֶיךָ
רֹאוֹת אֹתָנוּ:

va-yo-m'-RU el yir-m'-YA-hu ha-na-VEE ti-pol NA t'-khi-na-TAY-nu
l'-fa-NE-kha v'-hit-pa-LAYL ba-a-DAY-nu el a-do-NAI e-lo-HE-kha
b'-AD kol ha-sh'-ay-REET ha-ZOT kee nish-AR-nu m'-AT
may-har-BAY ka-a-SHER ay-NE-kha ro-OT o-TA-nu

3 Let *Hashem* your God tell us where we should go
and what we should do."

ג וְיַגֶּד־לָנוּ יְהוָה אֱלֹהֶיךָ אֶת־הַדֶּרֶךְ אֲשֶׁר
נֵלֶךְ־בָּהּ וְאֶת־הַדָּבָר אֲשֶׁר נַעֲשֶׂה:

Stones from the Second *Beit Hamikdash* thrown by the Romans

42:2 For we remain but a few out of many The people, in panic over the upcoming invasion from Babylonia, turn to the prophet and ask him to pray for guidance. *Yirmiyahu* counsels them against going down to Egypt. However, in their final act of disobedience against God, they flee to Egypt, forcefully taking *Yirmiyahu* with them. Their statement that they were once many, but now have become few, represents an undoing of the divine promises. *Sefer Devarim* (10:22) describes how God took a few people, made them many, and brought them from Egypt to the Land of Israel. Now, they leave *Eretz Yisrael* headed for Egypt, few instead of many; a painful reminder of the damage caused by refusing to listen to the word of God.

4 The *Navi Yirmiyahu* answered them, "Agreed: I will pray to *Hashem* your God as you request, and I will tell you whatever response *Hashem* gives for you. I will withhold nothing from you."

5 Thereupon they said to *Yirmiyahu*, "Let *Hashem* be a true and faithful witness against us! We swear that we will do exactly as *Hashem* your God instructs us through you –

6 Whether it is pleasant or unpleasant, we will obey *Hashem* our God to whom we send you, in order that it may go well with us when we obey *Hashem* our God."

7 After ten days, the word of *Hashem* came to *Yirmiyahu*.

8 He called *Yochanan* son of Kareah and all the army officers, and the rest of the people, great and small,

9 and said to them, "Thus said *Hashem*, the God of *Yisrael*, to whom you sent me to present your supplication before Him:

10 If you remain in this land, I will build you and not overthrow, I will plant you and not uproot; for I regret the punishment I have brought upon you.

11 Do not be afraid of the king of Babylon, whom you fear; do not be afraid of him – declares *Hashem* – for I am with you to save you and to rescue you from his hands.

12 I will dispose him to be merciful to you: he shall show you mercy and bring you back to your own land.

13 "But if you say, 'We will not stay in this land' – thus disobeying *Hashem* your God –

14 if you say, 'No! We will go to the land of Egypt, so that we may not see war or hear the sound of the *shofar*, and so that we may not hunger for bread; there we will stay,'

15 then hear the word of *Hashem*, O remnant of *Yehuda*! Thus said the Lord of Hosts, the God of *Yisrael*: If you turn your faces toward Egypt, and you go and sojourn there,

ד וַיֹּאמֶר אֲלֵיהֶם יִרְמְיָהוּ הַנָּבִיא שָׁמַעְתִּי הִנְנִי מִתְפַּלֵּל אֶל־יְהֹוָה אֱלֹהֵיכֶם כְּדִבְרֵיכֶם וְהָיָה כָּל־הַדָּבָר אֲשֶׁר־יַעֲנֶה יְהֹוָה אֶתְכֶם אַגִּיד לָכֶם לֹא־אֶמְנַע מִכֶּם דָּבָר:

ה וְהֵמָּה אָמְרוּ אֶל־יִרְמְיָהוּ יְהִי יְהֹוָה בָּנוּ לְעֵד אֱמֶת וְנֶאֱמָן אִם־לֹא כְּכָל־הַדָּבָר אֲשֶׁר יִשְׁלָחֲךָ יְהֹוָה אֱלֹהֶיךָ אֵלֵינוּ כֵּן נַעֲשֶׂה:

ו אִם־טוֹב וְאִם־רָע בְּקוֹל יְהֹוָה אֱלֹהֵינוּ אֲשֶׁר אֲנוּ [אֲנַחְנוּ] שֹׁלְחִים אֹתְךָ אֵלָיו נִשְׁמָע לְמַעַן אֲשֶׁר יִיטַב־לָנוּ כִּי נִשְׁמַע בְּקוֹל יְהֹוָה אֱלֹהֵינוּ:

ז וַיְהִי מִקֵּץ עֲשֶׂרֶת יָמִים וַיְהִי דְבַר־יְהֹוָה אֶל־יִרְמְיָהוּ:

ח וַיִּקְרָא אֶל־יוֹחָנָן בֶּן־קָרֵחַ וְאֶל כָּל־שָׂרֵי הַחֲיָלִים אֲשֶׁר אִתּוֹ וּלְכָל־הָעָם לְמִקָּטֹן וְעַד־גָּדוֹל:

ט וַיֹּאמֶר אֲלֵיהֶם כֹּה־אָמַר יְהֹוָה אֱלֹהֵי יִשְׂרָאֵל אֲשֶׁר שְׁלַחְתֶּם אֹתִי אֵלָיו לְהַפִּיל תְּחִנַּתְכֶם לְפָנָיו:

י אִם־שׁוֹב תֵּשְׁבוּ בָּאָרֶץ הַזֹּאת וּבָנִיתִי אֶתְכֶם וְלֹא אֶהֱרֹס וְנָטַעְתִּי אֶתְכֶם וְלֹא אֶתּוֹשׁ כִּי נִחַמְתִּי אֶל־הָרָעָה אֲשֶׁר עָשִׂיתִי לָכֶם:

יא אַל־תִּירְאוּ מִפְּנֵי מֶלֶךְ בָּבֶל אֲשֶׁר־אַתֶּם יְרֵאִים מִפָּנָיו אַל־תִּירְאוּ מִמֶּנּוּ נְאֻם־יְהֹוָה כִּי־אִתְּכֶם אָנִי לְהוֹשִׁיעַ אֶתְכֶם וּלְהַצִּיל אֶתְכֶם מִיָּדוֹ:

יב וְאֶתֵּן לָכֶם רַחֲמִים וְרִחַם אֶתְכֶם וְהֵשִׁיב אֶתְכֶם אֶל־אַדְמַתְכֶם:

יג וְאִם־אֹמְרִים אַתֶּם לֹא נֵשֵׁב בָּאָרֶץ הַזֹּאת לְבִלְתִּי שְׁמֹעַ בְּקוֹל יְהֹוָה אֱלֹהֵיכֶם:

יד לֵאמֹר לֹא כִּי אֶרֶץ מִצְרַיִם נָבוֹא אֲשֶׁר לֹא־נִרְאֶה מִלְחָמָה וְקוֹל שׁוֹפָר לֹא נִשְׁמָע וְלַלֶּחֶם לֹא־נִרְעָב וְשָׁם נֵשֵׁב:

טו וְעַתָּה לָכֵן שִׁמְעוּ דְבַר־יְהֹוָה שְׁאֵרִית יְהוּדָה כֹּה־אָמַר יְהֹוָה צְבָאוֹת אֱלֹהֵי יִשְׂרָאֵל אִם־אַתֶּם שׂוֹם תְּשִׂמוּן פְּנֵיכֶם לָבֹא מִצְרַיִם וּבָאתֶם לָגוּר שָׁם:

16 the sword that you fear shall overtake you there, in the land of Egypt, and the famine you worry over shall follow at your heels in Egypt too; and there you shall die.

טז וְהָיְתָה הַחֶרֶב אֲשֶׁר אַתֶּם יְרֵאִים מִמֶּנָּה שָׁם תַּשִּׂיג אֶתְכֶם בְּאֶרֶץ מִצְרָיִם וְהָרָעָב אֲשֶׁר־אַתֶּם דֹּאֲגִים מִמֶּנּוּ שָׁם יִדְבַּק אַחֲרֵיכֶם מִצְרַיִם וְשָׁם תָּמֻתוּ:

17 All the men who turn their faces toward Egypt, in order to sojourn there, shall die by the sword, by famine, and by pestilence. They shall have no surviving remnant of the disaster that I will bring upon them.

יז וְיִהְיוּ כָל־הָאֲנָשִׁים אֲשֶׁר־שָׂמוּ אֶת־פְּנֵיהֶם לָבוֹא מִצְרַיִם לָגוּר שָׁם יָמוּתוּ בַּחֶרֶב בָּרָעָב וּבַדָּבֶר וְלֹא־יִהְיֶה לָהֶם שָׂרִיד וּפָלִיט מִפְּנֵי הָרָעָה אֲשֶׁר אֲנִי מֵבִיא עֲלֵיהֶם:

18 For thus said the Lord of Hosts, the God of *Yisrael*: As My anger and wrath were poured out upon the inhabitants of *Yerushalayim*, so will My wrath be poured out on you if you go to Egypt. You shall become an execration of woe, a curse and a mockery; and you shall never again see this place.

יח כִּי כֹה אָמַר יְהֹוָה צְבָאוֹת אֱלֹהֵי יִשְׂרָאֵל כַּאֲשֶׁר נִתַּךְ אַפִּי וַחֲמָתִי עַל־יֹשְׁבֵי יְרוּשָׁלַ͏ִם כֵּן תִּתַּךְ חֲמָתִי עֲלֵיכֶם בְּבֹאֲכֶם מִצְרָיִם וִהְיִיתֶם לְאָלָה וּלְשַׁמָּה וְלִקְלָלָה וּלְחֶרְפָּה וְלֹא־תִרְאוּ עוֹד אֶת־הַמָּקוֹם הַזֶּה:

19 *Hashem* has spoken against you, O remnant of *Yehuda*! Do not go to Egypt! Know well, then – for I warn you this day

יט דִּבֶּר יְהֹוָה עֲלֵיכֶם שְׁאֵרִית יְהוּדָה אַל־תָּבֹאוּ מִצְרָיִם יָדֹעַ תֵּדְעוּ כִּי־הַעִידֹתִי בָכֶם הַיּוֹם:

20 that you were deceitful at heart when you sent me to *Hashem* your God, saying, 'Pray for us to *Hashem* our God; and whatever *Hashem* our God may say, just tell us and we will do it.'

כ כִּי הִתְעֵתֶים [הִתְעֵיתֶם] בְּנַפְשׁוֹתֵיכֶם כִּי־אַתֶּם שְׁלַחְתֶּם אֹתִי אֶל־יְהֹוָה אֱלֹהֵיכֶם לֵאמֹר הִתְפַּלֵּל בַּעֲדֵנוּ אֶל־יְהֹוָה אֱלֹהֵינוּ וּכְכֹל אֲשֶׁר יֹאמַר יְהֹוָה אֱלֹהֵינוּ כֵּן הַגֶּד־לָנוּ וְעָשִׂינוּ:

21 I told you today, and you have not obeyed *Hashem* your God in respect to all that He sent me to tell you –

כא וָאַגִּד לָכֶם הַיּוֹם וְלֹא שְׁמַעְתֶּם בְּקוֹל יְהֹוָה אֱלֹהֵיכֶם וּלְכֹל אֲשֶׁר־שְׁלָחַנִי אֲלֵיכֶם:

22 know well, then, that you shall die by the sword, by famine, and by pestilence in the place where you want to go and sojourn."

כב וְעַתָּה יָדֹעַ תֵּדְעוּ כִּי בַּחֶרֶב בָּרָעָב וּבַדֶּבֶר תָּמוּתוּ בַּמָּקוֹם אֲשֶׁר חֲפַצְתֶּם לָבוֹא לָגוּר שָׁם:

43 ¹ When *Yirmiyahu* had finished speaking all these words to all the people – all the words of *Hashem* their God, with which *Hashem* their God had sent him to them –

מג א וַיְהִי כְּכַלּוֹת יִרְמְיָהוּ לְדַבֵּר אֶל־כָּל־הָעָם אֶת־כָּל־דִּבְרֵי יְהֹוָה אֱלֹהֵיהֶם אֲשֶׁר שְׁלָחוֹ יְהֹוָה אֱלֹהֵיהֶם אֲלֵיהֶם אֵת כָּל־הַדְּבָרִים הָאֵלֶּה:

2 *Azarya* son of Hoshaiah and *Yochanan* son of Kareah and all the arrogant men said to *Yirmiyahu*, "You are lying! *Hashem* our God did not send you to say, 'Don't go to Egypt and sojourn there'!

ב וַיֹּאמֶר עֲזַרְיָה בֶן־הוֹשַׁעְיָה וְיוֹחָנָן בֶּן־קָרֵחַ וְכָל־הָאֲנָשִׁים הַזֵּדִים אֹמְרִים אֶל־יִרְמְיָהוּ שֶׁקֶר אַתָּה מְדַבֵּר לֹא שְׁלָחֲךָ יְהֹוָה אֱלֹהֵינוּ לֵאמֹר לֹא־תָבֹאוּ מִצְרַיִם לָגוּר שָׁם:

3 It is *Baruch* son of *Nerya* who is inciting you against us, so that we will be delivered into the hands of the Chaldeans to be killed or to be exiled to Babylon!"

ג כִּי בָּרוּךְ בֶּן־נֵרִיָּה מַסִּית אֹתְךָ בָּנוּ לְמַעַן תֵּת אֹתָנוּ בְיַד־הַכַּשְׂדִּים לְהָמִית אֹתָנוּ וּלְהַגְלוֹת אֹתָנוּ בָּבֶל:

Jeremiah

⁴ So *Yochanan* son of Kareah and all the army officers and the rest of the people did not obey *Hashem's* command to remain in the land of *Yehuda*.

ד וְלֹא־שָׁמַע יוֹחָנָן בֶּן־קָרֵחַ וְכָל־שָׂרֵי הַחֲיָלִים וְכָל־הָעָם בְּקוֹל יְהוָה לָשֶׁבֶת בְּאֶרֶץ יְהוּדָה:

⁵ Instead, *Yochanan* son of Kareah and all the army officers took the entire remnant of *Yehuda* – those who had returned from all the countries to which they had been scattered and had sojourned in the land of *Yehuda*,

ה וַיִּקַּח יוֹחָנָן בֶּן־קָרֵחַ וְכָל־שָׂרֵי הַחֲיָלִים אֵת כָּל־שְׁאֵרִית יְהוּדָה אֲשֶׁר־שָׁבוּ מִכָּל־הַגּוֹיִם אֲשֶׁר נִדְּחוּ־שָׁם לָגוּר בְּאֶרֶץ יְהוּדָה:

⁶ men, women, and children; and the daughters of the king and all the people whom Nebuzaradan the chief of the guards had left with *Gedalya* son of *Achikam* son of *Shafan*, as well as the *Navi Yirmiyahu* and *Baruch* son of *Nerya* –

ו אֶת־הַגְּבָרִים וְאֶת־הַנָּשִׁים וְאֶת־הַטַּף וְאֶת־בְּנוֹת הַמֶּלֶךְ וְאֵת כָּל־הַנֶּפֶשׁ אֲשֶׁר הִנִּיחַ נְבוּזַרְאֲדָן רַב־טַבָּחִים אֶת־גְּדַלְיָהוּ בֶּן־אֲחִיקָם בֶּן־שָׁפָן וְאֵת יִרְמְיָהוּ הַנָּבִיא וְאֶת־בָּרוּךְ בֶּן־נֵרִיָּהוּ:

⁷ and they went to Egypt. They did not obey *Hashem*. They arrived at Tahpanhes,

ז וַיָּבֹאוּ אֶרֶץ מִצְרַיִם כִּי לֹא שָׁמְעוּ בְּקוֹל יְהוָה וַיָּבֹאוּ עַד־תַּחְפַּנְחֵס:

⁸ and the word of *Hashem* came to *Yirmiyahu* in Tahpanhes:

ח וַיְהִי דְבַר־יְהוָה אֶל־יִרְמְיָהוּ בְּתַחְפַּנְחֵס לֵאמֹר:

⁹ Get yourself large stones, and embed them in mortar in the brick structure at the entrance to Pharaoh's palace in Tahpanhes, with some Judeans looking on.

ט קַח בְּיָדְךָ אֲבָנִים גְּדֹלוֹת וּטְמַנְתָּם בַּמֶּלֶט בַּמַּלְבֵּן אֲשֶׁר בְּפֶתַח בֵּית־פַּרְעֹה בְּתַחְפַּנְחֵס לְעֵינֵי אֲנָשִׁים יְהוּדִים:

¹⁰ And say to them: "Thus said the LORD of Hosts, the God of *Yisrael*: I am sending for My servant King Nebuchadrezzar of Babylon, and I will set his throne over these stones which I have embedded. He will spread out his pavilion over them.

י וְאָמַרְתָּ אֲלֵיהֶם כֹּה־אָמַר יְהוָה צְבָאוֹת אֱלֹהֵי יִשְׂרָאֵל הִנְנִי שֹׁלֵחַ וְלָקַחְתִּי אֶת־נְבוּכַדְרֶאצַּר מֶלֶךְ־בָּבֶל עַבְדִּי וְשַׂמְתִּי כִסְאוֹ מִמַּעַל לָאֲבָנִים הָאֵלֶּה אֲשֶׁר טָמָנְתִּי וְנָטָה אֶת־שפרורו [שַׁפְרִירוֹ] עֲלֵיהֶם:

v'-a-mar-TA a-lay-HEM koh a-MAR a-do-NAI tz'-va-OT e-lo-HAY
yis-ra-AYL hi-n'-NEE sho-LAY-akh v'-la-kakh-TEE et n'-vu-khad-RE-tzar
me-lekh ba-VEL av-DEE v'-sam-TEE khis-O mi-MA-al la-a-va-NEEM
ha-AY-leh a-SHER ta-MAN-tee v'-na-TAH et shaf-ree-RO a-lay-HEM

¹¹ He will come and attack the land of Egypt, delivering Those destined for the plague, to the plague, Those destined for captivity, to captivity, And those destined for the sword, to the sword.

יא וּבָא [וּבָא] וְהִכָּה אֶת־אֶרֶץ מִצְרָיִם אֲשֶׁר לַמָּוֶת לַמָּוֶת וַאֲשֶׁר לַשְּׁבִי לַשֶּׁבִי וַאֲשֶׁר לַחֶרֶב לֶחָרֶב:

43:10 And I will set his throne over these stones *Yirmiyahu* is commanded to embed giant stones into the mortar in front of Pharaoh's palace while men from *Yehuda* look on. This final symbolic act was performed with the hopes that the Jews who had fled to Egypt would regret their actions and return to Israel. The prophet declares that the gates of Egypt will not provide them protection, as the Babylonians will conquer Egypt as well. The only protection they can rely on is a return to *Hashem's* will and the Land of Israel, or they too will be captured and destroyed. God's dominion, while concentrated in the Holy Land, extends everywhere; they cannot flee from His bidding.

Greeting new immigrants to Israel at Ben Gurion airport

12 And I will set fire to the temples of the gods of Egypt; he will burn them down and carry them off. He shall wrap himself up in the land of Egypt, as a shepherd wraps himself up in his garment. And he shall depart from there in safety.

יב וְהִצַּתִּי אֵשׁ בְּבָתֵּי אֱלֹהֵי מִצְרַיִם וּשְׂרָפָם וְשָׁבָם וְעָטָה אֶת־אֶרֶץ מִצְרַיִם כַּאֲשֶׁר־יַעְטֶה הָרֹעֶה אֶת־בִּגְדוֹ וְיָצָא מִשָּׁם בְּשָׁלוֹם:

13 He shall smash the obelisks of the Temple of the Sun which is in the land of Egypt, and he shall burn down the temples of the gods of Egypt.

יג וְשִׁבַּר אֶת־מַצְּבוֹת בֵּית שֶׁמֶשׁ אֲשֶׁר בְּאֶרֶץ מִצְרַיִם וְאֶת־בָּתֵּי אֱלֹהֵי־מִצְרַיִם יִשְׂרֹף בָּאֵשׁ:

44 1 The word which came to *Yirmiyahu* for all the Judeans living in the land of Egypt, living in Migdol, Tahpanhes, and Noph, and in the land of Pathros:

מד א הַדָּבָר אֲשֶׁר הָיָה אֶל־יִרְמְיָהוּ אֶל כָּל־הַיְּהוּדִים הַיֹּשְׁבִים בְּאֶרֶץ מִצְרָיִם הַיֹּשְׁבִים בְּמִגְדֹּל וּבְתַחְפַּנְחֵס וּבְנֹף וּבְאֶרֶץ פַּתְרוֹס לֵאמֹר:

2 Thus said the Lord of Hosts, the God of *Yisrael*: You have seen all the disaster that I brought on *Yerushalayim* and on all the towns of *Yehuda*. They are a ruin today, and no one inhabits them,

ב כֹּה־אָמַר יְהֹוָה צְבָאוֹת אֱלֹהֵי יִשְׂרָאֵל אַתֶּם רְאִיתֶם אֵת כָּל־הָרָעָה אֲשֶׁר הֵבֵאתִי עַל־יְרוּשָׁלַם וְעַל כָּל־עָרֵי יְהוּדָה וְהִנָּם חָרְבָּה הַיּוֹם הַזֶּה וְאֵין בָּהֶם יוֹשֵׁב:

3 on account of the wicked things they did to vex Me, going to make offerings in worship of other gods which they had not known – neither they nor you nor your fathers.

ג מִפְּנֵי רָעָתָם אֲשֶׁר עָשׂוּ לְהַכְעִסֵנִי לָלֶכֶת לְקַטֵּר לַעֲבֹד לֵאלֹהִים אֲחֵרִים אֲשֶׁר לֹא יְדָעוּם הֵמָּה אַתֶּם וַאֲבֹתֵיכֶם:

4 Yet I persistently sent to you all My servants the *Neviim*, to say, "I beg you not to do this abominable thing which I hate."

ד וָאֶשְׁלַח אֲלֵיכֶם אֶת־כָּל־עֲבָדַי הַנְּבִיאִים הַשְׁכֵּים וְשָׁלֹחַ לֵאמֹר אַל־נָא תַעֲשׂוּ אֵת דְּבַר־הַתֹּעֵבָה הַזֹּאת אֲשֶׁר שָׂנֵאתִי:

5 But they would not listen or give ear, to turn back from their wickedness and not make offerings to other gods;

ה וְלֹא שָׁמְעוּ וְלֹא־הִטּוּ אֶת־אָזְנָם לָשׁוּב מֵרָעָתָם לְבִלְתִּי קַטֵּר לֵאלֹהִים אֲחֵרִים:

6 so My fierce anger was poured out, and it blazed against the towns of *Yehuda* and the streets of *Yerushalayim*. And they became a desolate ruin, as they still are today.

ו וַתִּתַּךְ חֲמָתִי וְאַפִּי וַתִּבְעַר בְּעָרֵי יְהוּדָה וּבְחֻצוֹת יְרוּשָׁלָם וַתִּהְיֶינָה לְחָרְבָּה לִשְׁמָמָה כַּיּוֹם הַזֶּה:

7 And now, thus said *Hashem*, the the Lord of Hosts, the God of *Yisrael*: Why are you doing such great harm to yourselves, so that every man and woman, child and infant of yours shall be cut off from the midst of *Yehuda*, and no remnant shall be left of you?

ז וְעַתָּה כֹּה־אָמַר יְהֹוָה אֱלֹהֵי צְבָאוֹת אֱלֹהֵי יִשְׂרָאֵל לָמָה אַתֶּם עֹשִׂים רָעָה גְדוֹלָה אֶל־נַפְשֹׁתְכֶם לְהַכְרִית לָכֶם אִישׁ־וְאִשָּׁה עוֹלֵל וְיוֹנֵק מִתּוֹךְ יְהוּדָה לְבִלְתִּי הוֹתִיר לָכֶם שְׁאֵרִית:

8 For you vex me by your deeds, making offering to other gods in the land of Egypt where you have come to sojourn, so that you shall be cut off and become a curse and a mockery among all the nations of earth.

ח לְהַכְעִסֵנִי בְּמַעֲשֵׂי יְדֵיכֶם לְקַטֵּר לֵאלֹהִים אֲחֵרִים בְּאֶרֶץ מִצְרַיִם אֲשֶׁר־אַתֶּם בָּאִים לָגוּר שָׁם לְמַעַן הַכְרִית לָכֶם וּלְמַעַן הֱיוֹתְכֶם לִקְלָלָה וּלְחֶרְפָּה בְּכֹל גּוֹיֵי הָאָרֶץ:

9 Have you forgotten the wicked acts of your forefathers, of the kings of *Yehuda* and their wives, and your own wicked acts and those of your wives, which were committed in the land of *Yehuda* and in the streets of *Yerushalayim*?

10 No one has shown contrition to this day, and no one has shown reverence. You have not followed the Teaching and the laws that I set before you and before your fathers.

11 Assuredly, thus said the Lord of Hosts, the God of *Yisrael*: I am going to set My face against you for punishment, to cut off all of *Yehuda*.

12 I will take the remnant of *Yehuda* who turned their faces toward the land of Egypt, to go and sojourn there, and they shall be utterly consumed in the land of Egypt. They shall fall by the sword, they shall be consumed by famine; great and small alike shall die by the sword and by famine, and they shall become an execration and a desolation, a curse and a mockery.

13 I will punish those who live in the land of Egypt as I punished *Yerushalayim*, with the sword, with famine, and with pestilence.

14 Of the remnant of *Yehuda* who came to sojourn here in the land of Egypt, no survivor or fugitive shall be left to return to the land of *Yehuda*. Though they all long to return and dwell there, none shall return except [a few] survivors.

15 Thereupon they answered *Yirmiyahu* – all the men who knew that their wives made offerings to other gods; all the women present, a large gathering; and all the people who lived in Pathros in the land of Egypt:

16 "We will not listen to you in the matter about which you spoke to us in the name of *Hashem*.

17 On the contrary, we will do everything that we have vowed – to make offerings to the Queen of Heaven and to pour libations to her, as we used to do, we and our fathers, our kings and our officials, in the towns of *Yehuda* and the streets of *Yerushalayim*. For then we had plenty to eat, we were well-off, and suffered no misfortune.

ט הַשְׁכַחְתֶּם אֶת־רָעוֹת אֲבוֹתֵיכֶם וְאֶת־רָעוֹת מַלְכֵי יְהוּדָה וְאֵת רָעוֹת נָשָׁיו וְאֵת רָעֹתְכֶם וְאֵת רָעֹת נְשֵׁיכֶם אֲשֶׁר עָשׂוּ בְּאֶרֶץ יְהוּדָה וּבְחֻצוֹת יְרוּשָׁלָם:

י לֹא דֻכְּאוּ עַד הַיּוֹם הַזֶּה וְלֹא יָרְאוּ וְלֹא־הָלְכוּ בְתוֹרָתִי וּבְחֻקֹּתַי אֲשֶׁר־נָתַתִּי לִפְנֵיכֶם וְלִפְנֵי אֲבוֹתֵיכֶם:

יא לָכֵן כֹּה־אָמַר יְהוָה צְבָאוֹת אֱלֹהֵי יִשְׂרָאֵל הִנְנִי שָׂם פָּנַי בָּכֶם לְרָעָה וּלְהַכְרִית אֶת־כָּל־יְהוּדָה:

יב וְלָקַחְתִּי אֶת־שְׁאֵרִית יְהוּדָה אֲשֶׁר־שָׂמוּ פְנֵיהֶם לָבוֹא אֶרֶץ־מִצְרַיִם לָגוּר שָׁם וְתַמּוּ כֹל בְּאֶרֶץ מִצְרַיִם יִפֹּלוּ בַּחֶרֶב בָּרָעָב יִתַּמּוּ מִקָּטֹן וְעַד־גָּדוֹל בַּחֶרֶב וּבָרָעָב יָמֻתוּ וְהָיוּ לְאָלָה לְשַׁמָּה וְלִקְלָלָה וּלְחֶרְפָּה:

יג וּפָקַדְתִּי עַל הַיּוֹשְׁבִים בְּאֶרֶץ מִצְרַיִם כַּאֲשֶׁר פָּקַדְתִּי עַל־יְרוּשָׁלָם בַּחֶרֶב בָּרָעָב וּבַדָּבֶר:

יד וְלֹא יִהְיֶה פָּלִיט וְשָׂרִיד לִשְׁאֵרִית יְהוּדָה הַבָּאִים לָגוּר־שָׁם בְּאֶרֶץ מִצְרַיִם וְלָשׁוּב אֶרֶץ יְהוּדָה אֲשֶׁר־הֵמָּה מְנַשְּׂאִים אֶת־נַפְשָׁם לָשׁוּב לָשֶׁבֶת שָׁם כִּי לֹא־יָשׁוּבוּ כִּי אִם־פְּלֵטִים:

טו וַיַּעֲנוּ אֶת־יִרְמְיָהוּ כָּל־הָאֲנָשִׁים הַיֹּדְעִים כִּי־מְקַטְּרוֹת נְשֵׁיהֶם לֵאלֹהִים אֲחֵרִים וְכָל־הַנָּשִׁים הָעֹמְדוֹת קָהָל גָּדוֹל וְכָל־הָעָם הַיֹּשְׁבִים בְּאֶרֶץ־מִצְרַיִם בְּפַתְרוֹס לֵאמֹר:

טז הַדָּבָר אֲשֶׁר־דִּבַּרְתָּ אֵלֵינוּ בְּשֵׁם יְהוָה אֵינֶנּוּ שֹׁמְעִים אֵלֶיךָ:

יז כִּי עָשֹׂה נַעֲשֶׂה אֶת־כָּל־הַדָּבָר אֲשֶׁר־יָצָא מִפִּינוּ לְקַטֵּר לִמְלֶכֶת הַשָּׁמַיִם וְהַסֵּיךְ־לָהּ נְסָכִים כַּאֲשֶׁר עָשִׂינוּ אֲנַחְנוּ וַאֲבֹתֵינוּ מְלָכֵינוּ וְשָׂרֵינוּ בְּעָרֵי יְהוּדָה וּבְחֻצוֹת יְרוּשָׁלָם וַנִּשְׂבַּע־לֶחֶם וַנִּהְיֶה טוֹבִים וְרָעָה לֹא רָאִינוּ:

Jeremiah

18 But ever since we stopped making offerings to the Queen of Heaven and pouring libations to her, we have lacked everything, and we have been consumed by the sword and by famine.

יח וּמִן־אָז חָדַלְנוּ לְקַטֵּר לִמְלֶכֶת הַשָּׁמַיִם וְהַסֵּךְ־לָהּ נְסָכִים חָסַרְנוּ כֹל וּבַחֶרֶב וּבָרָעָב תָּמְנוּ:

19 And when we make offerings to the Queen of Heaven and pour libations to her, is it without our husbands' approval that we have made cakes in her likeness and poured libations to her?"

יט וְכִי־אֲנַחְנוּ מְקַטְּרִים לִמְלֶכֶת הַשָּׁמַיִם וּלְהַסֵּךְ לָהּ נְסָכִים הֲמִבַּלְעֲדֵי אֲנָשֵׁינוּ עָשִׂינוּ לָהּ כַּוָּנִים לְהַעֲצִבָה וְהַסֵּךְ לָהּ נְסָכִים:

20 *Yirmiyahu* replied to all the people, men and women – all the people who argued with him. He said,

כ וַיֹּאמֶר יִרְמְיָהוּ אֶל־כָּל־הָעָם עַל־ הַגְּבָרִים וְעַל־הַנָּשִׁים וְעַל־כָּל־הָעָם הָעֹנִים אֹתוֹ דָּבָר לֵאמֹר:

21 "Indeed, the offerings you presented in the towns of *Yehuda* and the streets of *Yerushalayim* – you, your fathers, your kings, your officials, and the people of the land – were remembered by *Hashem* and brought to mind!

כא הֲלוֹא אֶת־הַקִּטֵּר אֲשֶׁר קִטַּרְתֶּם בְּעָרֵי יְהוּדָה וּבְחֻצוֹת יְרוּשָׁלַםִ אַתֶּם וַאֲבוֹתֵיכֶם מַלְכֵיכֶם וְשָׂרֵיכֶם וְעַם הָאָרֶץ אֹתָם זָכַר יְהוָה וַתַּעֲלֶה עַל־לִבּוֹ:

22 When *Hashem* could no longer bear your evil practices and the abominations you committed, your land became a desolate ruin and a curse, without inhabitant, as is still the case.

כב וְלֹא־יוּכַל יְהוָה עוֹד לָשֵׂאת מִפְּנֵי רֹעַ מַעַלְלֵיכֶם מִפְּנֵי הַתּוֹעֵבֹת אֲשֶׁר עֲשִׂיתֶם וַתְּהִי אַרְצְכֶם לְחָרְבָּה וּלְשַׁמָּה וְלִקְלָלָה מֵאֵין יוֹשֵׁב כְּהַיּוֹם הַזֶּה:

v'-lo yu-KHAL a-do-NAI OD la-SAYT mi-p'-NAY RO-a ma-a-l'-lay-KHEM
mi-p'-NAY ha-to-ay-VOT a-SHER a-see-TEM va-t'-HEE ar-tz-KHEM
l'-khor-BAH ul-sha-MAH v'-lik-la-LAH may-AYN yo-SHAYV k'-ha-YOM ha-ZEH

23 Because you burned incense and sinned against *Hashem* and did not obey *Hashem*, and because you did not follow His Teaching, His laws, and His exhortations, therefore this disaster has befallen you, as is still the case."

כג מִפְּנֵי אֲשֶׁר קִטַּרְתֶּם וַאֲשֶׁר חֲטָאתֶם לַיהוָה וְלֹא שְׁמַעְתֶּם בְּקוֹל יְהוָה וּבְתֹרָתוֹ וּבְחֻקֹּתָיו וּבְעֵדְוֹתָיו לֹא הֲלַכְתֶּם עַל־כֵּן קָרָאת אֶתְכֶם הָרָעָה הַזֹּאת כַּיּוֹם הַזֶּה:

24 *Yirmiyahu* further said to all the people and to all the women: "Hear the word of *Hashem*, all Judeans in the land of Egypt!

כד וַיֹּאמֶר יִרְמְיָהוּ אֶל־כָּל־הָעָם וְאֶל כָּל־ הַנָּשִׁים שִׁמְעוּ דְּבַר־יְהוָה כָּל־יְהוּדָה אֲשֶׁר בְּאֶרֶץ מִצְרָיִם:

Introspective religious man at the Mediterranean Sea

44:22 Your land became a desolate ruin Even in Egypt, their country overrun by Babylon and their *Beit Hamikdash* destroyed, the remaining Jews turn to *Yirmiyahu* and say, "We will not listen to you in the matter about which you spoke to us in the name of *Hashem*" (verse 16). Despite the destruction and exile, they choose to maintain their wrongdoing and wayward belief in idolatry. *Yirmiyahu* responds that their land has been destroyed because of their sins. The connection between the Jewish people and *Eretz Yisrael* is not happenstance. Whether or not they are able to remain in the land is directly dependent on their behavior. Sinful behavior caused them to be kicked out, and their re-entry into the land is dependent upon prayer and repentance. As soon as the People of Israel are willing to change, God will bring them back with open arms. This is one of the most enduring lessons repeated throughout the *Tanakh*.

25 Thus said the LORD of Hosts, the God of *Yisrael*: You and your wives have confirmed by deed what you spoke in words: 'We will fulfill the vows which we made, to burn incense to the Queen of Heaven and to pour libations to her.' So fulfill your vows; perform your vows!

כה כֹּה־אָמַר יְהֹוָה־צְבָאוֹת אֱלֹהֵי יִשְׂרָאֵל לֵאמֹר אַתֶּם וּנְשֵׁיכֶם וַתְּדַבֵּרְנָה בְּפִיכֶם וּבִידֵיכֶם מִלֵּאתֶם לֵאמֹר עָשֹׂה נַעֲשֶׂה אֶת־נְדָרֵינוּ אֲשֶׁר נָדַרְנוּ לְקַטֵּר לִמְלֶכֶת הַשָּׁמַיִם וּלְהַסֵּךְ לָהּ נְסָכִים הָקֵים תָּקִימְנָה אֶת־נִדְרֵיכֶם וְעָשֹׂה תַעֲשֶׂינָה אֶת־נִדְרֵיכֶם:

26 "Yet hear the word of *Hashem*, all Judeans who dwell in the land of Egypt! Lo, I swear by My great name – said *Hashem* – that none of the men of *Yehuda* in all the land of Egypt shall ever again invoke My name, saying, 'As *Hashem* lives!'

כו לָכֵן שִׁמְעוּ דְבַר־יְהֹוָה כָּל־יְהוּדָה הַיֹּשְׁבִים בְּאֶרֶץ מִצְרָיִם הִנְנִי נִשְׁבַּעְתִּי בִּשְׁמִי הַגָּדוֹל אָמַר יְהֹוָה אִם־יִהְיֶה עוֹד שְׁמִי נִקְרָא בְּפִי כָּל־אִישׁ יְהוּדָה אֹמֵר חַי־אֲדֹנָי יְהֹוִה בְּכָל־אֶרֶץ מִצְרָיִם:

27 I will be watchful over them to their hurt, not to their benefit; all the men of *Yehuda* in the land of Egypt shall be consumed by sword and by famine, until they cease to be.

כז הִנְנִי שֹׁקֵד עֲלֵיהֶם לְרָעָה וְלֹא לְטוֹבָה וְתַמּוּ כָל־אִישׁ יְהוּדָה אֲשֶׁר בְּאֶרֶץ־מִצְרַיִם בַּחֶרֶב וּבָרָעָב עַד־כְּלוֹתָם:

28 Only the few who survive the sword shall return from the land of Egypt to the land of *Yehuda*. All the remnant of *Yehuda* who came to the land of Egypt to sojourn there shall learn whose word will be fulfilled – Mine or theirs!

כח וּפְלִיטֵי חֶרֶב יְשֻׁבוּן מִן־אֶרֶץ מִצְרַיִם אֶרֶץ יְהוּדָה מְתֵי מִסְפָּר וְיָדְעוּ כָּל־שְׁאֵרִית יְהוּדָה הַבָּאִים לְאֶרֶץ־מִצְרַיִם לָגוּר שָׁם דְּבַר־מִי יָקוּם מִמֶּנִּי וּמֵהֶם:

29 "And this shall be the sign to you – declares *Hashem* – that I am going to deal with you in this place, so that you may know that My threats of punishment against you will be fulfilled:

כט וְזֹאת־לָכֶם הָאוֹת נְאֻם־יְהֹוָה כִּי־פֹקֵד אֲנִי עֲלֵיכֶם בַּמָּקוֹם הַזֶּה לְמַעַן תֵּדְעוּ כִּי קוֹם יָקוּמוּ דְבָרַי עֲלֵיכֶם לְרָעָה:

30 Thus said *Hashem*: I will deliver Pharaoh Hophra, king of Egypt, into the hands of his enemies, those who seek his life, just as I delivered King *Tzidkiyahu* of *Yehuda* into the hands of King Nebuchadrezzar of Babylon, his enemy who sought his life."

ל כֹּה אָמַר יְהֹוָה הִנְנִי נֹתֵן אֶת־פַּרְעֹה חָפְרַע מֶלֶךְ־מִצְרַיִם בְּיַד אֹיְבָיו וּבְיַד מְבַקְשֵׁי נַפְשׁוֹ כַּאֲשֶׁר נָתַתִּי אֶת־צִדְקִיָּהוּ מֶלֶךְ־יְהוּדָה בְּיַד נְבוּכַדְרֶאצַּר מֶלֶךְ־בָּבֶל אֹיְבוֹ וּמְבַקֵּשׁ נַפְשׁוֹ:

45 1 The word which the *Navi Yirmiyahu* spoke to *Baruch* son of *Nerya*, when he was writing these words in a scroll at *Yirmiyahu*'s dictation, in the fourth year of King *Yehoyakim* son of *Yoshiyahu* of *Yehuda*:

מה א הַדָּבָר אֲשֶׁר דִּבֶּר יִרְמְיָהוּ הַנָּבִיא אֶל־בָּרוּךְ בֶּן־נֵרִיָּה בְּכָתְבוֹ אֶת־הַדְּבָרִים הָאֵלֶּה עַל־סֵפֶר מִפִּי יִרְמְיָהוּ בַּשָּׁנָה הָרְבִעִית לִיהוֹיָקִים בֶּן־יֹאשִׁיָּהוּ מֶלֶךְ יְהוּדָה לֵאמֹר:

2 Thus said *Hashem*, the God of *Yisrael*, concerning you, *Baruch*:

ב כֹּה־אָמַר יְהֹוָה אֱלֹהֵי יִשְׂרָאֵל עָלֶיךָ בָּרוּךְ:

3 You say, "Woe is me! *Hashem* has added grief to my pain. I am worn out with groaning, and I have found no rest."

ג אָמַרְתָּ אוֹי־נָא לִי כִּי־יָסַף יְהֹוָה יָגוֹן עַל־מַכְאֹבִי יָגַעְתִּי בְּאַנְחָתִי וּמְנוּחָה לֹא מָצָאתִי:

4 Thus shall you speak to him: "Thus said *Hashem*: I am going to overthrow what I have built, and uproot what I have planted – this applies to the whole land.

ד כֹּה תֹּאמַר אֵלָיו כֹּה אָמַר יְהֹוָה הִנֵּה אֲשֶׁר־בָּנִיתִי אֲנִי הֹרֵס וְאֵת אֲשֶׁר־נָטַעְתִּי אֲנִי נֹתֵשׁ וְאֶת־כָּל־הָאָרֶץ הִיא:

5 And do you expect great things for yourself? Don't expect them. For I am going to bring disaster upon all flesh – declares *Hashem* – but I will at least grant you your life in all the places where you may go."

ה וְאַתָּה תְּבַקֶּשׁ־לְךָ גְדֹלוֹת אַל־תְּבַקֵּשׁ
כִּי הִנְנִי מֵבִיא רָעָה עַל־כָּל־בָּשָׂר נְאֻם־
יְהֹוָה וְנָתַתִּי לְךָ אֶת־נַפְשְׁךָ לְשָׁלָל עַל
כָּל־הַמְּקֹמוֹת אֲשֶׁר תֵּלֶךְ־שָׁם:

v'-a-TAH t'-va-kesh l'-KHA g'-do-LOT al t'-va-KESH KEE hi-n'-NEE may-VEE ra-AH al kol ba-SAR n'-um a-do-NAI v'-na-ta-TEE l'-KHA et naf-sh'-KHA l'-sha-LAL AL kol ha-m'-ko-MOT a-SHER tay-lekh SHAM

46 1 The word of *Hashem* to the *Navi Yirmiyahu* concerning the nations.

מו א אֲשֶׁר הָיָה דְבַר־יְהֹוָה אֶל־יִרְמְיָהוּ הַנָּבִיא
עַל־הַגּוֹיִם:

2 Concerning Egypt, about the army of Pharaoh Neco, king of Egypt, which was at the river Euphrates near Carchemish, and which was defeated by King Nebuchadrezzar of Babylon, in the fourth year of King *Yehoyakim* son of *Yoshiyahu* of *Yehuda*.

ב לְמִצְרַיִם עַל־חֵיל פַּרְעֹה נְכוֹ מֶלֶךְ
מִצְרַיִם אֲשֶׁר־הָיָה עַל־נְהַר־פְּרָת
בְּכַרְכְּמִשׁ אֲשֶׁר הִכָּה נְבוּכַדְרֶאצַּר מֶלֶךְ
בָּבֶל בִּשְׁנַת הָרְבִיעִית לִיהוֹיָקִים בֶּן־
יֹאשִׁיָּהוּ מֶלֶךְ יְהוּדָה:

3 Get ready buckler and shield, And move forward to battle!

ג עִרְכוּ מָגֵן וְצִנָּה וּגְשׁוּ לַמִּלְחָמָה:

4 Harness the horses; Mount, you horsemen! Fall in line, helmets on! Burnish the lances, Don your armor!

ד אִסְרוּ הַסּוּסִים וַעֲלוּ הַפָּרָשִׁים וְהִתְיַצְּבוּ
בְּכוֹבָעִים מִרְקוּ הָרְמָחִים לִבְשׁוּ
הַסְּרִיֹנֹת:

5 Why do I see them dismayed, Yielding ground? Their fighters are crushed, They flee in haste And do not turn back – Terror all around! – declares *Hashem*.

ה מַדּוּעַ רָאִיתִי הֵמָּה חַתִּים נְסֹגִים אָחוֹר
וְגִבּוֹרֵיהֶם יֻכַּתּוּ וּמָנוֹס נָסוּ וְלֹא הִפְנוּ
מָגוֹר מִסָּבִיב נְאֻם־יְהֹוָה:

6 The swift cannot get away, The warrior cannot escape. In the north, by the river Euphrates, They stagger and fall.

ו אַל־יָנוּס הַקַּל וְאַל־יִמָּלֵט הַגִּבּוֹר צָפוֹנָה
עַל־יַד נְהַר־פְּרָת כָּשְׁלוּ וְנָפָלוּ:

7 Who is this that rises like the Nile, Like streams whose waters surge?

ז מִי־זֶה כַּיְאֹר יַעֲלֶה כַּנְּהָרוֹת יִתְגָּעֲשׁוּ
מֵימָיו:

8 It is Egypt that rises like the Nile, Like streams whose waters surge, That said, "I will rise, I will cover the earth, I will wipe out towns And those who dwell in them.

ח מִצְרַיִם כַּיְאֹר יַעֲלֶה וְכַנְּהָרוֹת יִתְגֹּעֲשׁוּ
מָיִם וַיֹּאמֶר אַעֲלֶה אֲכַסֶּה־אֶרֶץ אֹבִידָה
עִיר וְיֹשְׁבֵי בָהּ:

A father teaching his son the prayers at the Western Wall

45:5 And do you expect great things for yourself? In the midst of the calamity, *Yirmiyahu* rebukes his closest student, *Baruch* son of *Nerya*, for being concerned about his personal welfare at a time of national crisis. Some suggest that as his grandfather was *Maasayahu*, governor of *Yerushalayim* during *Yoshiyahu's* reign (ɪɪ Chronicles 34:8), *Baruch* also hoped for high office, only to see his aspirations dissipate. *Rashi*, however attributes a higher motivation to *Baruch*: He was hoping, like great students of prophets before him, such as *Yehoshua* and *Elisha*, to receive the gift of prophecy. However, *Yirmiyahu* reminds his student, at a time when the people are suffering, personal goals – even spiritual ones – must be set aside.

9 Advance, O horses, Dash madly, O chariots! Let the warriors go forth, Cush and Put, that grasp the shield, And the Ludim who grasp and draw the bow!"

ט עֲלוּ הַסּוּסִים וְהִתְהֹלְלוּ הָרֶכֶב וְיֵצְאוּ הַגִּבּוֹרִים כּוּשׁ וּפוּט תֹּפְשֵׂי מָגֵן וְלוּדִים תֹּפְשֵׂי דֹּרְכֵי קָשֶׁת:

10 But that day shall be for the LORD of Hosts a day when He exacts retribution from His foes. The sword shall devour; it shall be sated and drunk with their blood. For the LORD of Hosts is preparing a sacrifice in the northland, by the river Euphrates.

י וְהַיּוֹם הַהוּא לַאדֹנָי יְהֹוִה צְבָאוֹת יוֹם נְקָמָה לְהִנָּקֵם מִצָּרָיו וְאָכְלָה חֶרֶב וְשָׂבְעָה וְרָוְתָה מִדָּמָם כִּי זֶבַח לַאדֹנָי יְהֹוִה צְבָאוֹת בְּאֶרֶץ צָפוֹן אֶל־נְהַר־פְּרָת:

11 Go up to *Gilad* and get balm, Fair Maiden Egypt. In vain do you seek many remedies, There is no healing for you.

יא עֲלִי גִלְעָד וּקְחִי צֳרִי בְּתוּלַת בַּת־מִצְרָיִם לַשָּׁוְא הרביתי [הִרְבֵּית] רְפֻאוֹת תְּעָלָה אֵין לָךְ:

12 Nations have heard your shame; The earth resounds with your screams. For warrior stumbles against warrior; The two fall down together.

יב שָׁמְעוּ גוֹיִם קְלוֹנֵךְ וְצִוְחָתֵךְ מָלְאָה הָאָרֶץ כִּי־גִבּוֹר בְּגִבּוֹר כָּשָׁלוּ יַחְדָּיו נָפְלוּ שְׁנֵיהֶם:

13 The word which *Hashem* spoke to the *Navi Yirmiyahu* about the coming of King Nebuchadrezzar of Babylon to attack the land of Egypt:

יג הַדָּבָר אֲשֶׁר דִּבֶּר יְהֹוָה אֶל־יִרְמְיָהוּ הַנָּבִיא לָבוֹא נְבוּכַדְרֶאצַּר מֶלֶךְ בָּבֶל לְהַכּוֹת אֶת־אֶרֶץ מִצְרָיִם:

14 Declare in Egypt, proclaim in Migdol, Proclaim in Noph and Tahpanhes! Say: Take your posts and stand ready, For the sword has devoured all around you!

יד הַגִּידוּ בְמִצְרַיִם וְהַשְׁמִיעוּ בְמִגְדּוֹל וְהַשְׁמִיעוּ בְנֹף וּבְתַחְפַּנְחֵס אִמְרוּ הִתְיַצֵּב וְהָכֵן לָךְ כִּי־אָכְלָה חֶרֶב סְבִיבֶיךָ:

15 Why are your stalwarts swept away? They did not stand firm, For *Hashem* thrust them down;

טו מַדּוּעַ נִסְחַף אַבִּירֶיךָ לֹא עָמַד כִּי יְהֹוָה הֲדָפוֹ:

16 He made many stumble, They fell over one another. They said: "Up! let us return to our people, To the land of our birth, Because of the deadly sword."

טז הִרְבָּה כּוֹשֵׁל גַּם־נָפַל אִישׁ אֶל־רֵעֵהוּ וַיֹּאמְרוּ קוּמָה וְנָשֻׁבָה אֶל־עַמֵּנוּ וְאֶל־אֶרֶץ מוֹלַדְתֵּנוּ מִפְּנֵי חֶרֶב הַיּוֹנָה:

17 There they called Pharaoh king of Egypt: "Braggart who let the hour go by."

יז קָרְאוּ שָׁם פַּרְעֹה מֶלֶךְ־מִצְרַיִם שָׁאוֹן הֶעֱבִיר הַמּוֹעֵד:

18 As I live – declares the King, Whose name is LORD of Hosts – As surely as *Tavor* is among the mountains And *Carmel* is by the sea, So shall this come to pass.

יח חַי־אָנִי נְאֻם־הַמֶּלֶךְ יְהֹוָה צְבָאוֹת שְׁמוֹ כִּי כְּתָבוֹר בֶּהָרִים וּכְכַרְמֶל בַּיָּם יָבוֹא:

19 Equip yourself for exile, Fair Egypt, you who dwell secure! For Noph shall become a waste, Desolate, without inhabitants.

יט כְּלֵי גוֹלָה עֲשִׂי לָךְ יוֹשֶׁבֶת בַּת־מִצְרָיִם כִּי־נֹף לְשַׁמָּה תִהְיֶה וְנִצְּתָה מֵאֵין יוֹשֵׁב:

20 Egypt is a handsome heifer – A gadfly from the north is coming, coming!

כ עֶגְלָה יְפֵה־פִיָּה מִצְרָיִם קֶרֶץ מִצָּפוֹן בָּא בָא:

21 The mercenaries, too, in her midst Are like stall-fed calves; They too shall turn tail, Flee as one, and make no stand. Their day of disaster is upon them, The hour of their doom.

כא גַּם־שְׂכִרֶיהָ בְקִרְבָּהּ כְּעֶגְלֵי מַרְבֵּק כִּי־גַם־הֵמָּה הִפְנוּ נָסוּ יַחְדָּיו לֹא עָמָדוּ כִּי יוֹם אֵידָם בָּא עֲלֵיהֶם עֵת פְּקֻדָּתָם:

22 She shall rustle away like a snake As they come marching in force; They shall come against her with axes, Like hewers of wood.

קוֹלָהּ כַּנָּחָשׁ יֵלֵךְ כִּי־בְחַיִל יֵלֵכוּ וּבְקַרְדֻּמּוֹת בָּאוּ לָהּ כְּחֹטְבֵי עֵצִים:

23 They shall cut down her forest – declares *Hashem* – Though it cannot be measured; For they are more numerous than locusts, And cannot be counted.

כָּרְתוּ יַעְרָהּ נְאֻם־יְהֹוָה כִּי לֹא יֵחָקֵר כִּי רַבּוּ מֵאַרְבֶּה וְאֵין לָהֶם מִסְפָּר:

24 Fair Egypt shall be shamed, Handed over to the people of the north.

הֹבִישָׁה בַּת־מִצְרָיִם נִתְּנָה בְּיַד עַם־צָפוֹן:

25 The LORD of Hosts, the God of *Yisrael*, has said: I will inflict punishment on Ammon of No and on Pharaoh – on Egypt, her gods, and her kings – on Pharaoh and all who rely on him.

אָמַר יְהֹוָה צְבָאוֹת אֱלֹהֵי יִשְׂרָאֵל הִנְנִי פוֹקֵד אֶל־אָמוֹן מִנֹּא וְעַל־פַּרְעֹה וְעַל־מִצְרַיִם וְעַל־אֱלֹהֶיהָ וְעַל־מְלָכֶיהָ וְעַל־פַּרְעֹה וְעַל הַבֹּטְחִים בּוֹ:

26 I will deliver them into the hands of those who seek to kill them, into the hands of King Nebuchadrezzar of Babylon and into the hands of his subjects. But afterward she shall be inhabited again as in former days, declares *Hashem*.

וּנְתַתִּים בְּיַד מְבַקְשֵׁי נַפְשָׁם וּבְיַד נְבוּכַדְרֶאצַּר מֶלֶךְ־בָּבֶל וּבְיַד־עֲבָדָיו וְאַחֲרֵי־כֵן תִּשְׁכֹּן כִּימֵי־קֶדֶם נְאֻם־יְהֹוָה:

27 But you, Have no fear, My servant *Yaakov*, Be not dismayed, O *Yisrael*! I will deliver you from far away, Your folk from their land of captivity; And *Yaakov* again shall have calm And quiet, with none to trouble him.

וְאַתָּה אַל־תִּירָא עַבְדִּי יַעֲקֹב וְאַל־תֵּחַת יִשְׂרָאֵל כִּי הִנְנִי מוֹשִׁעֲךָ מֵרָחוֹק וְאֶת־זַרְעֲךָ מֵאֶרֶץ שִׁבְיָם וְשָׁב יַעֲקוֹב וְשָׁקַט וְשַׁאֲנַן וְאֵין מַחֲרִיד:

*v'-a-TAH al tee-RA av-DEE ya-a-KOV v'-al tay-KHAT yis-ra-AYL KEE
hin-n'-NEE mo-shi-a-KHA may-ra-KHOK v'-et zar-a-KHA may-E-retz shiv-YAM
v'-SHAV ya-a-KOV v'-sha-KAT v'-sha-a-NAN v'-AYN ma-kha-REED*

28 But you, have no fear, My servant *Yaakov* – declares *Hashem* – For I am with you. I will make an end of all the nations Among which I have banished you, But I will not make an end of you! I will not leave you unpunished, But I will chastise you in measure.

אַתָּה אַל־תִּירָא עַבְדִּי יַעֲקֹב נְאֻם־יְהֹוָה כִּי אִתְּךָ אָנִי כִּי אֶעֱשֶׂה כָלָה בְּכָל־הַגּוֹיִם אֲשֶׁר הִדַּחְתִּיךָ שָׁמָּה וְאֹתְךָ לֹא־אֶעֱשֶׂה כָלָה וְיִסַּרְתִּיךָ לַמִּשְׁפָּט וְנַקֵּה לֹא אֲנַקֶּךָ:

David Ben-Gurion declaring the State of Israel

46:27 I will deliver you from far away *Yirmiyahu* once again prophesies against the nations of the world. He begins with Egypt, upon whom the Israelites relied for protection from Babylonia, instead of re- lying on God. After harsh words of destruction and doom directed at the Egyptians, he then addresses the Jewish people. Given the harsh fate that awaits those peoples who defy God, *Yirmiyahu* turns to console the Children of Israel. Though they have sinned against God and have been punished, God's love for them is eternal, and they will eventually return to their homeland.

47 ¹ The word of *Hashem* that came to the *Navi Yirmiyahu* concerning the Philistines, before Pharaoh conquered *Azza*.

*a-SHER ha-YAH d'-var a-do-NAI el yir-m'-YA-hu ha-na-VEE
el p'-lish-TEEM b'-TE-rem ya-KEH far-OH et a-ZAH*

א מז אֲשֶׁר הָיָה דְבַר־יְהֹוָה אֶל־יִרְמְיָהוּ הַנָּבִיא אֶל־פְּלִשְׁתִּים בְּטֶרֶם יַכֶּה פַרְעֹה אֶת־עַזָּה:

² Thus said *Hashem*: See, waters are rising from the north, They shall become a raging torrent, They shall flood the land and its creatures, The towns and their inhabitants. Men shall cry out, All the inhabitants of the land shall howl,

ב כֹּה אָמַר יְהֹוָה הִנֵּה־מַיִם עֹלִים מִצָּפוֹן וְהָיוּ לְנַחַל שׁוֹטֵף וְיִשְׁטְפוּ אֶרֶץ וּמְלוֹאָהּ עִיר וְיֹשְׁבֵי בָהּ וְזָעֲקוּ הָאָדָם וְהֵילִל כֹּל יוֹשֵׁב הָאָרֶץ:

³ At the clatter of the stamping hoofs of his stallions, At the noise of his chariots, The rumbling of their wheels, Fathers shall not look to their children Out of sheer helplessness

ג מִקּוֹל שַׁעֲטַת פַּרְסוֹת אַבִּירָיו מֵרַעַשׁ לְרִכְבּוֹ הֲמוֹן גַּלְגִּלָּיו לֹא־הִפְנוּ אָבוֹת אֶל־בָּנִים מֵרִפְיוֹן יָדָיִם:

⁴ Because of the day that is coming For ravaging all the Philistines, For cutting off every last ally Of Tyre and Sidon. For *Hashem* will ravage the Philistines, The remnant from the island of Caphtor.

ד עַל־הַיּוֹם הַבָּא לִשְׁדוֹד אֶת־כָּל־פְּלִשְׁתִּים לְהַכְרִית לְצֹר וּלְצִידוֹן כֹּל שָׂרִיד עֹזֵר כִּי־שֹׁדֵד יְהֹוָה אֶת־פְּלִשְׁתִּים שְׁאֵרִית אִי כַפְתּוֹר:

⁵ Baldness has come upon *Azza*, Ashkelon is destroyed. O remnant of their valley, How long will you gash yourself?

ה בָּאָה קָרְחָה אֶל־עַזָּה נִדְמְתָה אַשְׁקְלוֹן שְׁאֵרִית עִמְקָם עַד־מָתַי תִּתְגּוֹדָדִי:

⁶ "O sword of *Hashem*, When will you be quiet at last? Withdraw into your sheath, Rest and be still!"

ו הוֹי חֶרֶב לַיהֹוָה עַד־אָנָה לֹא תִשְׁקֹטִי הֵאָסְפִי אַל־תַּעְרֵךְ הֵרָגְעִי וָדֹמִּי:

⁷ How can it be quiet When *Hashem* has given it orders Against *Ashkelon* and the seacoast, Given it assignment there?

ז אֵיךְ תִּשְׁקֹטִי וַיהֹוָה צִוָּה־לָהּ אֶל־אַשְׁקְלוֹן וְאֶל־חוֹף הַיָּם שָׁם יְעָדָהּ:

48 ¹ Concerning Moab. Thus said the LORD of Hosts, the God of *Yisrael*: Alas, that Nebo should be ravaged, Kiriathaim captured and shamed, The stronghold shamed and dismayed!

א מח לְמוֹאָב כֹּה־אָמַר יְהֹוָה צְבָאוֹת אֱלֹהֵי יִשְׂרָאֵל הוֹי אֶל־נְבוֹ כִּי שֻׁדָּדָה הֹבִישָׁה נִלְכְּדָה קִרְיָתָיִם הֹבִישָׁה הַמִּשְׂגָּב וָחָתָּה:

² Moab's glory is no more; In Heshbon they have planned evil against her: "Come, let us make an end of her as a nation!" You too, O Madmen, shall be silenced; The sword is following you.

ב אֵין עוֹד תְּהִלַּת מוֹאָב בְּחֶשְׁבּוֹן חָשְׁבוּ עָלֶיהָ רָעָה לְכוּ וְנַכְרִיתֶנָּה מִגּוֹי גַּם־מַדְמֵן תִּדֹּמִּי אַחֲרַיִךְ תֵּלֶךְ חָרֶב:

47:1 Concerning the *Philistines* *Yirmiyahu* now prophesies about the destruction of the Philistines. The Philistines lived on the southwestern coast of Israel, and occupied the five cities of *Azza*, Ashkelon, Ashdod, Ekron, and Gath. In the Bible, they continuously appear as an enemy of the Israelites. While *Yirmiyahu* depicts their destruction, he does not provide a reason for the harsh decree against them. *Yechezkel* (25:15), however, provides a possible insight into why they deserve this punishment: "because the Philistines, in their ancient hatred, acted vengefully, and with utter scorn sought revenge and destruction."

The modern city of *Ashdod*

Jeremiah

3 Hark! an outcry from Horonaim, Destruction and utter ruin!

ג קוֹל צְעָקָה מֵחֹרוֹנָיִם שֹׁד וָשֶׁבֶר גָּדוֹל:

4 Moab is broken; Her young ones cry aloud;

ד נִשְׁבְּרָה מוֹאָב הִשְׁמִיעוּ זְּעָקָה צְעוֹרֶיהָ [צְעִירֶיהָ]:

5 They climb to Luhith Weeping continually; On the descent to Horonaim A distressing cry of anguish is heard:

ה כִּי מַעֲלֵה הַלָּחוֹת [הַלּוּחִית] בִּבְכִי יַעֲלֶה־בֶּכִי כִּי בְּמוֹרַד חוֹרֹנַיִם צָרֵי צַעֲקַת־שֶׁבֶר שָׁמֵעוּ:

6 Flee, save your lives! And be like Aroer in the desert.

ו נֻסוּ מַלְּטוּ נַפְשְׁכֶם וְתִהְיֶינָה כַּעֲרוֹעֵר בַּמִּדְבָּר:

7 Surely, because of your trust In your wealth and in your treasures, You too shall be captured. And Chemosh shall go forth to exile, Together with his *Kohanim* and attendants.

ז כִּי יַעַן בִּטְחֵךְ בְּמַעֲשַׂיִךְ וּבְאוֹצְרוֹתַיִךְ גַּם־אַתְּ תִּלָּכֵדִי וְיָצָא כמיש [כְמוֹשׁ] בַּגּוֹלָה כֹּהֲנָיו וְשָׂרָיו יחד [יַחְדָּיו]:

8 The ravager shall come to every town; No town shall escape. The valley shall be devastated And the tableland laid waste – because *Hashem* has spoken.

ח וְיָבֹא שֹׁדֵד אֶל־כָּל־עִיר וְעִיר לֹא תִמָּלֵט וְאָבַד הָעֵמֶק וְנִשְׁמַד הַמִּישֹׁר אֲשֶׁר אָמַר יְהֹוָה:

9 Give wings to Moab, For she must go hence. Her towns shall become desolate, With no one living in them.

ט תְּנוּ־צִיץ לְמוֹאָב כִּי נָצֹא תֵּצֵא וְעָרֶיהָ לְשַׁמָּה תִהְיֶינָה מֵאֵין יוֹשֵׁב בָּהֵן:

10 Cursed be he who is slack in doing *Hashem*'s work! Cursed be he who withholds his sword from blood!

י אָרוּר עֹשֶׂה מְלֶאכֶת יְהֹוָה רְמִיָּה וְאָרוּר מֹנֵעַ חַרְבּוֹ מִדָּם:

11 Moab has been secure from his youth on – He is settled on his lees And has not been poured from vessel to vessel – He has never gone into exile. Therefore his fine flavor has remained And his bouquet is unspoiled.

יא שַׁאֲנַן מוֹאָב מִנְּעוּרָיו וְשֹׁקֵט הוּא אֶל־שְׁמָרָיו וְלֹא־הוּרַק מִכְּלִי אֶל־כֶּלִי וּבַגּוֹלָה לֹא הָלָךְ עַל־כֵּן עָמַד טַעְמוֹ בּוֹ וְרֵיחוֹ לֹא נָמָר:

12 But days are coming – declares *Hashem* – when I will send men against him to tip him over; they shall empty his vessels and smash his jars.

יב לָכֵן הִנֵּה־יָמִים בָּאִים נְאֻם־יְהֹוָה וְשִׁלַּחְתִּי־לוֹ צֹעִים וְצֵעֻהוּ וְכֵלָיו יָרִיקוּ וְנִבְלֵיהֶם יְנַפֵּצוּ:

13 And Moab shall be shamed because of Chemosh, as the House of *Yisrael* were shamed because of *Beit El*, on whom they relied.

יג וּבֹשׁ מוֹאָב מִכְּמוֹשׁ כַּאֲשֶׁר־בֹּשׁוּ בֵּית יִשְׂרָאֵל מִבֵּית אֵל מִבְטֶחָם:

*u-VOSH mo-AV mik-MOSH ka-a-sher BO-shu BAYT
yis-ra-AYL mi-BAYT AYL miv-te-KHAM*

🔲 **48:13 As the House of *Yisrael* were shamed because of *Beit El*** Yirmiyahu asserts that Moab will be as embarrassed about relying on their god, Chemosh, as the Jews were about relying on *Yerovam's* golden calves. According to contemporary Israeli scholar Rabbi Amnon Bazak, *Yerovam's* calves were intended to replace the two cherubs found on top of the ark in the *Beit Hamikdash*. He placed one in *Dan*, the northern border of his kingdom, and one in *Beit El*, at the southern border, to signify that

Aerial view of *Beit El*

14 How can you say: We are warriors, Valiant men for war?

יד אֵיךְ תֹּאמְרוּ גִּבּוֹרִים אֲנָחְנוּ וְאַנְשֵׁי־חַיִל לַמִּלְחָמָה:

15 Moab is ravaged, His towns have been entered, His choice young men Have gone down to the slaughter – declares the King whose name is LORD of Hosts.

טו שֻׁדַּד מוֹאָב וְעָרֶיהָ עָלָה וּמִבְחַר בַּחוּרָיו יָרְדוּ לַטָּבַח נְאֻם־הַמֶּלֶךְ יְהֹוָה צְבָאוֹת שְׁמוֹ:

16 The doom of Moab is coming close, His downfall is approaching swiftly.

טז קָרוֹב אֵיד־מוֹאָב לָבוֹא וְרָעָתוֹ מִהֲרָה מְאֹד:

17 Condole with him, all who live near him, All you who know him by name! Say: "Alas, the strong rod is broken, The lordly staff!"

יז נֻדוּ לוֹ כׇּל־סְבִיבָיו וְכֹל יֹדְעֵי שְׁמוֹ אִמְרוּ אֵיכָה נִשְׁבַּר מַטֵּה־עֹז מַקֵּל תִּפְאָרָה:

18 Descend from glory And sit in thirst, O inhabitant of Fair Dibon; For the ravager of Moab has entered your town, He has destroyed your fortresses.

יח רְדִי מִכָּבוֹד ישבי [וּשְׁבִי] בַצָּמָא יֹשֶׁבֶת בַּת־דִּיבוֹן כִּי־שֹׁדֵד מוֹאָב עָלָה בָךְ שִׁחֵת מִבְצָרָיִךְ:

19 Stand by the road and look out, O inhabitant of Aroer. Ask of him who is fleeing And of her who is escaping: Say, "What has happened?"

יט אֶל־דֶּרֶךְ עִמְדִי וְצַפִּי יוֹשֶׁבֶת עֲרוֹעֵר שַׁאֲלִי־נָס וְנִמְלָטָה אִמְרִי מַה־נִּהְיָתָה:

20 Moab is shamed and dismayed; Howl and cry aloud! Tell at the Arnon That Moab is ravaged!

כ הֹבִישׁ מוֹאָב כִּי־חַתָּה הילילי [הֵילִילוּ] וזעקי [וּזְעָקוּ] הַגִּידוּ בְאַרְנוֹן כִּי שֻׁדַּד מוֹאָב:

21 Judgment has come upon the tableland – upon Holon, Jahzah, and Mephaath;

כא וּמִשְׁפָּט בָּא אֶל־אֶרֶץ הַמִּישֹׁר אֶל־חֹלוֹן וְאֶל־יַהְצָה וְעַל־מופעת [מֵיפָעַת:]

22 upon Dibon, Nebo, and Beth-diblathaim;

כב וְעַל־דִּיבוֹן וְעַל־נְבוֹ וְעַל־בֵּית דִּבְלָתָיִם:

23 upon Kiriathaim, Beth-gamul, and Beth-meon;

כג וְעַל קִרְיָתַיִם וְעַל־בֵּית גָּמוּל וְעַל־בֵּית מְעוֹן:

24 upon Kerioth and Bozrah – upon all the towns of the land of Moab, far and near.

כד וְעַל־קְרִיּוֹת וְעַל־בׇּצְרָה וְעַל כׇּל־עָרֵי אֶרֶץ מוֹאָב הָרְחֹקוֹת וְהַקְּרֹבוֹת:

25 The might of Moab has been cut down, His strength is broken, – declares *Hashem*.

כה נִגְדְּעָה קֶרֶן מוֹאָב וּזְרֹעוֹ נִשְׁבָּרָה נְאֻם יְהֹוָה:

26 Get him drunk For he vaunted himself against *Hashem*. Moab shall vomit till he is drained, And he too shall be a laughingstock.

כו הַשְׁכִּירֻהוּ כִּי עַל־יְהֹוָה הִגְדִּיל וְסָפַק מוֹאָב בְּקִיאוֹ וְהָיָה לִשְׂחֹק גַּם־הוּא:

27 Wasn't *Yisrael* a laughingstock to you? Was he ever caught among thieves, That you should shake your head Whenever you speak of him?

כז וְאִם לוֹא הַשְּׂחֹק הָיָה לְךָ יִשְׂרָאֵל אִם־בְּגַנָּבִים נמצאה [נִמְצָא] כִּי־מִדֵּי דְבָרֶיךָ בּוֹ תִּתְנוֹדָד:

---

the Divine Presence shall rest between the two calves, throughout his entire kingdom, just as it rests between the two cherubs on top of the ark. *Yerovam* hoped that instead of viewing *Yerushalayim* and the *Beit Hamikdash* as the sole place of God's Presence, they would see the entire Land of Israel as the resting place for God's glory. The people, however, failed to internalize *Yerovam's* intended message and instead of worshipping *Hashem* throughout the land, they worshiped the calves themselves, angering God and eventually leading to their exile.

28 Desert the cities And dwell in the crags, O inhabitants of Moab! Be like a dove that nests In the sides of a pit.

כח עִזְבוּ עָרִים וְשִׁכְנוּ בַּסֶּלַע יֹשְׁבֵי מוֹאָב וִהְיוּ כְיוֹנָה תְּקַנֵּן בְּעֶבְרֵי פִי־פָחַת:

29 We have heard of Moab's pride – Most haughty is he – Of his arrogance and pride, His haughtiness and self-exaltation.

כט שָׁמַעְנוּ גְאוֹן־מוֹאָב גֵּאֶה מְאֹד גָּבְהוֹ וּגְאוֹנוֹ וְגַאֲוָתוֹ וְרֻם לִבּוֹ:

30 I know his insolence – declares *Hashem* – the wickedness that is in him, th wickedness he has committed.

ל אֲנִי יָדַעְתִּי נְאֻם־יְהֹוָה עֶבְרָתוֹ וְלֹא־כֵן בַּדָּיו לֹא־כֵן עָשׂוּ:

31 Therefore I will howl for Moab, I will cry out for all Moab, I will moan for the men of Kir-heres.

לא עַל־כֵּן עַל־מוֹאָב אֲיֵלִיל וּלְמוֹאָב כֻּלֹּה אֶזְעָק אֶל־אַנְשֵׁי קִיר־חֶרֶשׂ יֶהְגֶּה:

32 With greater weeping than for Jazer I weep for you, O vine of Sibmah, Whose tendrils crossed the sea, Reached to the sea, to Jazer. A ravager has come down Upon your fig and grape harvests.

לב מִבְּכִי יַעְזֵר אֶבְכֶּה־לָּךְ הַגֶּפֶן שִׂבְמָה נְטִישֹׁתַיִךְ עָבְרוּ יָם עַד יָם יַעְזֵר נָגָעוּ עַל־קֵיצֵךְ וְעַל־בְּצִירֵךְ שֹׁדֵד נָפָל:

33 Rejoicing and gladness Are gone from the farm land, From the country of Moab; I have put an end to wine in the presses, No one treads [the grapes] with shouting – The shout is a shout no more.

לג וְנֶאֶסְפָה שִׂמְחָה וָגִיל מִכַּרְמֶל וּמֵאֶרֶץ מוֹאָב וְיַיִן מִיקָבִים הִשְׁבַּתִּי לֹא־יִדְרֹךְ הֵידָד הֵידָד לֹא הֵידָד:

34 There is an outcry from Heshbon to Elealeh, They raise their voices as far as Jahaz, From Zoar to Horonaim and Eglathshelishiah. The waters of Nimrim Shall also become desolation.

לד מִזַּעֲקַת חֶשְׁבּוֹן עַד־אֶלְעָלֵה עַד־יַהַץ נָתְנוּ קוֹלָם מִצֹּעַר עַד־חֹרֹנַיִם עֶגְלַת שְׁלִשִׁיָּה כִּי גַּם־מֵי נִמְרִים לִמְשַׁמּוֹת יִהְיוּ:

35 And I will make an end in Moab – declares *Hashem* – Of those who offer at a shrine And burn incense to their god.

לה וְהִשְׁבַּתִּי לְמוֹאָב נְאֻם־יְהֹוָה מַעֲלֶה בָמָה וּמַקְטִיר לֵאלֹהָיו:

36 Therefore, My heart moans for Moab like a flute; Like a flute my heart moans For the men of Kir-heres – Therefore, The gains they have made shall vanish –

לו עַל־כֵּן לִבִּי לְמוֹאָב כַּחֲלִלִים יֶהֱמֶה וְלִבִּי אֶל־אַנְשֵׁי קִיר־חֶרֶשׂ כַּחֲלִילִים יֶהֱמֶה עַל־כֵּן יִתְרַת עָשָׂה אָבָדוּ:

37 For every head is bald And every beard is shorn; On all hands there are gashes, And on the loins sackcloth.

לז כִּי כָל־רֹאשׁ קָרְחָה וְכָל־זָקָן גְּרֻעָה עַל כָּל־יָדַיִם גְּדֻדֹת וְעַל־מָתְנַיִם שָׂק:

38 On all the roofs of Moab, And in its squares There is naught but lamentation; For I have broken Moab Like a vessel no one wants – declares *Hashem*.

לח עַל כָּל־גַּגּוֹת מוֹאָב וּבִרְחֹבֹתֶיהָ כֻּלֹּה מִסְפֵּד כִּי־שָׁבַרְתִּי אֶת־מוֹאָב כִּכְלִי אֵין־חֵפֶץ בּוֹ נְאֻם־יְהֹוָה:

39 How he is dismayed! Wail! How Moab has turned his back in shame! Moab shall be a laughingstock And a shock to all those near him.

לט אֵיךְ חַתָּה הֵילִילוּ אֵיךְ הִפְנָה־עֹרֶף מוֹאָב בּוֹשׁ וְהָיָה מוֹאָב לִשְׂחֹק וְלִמְחִתָּה לְכָל־סְבִיבָיו:

40 For thus said *Hashem*: See, he soars like an eagle And spreads out his wings against Moab!

מ כִּי־כֹה אָמַר יְהֹוָה הִנֵּה כַנֶּשֶׁר יִדְאֶה וּפָרַשׂ כְּנָפָיו אֶל־מוֹאָב:

⁴¹ Kerioth shall be captured And the strongholds shall be seized. In that day, the heart of Moab's warriors Shall be like the heart of a woman in travail.

נִלְכְּדָה הַקְּרִיּוֹת וְהַמְּצָדוֹת נִתְפָּשָׂה וְהָיָה לֵב גִּבּוֹרֵי מוֹאָב בַּיּוֹם הַהוּא כְּלֵב אִשָּׁה מְצֵרָה: מא

⁴² And Moab shall be destroyed as a people, For he vaunted himself against *Hashem*.

וְנִשְׁמַד מוֹאָב מֵעָם כִּי עַל־יְהֹוָה הִגְדִּיל: מב

⁴³ Terror, and pit, and trap Upon you who dwell in Moab! – declares *Hashem*.

פַּחַד וָפַחַת וָפָח עָלֶיךָ יוֹשֵׁב מוֹאָב נְאֻם־יְהֹוָה: מג

⁴⁴ He who flees from the terror Shall fall into the pit; And he who climbs out of the pit Shall be caught in the trap. For I will bring upon Moab The year of their doom – declares *Hashem*.

הַנִּיס [הַנָּס] מִפְּנֵי הַפַּחַד יִפֹּל אֶל־הַפַּחַת וְהָעֹלֶה מִן־הַפַּחַת יִלָּכֵד בַּפָּח כִּי־אָבִיא אֵלֶיהָ אֶל־מוֹאָב שְׁנַת פְּקֻדָּתָם נְאֻם־יְהֹוָה: מד

⁴⁵ In the shelter of Heshbon Fugitives halt exhausted; For fire went forth from Heshbon, Flame from the midst of Sihon, Consuming the brow of Moab, The pate of the people of Shaon.

בְּצֵל חֶשְׁבּוֹן עָמְדוּ מִכֹּחַ נָסִים כִּי־אֵשׁ יָצָא מֵחֶשְׁבּוֹן וְלֶהָבָה מִבֵּין סִיחוֹן וַתֹּאכַל פְּאַת מוֹאָב וְקָדְקֹד בְּנֵי שָׁאוֹן: מה

⁴⁶ Woe to you, O Moab! The people of Chemosh are undone, For your sons are carried off into captivity, Your daughters into exile.

אוֹי־לְךָ מוֹאָב אָבַד עַם־כְּמוֹשׁ כִּי־לֻקְּחוּ בָנֶיךָ בַּשֶּׁבִי וּבְנֹתֶיךָ בַּשִּׁבְיָה: מו

⁴⁷ But I will restore the fortunes of Moab in the days to come – declares *Hashem*. Thus far is the judgment on Moab.

וְשַׁבְתִּי שְׁבוּת־מוֹאָב בְּאַחֲרִית הַיָּמִים נְאֻם־יְהֹוָה עַד־הֵנָּה מִשְׁפַּט מוֹאָב: מז

49 ¹ Concerning the Amonites. Thus said *Hashem*: Has *Yisrael* no sons, Has he no heir? Then why has Milcom dispossessed *Gad*, And why have his people settled in *Gad*'s towns?

לִבְנֵי עַמּוֹן כֹּה אָמַר יְהֹוָה הֲבָנִים אֵין לְיִשְׂרָאֵל אִם־יוֹרֵשׁ אֵין לוֹ מַדּוּעַ יָרַשׁ מַלְכָּם אֶת־גָּד וְעַמּוֹ בְּעָרָיו יָשָׁב: א מט

*liv-NAY a-MON KOH a-MAR a-do-NAI ha-va-NEEM AYN
l'-yis-ra-AYL im yo-RAYSH AYN LO ma-DU-a ya-RASH
mal-KAM et GAD v'-a-MO b'-a-RAV ya-SHAV*

² Assuredly, days are coming – declares *Hashem* – When I will sound the alarm of war Against Rabbah of the Amonites; It shall become a desolate mound, And its villages shall be set on fire. And *Yisrael* shall dispossess Those who dispossessed him – said *Hashem*.

לָכֵן הִנֵּה יָמִים בָּאִים נְאֻם־יְהֹוָה וְהִשְׁמַעְתִּי אֶל־רַבַּת בְּנֵי־עַמּוֹן תְּרוּעַת מִלְחָמָה וְהָיְתָה לְתֵל שְׁמָמָה וּבְנֹתֶיהָ בָּאֵשׁ תִּצַּתְנָה וְיָרַשׁ יִשְׂרָאֵל אֶת־יֹרְשָׁיו אָמַר יְהֹוָה: ב

Jeremiah

49:1 Has *Yisrael* no sons After the deportation of the ten tribes of Israel to Assyria by Tiglat-pileser, Ammon occupies some of the lands that have been vacated. *Yirmiyahu* criticizes the Ammonites for taking Israeli land. The Ammonites assume that the tribes of Israel have disappeared, never to return. However, this reflects a misunderstanding of the eternal bond between the People of Israel and their inherited land. Even if the exiles themselves do not return, eventually their children will. Therefore, *Yirmiyahu* asks Ammon if Israel has no sons – do they not understand that the ancestral link between the People of Israel and the Land of Israel spans all generations?

Members of the lost tribe of *Menashe* arrive at Ben Gurion airport

114

3 Howl, O Heshbon, for Ai is ravaged! Cry out, O daughters of Rabbah! Gird on sackcloth, lament, And run to and fro in the sheepfolds. For Milcom shall go into exile, Together with his *Kohanim* and attendants.

ג הֵילִילִי חֶשְׁבּוֹן כִּי שֻׁדְּדָה־עַי צְעַקְנָה בְּנוֹת רַבָּה חֲגֹרְנָה שַׂקִּים סְפֹדְנָה וְהִתְשׁוֹטַטְנָה בַּגְּדֵרוֹת כִּי מַלְכָּם בַּגּוֹלָה יֵלֵךְ כֹּהֲנָיו וְשָׂרָיו יַחְדָּיו:

4 Why do you glory in strength, Your strength is drained, O rebellious daughter, You who relied on your treasures, [Who said:] Who dares attack me?

ד מַה־תִּתְהַלְלִי בָּעֲמָקִים זָב עִמְקֵךְ הַבַּת הַשּׁוֹבֵבָה הַבֹּטְחָה בְּאֹצְרֹתֶיהָ מִי יָבוֹא אֵלָי:

5 I am bringing terror upon you – declares the Lord of Hosts – From all those around you. Every one of you shall be driven in every direction, And none shall gather in the fugitives.

ה הִנְנִי מֵבִיא עָלַיִךְ פַּחַד נְאֻם־אֲדֹנָי יְהוִה צְבָאוֹת מִכָּל־סְבִיבָיִךְ וְנִדַּחְתֶּם אִישׁ לְפָנָיו וְאֵין מְקַבֵּץ לַנֹּדֵד:

6 But afterward I will restore the fortunes of the Amonites – declares *Hashem*.

ו וְאַחֲרֵי־כֵן אָשִׁיב אֶת־שְׁבוּת בְּנֵי־עַמּוֹן נְאֻם־יְהוָה:

7 Concerning Edom. Thus said the Lord of Hosts: Is there no more wisdom in Teman? Has counsel vanished from the prudent? Has their wisdom gone stale?

ז לֶאֱדוֹם כֹּה אָמַר יְהוָה צְבָאוֹת הַאֵין עוֹד חָכְמָה בְּתֵימָן אָבְדָה עֵצָה מִבָּנִים נִסְרְחָה חָכְמָתָם:

8 Flee, turn away, sit down low, O inhabitants of Dedan, For I am bringing Esau's doom upon him, The time when I deal with him.

ח נֻסוּ הָפְנוּ הֶעְמִיקוּ לָשֶׁבֶת יֹשְׁבֵי דְּדָן כִּי אֵיד עֵשָׂו הֵבֵאתִי עָלָיו עֵת פְּקַדְתִּיו:

9 If vintagers were to come upon you, Would they leave no gleanings? Even thieves in the night Would destroy only for their needs!

ט אִם־בֹּצְרִים בָּאוּ לָךְ לֹא יַשְׁאִרוּ עוֹלֵלוֹת אִם־גַּנָּבִים בַּלַּיְלָה הִשְׁחִיתוּ דַיָּם:

10 But it is I who have bared Esau, Have exposed his place of concealment; He cannot hide. His offspring is ravaged, His kin and his neighbors – He is no more.

י כִּי־אֲנִי חָשַׂפְתִּי אֶת־עֵשָׂו גִּלֵּיתִי אֶת־מִסְתָּרָיו וְנֶחְבָּה לֹא יוּכָל שֻׁדַּד זַרְעוֹ וְאֶחָיו וּשְׁכֵנָיו וְאֵינֶנּוּ:

11 "Leave your orphans with me, I will rear them; Let your widows rely on me!"

יא עָזְבָה יְתֹמֶיךָ אֲנִי אֲחַיֶּה וְאַלְמְנֹתֶיךָ עָלַי תִּבְטָחוּ:

12 For thus said *Hashem*: If they who rightly should not drink of the cup must drink it, are you the one to go unpunished? You shall not go unpunished: you will have to drink!

יב כִּי־כֹה אָמַר יְהוָה הִנֵּה אֲשֶׁר־אֵין מִשְׁפָּטָם לִשְׁתּוֹת הַכּוֹס שָׁתוֹ יִשְׁתּוּ וְאַתָּה הוּא נָקֹה תִּנָּקֶה לֹא תִנָּקֶה כִּי שָׁתֹה תִּשְׁתֶּה:

13 For by Myself I swear – declares *Hashem* – Bozrah shall become a desolation, a mockery, a ruin, and a curse; and all its towns shall be ruins for all time.

יג כִּי בִי נִשְׁבַּעְתִּי נְאֻם־יְהוָה כִּי־לְשַׁמָּה לְחֶרְפָּה לְחֹרֶב וְלִקְלָלָה תִּהְיֶה בָצְרָה וְכָל־עָרֶיהָ תִהְיֶינָה לְחָרְבוֹת עוֹלָם:

14 I have received tidings from *Hashem*, And an envoy is sent out among the nations: Assemble, and move against her, And rise up for war!

יד שְׁמוּעָה שָׁמַעְתִּי מֵאֵת יְהוָה וְצִיר בַּגּוֹיִם שָׁלוּחַ הִתְקַבְּצוּ וּבֹאוּ עָלֶיהָ וְקוּמוּ לַמִּלְחָמָה:

15 For I will make you least among nations, Most despised among men.

טו כִּי־הִנֵּה קָטֹן נְתַתִּיךָ בַּגּוֹיִם בָּזוּי בָּאָדָם:

16 Your horrible nature, Your arrogant heart has seduced you, You who dwell in clefts of the rock, Who occupy the height of the hill! Should you nest as high as the eagle, From there I will pull you down – declares *Hashem*.

טז תִּפְלַצְתְּךָ הִשִּׁיא אֹתָךְ זְדוֹן לִבֶּךָ שֹׁכְנִי בְּחַגְוֵי הַסֶּלַע תֹּפְשִׂי מְרוֹם גִּבְעָה כִּי־תַגְבִּיהַ כַּנֶּשֶׁר קִנֶּךָ מִשָּׁם אוֹרִידְךָ נְאֻם־יְהֹוָה׃

17 And Edom shall be a cause of appallment; whoever passes by will be appalled and will hiss at all its wounds.

יז וְהָיְתָה אֱדוֹם לְשַׁמָּה כֹּל עֹבֵר עָלֶיהָ יִשֹּׁם וְיִשְׁרֹק עַל־כָּל־מַכּוֹתֶהָ׃

18 It shall be like the overthrow of Sodom and Gomorrah and their neighbors – said *Hashem*: no man shall live there, no human shall sojourn there.

יח כְּמַהְפֵּכַת סְדֹם וַעֲמֹרָה וּשְׁכֵנֶיהָ אָמַר יְהֹוָה לֹא־יֵשֵׁב שָׁם אִישׁ וְלֹא־יָגוּר בָּהּ בֶּן־אָדָם׃

19 It shall be as when a lion comes up out of the jungle of the *Yarden* against a secure pasture: in a moment I can harry him out of it and appoint over it anyone I choose. Then who is like Me? Who can summon Me? Who is the shepherd that can stand up against Me?

יט הִנֵּה כְּאַרְיֵה יַעֲלֶה מִגְּאוֹן הַיַּרְדֵּן אֶל־נְוֵה אֵיתָן כִּי־אַרְגִּיעָה אֲרִיצֶנּוּ מֵעָלֶיהָ וּמִי בָחוּר אֵלֶיהָ אֶפְקֹד כִּי מִי כָמוֹנִי וּמִי יֹעִידֶנִּי וּמִי־זֶה רֹעֶה אֲשֶׁר יַעֲמֹד לְפָנָי׃

20 Hear, then, the plan which *Hashem* has devised against Edom, and what He has purposed against the inhabitants of Teman: Surely the shepherd boys Shall drag them away; Surely the pasture shall be Aghast because of them.

כ לָכֵן שִׁמְעוּ עֲצַת־יְהֹוָה אֲשֶׁר יָעַץ אֶל־אֱדוֹם וּמַחְשְׁבוֹתָיו אֲשֶׁר חָשַׁב אֶל־יֹשְׁבֵי תֵימָן אִם־לֹא יִסְחָבוּם צְעִירֵי הַצֹּאן אִם־לֹא יַשִּׁים עֲלֵיהֶם נְוֵהֶם׃

21 At the sound of their downfall The earth shall shake; The sound of screaming Shall be heard at the Sea of Reeds.

כא מִקּוֹל נִפְלָם רָעֲשָׁה הָאָרֶץ צְעָקָה בְּיַם־סוּף נִשְׁמַע קוֹלָהּ׃

22 See, like an eagle he flies up, He soars and spreads his wings against Bozrah; And the heart of Edom's warriors in that day Shall be like the heart of a woman in travail.

כב הִנֵּה כַנֶּשֶׁר יַעֲלֶה וְיִדְאֶה וְיִפְרֹשׂ כְּנָפָיו עַל־בָּצְרָה וְהָיָה לֵב גִּבּוֹרֵי אֱדוֹם בַּיּוֹם הַהוּא כְּלֵב אִשָּׁה מְצֵרָה׃

23 Concerning Damascus. Hamath and Arpad are shamed, For they have heard bad news. They shake with anxiety, Like the sea which cannot rest.

כג לְדַמֶּשֶׂק בּוֹשָׁה חֲמָת וְאַרְפָּד כִּי־שְׁמֻעָה רָעָה שָׁמְעוּ נָמֹגוּ בַּיָּם דְּאָגָה הַשְׁקֵט לֹא יוּכָל׃

24 Damascus has grown weak, She has turned around to flee; Trembling has seized her, Pain and anguish have taken hold of her, Like a woman in childbirth.

כד רָפְתָה דַמֶּשֶׂק הִפְנְתָה לָנוּס וְרֶטֶט הֶחֱזִיקָה צָרָה וַחֲבָלִים אֲחָזַתָּה כַּיּוֹלֵדָה׃

25 How has the glorious city not been deserted, The citadel of my joy!

כה אֵיךְ לֹא־עֻזְּבָה עִיר תהלה [תְּהִלָּת] קִרְיַת מְשׂוֹשִׂי׃

26 Assuredly, her young men shall lie fallen in her squares. And all her warriors shall be stilled in that day – declares the Lord of Hosts.

כו לָכֵן יִפְּלוּ בַחוּרֶיהָ בִּרְחֹבֹתֶיהָ וְכָל־אַנְשֵׁי הַמִּלְחָמָה יִדַּמּוּ בַּיּוֹם הַהוּא נְאֻם יְהֹוָה צְבָאוֹת׃

27 I will set fire to the wall of Damascus, And it shall consume the fortresses of Ben-hadad.

כז וְהִצַּתִּי אֵשׁ בְּחוֹמַת דַּמָּשֶׂק וְאָכְלָה אַרְמְנוֹת בֶּן־הֲדָד׃

28 Concerning Kedar and the kingdoms of Hazor, which King Nebuchadrezzar of Babylon conquered. Thus said *Hashem*: Arise, march against Kedar, And ravage the Kedemites!

לְקֵדָר וּלְמַמְלְכוֹת חָצוֹר אֲשֶׁר הִכָּה נְבוּכַדְרֶאצּוֹר [נְבוּכַדְרֶאצַּר] מֶלֶךְ־בָּבֶל כֹּה אָמַר יְהֹוָה קוּמוּ עֲלוּ אֶל־קֵדָר וְשָׁדְדוּ אֶת־בְּנֵי־קֶדֶם: כח

29 They will take away their tents and their flocks, Their tent cloths and all their gear; They shall carry off their camels, And shall proclaim against them: Terror all around!

אָהֳלֵיהֶם וְצֹאנָם יִקָּחוּ יְרִיעוֹתֵיהֶם וְכָל־כְּלֵיהֶם וּגְמַלֵּיהֶם יִשְׂאוּ לָהֶם וְקָרְאוּ עֲלֵיהֶם מָגוֹר מִסָּבִיב: כט

30 Flee, wander far, Sit down low, O inhabitants of Hazor – says *Hashem*. For King Nebuchadrezzar of Babylon Has devised a plan against you And formed a purpose against you:

נֻסוּ נֻּדוּ מְאֹד הֶעְמִיקוּ לָשֶׁבֶת יֹשְׁבֵי חָצוֹר נְאֻם־יְהֹוָה כִּי־יָעַץ עֲלֵיכֶם נְבוּכַדְרֶאצַּר מֶלֶךְ־בָּבֶל עֵצָה וְחָשַׁב עֲלֵיהֶם [עֲלֵיכֶם] מַחֲשָׁבָה: ל

31 Rise up, attack a tranquil nation That dwells secure – says *Hashem* – That has no barred gates, That dwells alone.

קוּמוּ עֲלוּ אֶל־גּוֹי שְׁלֵיו יוֹשֵׁב לָבֶטַח נְאֻם־יְהֹוָה לֹא־דְלָתַיִם וְלֹא־בְרִיחַ לוֹ בָּדָד יִשְׁכֹּנוּ: לא

32 Their camels shall become booty, And their abundant flocks a spoil; And I will scatter to every quarter Those who have their hair clipped; And from every direction I will bring Disaster upon them – says *Hashem*.

וְהָיוּ גְמַלֵּיהֶם לָבַז וַהֲמוֹן מִקְנֵיהֶם לְשָׁלָל וְזֵרִתִים לְכָל־רוּחַ קְצוּצֵי פֵאָה וּמִכָּל־עֲבָרָיו אָבִיא אֶת־אֵידָם נְאֻם־יְהֹוָה: לב

33 Hazor shall become a lair of jackals, A desolation for all time. No man shall live there, No human shall sojourn there.

וְהָיְתָה חָצוֹר לִמְעוֹן תַּנִּים שְׁמָמָה עַד־עוֹלָם לֹא־יֵשֵׁב שָׁם אִישׁ וְלֹא־יָגוּר בָּהּ בֶּן־אָדָם: לג

34 The word of *Hashem* that came to the *Navi* *Yirmiyahu* concerning Elam, at the beginning of the reign of King *Tzidkiyahu* of *Yehuda*:

אֲשֶׁר הָיָה דְבַר־יְהֹוָה אֶל־יִרְמְיָהוּ הַנָּבִיא אֶל־עֵילָם בְּרֵאשִׁית מַלְכוּת צִדְקִיָּה מֶלֶךְ־יְהוּדָה לֵאמֹר: לד

35 Thus said the Lord of Hosts: I am going to break the bow of Elam, the mainstay of their strength.

כֹּה אָמַר יְהֹוָה צְבָאוֹת הִנְנִי שֹׁבֵר אֶת־קֶשֶׁת עֵילָם רֵאשִׁית גְּבוּרָתָם: לה

36 And I shall bring four winds against Elam from the four quarters of heaven, and scatter them to all those winds. There shall not be a nation to which the fugitives from Elam do not come.

וְהֵבֵאתִי אֶל־עֵילָם אַרְבַּע רוּחוֹת מֵאַרְבַּע קְצוֹת הַשָּׁמַיִם וְזֵרִתִים לְכֹל הָרֻחוֹת הָאֵלֶּה וְלֹא־יִהְיֶה הַגּוֹי אֲשֶׁר לֹא־יָבוֹא שָׁם נִדְּחֵי עוֹלָם [עֵילָם]: לו

37 And I will break Elam before their enemies, before those who seek their lives; and I will bring disaster upon them, My flaming wrath – declares *Hashem*. And I will dispatch the sword after them until I have consumed them.

וְהַחְתַּתִּי אֶת־עֵילָם לִפְנֵי אֹיְבֵיהֶם וְלִפְנֵי מְבַקְשֵׁי נַפְשָׁם וְהֵבֵאתִי עֲלֵיהֶם רָעָה אֶת־חֲרוֹן אַפִּי נְאֻם־יְהֹוָה וְשִׁלַּחְתִּי אַחֲרֵיהֶם אֶת־הַחֶרֶב עַד כַּלּוֹתִי אוֹתָם: לז

38 And I will set My throne in Elam, And wipe out from there king and officials – says *Hashem*.

וְשַׂמְתִּי כִסְאִי בְּעֵילָם וְהַאֲבַדְתִּי מִשָּׁם מֶלֶךְ וְשָׂרִים נְאֻם־יְהֹוָה: לח

39 But in the days to come I will restore the fortunes of Elam – declares *Hashem*.

וְהָיָה בְּאַחֲרִית הַיָּמִים אָשׁוּב [אָשִׁיב] אֶת־שְׁבִית [שְׁבוּת] עֵילָם נְאֻם־יְהֹוָה: לט

ירמיהו
פרק נ

50

¹ The word which *Hashem* spoke concerning Babylon, the land of the Chaldeans, through the *Navi Yirmiyahu*:

א הַדָּבָר אֲשֶׁר דִּבֶּר יְהֹוָה אֶל־בָּבֶל אֶל־אֶרֶץ כַּשְׂדִּים בְּיַד יִרְמְיָהוּ הַנָּבִיא:

² Declare among the nations, and proclaim; Raise a standard, proclaim; Hide nothing! Say: Babylon is captured, Bel is shamed, Merodach is dismayed. Her idols are shamed, Her fetishes dismayed.

ב הַגִּידוּ בַגּוֹיִם וְהַשְׁמִיעוּ וּשְׂאוּ־נֵס הַשְׁמִיעוּ אַל־תְּכַחֵדוּ אִמְרוּ נִלְכְּדָה בָבֶל הֹבִישׁ בֵּל חַת מְרֹדָךְ הֹבִישׁוּ עֲצַבֶּיהָ חַתּוּ גִּלּוּלֶיהָ:

³ For a nation from the north has attacked her, It will make her land a desolation. No one shall dwell in it, Both man and beast shall wander away.

ג כִּי עָלָה עָלֶיהָ גּוֹי מִצָּפוֹן הוּא־יָשִׁית אֶת־אַרְצָהּ לְשַׁמָּה וְלֹא־יִהְיֶה יוֹשֵׁב בָּהּ מֵאָדָם וְעַד־בְּהֵמָה נָדוּ הָלָכוּ:

⁴ In those days and at that time – declares *Hashem* – the people of *Yisrael* together with the people of *Yehuda* shall come, and they shall weep as they go to seek *Hashem* their God.

ד בַּיָּמִים הָהֵמָּה וּבָעֵת הַהִיא נְאֻם־יְהֹוָה יָבֹאוּ בְנֵי־יִשְׂרָאֵל הֵמָּה וּבְנֵי־יְהוּדָה יַחְדָּו הָלוֹךְ וּבָכוֹ יֵלֵכוּ וְאֶת־יְהֹוָה אֱלֹהֵיהֶם יְבַקֵּשׁוּ:

⁵ They shall inquire for *Tzion*; in that direction their faces shall turn; they shall come and attach themselves to *Hashem* by a covenant for all time, which shall never be forgotten.

ה צִיּוֹן יִשְׁאָלוּ דֶּרֶךְ הֵנָּה פְנֵיהֶם בֹּאוּ וְנִלְווּ אֶל־יְהֹוָה בְּרִית עוֹלָם לֹא תִשָּׁכֵחַ:

tzi-YON yish-A-lu DE-rekh HAY-nah f'-nay-HEM BO-u v'-nil-VU el a-do-NAI b'-REET o-LAM LO ti-sha-KHAY-akh

⁶ My people were lost sheep: their shepherds led them astray, they drove them out to the mountains, they roamed from mount to hill, they forgot their own resting place.

ו צֹאן אֹבְדוֹת הָיָה [הָיוּ] עַמִּי רֹעֵיהֶם הִתְעוּם הָרִים שׁוֹבֵבִים [שׁוֹבְבוּם] מֵהַר אֶל־גִּבְעָה הָלָכוּ שָׁכְחוּ רִבְצָם:

⁷ All who encountered them devoured them; and their foes said, "We shall not be held guilty, because they have sinned against *Hashem*, the true Pasture, the Hope of their fathers – *Hashem*."

ז כָּל־מוֹצְאֵיהֶם אֲכָלוּם וְצָרֵיהֶם אָמְרוּ לֹא נֶאְשָׁם תַּחַת אֲשֶׁר חָטְאוּ לַיהֹוָה נְוֵה־צֶדֶק וּמִקְוֵה אֲבוֹתֵיהֶם יְהֹוָה:

⁸ Flee from Babylon, Leave the land of the Chaldeans, And be like he-goats that lead the flock!

ח נֻדוּ מִתּוֹךְ בָּבֶל וּמֵאֶרֶץ כַּשְׂדִּים יצאו [צֵאוּ] וִהְיוּ כְּעַתּוּדִים לִפְנֵי־צֹאן:

⁹ For see, I am rousing and leading An assemblage of great nations against Babylon From the lands of the north. They shall draw up their lines against her, There she shall be captured. Their arrows are like those of a skilled warrior Who does not turn back without hitting the mark.

ט כִּי הִנֵּה אָנֹכִי מֵעִיר וּמַעֲלֶה עַל־בָּבֶל קְהַל־גּוֹיִם גְּדֹלִים מֵאֶרֶץ צָפוֹן וְעָרְכוּ לָהּ מִשָּׁם תִּלָּכֵד חִצָּיו כְּגִבּוֹר מַשְׁכִּיל לֹא יָשׁוּב רֵיקָם:

50:5 A covenant for all time, which shall never be forgotten
For most of *Yirmiyahu's* prophecies, the mighty nation of Babylonia serves as a messenger or agent, carrying out God's will. When the People of Israel wish to challenge Babylonia's rule over them, *Yirmiyahu* tells them that to do so is tantamount to challenging *Hashem* Himself. However, like the other nations before them, Babylonia will eventually be punished for its arrogance and sinful behavior. Like Israel, they shall face an enemy "from the north" (verse 3). When this occurs, Israel will once again be returned to its homeland. As *Yirmiyahu* says in verse 19, "And I will lead *Yisrael* back to his pasture." While nations come and go, the Jewish people remain connected to their beloved Land of Israel in "a covenant for all time, which shall never be forgotten."

Israel's "pasture," in the Golan Heights

¹⁰ Chaldea shall be despoiled, All her spoilers shall be sated – declares *Hashem*.

¹¹ For you rejoiced, you exulted, You who plundered My possession; You stamped like a heifer treading grain, You neighed like steeds.

¹² So your mother will be utterly shamed, She who bore you will be disgraced. Behold the end of the nations – Wilderness, desert, and steppe!

¹³ Because of *Hashem*'s wrath she shall not be inhabited; She shall be utterly desolate. Whoever passes by Babylon will be appalled And will hiss at all her wounds.

¹⁴ Range yourselves roundabout Babylon, All you who draw the bow; Shoot at her, don't spare arrows, For she has sinned against *Hashem*.

¹⁵ Raise a shout against her all about! She has surrendered; Her bastions have fallen, Her walls are thrown down – This is *Hashem*'s vengeance. Take vengeance on her, Do to her as she has done!

¹⁶ Make an end in Babylon of sowers, And of wielders of the sickle at harvest time. Because of the deadly sword, Each man shall turn back to his people, They shall flee every one to his land.

¹⁷ *Yisrael* are scattered sheep, harried by lions. First the king of Assyria devoured them, and in the end King Nebuchadrezzar of Babylon crunched their bones.

¹⁸ Assuredly, thus said the Lord of Hosts, the God of *Yisrael*: I will deal with the king of Babylon and his land as I dealt with the king of Assyria.

¹⁹ And I will lead *Yisrael* back to his pasture, and he shall graze in *Carmel* and Bashan, and eat his fill in the hill country of *Efraim* and in *Gilad*.

²⁰ In those days and at that time – declares *Hashem* – The iniquity of *Yisrael* shall be sought, And there shall be none; The sins of *Yehuda*, And none shall be found; For I will pardon those I allow to survive.

²¹ Advance against her – the land of Merathaim – And against the inhabitants of Pekod; Ruin and destroy after them to the last – says *Hashem* – Do just as I have commanded you.

²² Hark! War in the land And vast destruction!

י וְהָיְתָה כַשְׂדִּים לְשָׁלָל כָּל־שֹׁלְלֶיהָ יִשְׂבָּעוּ נְאֻם־יְהֹוָה:

יא כִּי תִשְׂמְחִי [תִשְׂמְחוּ] כִּי תַעַלְזִי [תַעַלְזוּ] שֹׁסֵי נַחֲלָתִי כִּי תָפוּשִׁי [תָפוּשׁוּ] כְּעֶגְלָה דָשָׁה וְתִצְהֲלִי [וְתִצְהֲלוּ] כָּאַבִּרִים:

יב בּוֹשָׁה אִמְּכֶם מְאֹד חָפְרָה יוֹלַדְתְּכֶם הִנֵּה אַחֲרִית גּוֹיִם מִדְבָּר צִיָּה וַעֲרָבָה:

יג מִקֶּצֶף יְהֹוָה לֹא תֵשֵׁב וְהָיְתָה שְׁמָמָה כֻּלָּהּ כֹּל עֹבֵר עַל־בָּבֶל יִשֹּׁם וְיִשְׁרֹק עַל־כָּל־מַכּוֹתֶיהָ:

יד עִרְכוּ עַל־בָּבֶל סָבִיב כָּל־דֹּרְכֵי קֶשֶׁת יְדוּ אֵלֶיהָ אַל־תַּחְמְלוּ אֶל־חֵץ כִּי לַיהֹוָה חָטָאָה:

טו הָרִיעוּ עָלֶיהָ סָבִיב נָתְנָה יָדָהּ נָפְלוּ אָשְׁיוֹתֶיהָ [אָשְׁיוֹתֶיהָ] נֶהֶרְסוּ חוֹמוֹתֶיהָ כִּי נִקְמַת יְהֹוָה הִיא הִנָּקְמוּ בָהּ כַּאֲשֶׁר עָשְׂתָה עֲשׂוּ־לָהּ:

טז כִּרְתוּ זוֹרֵעַ מִבָּבֶל וְתֹפֵשׂ מַגָּל בְּעֵת קָצִיר מִפְּנֵי חֶרֶב הַיּוֹנָה אִישׁ אֶל־עַמּוֹ יִפְנוּ וְאִישׁ לְאַרְצוֹ יָנֻסוּ:

יז שֶׂה פְזוּרָה יִשְׂרָאֵל אֲרָיוֹת הִדִּיחוּ הָרִאשׁוֹן אֲכָלוֹ מֶלֶךְ אַשּׁוּר וְזֶה הָאַחֲרוֹן עִצְּמוֹ נְבוּכַדְרֶאצַּר מֶלֶךְ בָּבֶל:

יח לָכֵן כֹּה־אָמַר יְהֹוָה צְבָאוֹת אֱלֹהֵי יִשְׂרָאֵל הִנְנִי פֹקֵד אֶל־מֶלֶךְ בָּבֶל וְאֶל־אַרְצוֹ כַּאֲשֶׁר פָּקַדְתִּי אֶל־מֶלֶךְ אַשּׁוּר:

יט וְשֹׁבַבְתִּי אֶת־יִשְׂרָאֵל אֶל־נָוֵהוּ וְרָעָה הַכַּרְמֶל וְהַבָּשָׁן וּבְהַר אֶפְרַיִם וְהַגִּלְעָד תִּשְׂבַּע נַפְשׁוֹ:

כ בַּיָּמִים הָהֵם וּבָעֵת הַהִיא נְאֻם־יְהֹוָה יְבֻקַּשׁ אֶת־עֲוֹן יִשְׂרָאֵל וְאֵינֶנּוּ וְאֶת־חַטֹּאת יְהוּדָה וְלֹא תִמָּצֶאינָה כִּי אֶסְלַח לַאֲשֶׁר אַשְׁאִיר:

כא עַל־הָאָרֶץ מְרָתַיִם עֲלֵה עָלֶיהָ וְאֶל־יוֹשְׁבֵי פְּקוֹד חֲרֹב וְהַחֲרֵם אַחֲרֵיהֶם נְאֻם־יְהֹוָה וַעֲשֵׂה כְּכֹל אֲשֶׁר צִוִּיתִיךָ:

כב קוֹל מִלְחָמָה בָּאָרֶץ וְשֶׁבֶר גָּדוֹל:

Jeremiah

23 How the hammer of the whole earth Has been hacked and shattered! How Babylon has become An appallment among the nations!

אֵיךְ נִגְדַּע וַיִּשָּׁבֵר פַּטִּישׁ כָּל־הָאָרֶץ אֵיךְ הָיְתָה לְשַׁמָּה בָּבֶל בַּגּוֹיִם: כג

24 I set a snare for you, O Babylon And you were trapped unawares; You were found and caught, Because you challenged *Hashem*.

יָקֹשְׁתִּי לָךְ וְגַם־נִלְכַּדְתְּ בָּבֶל וְאַתְּ לֹא יָדַעַתְּ נִמְצֵאת וְגַם־נִתְפַּשְׂתְּ כִּי בַיהֹוָה הִתְגָּרִית: כד

25 *Hashem* has opened His armory And brought out the weapons of His wrath; For that is the task Of my Lord God of Hosts In the land of the Chaldeans.

פָּתַח יְהֹוָה אֶת־אוֹצָרוֹ וַיּוֹצֵא אֶת־כְּלֵי זַעְמוֹ כִּי־מְלָאכָה הִיא לַאדֹנָי יְהֹוִה צְבָאוֹת בְּאֶרֶץ כַּשְׂדִּים: כה

26 Come against her from every quarter; Break open her granaries, Pile her up like heaps of grain, And destroy her, let her have no remnant!

בֹּאוּ־לָהּ מִקֵּץ פִּתְחוּ מַאֲבֻסֶיהָ סָלּוּהָ כְמוֹ־עֲרֵמִים וְהַחֲרִימוּהָ אַל־תְּהִי־לָהּ שְׁאֵרִית: כו

27 Destroy all her bulls, Let them go down to slaughter. Alas for them, their day is come, The hour of their doom!

חִרְבוּ כָּל־פָּרֶיהָ יֵרְדוּ לַטָּבַח הוֹי עֲלֵיהֶם כִּי־בָא יוֹמָם עֵת פְּקֻדָּתָם: כז

28 Hark! fugitives are escaping From the land of Babylon, To tell in *Tzion* of the vengeance of *Hashem* our God, Vengeance for His Temple.

קוֹל נָסִים וּפְלֵטִים מֵאֶרֶץ בָּבֶל לְהַגִּיד בְּצִיּוֹן אֶת־נִקְמַת יְהֹוָה אֱלֹהֵינוּ נִקְמַת הֵיכָלוֹ: כח

29 Summon archers against Babylon, All who draw the bow! Encamp against her roundabout, Let none of her people escape. Pay her back for her actions, Do to her just what she has done; For she has acted insolently against *Hashem*, The Holy One of *Yisrael*.

הַשְׁמִיעוּ אֶל־בָּבֶל רַבִּים כָּל־דֹּרְכֵי קֶשֶׁת חֲנוּ עָלֶיהָ סָבִיב אַל־יְהִי־[לָהּ] פְּלֵטָה שַׁלְּמוּ־לָהּ כְּפָעֳלָהּ כְּכֹל אֲשֶׁר עָשְׂתָה עֲשׂוּ־לָהּ כִּי אֶל־יְהֹוָה זָדָה אֶל־קְדוֹשׁ יִשְׂרָאֵל: כט

30 Assuredly, her young men shall fall in her squares, And all her warriors shall perish in that day – declares *Hashem*.

לָכֵן יִפְּלוּ בַחוּרֶיהָ בִּרְחֹבֹתֶיהָ וְכָל־אַנְשֵׁי מִלְחַמְתָּהּ יִדַּמּוּ בַּיּוֹם הַהוּא נְאֻם־יְהֹוָה: ל

31 I am going to deal with you, O Insolence – declares the Lord of Hosts – For your day is come, the time when I doom you:

הִנְנִי אֵלֶיךָ זָדוֹן נְאֻם־אֲדֹנָי יְהֹוִה צְבָאוֹת כִּי בָּא יוֹמְךָ עֵת פְּקַדְתִּיךָ: לא

32 Insolence shall stumble and fall, With none to raise her up. I will set her cities on fire, And it shall consume everything around her.

וְכָשַׁל זָדוֹן וְנָפַל וְאֵין לוֹ מֵקִים וְהִצַּתִּי אֵשׁ בְּעָרָיו וְאָכְלָה כָּל־סְבִיבֹתָיו: לב

33 Thus said the Lord of Hosts: The people of *Yisrael* are oppressed, And so too the people of *Yehuda*; All their captors held them, They refused to let them go.

כֹּה אָמַר יְהֹוָה צְבָאוֹת עֲשׁוּקִים בְּנֵי־יִשְׂרָאֵל וּבְנֵי־יְהוּדָה יַחְדָּו וְכָל־שֹׁבֵיהֶם הֶחֱזִיקוּ בָם מֵאֲנוּ שַׁלְּחָם: לג

34 Their Redeemer is mighty, His name is Lord of Hosts. He will champion their cause – So as to give rest to the earth, And unrest to the inhabitants of Babylon.

גֹּאֲלָם חָזָק יְהֹוָה צְבָאוֹת שְׁמוֹ רִיב יָרִיב אֶת־רִיבָם לְמַעַן הִרְגִּיעַ אֶת־הָאָרֶץ וְהִרְגִּיז לְיֹשְׁבֵי בָבֶל: לד

³⁵ A sword against the Chaldeans – declares *Hashem* – And against the inhabitants of Babylon, Against its officials and its wise men!

חֶ֤רֶב עַל־כַּשְׂדִּים֙ נְאֻם־יְהֹוָ֔ה וְאֶל־יֹשְׁבֵ֖י בָּבֶ֑ל וְאֶל־שָׂרֶ֖יהָ וְאֶל־חֲכָמֶֽיהָ׃

³⁶ A sword against the diviners, that they be made fools of! A sword against the warriors, that they be dismayed!

חֶ֥רֶב אֶל־הַבַּדִּ֖ים וְנֹאָ֑לוּ חֶ֥רֶב אֶל־גִּבּוֹרֶ֖יהָ וָחָֽתּוּ׃

³⁷ A sword against its horses and chariots, And against all the motley crowd in its midst, That they become like women! A sword against its treasuries, that they be pillaged!

חֶ֜רֶב אֶל־סוּסָ֣יו וְאֶל־רִכְבּ֗וֹ וְאֶל־כׇּל־הָעֶ֙רֶב֙ אֲשֶׁ֣ר בְּתוֹכָ֔הּ וְהָי֖וּ לְנָשִׁ֑ים חֶ֥רֶב אֶל־אוֹצְרֹתֶ֖יהָ וּבֻזָּֽזוּ׃

³⁸ A drought against its waters, that they be dried up! For it is a land of idols; They are besotted by their dread images.

חֹ֥רֶב אֶל־מֵימֶ֖יהָ וְיָבֵ֑שׁוּ כִּ֣י אֶ֤רֶץ פְּסִלִים֙ הִ֔יא וּבָאֵימִ֖ים יִתְהֹלָֽלוּ׃

³⁹ Assuredly, Wildcats and hyenas shall dwell [there], And ostriches shall dwell there; It shall never be settled again, Nor inhabited throughout the ages.

לָכֵ֗ן יֵשְׁב֤וּ צִיִּים֙ אֶת־אִיִּ֔ים וְיָ֥שְׁבוּ בָ֖הּ בְּנ֣וֹת יַעֲנָ֑ה וְלֹֽא־תֵשֵׁ֥ב עוֹד֙ לָנֶ֔צַח וְלֹ֥א תִשְׁכּ֖וֹן עַד־דּ֥וֹר וָדֽוֹר׃

⁴⁰ It shall be as when *Hashem* overthrew Sodom and Gomorrah and their neighbors – declares *Hashem*; no man shall live there, no human shall sojourn there.

כְּמַהְפֵּכַ֨ת אֱלֹהִ֜ים אֶת־סְדֹ֧ם וְאֶת־עֲמֹרָ֛ה וְאֶת־שְׁכֵנֶ֖יהָ נְאֻם־יְהֹוָ֑ה לֹֽא־יֵשֵׁ֥ב שָׁם֙ אִ֔ישׁ וְלֹא־יָג֥וּר בָּ֖הּ בֶּן־אָדָֽם׃

⁴¹ Lo, a people comes from the northland; A great nation and many kings are roused From the remotest parts of the earth.

הִנֵּ֛ה עַ֥ם בָּ֖א מִצָּפ֑וֹן וְג֤וֹי גָּדוֹל֙ וּמְלָכִ֣ים רַבִּ֔ים יֵעֹ֖רוּ מִיַּרְכְּתֵי־אָֽרֶץ׃

⁴² They grasp the bow and javelin, They are cruel, they show no mercy; The sound of them is like the roaring sea. They ride upon horses, Accoutered like a man for battle, Against you, O Fair Babylon!

קֶ֣שֶׁת וְכִידֹ֞ן יַחֲזִ֗יקוּ אַכְזָרִ֥י הֵ֙מָּה֙ וְלֹ֣א יְרַחֵ֔מוּ קוֹלָם֙ כַּיָּ֣ם יֶהֱמֶ֔ה וְעַל־סוּסִ֖ים יִרְכָּ֑בוּ עָר֗וּךְ כְּאִישׁ֙ לַמִּלְחָמָ֔ה עָלַ֖יִךְ בַּת־בָּבֶֽל׃

⁴³ The king of Babylon has heard the report of them And his hands are weakened; Anguish seizes him, Pangs like a woman in childbirth.

שָׁמַ֧ע מֶלֶךְ־בָּבֶ֛ל אֶת־שִׁמְעָ֖ם וְרָפ֣וּ יָדָ֑יו צָרָה֙ הֶחֱזִיקַ֔תְהוּ חִ֖יל כַּיּֽוֹלֵדָֽה׃

⁴⁴ It shall be as when a lion comes out of the jungle of the *Yarden* against a secure pasture: in a moment I can harry them out of it and appoint over it anyone I choose. Then who is like Me? Who can summon Me? Who is the shepherd that can stand up against Me?

הִ֠נֵּ֠ה כְּאַרְיֵ֞ה יַעֲלֶ֨ה מִגְּא֣וֹן הַיַּרְדֵּן֮ אֶל־נְוֵ֣ה אֵיתָן֒ כִּֽי־אַרְגִּ֤עָה אֲרוֹצֵ֣ם [אֲרִיצֵ֣ם] מֵֽעָלֶ֔יהָ וּמִ֥י בָח֖וּר אֵלֶ֣יהָ אֶפְקֹ֑ד כִּ֣י מִ֤י כָמ֙וֹנִי֙ וּמִ֣י יֹֽעִידֶ֔נִּי וּמִי־זֶ֣ה רֹעֶ֔ה אֲשֶׁ֥ר יַעֲמֹ֖ד לְפָנָֽי׃

⁴⁵ Hear, then, the plan that *Hashem* has devised against Babylon, and has purposed against the land of Chaldea: Surely the shepherd boys Shall drag them away; Surely the pasture shall be Aghast because of them.

לָכֵ֞ן שִׁמְע֣וּ עֲצַת־יְהֹוָ֗ה אֲשֶׁ֤ר יָעַץ֙ אֶל־בָּבֶ֔ל וּמַ֨חְשְׁבוֹתָ֔יו אֲשֶׁ֥ר חָשַׁ֖ב אֶל־אֶ֣רֶץ כַּשְׂדִּ֑ים אִם־לֹ֤א יִסְחָבוּם֙ צְעִירֵ֣י הַצֹּ֔אן אִם־לֹ֥א יַשִּׁ֛ים עֲלֵיהֶ֖ם נָוֶֽה׃

⁴⁶ At the sound of Babylon's capture The earth quakes, And an outcry is heard among the nations.

מִקּוֹל֙ נִתְפְּשָׂ֣ה בָבֶ֔ל נִרְעֲשָׁ֖ה הָאָ֑רֶץ וּזְעָקָ֖ה בַּגּוֹיִ֥ם נִשְׁמָֽע׃

Jeremiah

51 ¹ Thus said *Hashem*: See, I am rousing a destructive wind Against Babylon and the inhabitants of Leb-kamai.

² I will send strangers against Babylon, and they shall winnow her. And they shall strip her land bare; They shall beset her on all sides On the day of disaster.

³ Let the archer draw his bow, And let him stand ready in his coat of mail! Show no pity to her young men, Wipe out all her host!

⁴ Let them fall slain in the land of Chaldea, Pierced through in her streets.

⁵ For *Yisrael* and *Yehuda* were not bereft Of their God the Lord of Hosts, But their land was filled with guilt Before the Holy One of *Yisrael*.

⁶ Flee from the midst of Babylon And save your lives, each of you! Do not perish for her iniquity; For this is a time of vengeance for *Hashem*, He will deal retribution to her.

⁷ Babylon was a golden cup in *Hashem*'s hand, It made the whole earth drunk; The nations drank of her wine – That is why the nations are mad.

⁸ Suddenly Babylon has fallen and is shattered; Howl over her! Get balm for her wounds: Perhaps she can be healed.

⁹ We tried to cure Babylon But she was incurable. Let us leave her and go, Each to his own land; For her punishment reaches to heaven, It is as high as the sky.

¹⁰ *Hashem* has proclaimed our vindication; Come, let us recount in *Tzion* The deeds of *Hashem* our God.

¹¹ Polish the arrows, Fill the quivers! *Hashem* has roused the spirit of the kings of Media, For His plan against Babylon is to destroy her. This is the vengeance of *Hashem*, Vengeance for His Temple.

¹² Raise a standard against the walls of Babylon! Set up a blockade; station watchmen; Prepare those in ambush. For *Hashem* has both planned and performed What He decreed against the inhabitants of Babylon.

¹³ O you who dwell by great waters, With vast storehouses, Your time is come, the hour of your end.

נא א כֹּה אָמַר יְהֹוָה הִנְנִי מֵעִיר עַל־בָּבֶל וְאֶל־ יֹשְׁבֵי לֵב קָמָי רוּחַ מַשְׁחִית:

ב וְשִׁלַּחְתִּי לְבָבֶל זָרִים וְזֵרוּהָ וִיבֹקְקוּ אֶת־ אַרְצָהּ כִּי־הָיוּ עָלֶיהָ מִסָּבִיב בְּיוֹם רָעָה:

ג אֶל־יִדְרֹךְ יִדְרֹךְ הַדֹּרֵךְ קַשְׁתּוֹ וְאֶל־ יִתְעַל בְּסִרְיֹנוֹ וְאַל־תַּחְמְלוּ אֶל־בַּחֻרֶיהָ הַחֲרִימוּ כָּל־צְבָאָהּ:

ד וְנָפְלוּ חֲלָלִים בְּאֶרֶץ כַּשְׂדִּים וּמְדֻקָּרִים בְּחוּצוֹתֶיהָ:

ה כִּי לֹא־אַלְמָן יִשְׂרָאֵל וִיהוּדָה מֵאֱלֹהָיו מֵיְהֹוָה צְבָאוֹת כִּי אַרְצָם מָלְאָה אָשָׁם מִקְּדוֹשׁ יִשְׂרָאֵל:

ו נֻסוּ מִתּוֹךְ בָּבֶל וּמַלְּטוּ אִישׁ נַפְשׁוֹ אַל־ תִּדַּמּוּ בַּעֲוֹנָהּ כִּי עֵת נְקָמָה הִיא לַיהֹוָה גְּמוּל הוּא מְשַׁלֵּם לָהּ:

ז כּוֹס־זָהָב בָּבֶל בְּיַד־יְהֹוָה מְשַׁכֶּרֶת כָּל־ הָאָרֶץ מִיֵּינָהּ שָׁתוּ גוֹיִם עַל־כֵּן יִתְהֹלְלוּ גוֹיִם:

ח פִּתְאֹם נָפְלָה בָבֶל וַתִּשָּׁבֵר הֵילִילוּ עָלֶיהָ קְחוּ צֳרִי לְמַכְאוֹבָהּ אוּלַי תֵּרָפֵא:

ט רִפִּאנוּ [רִפִּינוּ] אֶת־בָּבֶל וְלֹא נִרְפָּתָה עִזְבוּהָ וְנֵלֵךְ אִישׁ לְאַרְצוֹ כִּי־נָגַע אֶל־ הַשָּׁמַיִם מִשְׁפָּטָהּ וְנִשָּׂא עַד־שְׁחָקִים:

י הוֹצִיא יְהֹוָה אֶת־צִדְקֹתֵינוּ בֹּאוּ וּנְסַפְּרָה בְצִיּוֹן אֶת־מַעֲשֵׂה יְהֹוָה אֱלֹהֵינוּ:

יא הָבֵרוּ הַחִצִּים מִלְאוּ הַשְּׁלָטִים הֵעִיר יְהֹוָה אֶת־רוּחַ מַלְכֵי מָדַי כִּי־עַל־בָּבֶל מְזִמָּתוֹ לְהַשְׁחִיתָהּ כִּי־נִקְמַת יְהֹוָה הִיא נִקְמַת הֵיכָלוֹ:

יב אֶל־חוֹמֹת בָּבֶל שְׂאוּ־נֵס הַחֲזִיקוּ הַמִּשְׁמָר הָקִימוּ שֹׁמְרִים הָכִינוּ הָאֹרְבִים כִּי גַּם־זָמַם יְהֹוָה גַּם־עָשָׂה אֵת אֲשֶׁר־ דִּבֶּר אֶל־יֹשְׁבֵי בָבֶל:

יג שֹׁכַנְתִּי [שֹׁכַנְתְּ] עַל־מַיִם רַבִּים רַבַּת אוֹצָרֹת בָּא קִצֵּךְ אַמַּת בִּצְעֵךְ:

Jeremiah

14 The LORD of Hosts has sworn by Himself: I will fill you with men like a locust swarm, They will raise a shout against you.

נִשְׁבַּע יְהֹוָה צְבָאוֹת בְּנַפְשׁוֹ כִּי אִם־מִלֵּאתִיךְ אָדָם כַּיֶּלֶק וְעָנוּ עָלַיִךְ הֵידָד: יד

15 He made the earth by His might, Established the world by His wisdom, And by His understanding stretched out the skies.

עֹשֵׂה אֶרֶץ בְּכֹחוֹ מֵכִין תֵּבֵל בְּחָכְמָתוֹ וּבִתְבוּנָתוֹ נָטָה שָׁמָיִם: טו

16 When He makes His voice heard, There is a rumbling of waters in the skies; He makes vapors rise from the end of the earth, He makes lightning for the rain, And brings forth wind from His treasuries.

לְקוֹל תִּתּוֹ הֲמוֹן מַיִם בַּשָּׁמַיִם וַיַּעַל נְשִׂאִים מִקְצֵה־אֶרֶץ בְּרָקִים לַמָּטָר עָשָׂה וַיּוֹצֵא רוּחַ מֵאֹצְרֹתָיו: טז

17 Every man is proved dull, without knowledge; Every goldsmith is put to shame because of the idol, For his molten image is a deceit – There is no breath in them.

נִבְעַר כָּל־אָדָם מִדַּעַת הֹבִישׁ כָּל־צֹרֵף מִפָּסֶל כִּי שֶׁקֶר נִסְכּוֹ וְלֹא־רוּחַ בָּם: יז

18 They are delusion, a work of mockery; In their hour of doom, they shall perish.

הֶבֶל הֵמָּה מַעֲשֵׂה תַּעְתֻּעִים בְּעֵת פְּקֻדָּתָם יֹאבֵדוּ: יח

19 Not like these in the Portion of *Yaakov*, For it is He who formed all things; And [*Yisrael* is] His very own tribe. LORD of Hosts is His name.

לֹא־כְאֵלֶּה חֵלֶק יַעֲקֹב כִּי־יוֹצֵר הַכֹּל הוּא וְשֵׁבֶט נַחֲלָתוֹ יְהֹוָה צְבָאוֹת שְׁמוֹ: יט

*lo kh'-AY-leh KHAY-lek ya-a-KOV kee -yo-TZAYR ha-KOL HU
v'-SHAY-vet na-kha-la-TO a-do-NAI tz'-va-OT sh'-MO*

20 You are My war club, [My] weapons of battle; With you I clubbed nations, With you I destroyed kingdoms;

מַפֵּץ־אַתָּה לִי כְּלֵי מִלְחָמָה וְנִפַּצְתִּי בְךָ גּוֹיִם וְהִשְׁחַתִּי בְךָ מַמְלָכוֹת: כ

21 With you I clubbed horse and rider, With you I clubbed chariot and driver,

וְנִפַּצְתִּי בְךָ סוּס וְרֹכְבוֹ וְנִפַּצְתִּי בְךָ רֶכֶב וְרֹכְבוֹ: כא

22 With you I clubbed man and woman, With you I clubbed graybeard and boy, With you I clubbed youth and maiden;

וְנִפַּצְתִּי בְךָ אִישׁ וְאִשָּׁה וְנִפַּצְתִּי בְךָ זָקֵן וָנָעַר וְנִפַּצְתִּי בְךָ בָּחוּר וּבְתוּלָה: כב

23 With you I clubbed shepherd and flock, With you I clubbed plowman and team, With you I clubbed governors and prefects.

וְנִפַּצְתִּי בְךָ רֹעֶה וְעֶדְרוֹ וְנִפַּצְתִּי בְךָ אִכָּר וְצִמְדּוֹ וְנִפַּצְתִּי בְךָ פַּחוֹת וּסְגָנִים: כג

24 But I will requite Babylon and all the inhabitants of Chaldea For all the wicked things they did to *Tzion* before your eyes – declares *Hashem*.

וְשִׁלַּמְתִּי לְבָבֶל וּלְכֹל יוֹשְׁבֵי כַשְׂדִּים אֵת כָּל־רָעָתָם אֲשֶׁר־עָשׂוּ בְצִיּוֹן לְעֵינֵיכֶם נְאֻם יְהֹוָה: כד

An Israeli soldier at the beach in *Tel Aviv*

51:19 Not like these in the Portion of Yaakov For two long chapters, *Yirmiyahu* describes the utter destruction that will befall the Babylonians. However, it is the future of Israel that ultimately concerns God. The Babylonians put their trust in their idols (verse 17–18) and are let down in the end. Israel's fate is different because they trust in *Hashem*. Since *Hashem* created the world, it is His to distribute as He pleases. He chose to give the Land of Israel to the people of Israle, the "Portion of *Yaakov*," as an eternal inheritance that will remain theirs forever.

25 See, I will deal with you, O mountain of the destroyer – declares *Hashem* – Destroyer of the whole earth! I will stretch out My hand against you And roll you down from the crags, And make you a burnt-out mountain.

כה הִנְנִי אֵלֶיךָ הַר הַמַּשְׁחִית נְאֻם־יְהֹוָה הַמַּשְׁחִית אֶת־כָּל־הָאָרֶץ וְנָטִיתִי אֶת־יָדִי עָלֶיךָ וְגִלְגַּלְתִּיךָ מִן־הַסְּלָעִים וּנְתַתִּיךָ לְהַר שְׂרֵפָה:

26 They shall never take from you A cornerstone or foundation stone; You shall be a desolation for all time – declares *Hashem*.

כו וְלֹא־יִקְחוּ מִמְּךָ אֶבֶן לְפִנָּה וְאֶבֶן לְמוֹסָדוֹת כִּי־שִׁמְמוֹת עוֹלָם תִּהְיֶה נְאֻם־יְהֹוָה:

27 Raise a standard on earth, Sound a *shofar* among the nations, Appoint nations against her, Assemble kingdoms against her – Ararat, Minni, and Ashkenaz – Designate a marshal against her, Bring up horses like swarming locusts!

כז שְׂאוּ־נֵס בָּאָרֶץ תִּקְעוּ שׁוֹפָר בַּגּוֹיִם קַדְּשׁוּ עָלֶיהָ גּוֹיִם הַשְׁמִיעוּ עָלֶיהָ מַמְלְכוֹת אֲרָרַט מִנִּי וְאַשְׁכְּנָז פִּקְדוּ עָלֶיהָ טִפְסָר הַעֲלוּ־סוּס כְּיֶלֶק סָמָר:

28 Appoint nations for war against her – The kings of Media, Her governors and all her prefects, And all the lands they rule!

כח קַדְּשׁוּ עָלֶיהָ גוֹיִם אֶת־מַלְכֵי מָדַי אֶת־פַּחוֹתֶיהָ וְאֶת־כָּל־סְגָנֶיהָ וְאֵת כָּל־אֶרֶץ מֶמְשַׁלְתּוֹ:

29 Then the earth quakes and writhes, For *Hashem*'s purpose is fulfilled against Babylon, To make the land of Babylon A waste without inhabitant.

כט וַתִּרְעַשׁ הָאָרֶץ וַתָּחֹל כִּי קָמָה עַל־בָּבֶל מַחְשְׁבוֹת יְהֹוָה לָשׂוּם אֶת־אֶרֶץ בָּבֶל לְשַׁמָּה מֵאֵין יוֹשֵׁב:

30 The warriors of Babylon stop fighting, They sit in the strongholds, Their might is dried up, They become women. Her dwellings are set afire, Her bars are broken.

ל חָדְלוּ גִבּוֹרֵי בָבֶל לְהִלָּחֵם יָשְׁבוּ בַּמְּצָדוֹת נָשְׁתָה גְבוּרָתָם הָיוּ לְנָשִׁים הִצִּיתוּ מִשְׁכְּנֹתֶיהָ נִשְׁבְּרוּ בְרִיחֶיהָ:

31 Runner dashes to meet runner, Messenger to meet messenger, To report to the king of Babylon That his city is captured, from end to end.

לא רָץ לִקְרַאת־רָץ יָרוּץ וּמַגִּיד לִקְרַאת מַגִּיד לְהַגִּיד לְמֶלֶךְ בָּבֶל כִּי־נִלְכְּדָה עִירוֹ מִקָּצֶה:

32 The fords are captured, And the swamp thickets are consumed in fire; And the fighting men are in panic.

לב וְהַמַּעְבָּרוֹת נִתְפָּשׂוּ וְאֶת־הָאֲגַמִּים שָׂרְפוּ בָאֵשׁ וְאַנְשֵׁי הַמִּלְחָמָה נִבְהָלוּ:

33 For thus said the LORD of Hosts, the God of *Yisrael*: Fair Babylon is like a threshing floor Ready to be trodden; In a little while her harvesttime will come.

לג כִּי כֹה אָמַר יְהֹוָה צְבָאוֹת אֱלֹהֵי יִשְׂרָאֵל בַּת־בָּבֶל כְּגֹרֶן עֵת הִדְרִיכָהּ עוֹד מְעַט וּבָאָה עֵת־הַקָּצִיר לָהּ:

34 "Nebuchadrezzar king of Babylon Devoured me and discomfited me; He swallowed me like a dragon, He filled his belly with my dainties, And set me down like an empty dish; Then he rinsed me out.

לד אֲכָלַנוּ [אֲכָלַנִי] הֲמָמַנוּ [הֲמָמַנִי] נְבוּכַדְרֶאצַּר מֶלֶךְ בָּבֶל הִצִּיגַנוּ [הִצִּיגַנִי] כְּלִי רִיק בְּלָעַנוּ [בְּלָעַנִי] כַּתַּנִּין מִלָּא כְרֵשׂוֹ מֵעֲדָנָי הֱדִיחָנוּ [הֱדִיחָנִי]:

35 Let the violence done me and my kindred Be upon Babylon," Says the inhabitant of *Tzion*; "And let my blood be upon the inhabitants of Chaldea," Says *Yerushalayim*.

לה חֲמָסִי וּשְׁאֵרִי עַל־בָּבֶל תֹּאמַר יֹשֶׁבֶת צִיּוֹן וְדָמִי אֶל־יֹשְׁבֵי כַשְׂדִּים תֹּאמַר יְרוּשָׁלָ͏ִם:

36 Assuredly, thus said *Hashem*: I am going to uphold your cause And take vengeance for you; I will dry up her sea And make her fountain run dry.

לו לָכֵן כֹּה אָמַר יְהֹוָה הִנְנִי־רָב אֶת־רִיבֵךְ וְנִקַּמְתִּי אֶת־נִקְמָתֵךְ וְהַחֲרַבְתִּי אֶת־יַמָּהּ וְהֹבַשְׁתִּי אֶת־מְקוֹרָהּ:

³⁷ Babylon shall become rubble, A den for jackals, An object of horror and hissing, Without inhabitant.

לז וְהָיְתָה בָבֶל לְגַלִּים מְעוֹן־תַּנִּים שַׁמָּה וּשְׁרֵקָה מֵאֵין יוֹשֵׁב:

³⁸ Like lions, they roar together, They growl like lion cubs.

לח יַחְדָּו כַּכְּפִרִים יִשְׁאָגוּ נָעֲרוּ כְּגוֹרֵי אֲרָיוֹת:

³⁹ When they are heated, I will set out their drink And get them drunk, that they may become hilarious And then sleep an endless sleep, Never to awake – declares *Hashem*.

לט בְּחֻמָּם אָשִׁית אֶת־מִשְׁתֵּיהֶם וְהִשְׁכַּרְתִּים לְמַעַן יַעֲלֹזוּ וְיָשְׁנוּ שְׁנַת־עוֹלָם וְלֹא יָקִיצוּ נְאֻם יְהֹוָה:

⁴⁰ I will bring them down like lambs for slaughter, Like rams and he-goats.

מ אוֹרִידֵם כְּכָרִים לִטְבוֹחַ כְּאֵילִים עִם־עַתּוּדִים:

⁴¹ How has Sheshach been captured, The praise of the whole earth been taken! How has Babylon become A horror to the nations!

מא אֵיךְ נִלְכְּדָה שֵׁשַׁךְ וַתִּתָּפֵשׂ תְּהִלַּת כָּל־הָאָרֶץ אֵיךְ הָיְתָה לְשַׁמָּה בָּבֶל בַּגּוֹיִם:

⁴² The sea has risen over Babylon, She is covered by its roaring waves.

מב עָלָה עַל־בָּבֶל הַיָּם בַּהֲמוֹן גַּלָּיו נִכְסָתָה:

⁴³ Her towns are a desolation, A land of desert and steppe, A land no man lives in And no human passes through.

מג הָיוּ עָרֶיהָ לְשַׁמָּה אֶרֶץ צִיָּה וַעֲרָבָה אֶרֶץ לֹא־יֵשֵׁב בָּהֵן כָּל־אִישׁ וְלֹא־יַעֲבֹר בָּהֵן בֶּן־אָדָם:

⁴⁴ And I will deal with Bel in Babylon, And make him disgorge what he has swallowed, And nations shall no more gaze on him with joy. Even the wall of Babylon shall fall.

מד וּפָקַדְתִּי עַל־בֵּל בְּבָבֶל וְהֹצֵאתִי אֶת־בִּלְעוֹ מִפִּיו וְלֹא־יִנְהֲרוּ אֵלָיו עוֹד גּוֹיִם גַּם־חוֹמַת בָּבֶל נָפָלָה:

⁴⁵ Depart from there, O My people, Save your lives, each of you, From the furious anger of *Hashem*.

מה צְאוּ מִתּוֹכָהּ עַמִּי וּמַלְּטוּ אִישׁ אֶת־נַפְשׁוֹ מֵחֲרוֹן אַף־יְהֹוָה:

⁴⁶ Do not be downhearted or afraid At the rumors heard in the land: A rumor will come one year, And another rumor the next year Of violence in the land, And of ruler against ruler.

מו וּפֶן־יֵרַךְ לְבַבְכֶם וְתִירְאוּ בַּשְּׁמוּעָה הַנִּשְׁמַעַת בָּאָרֶץ וּבָא בַשָּׁנָה הַשְּׁמוּעָה וְאַחֲרָיו בַּשָּׁנָה הַשְּׁמוּעָה וְחָמָס בָּאָרֶץ וּמֹשֵׁל עַל־מֹשֵׁל:

⁴⁷ Assuredly, days are coming, When I will deal with Babylon's images; Her whole land shall be shamed, And all her slain shall fall in her midst.

מז לָכֵן הִנֵּה יָמִים בָּאִים וּפָקַדְתִּי עַל־פְּסִילֵי בָבֶל וְכָל־אַרְצָהּ תֵּבוֹשׁ וְכָל־חֲלָלֶיהָ יִפְּלוּ בְתוֹכָהּ:

⁴⁸ Heavens and earth and all that is in them Shall shout over Babylon; For the ravagers shall come upon her from the north – declares *Hashem*.

מח וְרִנְּנוּ עַל־בָּבֶל שָׁמַיִם וָאָרֶץ וְכֹל אֲשֶׁר בָּהֶם כִּי מִצָּפוֹן יָבוֹא־לָהּ הַשּׁוֹדְדִים נְאֻם־יְהֹוָה:

⁴⁹ Yes, Babylon is to fall [For] the slain of *Yisrael*, As the slain of all the earth Have fallen through Babylon.

מט גַּם־בָּבֶל לִנְפֹּל חַלְלֵי יִשְׂרָאֵל גַּם־לְבָבֶל נָפְלוּ חַלְלֵי כָל־הָאָרֶץ:

⁵⁰ You fugitives from the sword, Go, don't delay! Remember *Hashem* from afar, And call *Yerushalayim* to mind.

נ פְּלֵטִים מֵחֶרֶב הִלְכוּ אַל־תַּעֲמֹדוּ זִכְרוּ מֵרָחוֹק אֶת־יְהֹוָה וִירוּשָׁלַ͏ִם תַּעֲלֶה עַל־לְבַבְכֶם:

51 "We were shamed, we heard taunts; Humiliation covered our faces, When aliens entered The sacred areas of *Hashem*'s House."

נא בֹּשְׁנוּ כִּי־שָׁמַעְנוּ חֶרְפָּה כִּסְּתָה כְלִמָּה פָּנֵינוּ כִּי בָּאוּ זָרִים עַל־מִקְדְּשֵׁי בֵּית יְהֹוָה:

52 Assuredly, days are coming – declares *Hashem* – When I will deal with her images, And throughout her land the dying shall groan.

נב לָכֵן הִנֵּה־יָמִים בָּאִים נְאֻם־יְהֹוָה וּפָקַדְתִּי עַל־פְּסִילֶיהָ וּבְכָל־אַרְצָהּ יֶאֱנֹק חָלָל:

53 Though Babylon should climb to the skies, Though she fortify her strongholds up to heaven, The ravagers would come against her from Me – declares *Hashem*.

נג כִּי־תַעֲלֶה בָבֶל הַשָּׁמַיִם וְכִי תְבַצֵּר מְרוֹם עֻזָּהּ מֵאִתִּי יָבֹאוּ שֹׁדְדִים לָהּ נְאֻם־יְהֹוָה:

54 Hark! an outcry from Babylon, Great destruction from the land of the Chaldeans.

נד קוֹל זְעָקָה מִבָּבֶל וְשֶׁבֶר גָּדוֹל מֵאֶרֶץ כַּשְׂדִּים:

55 For *Hashem* is ravaging Babylon; He will put an end to her great din, Whose roar is like waves of mighty waters, Whose tumultuous noise resounds.

נה כִּי־שֹׁדֵד יְהֹוָה אֶת־בָּבֶל וְאִבַּד מִמֶּנָּה קוֹל גָּדוֹל וְהָמוּ גַלֵּיהֶם כְּמַיִם רַבִּים נִתַּן שְׁאוֹן קוֹלָם:

56 For a ravager is coming upon Babylon, Her warriors shall be captured, their bows shall be snapped. For *Hashem* is a God of requital, He deals retribution.

נו כִּי בָא עָלֶיהָ עַל־בָּבֶל שׁוֹדֵד וְנִלְכְּדוּ גִּבּוֹרֶיהָ חִתְּתָה קַשְּׁתוֹתָם כִּי אֵל גְּמֻלוֹת יְהֹוָה שַׁלֵּם יְשַׁלֵּם:

57 I will make her officials and wise men drunk, Her governors and prefects and warriors; And they shall sleep an endless sleep, Never to awaken – declares the King whose name is LORD of Hosts.

נז וְהִשְׁכַּרְתִּי שָׂרֶיהָ וַחֲכָמֶיהָ פַּחוֹתֶיהָ וּסְגָנֶיהָ וְגִבּוֹרֶיהָ וְיָשְׁנוּ שְׁנַת־עוֹלָם וְלֹא יָקִיצוּ נְאֻם־הַמֶּלֶךְ יְהֹוָה צְבָאוֹת שְׁמוֹ:

58 Thus said the LORD of Hosts: Babylon's broad wall shall be knocked down, And her high gates set afire. Peoples shall labor for naught, And nations have wearied themselves for fire.

נח כֹּה־אָמַר יְהֹוָה צְבָאוֹת חֹמוֹת בָּבֶל הָרְחָבָה עַרְעֵר תִּתְעַרְעָר וּשְׁעָרֶיהָ הַגְּבֹהִים בָּאֵשׁ יִצַּתּוּ וְיִגְעוּ עַמִּים בְּדֵי־רִיק וּלְאֻמִּים בְּדֵי־אֵשׁ וְיָעֵפוּ:

59 The instructions that the *Navi Yirmiyahu* gave to *Seraya* son of *Nerya* son of *Machseya*, when the latter went with King *Tzidkiyahu* of *Yehuda* to Babylonia, in the fourth year of [*Tzidkiyahu*'s] reign. *Seraya* was quartermaster.

נט הַדָּבָר אֲשֶׁר־צִוָּה יִרְמְיָהוּ הַנָּבִיא אֶת־שְׂרָיָה בֶן־נֵרִיָּה בֶּן־מַחְסֵיָה בְּלֶכְתּוֹ אֶת־צִדְקִיָּהוּ מֶלֶךְ־יְהוּדָה בָּבֶל בִּשְׁנַת הָרְבִעִית לְמָלְכוֹ וּשְׂרָיָה שַׂר מְנוּחָה:

60 *Yirmiyahu* wrote down in one scroll all the disaster that would come upon Babylon, all these things that are written concerning Babylon.

ס וַיִּכְתֹּב יִרְמְיָהוּ אֵת כָּל־הָרָעָה אֲשֶׁר־תָּבוֹא אֶל־בָּבֶל אֶל־סֵפֶר אֶחָד אֵת כָּל־הַדְּבָרִים הָאֵלֶּה הַכְּתֻבִים אֶל־בָּבֶל:

61 And *Yirmiyahu* said to *Seraya*, "When you get to Babylon, see that you read out all these words.

סא וַיֹּאמֶר יִרְמְיָהוּ אֶל־שְׂרָיָה כְּבֹאֲךָ בָבֶל וְרָאִיתָ וְקָרָאתָ אֵת כָּל־הַדְּבָרִים הָאֵלֶּה:

62 And say, '*Hashem*, You Yourself have declared concerning this place that it shall be cut off, without inhabitant, man or beast; that it shall be a desolation for all time.'

סב וְאָמַרְתָּ יְהֹוָה אַתָּה דִבַּרְתָּ אֶל־הַמָּקוֹם הַזֶּה לְהַכְרִיתוֹ לְבִלְתִּי הֱיוֹת־בּוֹ יוֹשֵׁב לְמֵאָדָם וְעַד־בְּהֵמָה כִּי־שִׁמְמוֹת עוֹלָם תִּהְיֶה:

63 And when you finish reading this scroll, tie a stone to it and hurl it into the Euphrates.

סג וְהָיָה כְּכַלֹּתְךָ לִקְרֹא אֶת־הַסֵּפֶר הַזֶּה תִּקְשֹׁר עָלָיו אֶבֶן וְהִשְׁלַכְתּוֹ אֶל־תּוֹךְ פְּרָת:

64 And say, 'Thus shall Babylon sink and never rise again, because of the disaster that I will bring upon it. And [nations] shall have wearied themselves [for fire].'" Thus far the words of *Yirmiyahu*.

סד וְאָמַרְתָּ כָּכָה תִּשְׁקַע בָּבֶל וְלֹא־תָקוּם מִפְּנֵי הָרָעָה אֲשֶׁר אָנֹכִי מֵבִיא עָלֶיהָ וְיָעֵפוּ עַד־הֵנָּה דִּבְרֵי יִרְמְיָהוּ:

52 **1** *Tzidkiyahu* was twenty-one years old when he became king, and he reigned in *Yerushalayim* for eleven years. His mother's name was Hamutal, daughter of *Yirmiyahu* of Libnah.

נב א בֶּן־עֶשְׂרִים וְאַחַת שָׁנָה צִדְקִיָּהוּ בְמָלְכוֹ וְאַחַת עֶשְׂרֵה שָׁנָה מָלַךְ בִּירוּשָׁלָ͏ִם וְשֵׁם אִמּוֹ חֲמִיטַל [חֲמוּטַל] בַּת־יִרְמְיָהוּ מִלִּבְנָה:

2 He did what was displeasing to *Hashem*, just as *Yehoyakim* had done.

ב וַיַּעַשׂ הָרַע בְּעֵינֵי יְהֹוָה כְּכֹל אֲשֶׁר־עָשָׂה יְהוֹיָקִים:

3 Indeed, *Yerushalayim* and *Yehuda* were a cause of anger for *Hashem*, so that He cast them out of His presence. *Tzidkiyahu* rebelled against the king of Babylon.

ג כִּי עַל־אַף יְהֹוָה הָיְתָה בִּירוּשָׁלַ͏ִם וִיהוּדָה עַד־הִשְׁלִיכוֹ אוֹתָם מֵעַל פָּנָיו וַיִּמְרֹד צִדְקִיָּהוּ בְּמֶלֶךְ בָּבֶל:

KEE al AF a-do-NAI ha-y'-TAH bee-ru-sha-LA-im vee-hu-DAH ad hish-li-KHO o-TAM may-AL pa-NAV va-yim-ROD tzid-ki-YA-hu b'-ME-lekh ba-VEL

4 And in the ninth year of his reign, on the tenth day of the tenth month, King Nebuchadrezzar moved against *Yerushalayim* with his whole army. They besieged it and built towers against it all around.

ד וַיְהִי בַשָּׁנָה הַתְּשִׁעִית לְמָלְכוֹ בַּחֹדֶשׁ הָעֲשִׂירִי בֶּעָשׂוֹר לַחֹדֶשׁ בָּא נְבוּכַדְרֶאצַּר מֶלֶךְ־בָּבֶל הוּא וְכָל־חֵילוֹ עַל־יְרוּשָׁלַ͏ִם וַיַּחֲנוּ עָלֶיהָ וַיִּבְנוּ עָלֶיהָ דָּיֵק סָבִיב:

5 The city continued in a state of siege until the eleventh year of King *Tzidkiyahu*.

ה וַתָּבֹא הָעִיר בַּמָּצוֹר עַד עַשְׁתֵּי עֶשְׂרֵה שָׁנָה לַמֶּלֶךְ צִדְקִיָּהוּ:

6 By the ninth day of the fourth month, the famine had become acute in the city; there was no food left for the common people.

ו בַּחֹדֶשׁ הָרְבִיעִי בְּתִשְׁעָה לַחֹדֶשׁ וַיֶּחֱזַק הָרָעָב בָּעִיר וְלֹא־הָיָה לֶחֶם לְעַם הָאָרֶץ:

7 Then [the wall of] the city was breached. All the soldiers fled; they left the city by night through the gate between the double walls, which is near the king's garden – the Chaldeans were all around the city – and they set out for the Arabah.

ז וַתִּבָּקַע הָעִיר וְכָל־אַנְשֵׁי הַמִּלְחָמָה יִבְרְחוּ וַיֵּצְאוּ מֵהָעִיר לַיְלָה דֶּרֶךְ שַׁעַר בֵּין־הַחֹמֹתַיִם אֲשֶׁר עַל־גַּן הַמֶּלֶךְ וְכַשְׂדִּים עַל־הָעִיר סָבִיב וַיֵּלְכוּ דֶּרֶךְ הָעֲרָבָה:

"I love Jerusalem" near the Jaffa Gate in *Yerushalayim*

52:3 Indeed, *Yerushalayim* and *Yehuda* were a cause of anger for *Hashem* *Yirmiyahu's* final chapter repeats the description of the downfall of *Yehuda* and *Yerushalayim* at the hands of the Babylonians. One might be tempted to separate *Hashem* from history, and state that politics and theology do not mix. What *Yirmiyahu* teaches is that the two work hand-in-hand. On the surface, Babylonia is another superpower overrunning a minor, vassal state. However, *Yehuda* is vulnerable not because of its small army, but because it refuses to perform justice and righteousness, and worships idols in *Hashem's* holy land. It is their sinful behavior and God's corresponding anger that leads to Israel's exile, just as God's everlasting love for His people and His land will eventually lead to their full return and restoration, and to the redemption of the entire world.

8 But the Chaldean troops pursued the king, and they overtook *Tzidkiyahu* in the steppes of *Yericho*, as his entire force left him and scattered.

ח וַיִּרְדְּפוּ חֵיל־כַּשְׂדִּים אַחֲרֵי הַמֶּלֶךְ וַיַּשִּׂגוּ אֶת־צִדְקִיָּהוּ בְּעַרְבֹת יְרֵחוֹ וְכָל־חֵילוֹ נָפֹצוּ מֵעָלָיו:

9 They captured the king and brought him before the king of Babylon at Riblah, in the region of Hamath; and he put him on trial.

ט וַיִּתְפְּשׂוּ אֶת־הַמֶּלֶךְ וַיַּעֲלוּ אֹתוֹ אֶל־מֶלֶךְ בָּבֶל רִבְלָתָה בְּאֶרֶץ חֲמָת וַיְדַבֵּר אִתּוֹ מִשְׁפָּטִים:

10 The king of Babylon had *Tzidkiyahu*'s sons slaughtered before his eyes; he also had all the officials of *Yehuda* slaughtered at Riblah.

י וַיִּשְׁחַט מֶלֶךְ־בָּבֶל אֶת־בְּנֵי צִדְקִיָּהוּ לְעֵינָיו וְגַם אֶת־כָּל־שָׂרֵי יְהוּדָה שָׁחַט בְּרִבְלָתָה:

11 Then the eyes of *Tzidkiyahu* were put out, and he was chained in bronze fetters. The king of Babylon brought him to Babylon and put him in prison, [where he remained] to the day of his death.

יא וְאֶת־עֵינֵי צִדְקִיָּהוּ עִוֵּר וַיַּאַסְרֵהוּ בַנְחֻשְׁתַּיִם וַיְבִאֵהוּ מֶלֶךְ־בָּבֶל בָּבֶלָה וַיִּתְּנֵהוּ בבֵית־[בֵית־] הַפְּקֻדֹּת עַד־יוֹם מוֹתוֹ:

12 On the tenth day of the fifth month – that was the nineteenth year of King Nebuchadrezzar, the king of Babylon – Nebuzaradan, the chief of the guards, came to represent the king of Babylon in *Yerushalayim*.

יב וּבַחֹדֶשׁ הַחֲמִישִׁי בֶּעָשׂוֹר לַחֹדֶשׁ הִיא שְׁנַת תְּשַׁע־עֶשְׂרֵה שָׁנָה לַמֶּלֶךְ נְבוּכַדְרֶאצַּר מֶלֶךְ־בָּבֶל בָּא נְבוּזַרְאֲדָן רַב־טַבָּחִים עָמַד לִפְנֵי מֶלֶךְ־בָּבֶל בִּירוּשָׁלָם:

13 He burned the House of *Hashem*, the king's palace, and all the houses of *Yerushalayim*; he burned down the house of every notable person.

יג וַיִּשְׂרֹף אֶת־בֵּית־יְהֹוָה וְאֶת־בֵּית הַמֶּלֶךְ וְאֵת כָּל־בָּתֵּי יְרוּשָׁלַם וְאֶת־כָּל־בֵּית הַגָּדוֹל שָׂרַף בָּאֵשׁ:

14 The entire Chaldean force that was with the chief of the guards tore down all the walls of *Yerushalayim* on every side.

יד וְאֶת־כָּל־חֹמוֹת יְרוּשָׁלַם סָבִיב נָתְצוּ כָּל־חֵיל כַּשְׂדִּים אֲשֶׁר אֶת־רַב־טַבָּחִים:

15 The remnant of the people left in the city, the defectors who had gone over to the king of Babylon, and what remained of the craftsmen were taken into exile by Nebuzaradan, the chief of the guards. But some of the poorest elements of the population –

טו וּמִדַּלּוֹת הָעָם וְאֶת־יֶתֶר הָעָם הַנִּשְׁאָרִים בָּעִיר וְאֶת־הַנֹּפְלִים אֲשֶׁר נָפְלוּ אֶל־מֶלֶךְ בָּבֶל וְאֵת יֶתֶר הָאָמוֹן הֶגְלָה נְבוּזַרְאֲדָן רַב־טַבָּחִים:

16 some of the poorest in the land – were left by Nebuzaradan, the chief of the guards, to be vine-dressers and field hands.

טז וּמִדַּלּוֹת הָאָרֶץ הִשְׁאִיר נְבוּזַרְאֲדָן רַב־טַבָּחִים לְכֹרְמִים וּלְיֹגְבִים:

17 The Chaldeans broke up the bronze columns of the House of *Hashem*, the stands, and the bronze tank that was in the House of *Hashem*; and they carried all the bronze away to Babylon.

יז וְאֶת־עַמּוּדֵי הַנְּחֹשֶׁת אֲשֶׁר לְבֵית־יְהֹוָה וְאֶת־הַמְּכֹנוֹת וְאֶת־יָם הַנְּחֹשֶׁת אֲשֶׁר בְּבֵית־יְהֹוָה שִׁבְּרוּ כַשְׂדִּים וַיִּשְׂאוּ אֶת־כָּל־נְחֻשְׁתָּם בָּבֶלָה:

18 They also took the pails, scrapers, snuffers, sprinkling bowls, ladles, and all the other bronze vessels used in the service.

יח וְאֶת־הַסִּרוֹת וְאֶת־הַיָּעִים וְאֶת־הַמְזַמְּרוֹת וְאֶת־הַמִּזְרָקֹת וְאֶת־הַכַּפּוֹת וְאֵת כָּל־כְּלֵי הַנְּחֹשֶׁת אֲשֶׁר־יְשָׁרְתוּ בָהֶם לָקָחוּ:

Jeremiah

19 The chief of the guards took whatever was of gold and whatever was of silver: basins, fire pans, sprinkling bowls, pails, *menorah*s, ladles, and jars.

יט וְאֶת־הַסִּפִּים וְאֶת־הַמַּחְתּוֹת וְאֶת־הַמִּזְרָקוֹת וְאֶת־הַסִּירוֹת וְאֶת־הַמְּנֹרוֹת וְאֶת־הַכַּפּוֹת וְאֶת־הַמְּנַקִיּוֹת אֲשֶׁר זָהָב זָהָב וַאֲשֶׁר־כֶּסֶף כָּסֶף לָקַח רַב־טַבָּחִים:

20 The two columns, the one tank and the twelve bronze oxen which supported it, and the stands, which King *Shlomo* had provided for the House of *Hashem* – all these objects contained bronze beyond weighing.

כ הָעַמּוּדִים שְׁנַיִם הַיָּם אֶחָד וְהַבָּקָר שְׁנֵים־עָשָׂר נְחֹשֶׁת אֲשֶׁר־תַּחַת הַמְּכֹנוֹת אֲשֶׁר עָשָׂה הַמֶּלֶךְ שְׁלֹמֹה לְבֵית יְהֹוָה לֹא־הָיָה מִשְׁקָל לִנְחֻשְׁתָּם כָּל־הַכֵּלִים הָאֵלֶּה:

21 As for the columns, each was eighteen *amot* high and twelve *amot* in circumference; it was hollow, and [the metal] was four fingers thick.

כא וְהָעַמּוּדִים שְׁמֹנֶה עֶשְׂרֵה אַמָּה קוֹמָה [קוֹמַת] הָעַמֻּד הָאֶחָד וְחוּט שְׁתֵּים־עֶשְׂרֵה אַמָּה יְסֻבֶּנּוּ וְעָבְיוֹ אַרְבַּע אַצְבָּעוֹת נָבוּב:

22 It had a bronze capital above it; the height of each capital was five *amot*, and there was a meshwork [decorated] with pomegranates about the capital, all made of bronze; and so for the second column, also with pomegranates.

כב וְכֹתֶרֶת עָלָיו נְחֹשֶׁת וְקוֹמַת הַכֹּתֶרֶת הָאַחַת חָמֵשׁ אַמּוֹת וּשְׂבָכָה וְרִמּוֹנִים עַל־הַכּוֹתֶרֶת סָבִיב הַכֹּל נְחֹשֶׁת וְכָאֵלֶּה לָעַמּוּד הַשֵּׁנִי וְרִמּוֹנִים:

23 There were ninety-six pomegranates facing outward; all the pomegranates around the meshwork amounted to one hundred.

כג וַיִּהְיוּ הָרִמֹּנִים תִּשְׁעִים וְשִׁשָּׁה רוּחָה כָּל־הָרִמּוֹנִים מֵאָה עַל־הַשְּׂבָכָה סָבִיב:

24 The chief of the guards also took *Seraya* the chief *Kohen* and *Tzefanya*, the deputy *Kohen*, and the three guardians of the threshold.

כד וַיִּקַּח רַב־טַבָּחִים אֶת־שְׂרָיָה כֹּהֵן הָרֹאשׁ וְאֶת־צְפַנְיָה כֹּהֵן הַמִּשְׁנֶה וְאֶת־שְׁלֹשֶׁת שֹׁמְרֵי הַסַּף:

25 And from the city he took a eunuch who was in command of the soldiers; seven royal privy councilors, who were present in the city; the scribe of the army commander, who was in charge of mustering the people of the land; and sixty of the common people who were inside the city.

כה וּמִן־הָעִיר לָקַח סָרִיס אֶחָד אֲשֶׁר־הָיָה פָקִיד עַל־אַנְשֵׁי הַמִּלְחָמָה וְשִׁבְעָה אֲנָשִׁים מֵרֹאֵי פְנֵי־הַמֶּלֶךְ אֲשֶׁר נִמְצְאוּ בָעִיר וְאֵת סֹפֵר שַׂר הַצָּבָא הַמַּצְבִּא אֶת־עַם הָאָרֶץ וְשִׁשִּׁים אִישׁ מֵעַם הָאָרֶץ הַנִּמְצְאִים בְּתוֹךְ הָעִיר:

26 Nebuzaradan, the chief of the guards, took them and brought them to the king of Babylon at Riblah.

כו וַיִּקַּח אוֹתָם נְבוּזַרְאֲדָן רַב־טַבָּחִים וַיֹּלֶךְ אוֹתָם אֶל־מֶלֶךְ בָּבֶל רִבְלָתָה:

27 The king of Babylon had them struck down and put to death at Riblah, in the region of Hamath. Thus *Yehuda* was exiled from its land.

כז וַיַּכֶּה אוֹתָם מֶלֶךְ בָּבֶל וַיְמִתֵם בְּרִבְלָה בְּאֶרֶץ חֲמָת וַיִּגֶל יְהוּדָה מֵעַל אַדְמָתוֹ:

28 This is the number of those whom Nebuchadrezzar exiled in the seventh year: 3,023 Judeans.

כח זֶה הָעָם אֲשֶׁר הֶגְלָה נְבוּכַדְרֶאצַּר בִּשְׁנַת־שֶׁבַע יְהוּדִים שְׁלֹשֶׁת אֲלָפִים וְעֶשְׂרִים וּשְׁלֹשָׁה:

29 In the eighteenth year of Nebuchadrezzar, 832 persons [were exiled] from *Yerushalayim*.

כט בִּשְׁנַת שְׁמוֹנֶה עֶשְׂרֵה לִנְבוּכַדְרֶאצַּר מִירוּשָׁלַ͏ִם נֶפֶשׁ שְׁמֹנֶה מֵאוֹת שְׁלֹשִׁים וּשְׁנָיִם:

30 And in the twenty-third year of Nebuchadrezzar,
Nebuzaradan, the chief of the guards, exiled 745
Judeans. The total amounted to 4,600 persons.

ל בִּשְׁנַת שָׁלֹשׁ וְעֶשְׂרִים לִנְבוּכַדְרֶאצַּר
הֶגְלָה נְבוּזַרְאֲדָן רַב־טַבָּחִים יְהוּדִים
נֶפֶשׁ שְׁבַע מֵאוֹת אַרְבָּעִים וַחֲמִשָּׁה כָּל־
נֶפֶשׁ אַרְבַּעַת אֲלָפִים וְשֵׁשׁ מֵאוֹת:

31 In the thirty-seventh year of the exile of King
Yehoyachin of *Yehuda*, on the twenty-fifth day of the
twelfth month, King Evil-merodach of Babylon,
in the year he became king, took note of King
Yehoyachin of *Yehuda* and released him from prison.

לא וַיְהִי בִשְׁלֹשִׁים וָשֶׁבַע שָׁנָה לְגָלוּת
יְהוֹיָכִן מֶלֶךְ־יְהוּדָה בִּשְׁנֵים עָשָׂר חֹדֶשׁ
בְּעֶשְׂרִים וַחֲמִשָּׁה לַחֹדֶשׁ נָשָׂא אֱוִיל
מְרֹדַךְ מֶלֶךְ בָּבֶל בִּשְׁנַת מַלְכֻתוֹ אֶת־
רֹאשׁ יְהוֹיָכִין מֶלֶךְ־יְהוּדָה וַיֹּצֵא אוֹתוֹ
מִבֵּית הַכְּלִיא [הַכְּלוֹא]:

32 He spoke kindly to him, and gave him a throne
above those of other kings who were with him in
Babylon.

לב וַיְדַבֵּר אִתּוֹ טֹבוֹת וַיִּתֵּן אֶת־כִּסְאוֹ
מִמַּעַל לְכִסֵּא מלכים [הַמְּלָכִים] אֲשֶׁר
אִתּוֹ בְּבָבֶל:

33 He removed his prison garments and [*Yehoyachin*]
ate regularly in his presence the rest of his life.

לג וְשִׁנָּה אֵת בִּגְדֵי כִלְאוֹ וְאָכַל לֶחֶם לְפָנָיו
תָּמִיד כָּל־יְמֵי חַיָּו:

34 A regular allotment of food was given him by order
of the king of Babylon, an allotment for each day,
to the day of his death – all the days of his life.

לד וַאֲרֻחָתוֹ אֲרֻחַת תָּמִיד נִתְּנָה־לּוֹ מֵאֵת
מֶלֶךְ־בָּבֶל דְּבַר־יוֹם בְּיוֹמוֹ עַד־יוֹם מוֹתוֹ
כֹּל יְמֵי חַיָּיו:

Jeremiah

List of Transliterated Words in *The Israel Bible*

The following is a list of nouns which have been transliterated into Hebrew in the English translation and commentary of *The Israel Bible*:

Hebrew Name	English Name	Pronunciation	Hebrew
Achan	Achan	a-KHAN	עָכָן
Achav	Ahab	akh-AV	אַחְאָב
Achaz	Ahaz	a-KHAZ	אָחָז
Achazyahu	Ahaziah	a-khaz-YA-hu	אֲחַזְיָהוּ
Achiezer	Ahiezer	a-khee-E-zer	אֲחִיעֶזֶר
Achihud	Ahihud	a-khee-HUD	אֲחִיהוּד
Achikam	Ahikam	a-khee-KAM	אֲחִיקָם
Achilud	Ahilud	a-khee-LUD	אֲחִילוּד
Achimelech	Ahimelech	a-khee-ME-lekh	אֲחִימֶלֶךְ
Achira	Ahira	a-khee-RA	אֲחִירַע
Achisamach	Ahisamach	a-khee-sa-MAKH	אֲחִיסָמָךְ
Achitofel	Ahithophel	a-khee-TO-fel	אֲחִיתֹפֶל
Achituv	Ahitub	a-khee-TUV	אֲחִיטוּב
Achiya	Ahijah	a-khi-YAH	אֲחִיָּה
Adam	Adam	a-DAM	אָדָם
Adar	Adar	a-DAR	אֲדָר
Adoniyahu	Adonijah	a-do-ni-YA-hu	אֲדֹנִיָּהוּ
Adulam	Adullam	a-du-LAM	עֲדֻלָּם
Agur	Agur	a-GUR	אָגוּר
Aharon	Aaron	a-ha-RON	אַהֲרֹן
Amasa	Amasa	a-ma-SA	עֲמָשָׂא
Amatzya	Amaziah	a-matz-YAH	אֲמַצְיָה
Amen	Amen	a-MAYN	אָמֵן
Amiel	Ammiel	a-mee-AYL	עַמִּיאֵל
Aminadav	Amminadab	a-mee-na-DAV	עַמִּינָדָב
Amitai	Amittai	a-mi-TAI	אֲמִתַּי
Amnon	Amnon	am-NON	אַמְנֹן

Hebrew Name	English Name	Pronunciation	Hebrew
Amon	Amon	a-MON	אָמוֹן
Amos	Amos	a-MOS	עָמוֹס
Amotz	Amoz	a-MOTZ	אָמוֹץ
Amram	Amram	am-RAM	עַמְרָם
Anatot	Anathoth	a-na-TOT	עֲנָתוֹת
Aron	Ark	a-RON	אֲרוֹן
Aron HaBrit	Ark of the Covenant	a-RON ha-b'-REET	אֲרוֹן הַבְּרִית
Arpachshad	Arpachshad	ar-pakh-SHAD	אַרְפַּכְשַׁד
Asa	Asa	a-SA	אָסָא
Asael	Asahel	a-sah-AYL	עֲשָׂהאֵל
Asaf	Asaph	a-SAF	אָסָף
Ashdod	Ashdod	ash-DOD	אַשְׁדּוֹד
Asher	Asher	a-SHAYR	אָשֵׁר
Ashkelon	Ashkelon	ash-k'-LON	אַשְׁקְלוֹן
Atalya	Athaliah	a-tal-YAH	עֲתַלְיָה
Avdon	Abdon	av-DON	עַבְדּוֹן
Avichayil	Abihail	a-vee-KHA-yil	אֲבִיחַיִל
Avidan	Abidan	a-vee-DAN	אֲבִידָן
Avigail	Abigail	a-vee-GA-yil	אֲבִיגַיִל
Avihu	Abihu	a-vee-HU	אֲבִיהוּא
Avimelech	Abimelech	a-vee-ME-lekh	אֲבִימֶלֶךְ
Avinadav	Abinadab	a-vee-na-DAV	אֲבִינָדָב
Aviram	Abiram	a-vee-RAM	אֲבִירָם
Avishai	Abishai	a-vee-SHAI	אֲבִישַׁי
Aviya	Abijah	a-vi-YAH	אֲבִיָּה
Aviyam	Abijam	a-vi-YAM	אֲבִיָּם
Avner	Abner	av-NAYR	אַבְנֵר
Avraham	Abraham	av-ra-HAM	אַבְרָהָם
Avram	Abram	av-RAM	אַבְרָם
Avshalom	Absalom	av-sha-LOM	אַבְשָׁלוֹם
Azarya	Azariah	a-zar-YAH	עֲזַרְיָה
Azeika	Azekah	a-zay-KAH	עֲזֵקָה
Azza	Gaza	a-ZAH	עַזָּה

Hebrew Name	English Name	Pronunciation	Hebrew
B'nei Yisrael	The Children of Israel	b'-NAY yis-ra-AYL	בְּנֵי יִשְׂרָאֵל
Barak	Barak	ba-rakh-AYL	בָּרָק
Baruch	Baruch	ba-RUKH	בָּרוּךְ
Barzilai	Barzillai	bar-zi-LAI	בַּרְזִלַּי
Basha	Baasa	ba-SHA	בַּעְשָׁא
Batsheva	Bath-sheba	bat-SHE-va	בַּת־שֶׁבַע
Be'er Sheva	Beer-sheba	b'-AYR SHE-va	בְּאֵר שֶׁבַע
Be'eri	Beeri	b'-ay-REE	בְּאֵרִי
Beit Aven	Beth-aven	bayt A-ven	בֵּית אָוֶן
Beit El	Beth-el	bayt el	בֵּית אֵל
Beit Hamikdash	Temple	bayt ha-mik-DASH	בֵּית הַמִּקְדָּשׁ
Beit Lechem	Beth-lehem	bayt LE-khem	בֵּית לָחֶם
Beit Shean	Beth-shean	bayt sh'-AN	בֵּית שְׁאָן
Beit Shemesh	Beth-shemesh	bayt SHE-mesh	בֵּית שֶׁמֶשׁ
Berechya	Berechiah	be-rekh-YAH	בֶּרֶכְיָה
Betzalel	Bezalel	b'-tzal-AYL	בְּצַלְאֵל
Bilha	Bilhah	bil-HAH	בִּלְהָה
Binyamin	Benjamin	bin-ya-MIN	בִּנְיָמִין
Boaz	Boaz	BO-az	בֹּעַז
Buki	Bukki	bu-KEE	בֻּקִּי
Buzi	Buzi	bu-ZEE	בּוּזִי
Carmel	Carmel	kar-MEL	כַּרְמֶל
Chachalya	Hacaliah	kha-khal-YAH	חֲכַלְיָה
Chagai	Haggai	kha-GAI	חַגַּי
Chana	Hannah	kha-NAH	חַנָּה
Chanamel	Hanamel	kha-nam-AYL	חֲנַמְאֵל
Chanani	Hanani	kha-NA-nee	חֲנָנִי
Chananya	Hananiah	kha-nan-YAH	חֲנַנְיָה
Chaniel	Hanniel	kha-nee-AYL	חַנִּיאֵל
Chanoch	Enoch	kha-NOKH	חֲנוֹךְ
Chava	Eve	kha-VAH	חַוָּה
Chavakuk	Habakkuk	kha-va-KUK	חֲבַקּוּק
Chermon	Hermon	kher-MON	חֶרְמוֹן

Hebrew Name	English Name	Pronunciation	Hebrew
Chetzron	Hezron	khetz-RON	חֶצְרוֹן
Chever	Heber	KHE-ver	חֶבֶר
Chevron	Hebron	khev-RON	חֶבְרוֹן
Chilkiyahu	Hilkiah	khil-ki-YA-hu	חִלְקִיָּהוּ
Chizkiyahu	Hezekiah	khiz-ki-YA-hu	חִזְקִיָּהוּ
Chofni	Hophni	khof-NEE	חָפְנִי
Chogla	Hoglah	khog-LAH	חָגְלָה
Chulda	Hulda	khul-DAH	חֻלְדָּה
Chur	Hur	Khur	חוּר
Dan	Dan	Dan	דָּן
Daniel	Daniel	da-ni-YAYL	דָּנִיֵּאל
Datan	Dathan	da-TAN	דָּתָן
David	David	da-VID	דָּוִד
Devora	Deborah	d'-vo-RAH	דְּבוֹרָה
Dina	Dinah	DEE-nah	דִּינָה
Doeg Ha'adomi	Doeg the Edomite	do-AYG ha-a-do-MEE	דּוֹאֵג הָאֲדֹמִי
Efraim	Ephraim	ef-RA-yim	אֶפְרַיִם
Efrat	Ephrat	ef-RAT	אֶפְרָתָה
Efrat	Ephrathah	ef-RA-tah	אֶפְרָתָה
Ehud	Ehud	ay-HUD	אֵהוּד
Eila	Elah	AY-lah	אֵלָה
Eilon	Elon	ay-LON	אֵילוֹן
Ein Gedi	En-gedi	ayn GE-dee	עֵין גֶּדִי
Elazar	Eleazar	el-a-ZAR	אֶלְעָזָר
Elchanan	Elhanan	el-kha-NAN	אֶלְחָנָן
Eli	Eli	ay-LEE	עֵלִי
Eliav	Eliab	e-lee-AV	אֱלִיאָב
Elidad	Elidad	e-lee-DAD	אֱלִידָד
Eliezer	Eliezer	e-lee-E-zer	אֱלִיעֶזֶר
Elimelech	Elimelech	e-lee-ME-lekh	אֱלִימֶלֶךְ
Elisha	Elisha	e-lee-SHA	אֱלִישָׁע
Elishama	Elishama	e-lee-sha-MA	אֱלִישָׁמָע
Elisheva	Elisheba	e-lee-SHE-va	אֱלִישֶׁבַע

Hebrew Name	English Name	Pronunciation	Hebrew
Elitzafan	Eli-zaphan	e-lee-tza-FAN	אֱלִיצָפָן
Elitzur	Elizur	e-lee-TZUR	אֱלִיצוּר
Eliyahu	Elijah	ay-li-YA-hu	אֵלִיָּהוּ
Elkana	Elkanah	el-ka-NAH	אֶלְקָנָה
Elyasaf	Eliasaph	el-ya-SAF	אֶלְיָסָף
Elyashiv	Eliashib	el-ya-SHEEV	אֶלְיָשִׁיב
Enosh	Enosh	e-NOSH	אֱנוֹשׁ
Er	Er	ayr	עֵר
Eshtaol	Eshtaol	esh-ta-OL	אֶשְׁתָּאֹל
Esther	Esther	es-TAYR	אֶסְתֵּר
Eved Melech	Ebed-melech	E-ved ME-lekh	עֶבֶד־מֶלֶךְ
Even Ha-Ezer	Eben-Ezer	E-ven ha-E-zer	אֶבֶן הָעֵזֶר
Ever	Eber	AY-ver	עֵבֶר
Evyatar	Abiathar	ev-ya-TAR	אֶבְיָתָר
Ezra	Ezra	ez-RA	עֶזְרָא
Gad	Gad	gad	גָּד
Gadi	Gaddi	ga-DEE	גַּדִּי
Gadiel	Gaddiel	ga-dee-AYL	גַּדִּיאֵל
Gamliel	Gamaliel	gam-lee-AYL	גַּמְלִיאֵל
Gedalia	Gedaliah	g'-dal-YA (hu)	גְּדַלְיָהוּ
Gedera	Gederah	g'-day-RAH	גְּדֵרָה
Gershom	Gershom	gay-r'-SHOM	גֵּרְשׁוֹם
Gershon	Gershon	gay-r'-SHON	גֵּרְשׁוֹן
Geshem	Geshem	GE-shem	גֶּשֶׁם
Geuel	Geuel	g'-u-AYL	גְּאוּאֵל
Gidon	Gideon	gid-ON	גִּדְעוֹן
Gilad	Gilead	gil-AD	גִּלְעָד
Gilgal	Gilgal	gil-GAL	גִּלְגָּל
Giva	Gibeah	giv-AH	גִּבְעָה
Givon	Gibeon	giv-ON	גִּבְעוֹן
Hadassa	Hadassah	ha-da-SAH	הֲדַסָּה
Har Eival	Mount Ebal	ay-VAL	הַר עֵיבָל
Har Gerizim	Mount Gerizim	g'-ri-ZEEM	הַר גְּרִזִים

Hebrew Name	English Name	Pronunciation	Hebrew
Har HaBayit	Temple Mount	har ha-BA-yit	הַר הַבַּיִת
Har HaZeitim	the Mount of Olives	har ha-zay-TEEM	הַר הַזֵּיתִים
Hashem	Lord/God		
Hayman	Heman	hay-MAN	הֵימָן
Hoshea	Hosea	ho-SHAY-a	הוֹשֵׁעַ
Ido	Iddo	i-DO	עִדּוֹ
Imanu-El	Immanuel	i-MA-nu ayl	עִמָּנוּ אֵל
Ish-boshet	Ish-bosheth	eesh BO-shet	אִישׁ־בֹּשֶׁת
Itamar	Ithamar	ee-ta-MAR	אִיתָמָר
Itiel	Ithiel	ee-tee-AYL	אִיתִיאֵל
Ivtzan	Ibzan	iv-TZAN	אִבְצָן
Iyov	Job	i-YOV	אִיּוֹב
Kadmiel	Kadmiel	kad-mee-AYL	קַדְמִיאֵל
Kalev	Caleb	ka-LAYV	כָּלֵב
Keesh	Kish	keesh	קִישׁ
Kehat	Kohath	k'-HAT	קְהָת
Keinan	Kenan	kay-NAN	קֵינָן
Kemuel	Kemuel	k'-mu-AYL	קְמוּאֵל
Keruvim	Cherubim	k'-ru-VEEM	כְּרוּבִים
Kilyon	Chilion	kil-YON	כִּלְיוֹן
Kiryat Arba	Kiriath-arba	keer-YAT AR-bah	קִרְיַת אַרְבַּע
Kiryat Sefer	Kiriath-sepher	keer-YAT SAY-fer	קִרְיַת־סֵפֶר
Kiryat Ye'arim	Kiriath-jearim	keer-YAT y'-a-REEM	קִרְיַת יְעָרִים
Kislev	Chislev	kis-LAYV	כִּסְלֵו
Kohanim	Priests	ko-ha-NEEM	כֹּהֲנִים
Kohelet	Koheleth	ko-HE-let	קֹהֶלֶת
Kohen	Priest	ko-HAYN	כֹּהֵן
Kohen Gadol	High Priest	ko-HAYN ga-DOL	כֹּהֵן גָּדוֹל
Korach	Korah	KO-rakh	קֹרַח
Kushi	Cushi	ku-SHEE	כּוּשִׁי
Lachish	Lachish	la-KHEESH	לָכִישׁ
Leah	Leah	lay-AH	לֵאָה
Lemech	Lamech	LE-mekh	לֶמֶךְ

Hebrew Name	English Name	Pronunciation	Hebrew
Lemuel	Lemuel	l'-mu-AYL	לְמוֹאֵל
Levi	Levi	lay-VEE	לֵוִי
Leviim	Levites	l'-vee-IM	לְוִיִּם
Machla	Mahlah	makh-LAH	מַחְלָה
Machlon	Mahlon	makh-LON	מַחְלוֹן
Machseya	Mahseiah	makh-say-YAH	מַחְסֵיָה
Malachi	Malachi	mal-a-KHEE	מַלְאָכִי
Manoach	Manoah	ma-NO-akh	מָנוֹחַ
Mashiach	Messiah	ma-SHEE-akh	מָשִׁיחַ
Mefiboshet	Mephibosheth	m'-fee-VO-shet	מְפִיבֹשֶׁת
Mehalalel	Mahalalel	ma-ha-lal-AYL	מַהֲלַלְאֵל
Menachem	Menahem	m'-na-KHAYM	מְנַחֵם
Menashe	Menasseh	m'-na-SHEH	מְנַשֶּׁה
Menorah	Candlestick	m'-no-RAH	מְנֹרָה
Merari	Merari	m'-ra-REE	מְרָרִי
Metushelach	Methusaleh	m'-tu-SHE-lakh	מְתוּשָׁלַח
Micha	Micah	mee-KHAH	מִיכָה
Michael	Michael	mee-kha-AYL	מִיכָאֵל
Michaihu	Micaiah	mee-KHAI-hu	מִיכָיְהוּ
Michal	Michal	mee-KHAL	מִיכַל
Milka	Milcah	mil-KAH	מִלְכָּה
Miriam	Miriam	mir-YAM	מִרְיָם
Mishael	Mishael	mee-sha-AYL	מִישָׁאֵל
Mishkan	Tabernacle	mish-KAN	מִשְׁכָּן
Mitzpa	Mizpah	mitz-PAH	מִצְפָּה
Mizbayach	Altar	miz-BAY-akh	מִזְבֵּחַ
Mordechai	Mordecai	mor-d'-KHAI	מָרְדֳּכַי
Moriah	Moriah	mo-ri-YAH	מוֹרִיָה
Moshe	Moses	mo-SHEH	מֹשֶׁה
Nachbi	Nahbi	nakh-BEE	נַחְבִּי
Nachor	Nahor	na-KHOR	נָחוֹר
Nachshon	Nahshon	nakh-SHON	נַחְשׁוֹן
Nachum	Nahum	na-KHUM	נַחוּם

Hebrew Name	English Name	Pronunciation	Hebrew
Nadav	Nadab	na-DAV	נָדָב
Naftali	Naphtali	naf-ta-LEE	נַפְתָּלִי
Naomi	Naomi	na-o-MEE	נָעֳמִי
Natan	Nathan	na-TAN	נָתָן
Naval	Nabal	na-VAL	נָבָל
Navi	Prophet	na-VEE	נָבִיא
Navot	Naboth	na-VAL	נָבָל
Nechemya	Nehemiah	n'-khem-YAH	נְחֶמְיָה
Negev	Negeb	NE-gev	נֶגֶב
Nerya	Neriah	nay-ri-YAH	נֵרִיָּה
Netanel	Nethanel	n'-tan-AYL	נְתַנְאֵל
Neviah	Prophetess	n'-vee-AH	נְבִיאָה
Neviim	Prophets	n'-vee-EEM	נְבִיאִים
Nisan	Nisan	nee-SAN	נִיסָן
Noa	Noah	no-AH	נֹעָה
Noach	Noah	NO-akh	נֹחַ
Nov	Nob	nov	נֹב
Nun	Nun	nun	נוּן
Oded	Oded	o-DAYD	עוֹדֵד
Ohola	Oholah	a-ho-LAH	אָהֳלָה
Oholiav	Oholiab	o-ha-lee-AV	אָהֳלִיאָב
Oholiva	Oholibah	a-ho-lee-VAH	אָהֳלִיבָה
Omri	Omri	om-REE	עָמְרִי
Onan	Onan	o-NAN	אוֹנָן
Otniel	Othniel	ot-nee-AYL	עָתְנִיאֵל
Ovadya	Obadiah	o-vad-YAH	עֹבַדְיָה
Oved	Obed	o-VAYD	עוֹבֵד
Oved Edom	Obed Edom	o-VAYD e-DOM	עוֹבֵד אֱדוֹם
Pagiel	Pagiel	pag-ee-AYL	פַּגְעִיאֵל
Palti	Palti	pal-TEE	פַּלְטִי
Paltiel	Paltiel	pal-tee-AYL	פַּלְטִיאֵל
Pekach	Pekah	PE-kakh	פֶּקַח
Pedael	Pedahel	p'-da-AYL	פְּדַהְאֵל

Hebrew Name	English Name	Pronunciation	Hebrew
Pekachya	Pekahiah	p'-kakh-YAH	פְּקַחְיָה
Peleg	Peleg	PE-leg	פֶּלֶג
Penina	Peninnah	p'-ni-NAH	פְּנִנָּה
Peretz	Perez	PE-retz	פֶּרֶץ
Petuel	Pethuel	p'-tu-AYL	פְּתוּאֵל
Pinchas	Phinehas	peen-KHAS	פִּינְחָס
Rachel	Rachel	ra-KHAYL	רָחֵל
Ram	Ram	ram	רָם
Rama	Ramah	ra-MAH	רָמָה
Re'u	Reu	r'-U	רְעוּ
Rechovam	Rehoboam	r'-khav-AM	רְחַבְעָם
Reuven	Reuben	r'-u-VAYN	רְאוּבֵן
Rivka	Rebecca	riv-KAH	רִבְקָה
Rut	Ruth	rut	רוּת
Salma	Salmon/Salmah	sal-MAH	שַׂלְמָה
Salmon	Salmon	sal-MON	שַׂלְמוֹן
Sara	Sarah	sa-RAH	שָׂרָה
Sarai	Sarai	sa-RAI	שָׂרַי
Selah	Selah	SE-lah	סֶלָה
Seraya	Seraiah	s'-ra-YAH	שְׂרָיָה
Serug	Serug	s'-RUG	שְׂרוּג
Setur	Sethur	s'-TUR	סְתוּר
Shaarayim	Shaaraim	sha-a-RA-yim	שַׁעֲרַיִם
Shabbat	Sabbath	sha-BAT	שַׁבַּת
Shabbatot	Sabbaths	sha-ba-TOT	שַׁבְּתוֹת
Shafan	Shaphan	sha-FAN	שָׁפָן
Shafat	Shaphat	sha-FAT	שָׁפָט
Shalem	Salem	sha-LAYM	שָׁלֵם
Shalum	Shallum	sha-LUM	שַׁלּוּם
Shamgar	Shamgar	sham-GAR	שַׁמְגַּר
Shamua	Shammua	sha-MU-a	שַׁמּוּעַ
Shaul	Saul	sha-UL	שָׁאוּל
Shealtiel	Shealtiel	sh'-al-tee-AYL	שְׁאַלְתִּיאֵל

Hebrew Name	English Name	Pronunciation	Hebrew
Shear Yashuv	Shear-Jashub	sh'-AR ya-SHUV	שְׁאָר יָשׁוּב
Shechanya	Shecaniah	sh'-khan-YAH	שְׁכַנְיָה
Shechem	Shechem	sh'-KHEM	שְׁכֶם
Sheila	Shelah	shay-LAH	שֵׁלָה
Shelach	Shelah	SHE-lakh	שָׁלַח
Shelumiel	Shelumiel	sh'-lu-mee-AYL	שְׁלֻמִיאֵל
Shem	Shem	Shaym	שֵׁם
Shemaya	Shemaiah	sh'-ma-YAH	שְׁמַעְיָה
Sheshbatzar	Sheshbazzar	shaysh-ba-TZAR	שֵׁשְׁבַּצַּר
Shet	Seth	Shayt	שֵׁת
Shevat	Shebat	sh'-VAT	שְׁבָט
Shilo	Shiloh	shi-LOH	שִׁלֹה
Shim'i	Shimei	shim-EE	שִׁמְעִי
Shimon	Simeon	shim-ON	שִׁמְעוֹן
Shimshon	Samson	shim-SHON	שִׁמְשׁוֹן
Shlomo	Solomon	sh'-lo-MOH	שְׁלֹמֹה
Shmuel	Samuel	sh'-mu-AYL	שְׁמוּאֵל
Shofar	Horn	sho-FAR	שׁוֹפָר
Shofarot	Horns	sho-fa-ROT	שׁוֹפָרוֹת
Shomron	Samaria	sho-m'-RON	שֹׁמְרוֹן
Sivan	Sivan	see-VAN	סִיוָן
Tamar	Tamar	ta-MAR	תָּמָר
Tanakh	Hebrew Bible	ta-NAKH	תָּנָ"ךְ
Tapuach	Tappuah	ta-PU-akh	תַּפּוּחַ
Tavor	Tabor	ta-VOR	תָּבוֹר
Tekoa	Tekoa	t'-KO-a	תְּקוֹעָה
Terach	Terah	TE-rakh	תֶּרַח
Teveria	Tiberias	t'-ver-YAH	טְבֶרְיָה
Tevet	Tebeth	tay-VAYT	טֵבֵת
Tirtza	Tirzah	tir-TZAH	תִּרְצָה
Tola	Tola	to-LA	תּוֹלָע
Tzadok	Zadok	tza-DOK	צָדוֹק
Tzefanya	Zephaniah	tz'-fan-YAH	צְפַנְיָה

Hebrew Name	English Name	Pronunciation	Hebrew
Tzelofchad	Zelophehad	tz'-lo-f-KHAD	צְלָפְחָד
Tzeruya	Zeruiah	tz'-ru-YAH	צְרוּיָה
Tzfat	Safed	tz'-FAT	צְפַת
Tzidkiyahu	Zedekiah	tzid-ki-YA-hu	צִדְקִיָּהוּ
Tziklag	Ziklag	tzi-k'-LAG	צִקְלַג
Tzion	Zion	tzi-YON	צִיּוֹן
Tzipora	Zipporah	tzi-po-RAH	צִפֹּרָה
Tzora	Zorah	tzor-AH	צָרְעָה
Tzuriel	Zuriel	tzu-ree-AYL	צוּרִיאֵל
Ukal	Ucal	u-KAL	אֻכָל
Uri	Uri	u-REE	אוּרִי
Uriya	Uriah	u-ri-YAH	אוּרִיָּה
Utz	Uz	Utz	עוּץ
Uzziyahu	Uzziah	u-zi-YA-hu	עֻזִּיָּהוּ
Yaakov	Jacob	ya-a-KOV	יַעֲקֹב
Yachaziel	Jahaziel	ya-kha-zee-AYL	יַחֲזִיאֵל
Yael	Jael	ya-AYL	יָעֵל
Yaffo	Joppa/Jaffa	ya-FO	יָפוֹ
Yair	Jair	ya-EER	יָאִיר
Yakeh	Jakeh	ya-KEH	יָקֶה
Yarden	Jordan	yar-DAYN	יַרְדֵּן
Yarmut	Jarmuth	yar-MUT	יַרְמוּת
Yechezkel	Ezekiel	y'-khez-KAYL	יְחֶזְקֵאל
Yechiel	Jehiel	y'-khee-AYL	יְחִיאֵל
Yechonya	Jeconiah	y'-khon-YAH	יְכָנְיָה
Yedutun	Jeduthun	y'-du-TUN	יְדוּתוּן
Yehoachaz	Jehoahaz	y'-ho-a-KHAZ	יְהוֹאָחָז
Yehoash	Jehoash	y'-ho-ASH	יְהוֹאָשׁ
Yehochanan	Jehohanan	y'-ho-kha-NAN	יְהוֹחָנָן
Yehonatan	Jonathan	y'-ho-na-TAN	יְהוֹנָתָן
Yehoram	Jehoram	y'-ho-RAM	יְהוֹרָם
Yehoshafat	Jehoshaphat	y'-ho-sha-FAT	יְהוֹשָׁפָט
Yehoshavat	Jehoshabeath	y'-ho-shav-AT	יְהוֹשַׁבְעַת

Hebrew Name	English Name	Pronunciation	Hebrew
Yehosheva	Jehosheba	y-ho-SHE-va	יְהוֹשֶׁבַע
Yehoshua	Joshua	y'-ho-SHU-a	יְהוֹשֻׁעַ
Yehotzadak	Jehozadak	y'-ho-tza-DAK	יְהוֹצָדָק
Yehoyachin	Jehoiachin	y'-ho-ya-KHEEN	יְהוֹיָכִין
Yehoyada	Jehoiada	y'-ho-ya-DA	יְהוֹיָדָע
Yehoyakim	Jehoiakim	y'-ho-ya-KEEM	יְהוֹיָקִים
Yehu	Jehu	yay-HU	יֵהוּא
Yehuda	Judah	y'-hu-DAH	יְהוּדָה
Yehudi	Jew	y'-hu-DEE	יְהוּדִי
Yehudim	Jews	y'-hu-DEEM	יְהוּדִים
Yered	Jared	YE-red	יֶרֶד
Yericho	Jericho	y'-ree-KHO	יְרִיחוֹ
Yerovam	Jeroboam	ya-rov-AM	יָרָבְעָם
Yerubaal	Jerubbaal	y'-ru-BA-al	יְרֻבַּעַל
Yerushalayim	Jerusalem	y'-ru-sha-LA-yim	יְרוּשָׁלַיִם
Yeshayahu	Isaiah	y'-sha-YA-hu	יְשַׁעְיָהוּ
Yeshua	Jeshua	yay-SHU-a	יֵשׁוּעַ
Yiftach	Jephthah	yif-TAKH	יִפְתָּח
Yigal	Igal	yig-AL	יִגְאָל
Yirmiyahu	Jeremiah	yir-m'-YA-hu	יִרְמְיָהוּ
Yishai	Jesse	yi-SHAI	יִשַׁי
Yisrael	Israel	yis-ra-AYL	יִשְׂרָאֵל
Yissachar	Issachar	yi-sa-KHAR	יִשָּׂשכָר
Yitzchak	Issac	yitz-KHAK	יִצְחָק
Yizrael	Jezreel	yiz-r'-EL	יִזְרְעָאל
Yoash	Joash	yo-ASH	יוֹאָשׁ
Yoav	Joab	yo-AV	יוֹאָב
Yochanan	Johanan	yo-kha-NAN	יוֹחָנָן
Yocheved	Jochebed	yo-KHE-ved	יוֹכֶבֶד
Yoel	Joel	yo-AYL	יוֹאֵל
Yona	Jonah	yo-NAH	יוֹנָה
Yonadav	Jonadab	yo-na-DAV	יוֹנָדָב
Yonatan	Jonathan	yo-na-TAN	יוֹנָתָן

Hebrew Name	English Name	Pronunciation	Hebrew
Yoram	Joram	yo-RAM	יוֹרָם
Yosef	Joseph	yo-SAYF	יוֹסֵף
Yoshiyahu	Josiah	yo-shi-YA-hu	יֹאשִׁיָּהוּ
Yotam	Jotham	yo-TAM	יוֹתָם
Yotzadak	Jozadak	yo-tza-DAK	יוֹצָדָק
Yozavad	Jozabad	yo-za-VAD	יוֹזָבָד
Zanoach	Zanoah	za-NO-akh	זָנוֹחַ
Zecharya	Zechariah	z'-khar-YAH	זְכַרְיָה
Zerach	Zerah	ZE-rakh	זֶרַח
Zerubavel	Zerubbabel	z'-ru-ba-VEL	זְרֻבָּבֶל
Zevulun	Zebulun	z'-vu-LUN	זְבוּלֻן
Zilpa	Zilpah	zil-PAH	זִלְפָּה
Zimri	Zimri	zim-REE	זִמְרִי

Jewish Holidays

Chanukah	Hanukkah	kha-nu-KAH	חֲנוּכָּה
Pesach	Passover	PE-sakh	פֶּסַח
Purim	Purim	pu-REEM	פּוּרִים
Rosh Hashana	Jewish New Year	rosh ha-sha-NAH	רֹאשׁ הַשָּׁנָה
Shavuot	Feast of Weeks	sha-vu-OT	שָׁבוּעוֹת
Shemini Atzeret	Eight Day of Assembly	sh'-mee-NEE a-TZE-ret	שְׁמִינִי עֲצֶרֶת
Sukkot	Feast of Tabernacles	su-KOT	סֻכּוֹת
Yom Kippur	Day of Atonement	yom kee-PUR	יוֹם כִּיפּוּר

Biblical Measurements

Amah	Cubit	a-MAH	אַמָּה
Amot	Cubits	a-MOT	אַמּוֹת
Bat	Bath	bat	בַּת
Batim	Baths	ba-TEEM	בַּתִּים
Beka	half-shekel	BE-ka	בֶּקַע
Chomarim	Homers	kho-ma-REEM	חֳמָרִים
Chomer	Homer	KHO-mer	חֹמֶר
Efah	Ephah	ay-FAH	אֵיפָה
Geira	Gerah	gay-RAH	גֵּרָה

Hebrew Name	English Name	Pronunciation	Hebrew
Gomed	Gomed	GO- med	גֹּמֶד
Hin	Hin	heen	הִין
Kav	kab	kav	קַב
Kesita	kesitah	k'-see-TAH	קְשִׂיטָה
Kikar	talent	ki-KAR	כִּכָּר
Kikarim	talents	ki-ka-RIM	כִּכָּרִים
Kor	kor	kor	כֹּר
Letek	lethech	LE-tek	לֶתֶךְ
Log	Log	log	לֹג
Maneh	Mina	ma-NEH	מָנֶה
Manim	Minas	ma-NEEM	מָנִים
Omer	Omer	O-mer	עֹמֶר
Pim	Pim	peem	פִּים
Se'ah	Seah	say-AH	סְאָה
Se'eem	Seahs	s'-EEM	סְאִים
Shekalim	Shekels	sh'-ka-LEEM	שְׁקָלִים
Shekel	Shekel	SHE-kel	שֶׁקֶל
Tefach	Handbreadth	TE-fakh	טֶפַח
Zeret	Span	ZE-ret	זֶרֶת

Photo Credits

1:11 Mark Neyman, Government Press Office (Israel), **2:13** Avishai Teicher, Wikimedia Commons, **3:19** Courtesy of Israel365, **4:6** By Amos Meron – Own work, CC BY-SA 3.0, https://commons.wikimedia.org/w/index.php?curid=23523729, **5:6** Evgeny Meerson/Shutterstock.com, **6:2** Moshe EINHORN/Shutterstock.com, **7:4** Mikhail Semenov/Shutterstock.com, **8:22** By Spaza-Bozo (talk) – I (Spaza-Bozo 20px|link=|alt= (talk)) created this work entirely by myself., WTFPL, https://commons.wikimedia.org/w/index.php?curid=12862866, **9:23** Courtesy of Israel365, **11:16** Dubova/Shutterstock.com **12:14** By Unknown author – The Israel Internet Association via the PikiWiki – Israel free image collection project, Public Domain, https://commons.wikimedia.org/w/index.php?curid=64758668, **13:12** Yair Aronshtam, Wikimedia Commons, **14:7** Protasov AN/Shutterstock.com, **15:1** Poleznova/Shutterstock.com, **16:15** NathanNT/Shutterstock.com, **17:6** Rostislav Glinsky/Shutterstock.com, **18:14** maratr/Shutterstock.com, **19:2** Dror Feitelson, Wikimedia Commons, **20:3** Arkady Mazor/Shutterstock.com, **21:12** קובי גדעון, לשכת העיתונות הממשלתית, CC BY-SA 3.0 via Wikimedia Commons, **22:15** Courtesy of Israel365, **23:6** Jason Busa/Shutterstock.com, **24:2** Kvita Fabian/Shutterstock.com, **25:30** Evgeny Meerson/Shutterstock.com, **27:2** Slavoljub Pantelic/Shutterstock.com, **28:8** By https://www.flickr.com/photos/andrewscheer/ – https://www.flickr.com/photos/andrewscheer/40600599240/, CC0, https://commons.wikimedia.org/w/index.php?curid=69851562, **29:13** Wikimedia Commons, **30:3** Protasov AN/Shutterstock.com, **31:16** Moshe Milner, Government Press Office (Israel), **32:7** Ya'acov Sa'ar, Government Press Office (Israel), **33:11** Hans Pinn, Government Press Offices, Jerusalem, **35:2** Yair Aronshtam/Shutterstock.com, **36:22** Amos Ben Gershom, Government Press Office (Israel), **37:12** John Theodor/Shutterstock.com, **38:5** By Proesi at German Wikipedia – Self-photographed, CC BY-SA 2.0 de, https://commons.wikimedia.org/w/index.php?curid=16231918, **39:5** Avishai Teicher, Wikimedia Commons, **40:1** CC BY-SA 2.5, https://commons.wikimedia.org/w/index.php?curid=792661, **41:2** Courtesy of Israel365, **42:2** Sarit Richerson/Shutterstock.com, **43:10** Moshe Milner, Government Press Office (Israel), **44:22** Max Zalevsky/Shutterstock.com, **45:5** mikhail/Shutterstock.com, **46:27** By Melery821976 – Own work, CC BY-SA 4.0, https://commons.wikimedia.org/w/index.php?curid=107017921, **47:1** Mapic Aerials/Shutterstock.com, **48:13** Par Dvirraz – Travail personnel, CC BY-SA 3.0, https://commons.wikimedia.org/w/index.php?curid=31220250, **49:1** Moshe Milner, Government Press Office (Israel), **50:5** John Theodor/Shutterstock.com, **51:19** Natalia Bratslavsky/Shutterstock.com, **52:3** KiyechkaSo/Shutterstock.com

Map of Modern-Day Israel and its Neighbors

The following is a map of modern-day Israel and the surrounding countries

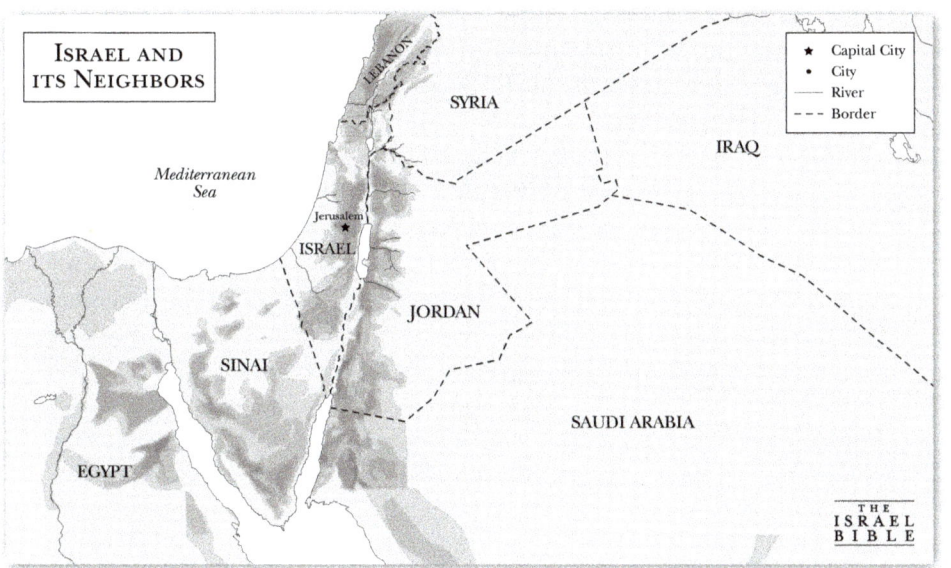

NOTES

NOTES

NOTES

NOTES

NOTES

For more inspiring commentary,
interactive maps, educational videos,
vivid photographs and more,
please visit our website

www.TheIsraelBible.com

THE
ISRAEL
BIBLE